THE PLURALITY OF TRUTH: A CRITIQUE OF RESEARCH ON THE STATE AND EUROPEAN INTEGRATION

"Così è (se vi pare)"
Pirandello

The Plurality of Truth: A Critique of Research on the State and European Integration

DR. HANNA OJANEN
The Finnish Institute of International Affairs

Routledge
Taylor & Francis Group
LONDON AND NEW YORK

First published 1998 by Ashgate Publishing

Reissued 2018 by Routledge
2 Park Square, Milton Park, Abingdon, Oxon, OX14 4RN
711 Third Avenue, New York, NY 10017, USA

Routledge is an imprint of the Taylor & Francis Group, an informa business

Copyright © Hanna Ojanen 1998

All rights reserved. No part of this book may be reprinted or reproduced or utilised in any form or by any electronic, mechanical, or other means, now known or hereafter invented, including photocopying and recording, or in any information storage or retrieval system, without permission in writing from the publishers.

Notice:
Product or corporate names may be trademarks or registered trademarks, and are used only for identification and explanation without intent to infringe.

Publisher's Note
The publisher has gone to great lengths to ensure the quality of this reprint but points out that some imperfections in the original copies may be apparent.

Disclaimer
The publisher has made every effort to trace copyright holders and welcomes correspondence from those they have been unable to contact.

A Library of Congress record exists under LC control number: 98024497

ISBN 13: 978-1-138-34147-0 (hbk)
ISBN 13: 978-1-138-34148-7 (pbk)
ISBN 13: 978-0-429-44011-3 (ebk)

Contents

Preface	vii
Acknowledgements	xi

1 **Introduction: troubling concepts and theories**   1
    Are there inadmissible concepts?   1
    Conventional research practice and its consequences for
        the study of the state and integration   16
    Depicting plurality   21

2 **Approaches to the relationship between
the state and integration**   33
    Integration as a solution to the problems of the state and
        the system of states   34
    Integration as a process in which the state is weakened or
        replaced   40
    The state which strengthens itself through integration   53
    Integration which transforms the state   79

3 **Causes and consequences**   105
    The state of the art in integration studies: a self-portrait
        with some corrective remarks   105
    The crucial assumptions and questions   115
    Origins of the assumptions   119

4 **Opting for integration: the slow retreat of Nordic cooperation**   189
    EU enlargement: a push towards a necessary reappraisal
        of Nordic cooperation   189
    The symptomatic failures of the grand designs in security
        and economy   190
    The low profile of Nordic achievements   198
    Nordic institutions: deliberately in a minor role   203
    Implications for the encounter with European integration   209
    The challenge of the EU: increasing incompatibility   210

5	**Nordic integration: elements of a model**	229
	The 1990s: new dynamism for Nordic cooperation	229
	The peculiar extent and methods of Nordic integration	231
	The *acquis nordique*	246
	Meeting of two methods of integration	256
6	**Finnish EU membership: an integration policy turned on its head**	269
	The customary principles of neutrality and sovereignty in Finnish integration policy	269
	The EEA: a step into a whirlpool	276
	The rhetoric of application and the implications of membership	284
7	**EU membership: a new dimension to Finland's integration**	303
	The logic of membership	303
	Neutrality: the cold war means in Finnish integration policy	306
	The implications of membership	320
8	**Conclusion: the plurality of interpretation**	331
	Constructing knowledge	331
	Possibilities and limits of scientific analysis	344
	The plurality of truth and credibility of research	347

Bibliography 353

Preface

At first, this study started from the assumption that European integration could help to solve the problem of how to redefine the term 'the state' in international relations. Having devoted considerable time to the study of the concept and having subsequently turned her attention to integration, the present author was inclined to see in this latter phenomena a most suitable candidate for being something which definitively requires a change in the established understanding of the state in international relations theory. How could one, in fact, continue talking in the conventional terms of a sovereign, omnipotent state in a context in which the state was clearly becoming a part of a larger unit? It seemed that a wholly new and much more useful concept of state could be discovered when analysing the process of integration.

That this belief was a rather paradigmatic if not altogether an archetypal starting point for a study occurred to the author much later. A considerable part of the studies on the state indeed makes the same discovery, namely, that (other) researchers tend to subscribe to a specific understanding of the state which is obsolete in the current international environment. As a rule, efforts are directed towards developing new and, by implication, better ones.

This aim is hardly useless; nor is the task necessarily difficult. When studying the relationship between the state and European integration, it became apparent that one indeed could see a new understanding emerging. Strikingly, the state was increasingly becoming defined as a part of a larger unit, its structures and policies being increasingly exposed to decisive influence from the outside.

Nonetheless, what was even more striking was that not only the envisaged new understanding was possible but that the old ones also persisted. The state had, for many an observer, not altered at all: it continued to be an independent unit controlling whatever consequences the processes of integration might have. This fact challenged the original research design of this study and redirected it towards an analysis of the *conditions* of the validity of specific understandings. Thus, this project became a piece of research on research itself, on the development of integration theories and on the formation of knowledge of integration.

In analysing research on integration, the book draws attention to some typical features of research practice, in particular the pervasive search for *one* answer or one truth and the almost anxious reactions that plural and diverging outcomes may cause. The coexistence of different, contradictory theories is often seen as a major problem to be resolved or as an imperfection to be removed, if not altogether as a stain on the reputation of the whole scientific enterprise which jeopardises its very trustworthiness. When the search for one correct answer seems futile and efforts at synthesising existing research results fail due to their incompatibility, what seemingly remains is complete relativism, difficult to accept for many reasons. What should be deduced from plurality, in fact, is a question less often dwelled upon: the normal 'consumer' or 'producer' of academic knowledge in a similar field might not be particularly well-equipped to deal with it.

A proper evaluation requires understanding the way theories emerge: assessing the different results requires knowledge on how they actually have been attained. This understanding can be reached through steps towards realising that any single theory depends on something, stems from something, and leads to something; in particular, it depends on other theories and stems from the choices made by the scholar.

Thus, this study gives an account of how and why different views emerge, get consolidated and coexist in research on the state and European integration. As such, the book is aimed at gathering readers with different interests areas, and it hopes to engage them in discussions partly outside the realm of their own, immediate concerns. The reader interested in the question of the state-integration relationship will be led to larger problems concerning the bases of knowledge on the question, while the one interested in general aspects of research practice in social sciences will find a concrete example in the specific question of the relationship between the state and the process of European integration. Yet, it is perhaps particularly the reader interested in the two case studies who will be led to an unexpected path. This reader will find ample evidence and thorough accounts, yet possibly at the expense of some previously held certainties and a risk of increased frustration. Through the case studies, in fact, the book teases the reader with two competing accounts on the cases. In addition to being an issue of theoretical debate, the plurality of truth is also, and above all, a question of interpretation of reality, of finding answers to particular inquiries. Through the case studies, the book therefore proves attitudes towards the plurality of outcomes or results in practice. It prompts us to question whether we want and whether we are able to come to terms with plurality, and how, finally, this plurality relates to our views about the credibility of research.

Acknowledgements

It is close to impossible to encompass in the acknowledgements all those who have contributed to a work that has evolved over a long period of time and in different places. Many people have contributed to this study decisively without their noticing it, and others without my recognising their contribution. Some have, however, had a particularly important role in the process. Above all, I would like to thank Professor Susan Strange, outstanding both in her criticism and in her support, for having several times deservedly questioned the enterprise with a pungent critique while nonetheless showing an understanding of and a confidence in the study often far clearer than the author's. I would also like to recognise the inspiration and encouragement given by Professor Martti Koskenniemi.

I have further drawn great benefit from the unique research milieu offered by the European University Institute in Florence. There, I would like to thank in particular professors Roger Morgan, John Krige, Alan W. Cafruny and Giandomenico Majone for their stimulating seminars and comments. I have also had the opportunity to discuss with or receive comments from several other scholars, among whom I am glad to mention Iver B. Neumann, Stefano Guzzini and Helge Hveem. For the financing of my stay at the EUI, recognition is due to the Academy of Finland.

I owe a debt of gratitude no less to the Finnish Institute of International Affairs and its personnel for providing both a very pleasant working environment and warm support, as well as to my friends and colleagues both in Florence and at the Department of Political Science at the University of Helsinki.

For the case study on Nordic cooperation, I am indebted to the Nordic Council and the Nordic Council of Ministers in Stockholm and Copenhagen for their generous help with both interviews and documentary material.

The book as it now stands would certainly have been both less accessible and less thoroughly thought out if it had not been for the precious linguistic advice I have received at the EUI and in Helsinki. I am particularly grateful to Mark Waller who checked with great care and efficiency the final manuscript. All remaining errors and imprecisions, be they linguistic or substantial, are, of course, mine.

Finally, both my friends and family have been an outstanding source of inspiration. Particular thanks go to my mother, to Aira, and of course to Mikael, by no means just for taming some of my wildest misinterpretations of contemporary history.

Helsinki, February 1998
Hanna Ojanen

1 Introduction: troubling concepts and theories

Are there inadmissible concepts?

The relationship between the state and European integration is with good reason a central concern in current political sciences. Scholars approach the subject in different ways: some study how integration influences the state, others take the converse approach. In dealing with the question of how the state and integration relate to each other, all of them are concerned with a problem that is particularly important because of its tangible implications, but is also particularly difficult to resolve.

The empirical questions of what happens to the state in the process of integration, or what its role is in this process, are essential for understanding the nature and functioning of present European political systems. If the states' functions change, one can also expect changes in their political, administrative and judiciary systems and structures. Changes in functions and practices can also be seen as amounting to gradual changes in political culture. Through changes in the role and nature of the state, the substance of citizenship as well as the forms of political participation may be expected to alter. Finally, the understanding of democracy and identity will be modified. On the other hand, if states guide the process of integration, they can be seen to do so on the basis of their own characteristics, and to be able to halt the process when they wish. The empirical relevance of the understanding of the relationship between the state and integration is, however, not based only on these long-term effects. In some situations, it has an immediate and decisive importance in political decision-making. For example, a country's decision to join the European Union is based on an evaluation of the consequences of membership. The understanding of these consequences, then, depends on how the relationship between the state and integration is seen.

The relationship is also important as a part of the larger, and in some sense classic, theme of the future of the state. Integration can be seen as a factor which influences the position of the state, together with such phenomena as technological development and economic internationalisation.

Moreover, as 'state' and 'integration' are both central concepts constantly employed in research, the question of how the two relate to one another arises in a variety of different contexts.

At the same time, the question is from the outset difficult, and, indeed, an illustrative example of conceptual research problems. Obviously, the answer to the question depends on how the two terms are understood, and it is well-known that both have many meanings. 'State' and 'integration' are abstract entities which lack a single concrete referent in the real world; they are often used in research as basic assumptions without any explicit definitions, and, moreover, both also feature in value-laden concepts.

Time and again, research has wrestled with the task of finding a general agreement on the definition of the state and on the explanation of integration, but it has never gained a lasting advantage over the problem. Rather, an increasing sense of despondency has characterised the pleas for common agreement. It is argued that even if 'the state' at some point in time still had a referent, amidst the changed political landscape the concept is now increasingly outdated hampering or distorting analyses. Repeatedly, these problems have led scholars to conclude that the terms are unsuitable for research, since they cannot be appropriately defined, and that they should therefore be avoided.

Yet, the two terms continue to play a central role: their assumed meanings guide research in an often unnoticeable but not for that reason less consequential way. For despite assurances to the contrary, research on the difficult question of how the state and European integration relate to one another has never failed to produce a response. Answers abound. These diverse answers should not be difficult to understand, either, when we take into account the variety of meanings both terms have. This plurality of answers renders the vast field of integration studies conflicting in outlook, and also particularly interesting to explore.

This study is a critical examination of this plurality of answers to the question of what is the relationship between the state and integration. Instead of aiming to give a specific reply to the question, as is the case in the existing literature, the study shows by drawing on examples of research how certain views and responses emerge in certain contexts. It aims to identify factors which lead to the adoption of a certain understanding, to explain how and why a certain result is achieved. The aim here is also to evaluate the consequences of that understanding for further research, to see what follows from its application. In essence, thus, this book hopes to shed light on the research process with a view to attaining an improved understanding of the variety of different results. This introductory chapter grounds this analysis in some general considerations on the conceptual and methodological problems related to research concerning 'the state' and 'integration', considerations which in part explain why the relationship between the state and integration is so complicated and so central a research problem.

The 'chaotic' variety of meanings of 'the state'

When the two concepts of 'state' and 'integration' are analysed separately, disputes about their respective meanings immediately attract attention. In particular, 'the state' is well-known in this respect: few would counter the claim that the concept of 'state' belongs to the most controversial concepts in political sciences. Characteristically, it is often used without definition as any explicit definition seems to provoke a disagreement on its appropriateness.

Some definitions of the concept are regarded as benchmarks in some sense and are used more often than other, more honed ones. Some definitions are purposively very general while others aim at nailing the matter down as narrowly and exactly as possible. Any reader would be familiar with definitions such as Weber's, for whom the state has the monopoly of legitimate physical violence in society[1] but would also recognise the definition of the state in the specific characteristics arrived at in international law,[2] according to which the state has a permanent territory, a permanent population living in it, a government capable of governing the territory and the population, and the capacity of entering into relations with other states.

In addition to seeing the state as a territorial entity, a political, administrative and judicial unit, level or machinery, it can be seen as a normative or institutional legal order or as a functional unit, a provider of common goods such as security or welfare. Further, one can view the state as an arena of contention for different interest or social groups; it can be identified with bureaucracy, the executive, or a single leader. Or the state can appear as a network or source of authority and power which competes with other similar ones for resources and loyalty. One can also highlight the state as an ethnic-cultural unit, a community of people, or an object of identification; one can see it as a fulfilment of human nature, as well as an apparatus which furthers the aims of some groups or classes, inherently shaped by classes or class struggles and functioning to preserve and expand modes of production. What is more, the state can be seen either as the main actor in international relations, a sovereign among sovereigns or as a part of a system, interdependent with others, or then a dependent subsystem of a larger system. (Cf. Ferguson and Mansbach 1989: 41-79.)

Often, more detailed definitions of the state are propounded with some particular purpose. Then, the applicability of the concept is restricted by the use of specific conditions. By way of example we can turn to Grieco's (1990: 24) definition of the state as the institutions and roles responsible for foreign policies, or the example given by Poggi (1990: 19) according to which an organisation which controls the population in a definite territory is a state insofar as it is differentiated from other organisations operating in the same territory, autonomous and centralised, and its divisions are formally coordinated with one another.

The question of how to define or understand the state can be somewhat confusing. However, the problem can be made to seem even more confusing than it really is. A good example is the inventory of meanings of the term 'state' compiled by Ferguson and Mansbach. The authors seem to want to show that the question of the definition of the state can be characterised as 'conceptual chaos', and indeed they succeed in doing so, and add to the chaos by a convincingly chaotic presentation, and magnifying it by reference to some anecdotal records in counting the different meanings of the state where impressive numbers have been achieved.[3]

It is also customary in the literature to arrive at a certain conclusion about this state of affairs. Not only is it recalled that the concept has many meanings, and that this makes the analysis of the state particularly complicated; it is also often pointed out that finding the proper meaning of the term is a formidably difficult, even impossible task. So, the conclusion reached is that it is best to avoid using the term at all, or perhaps to replace it with a more suitable one. As Ferguson and Mansbach put it, the concept of state has so many meanings that it is practically useless as a tool for analysis and a part of theory. Instead of 'the state', one could, in their view, use a term like 'power centre'. They propose to direct attention to shifting patterns of authority and recommend historically grounded analyses of what these have been and how and why they have changed. (Ferguson and Mansbach 1989: 1-3, 84-88.)

In a similar vein, Easton (1971: 107, 112-113) concludes from the sheer amount of different definitions of the state that a satisfactory definition cannot be found. Palan, in turn, locates the problem of the 'state' in its not being a discrete entity that is separate from society or government, and instead proposes the political process as a unit of analysis. (Palan 1990: esp. 15, 89, 96, 146.)

Others argue that the state is rendered obsolete as a concept by the various changes in the contemporary world which have deprived it of its former defining characteristics. In Czempiel's view, one has to give up the notion and the concept of the state: since there are no 'states' acting in the transnational world, nor 'states' as actors in domestic politics, there is no use in preserving the terminology. In its place, Czempiel proposes the notion of a 'demand-conversion relationship between a society and its political system'. (Czempiel 1989: esp. 124, 132.) For Schmitter, too, the term 'state' should not be used in political analysis or in the analysis of integration. The state has simply changed too much: it is, for him, a waste of time speaking about it or redefining it. The state no longer resembles 'its historical self'; among other features, it has lost its differentiation from civil society, sovereignty, and capacity for unitary action. Moreover, Schmitter argues, the relevance of territoriality has changed; the contemporary context systematically favours the transformation of states into other political forms, such as *confederatii, condominii* or *federatii*. (Schmitter 1991: 3, 12, 15, footnote 15.)

As such, these observations cannot be said to be particularly new or current. Arguments about the decline of the state seem to have pursued the state continuously. We find, for example, Zimmern arguing some sixty years ago that the very notion of 'state' was perhaps obsolete or obsolescent (Zimmern 1939: 284), and Carr claiming in 1945 that the state has become an anachronism.[4] On the other hand, the conceptual substitutes proposed are not all that convincing either: they are hardly less ambiguous than 'the state', and their appropriateness can similarly be questioned. Moreover, abandoning the concept of 'state' seems a rather impetuous solution to the problem. Even those advocates of the rapid elimination of the concept leave a way open for its use, thereby confirming that the phenomenon still exists and may need to be called by its traditional name. Easton (1971) notes that even if the concept is not good as a tool of analysis, it is still important in practical politics as a means for achieving national cohesion. For Czempiel (1989), the state is still the most important, and the only authoritative, distributor of political values in a society, and he sees its role as especially uncontested in the realm of security. Even Schmitter (1991) sees that there are some cases, although rare, in which state capacity and action are wielded in ways that are distinct from the powers of government, bureaucracy, parties, individuals or the like, therefore prompting the use of the concept.

As we will see, exactly the same problems characterise the discussion on the concept of integration, where the lack of agreement on its definition is similarly reckoned to be a major problem. It is not difficult to encounter other examples either, such as the concept of 'sovereignty', which for Krasner (1989:88) has lost meaning and analytical relevance, and which for Carr should not be used scientifically because of its blurred meaning (see Bartelson 1993: 11). Ferguson and Mansbach (1989) point out the vagueness of a number of other key concepts, such as 'autonomy', 'aggression', 'imperialism', 'interdependence', 'dependency' and 'regime'. Together, these examples allude to more general features in research concerning the attitude towards multifaceted concepts and the difficulties in dealing with the role and functions of definitions adequately.

'Integration' - scarcely less 'chaos'

One might expect the concept of integration to differ from that of the state. 'Integration' is obviously a term of recent origin compared to the concept of the state; one might suppose that it would be more precise and that it would be less prone to be taken for granted as an uncontested notion. On the other hand, integration could also be seen as a 'second order' concept that is not as central and basic as that of the state. Integration has also been predominantly a phenomenon to be explained, and therefore, the very definition of the term has been the aim, or part of the aim, of research even more than it has been for the concept of the state. Moreover, the fact that integration is often seen as an ongoing process has meant uncertainty about whether integration already is here or whether it is on the horizon, even as to whether it is here *to a certain extent*, with all the ensuing problems of measurement, indicators and quantification.

However, the same discourse is valid for both concepts: defining 'integration' is by no means less complicated and the ensuing disagreement not less vehement. There is an abundance of different meanings for both terms. Frustration over the difficulties in reaching a consensus about the meaning or shared definitions and the uneasiness sensed about the actual nature of the phenomena to be studied mirror each other, and so do attempts to find more suitable alternative concepts and advice to renounce the use of the term. Both concepts are value-laden and both are in practice often used as assumptions rather than being opened up for discussion. Moreover, both also seem subject to interesting trends in research concerning what is seen as a proper research object; every now and again, both 'state' and 'integration' emerge as objects of intensive debate, while at other times they are left out of the discussion. Both appear and disappear, as it were, in tides as focal objects of research interests, and they can even be seen to compete with each other in being the central element in conceptualising reality so that 'integration', when taking the lead, renders the state obsolete, and vice versa.[5]

Among the much quoted 'standard' understandings of integration, we have Haas' definition according to which integration is a process whereby political actors in several distinct national settings are persuaded to shift their loyalties, expectations and political activities towards a new centre, whose institutions possess or demand jurisdiction over the pre-existing national states, the end result of integration being a new political community superimposed over the existing ones (Haas 1958: 5, 16). For Deutsch, in turn, integration is the attainment, within a territory, of a 'sense of community' and of institutions and practices which are strong and widespread enough to assure stable and dependable expectations of 'peaceful change'. A central factor thus is an agreement on peaceful change and the peaceful settlement of disputes instead of resorting to large-scale physical force. (Deutsch *et al.* 1957: 5-7.) For Etzioni (1965: 12, 329-332), integration is the ability of a unit or system to maintain itself in the face of internal or external challenges, while for Galtung (1967: 368), integration is a process whereby two or more actors form a new actor.

The definitions of integration range, in fact, from the most lexical ones – combining something, becoming part of something else, previously separate units forming a new, composite unit – to more specific ones where the term is divided into subconcepts. Thus, for instance, one can distinguish between political, economic, social or juridical integration, and limit 'integration' to the process in the European Communities and European Union, or see it in a wider sense as encompassing other geographical areas and different forms of regional cooperation. Further, one can understand integration as a process, a structure or as a final result and end state.

A cursory look at the integration literature shows the extent to which the meaning of 'integration' is contested. It is common to find demands for more work towards a common understanding of the term in order to allow for both progress and more accurate results. Integration studies are often depicted as a field of widespread controversy when it comes to concepts and definitions, particularly concerning the notion of 'integration'. The problem of the lack of clear consensus on the delimitation of the field or the dependent variable, that is, what integration exactly is, is noted by several scholars. Puchala even compares integration scholars to blind men each examining a different part of an elephant and failing to agree on what is before them. In his view, the situation is made even worse by the fact that the elephant has been growing in size and complexity and that normative concerns have influenced intellectual efforts. (Puchala 1972: 267-268; cf. Haas 1970: 607, Caporaso 1971: 228, Dougherty and Pfaltzgraff 1981: 453, 459.)

As in the case of the state, if integration often appears 'underdefined', it can also be so 'overdefined' that the variety of different meanings inhibits the use of the concept. Remarks that a commonly agreed definition of integration can hardly be found have led to suggestions for a new conceptual framework to replace the original term. For instance, Puchala (1972) calls for new empirical research within a fresh descriptive framework, that of a 'concordance system'; Schmitter (1991) proposes speaking of a new form of political domination; still others have turned to classical conceptual frameworks, such as the distinction between *Gemeinschaft* and *Gesellschaft* (e.g., Kaiser 1972), or to what are seen as new and more interesting themes to be explored, such as Haas' (1975) 'interdependence' and 'systems change'.

The essential plurality

The problem dealt with in this book is not the complex character of the two terms but the general attitude towards and the conclusions drawn from this complexity. Generally, the plurality of meanings of 'the state' and 'integration' leads to conflicts between the different definitions, if not to the dismissal of the concepts as if they were useless. As a result, examining how two equally complex concepts relate to each other appears close to impossible. There is a tendency to leave the question of the relationship between the state and integration altogether unanswered, making it disappear from the central and explicit research concerns. This, however, only aggravates the conceptual confusion. In fact, attention is turned away from what is meant by the concepts while still continuing to use them, and also away from the range of possible and actual meanings present in research.

In a peculiar way, many scholars seem to look for definitions and theories in a wrong place as if they did not recognise them, or as if they did not understand the way they conduct research. It is as if definitions were presupposed to be clear and commonly shared, and theories to be faultless: when these conditions do not apply, concepts and theories are simply abandoned or replaced, as if conceptual and theoretical problems would vanish with them. The very idea that there should be only one commonly agreed meaning for a term in order for it to be usable is problematic. This reflects a rather narrow view of research. It means that the plurality of meanings cannot be dealt with, and so the possibilities to understand and evaluate research results are dramatically diminished.

It is essential to treat the complexity of concepts such as 'state' and 'integration' as an inherent feature of these terms rather than as a problem. That this complexity is inherent becomes understandable when one looks at the nature of the two major factors which render these concepts particularly complicated and increase the difficulties in finding a consensus about their 'proper' meaning. On the one hand, the very centrality of the concepts increases their ambiguity. Bartelson remarks that a central concept is bound to be ambiguous by the very fact of its centrality. When a concept becomes central to the extent that other concepts are defined in terms of it or depend on it for their coherent meaning and use, these linkages saturate the concept with multiple meanings and make it ambiguous; this ambiguity, then, is open to further logical and rhetorical exploitation. (Bartelson 1993: 11.)

On the other hand, these concepts consist of two different but equally essential elements, descriptive and normative, or formal and ethical, as Grant puts it. Thus, while the formal element of the concept of the state includes features which states may share and which distinguish the state from, for example, government, citizenship, institutions and sovereignty, the ethical component, then, concerns views about the nature of the state, closely related to values. Values determine the view of the state's functions, scope and limits. Here, widely different views notoriously coexist: the state can be seen as having a distributive function or the task of a guarantor of individual rights, but it can also be seen as the realisation of man's social nature, a power for its own sake, or a mere practical necessity. (Grant 1988: 691-692, 709.)

A discussion on how the state should be defined, thus, is not merely a question of the empirical characteristics of states or what they actually are; it is also intertwined with considerations about what the state should or should not be. Yet, scholars tend to perceive a fundamental contradiction between norms and theory: a concept which has an overtly normative side is considered unqualified for theory construction. This is for many the main reason for arguing that the concept of the state should not be used – with the consequence that the concept is disregarded as if analytical research on the state was impossible.

This is clearly reflected in Ferguson and Mansbach (1989: 41, 83-85) for whom not only the state but also other concepts in social sciences are inherently value-laden and reflect the normative biases of the theorists. They argue that social scientists are as a rule less 'objective' in their search for definitions than they like to admit or realise; definitions are shaped to conform to value preferences, to norms, ideologies or political aspirations, which are rarely articulated and serve as weapons in battles among scientists. Thus, they conclude that the conceptions of the state they have found in the literature are suitable for normative and ideological aims rather than for theory construction or achieving conceptual consensus. Similarly, it was seen, Puchala (1972) complained about the negative influence of normative concerns on intellectual efforts towards understanding integration. In fact, the concept of integration does not differ in this respect from that of the state. The ethical or normative aspect could be even more prominent in the case of 'integration' which was from the outset endorsed as a project by normative considerations about its possibilities in rendering relations between states more peaceful and increasing general welfare.

Due to this inherent ambiguity, a reduction of meanings for the sake of analysis may not necessarily be a way to increase the understanding of concepts such as the state and integration. It might even increase fragmentation and 'conceptual chaos'. In practice, or in the reality that is being analysed, these concepts have a plurality of meanings. Therefore, research which reduces the meanings to one risks never really catching this reality. It could be argued with Ferguson and Mansbach (1989: 84) that 'were the social scientists somehow able to develop a consensual body of concepts, that very triumph would serve to render their work even more irrelevant to practitioners [...]'. The ardent discussion on the proper meaning of 'integration', for instance, seems beside the point when one considers how the term was originally invented in the European context. In fact, those drafting written documents and treaties about the European arrangements were well aware of conceptual problems and the value-laden nature of political terms: the designation 'integration' was explicitly chosen because it was less precise and therefore far more suitable than, for example, the proposed 'union', which had overly profound connotations.[6] Finally, reduction of meanings might not be disconnected with questions of power and influence, either. Ferguson and Mansbach (1989: 41, 83-85) point to the link between the power to define and the power to control, arguing that for policy makers, the control of concepts is a source of unique authority and legitimacy.

The explicit definition of the concept is less important than the use to which it is put. In practice, explicit definitions are not always given and even if they are, these clarifications and what actually is meant by the concept in a particular piece of research might not coincide. Attention has to be paid to the function of the concept in the analysis. An important difference appears depending whether the concept is used as a tool for analysis or as an object of analysis, or, in other words, whether the state is seen as something to be explained or an explaining factor. As in the case of the term 'sovereignty', the more the term is thought to explain, the more it is itself withdrawn from explanation (cf. Bartelson 1993: 15). The very question of whether the definition becomes a problem is a question of the function of the concept. When used as an explaining (independent and isolable) variable, the state is often an assumed element in the theory – more a constant than a variable. It often forms the basis for the definition of other concepts or for a whole conceptual hierarchy. A series of concepts and understandings are built on it, such as 'state functions', 'state interest', 'intergovernmental', 'international', 'supranational', even 'citizenship'. As the terms 'international' and 'supranational' show, what is seen to be outside or above the state is a function of the understanding of the state itself. While it might be impossible to define the term itself explicitly, it has a fundamental role in serving as a basis for the definition of other concepts.[7] This role, again, cannot be fully understood without taking into account the plenitude of meanings.

It also seems that the role and functions of the two concepts, state and integration, as research objects are becoming more similar. Despite the difficulties in explaining integration, or perhaps because of these difficulties, 'integration' seems to be acquiring some of the features of 'the state' in terms of its functions in theory construction. Although there still is an ongoing debate between different ways of explaining integration, there seems to be a shift from integration as a dependent variable to integration as an independent variable: while it first was explained by different factors, it now explains different phenomena, such as regionalism or the strengthening of the executive in relation to the legislative. A look at the development of integration studies shows that through the process of theoretical accumulation, integration becomes something isolable or independent, an explanatory variable, while, at the same time, EU integration is increasingly analysed as unique or incomparable.

The 'essential contestability' and the role of choice

The notion of 'essential contestability' helps to articulate the prevailing view on concept definition and the problems stemming from it. Several terms central to political and social sciences have been described as 'essentially contested'; typically, these concepts involve endless disputes about their proper uses on the part of their users. For Gallie (1956), the characterisation as essentially contested applies when the concept involved is appraisive in that the state of affairs it describes is a valued achievement, when the practice described is internally complex in that its characterisation involves reference to several dimensions and when the agreed and contested rules of application are relatively open. Examples of these concepts could be 'democracy'[8] or 'politics' (see Connolly 1974); the two terms examined here certainly fit well in the category.

It is therefore argued that the problem with these concepts lies more in the attitude towards 'essential contestability' than in this contestability itself. Connolly's remarks about the way essentially contested concepts are approached support this view. He argues that according to the prevailing view, the concepts used in contemporary social sciences are not such contested concepts; rather, they are uncontested. This view is based on the idea that there are descriptive and normative concepts, and the former, which are noncontroversial, are those pertinent to scientific work. They are neutral and technically defined, designed to meet the conditions of objective inquiry; they allow for common definitions and impersonal tests, in short, for objectivity. As Connolly observes, for those representing this view, the notion of essentially contested concepts is difficult to assimilate and easy to ignore. (Connolly 1974: 11-12.)

Should the concepts used in research, nevertheless, present some ambiguities, the need arises to render them noncontroversial. It is not difficult to come across examples of scholars maintaining that ordinary language is too blunt a tool to be of use for scientific investigation and that the language used in political life is especially ill-suited for the purposes of political inquiry. For instance Oppenheim (1981: 177-178, 185-186) argues that it is therefore necessary to reconstruct the basic concepts in order to reach a language as free as possible of the imperfections of ordinary usage. In the realm of integration studies, examples of efforts at rendering the term 'integration' more precise and suitable for more technical theory construction stem from the same considerations.

Alternatively, research proceeds as if the concepts were uncontested. The concept of 'state' thus appears at the same time to be contested and fundamentally uncontested. When attention is focused on the explicit definition, disputation begins; however, in normal use, the concept can be used as if it had one unambiguous meaning. The same point is argued by Walker as regards state sovereignty. Far from its largely accepted status as an 'essentially contested' concept, state sovereignty is instead an essentially uncontested concept; it is treated as a ready settled question. (Walker 1990, quoted in Weber 1995: 2.)

Connolly points to three important elements which contradict this view on concepts and definition and which help to understand the problems related to 'the state' and 'integration'. The first element is the inherent importance of the normative element in the kinds of concepts alluded to above. Connolly sees problems in drawing a clear line between concepts that are acceptable in social inquiry and those to be excluded, and challenges the distinction between descriptive and normative concepts. Description, for Connolly, is not simply 'naming': to describe is to characterise a situation from the vantage point of certain interests, purposes or standards. Concepts such as 'democracy', 'politics' and 'freedom' are bounded by normative considerations. Their normative side, or 'moral component', is essential for the use of the concepts, and if it is not taken into account, their rationale and the possibility of applying them to new situations is lost. In fact, Connolly argues that disputes about concepts are not just about the concepts of politics but are part of politics itself. On the other hand, the concepts of ordinary discourse or language play a central role in the technical inquiries; one cannot devise a technical language which would minimise disagreement and troublesome features. (Connolly 1974: 23, 27-30, 36.)

Secondly, he stresses that an understanding of a concept requires that the concept be seen in a context. In other words, it requires an understanding of relations between concepts and conceptual systems. Connolly notes how the different dimensions of the term 'politics' refer to other concepts such as 'institution', 'decision', 'motive', 'interest', or 'consensus'; in order to clarify the concept of politics or to make it intelligible, he argues, its connections with a host of other concepts have to be displayed, and an elaboration of the broader conceptual system within which it is implicated is needed (*idem:* 12-14).

Thirdly, Connolly doubts whether uncontestability, or very precise definitions, at all can be seen as an asset, and whether, accordingly, definitions can be compared using their exactness as a yardstick. It is often thought that interpretations could be judged against some standard operationalistic definitions. In that case, however, all invoked concepts of the conceptual system should be made operationalistic, which would already be close to impossible. Even more importantly, even if it were established that one proposed definition of politics were more operational than another, this in itself would not be sufficient to establish it as the preferred definition. Indeed, Connolly argues that the more operational definition might leave out elements central to our idea of politics. (Connolly 1974: 15-16.)

This entails two major points: first, the more operationalistic a definition is, the less faithfully it probably depicts reality, and second, that an ultimate point of reference in the evaluation of the definition is 'our' view, our own preferences. To assess the relative merits of different definitions, one should, in Connolly's view, look at the point or purpose of the definition. Thus, the perplexing question of subjectivity, of choice and purpose, arises. It seems reasonable to argue that sufficient definitions can only be achieved if the purpose of the definition is known (e.g., Bayles 1991: 253). Yet, the question of purpose in political analysis is obviously complicated: a definition formed according to the purposes of the researcher can be seen as a negation of objective research, at least if one thinks that the purpose in finding a proper definition in order to be able to answer a certain question is directly linked to the purpose of arriving at a certain answer.

The prevailing attitude towards definitions, as Connolly depicts it, seems thus to involve a contradiction in that concepts are expected to be and are treated as an objective, technical matter, while at the same time, they reflect important theoretical and normative commitments. As Connolly explains:

> But why doesn't each investigator simply stipulate definitions suitable to his particular purposes and leave matters at that? Why do *differences* in interpretation of a key concept so often become *disputes* over its proper meaning? Why, when these disputes occur, are they *essential* in the twofold sense that the prevailing use is continually vulnerable to challenge and reassessment and that the disputants find themselves treating the issue as important rather than merely irksome? It is widely known that even social scientists who formally state that the definitions they advance are merely 'arbitrary' stipulations preceding the important questions of inquiry become quite disturbed when their own favored definitions of key concepts are challenged; but the model of inquiry accepted by these social scientists makes it difficult to locate the source of that irritation. (Connolly 1974: 20-21).

In all, Connolly sees conceptual disputes as neither a mere prelude to inquiry nor peripheral to it, but when they involve the central concepts of a field of investigation, they are surface manifestations of fundamental theoretical differences. The conceptual debates are often intense because of the tacit understanding of the relation of these debates to deep commitments and the import that the outcome of such contests has for the politics of the society. (Connolly 1974: 20-21, 40.)

That differences concerning concept definition easily lead to stagnating disputes may well depend on factors linked to the 'model of inquiry' alluded to by Connolly – in particular, it could be argued, to an inadequate consideration of the role of *choice*. The very idea that research involves choice seems, in fact, often to meet with an ambivalent reception. Choice seems to be too subjective and arbitrary an element to fit in the common picture of research as something objective and definite. The role of choice in research is seen to be minimal if it exists at all. At the same time, however, many admit that research results do not stem automatically from reality or from the material at hand, and that the material does not automatically constitute itself: at all stages, the scholar makes choices, both conscious and unconscious. Reality is necessarily 'mediated' through the active role of the researcher. Concepts can be seen as introducing an element of choice which intervenes between reality and the result of the research. In a situation in which there is no single 'real' meaning for these concepts, but instead a variety of meanings, and in which the framing of research questions implies a decision on the meaning, the understanding adapted is not obvious and cannot be taken for granted. Therefore, it is illuminating to try to assess both the array of choice and the different constraints that might reduce the number of possible choices.

Being aware of the manifold meanings or definitions that both 'the state' and 'integration' may have, one can assume that the different views concerning how the two affect each other depend on how both terms are defined, or, in other words, what definitions are chosen for the terms. The point is simple, but it deserves attention in that the link between definitions and results is not always recognised. It is not completely clear whether research results should be judged against some objective, external point of reference, such as a particular definition, or against the choices made in the piece of research itself, respecting its integrity. Research results are sometimes criticised because they do not reflect the views of the reader, although they might well be consonant with those of the writer. Secondly, and more importantly, the link between definitions and results deserves attention in that the choice available seems to be, after all, rather limited: not all definitions will do, and a choice made will subsequently act as a constraint on other choices.

The choice made, in fact, might not be 'free' at all. Moreover, it might not be intentional. One can see that there is an array of possible choices, which in the case of the state and integration is certainly not modest. In practice, though, such choice is restricted by various factors, in particular the position of the scholar and the study in terms of methodology and academic disciplines. Finally, the choice made is crucial in the sense that there is not only the possibility of choice, but also a necessity of choice. It is apparent and somehow commonsensical that scholars should always determine what they mean by the concepts they use; thus, they have to choose a meaning, and precisely one meaning, to which they are then expected to adhere. These general rules of what could be called 'research practice' are seldom seen as a constraint; rather, they seem to be the essence of the research itself.

Conventional research practice and its consequences for the study of the state and integration

The features of concept use outlined above can also be seen as a part of a 'research practice', of certain rules and understandings of what research is and how it is to be conducted, which can be assumed to influence the existing research on the relation between the state and integration. 'Research practice' is here used to mean a relatively limited and presupposed set of rules concerning the procedure of a study, norms and practices of research as a regulated activity involving expectations concerning the coherence, logic and proofs of a piece of research. It is a view of how research should be conducted and what counts as scientific knowledge in each field. It involves very practical matters linked to the definition of terms, internal coherence and the question of evidence.[9] It can also be seen to involve a general understanding of the process, also of what is 'scientific'.[10]

In that it is taken for granted and conventional, research practice can also be expected to resist change. It sets certain constraints on theorising and the scope of definitions and may influence our way of thinking to the extent that we might be unable to imagine different models or solutions, alternative conceptualisations and assumptions. Some of its rules may be particularly 'costly' to alter, in particular those concerning the definition and choice of objects of the discipline in question, as well as the rules of the 'scientific game' more generally. Among the most important rules, there are respect for the facts and obedience to the rules of coherence, as Morin (1982: 38) proposes.

The prevailing or conventional research practice could be characterised by the quest for objective, cumulative knowledge, and by the presentation of science as rational and progressive. The goal of objectivity seems further linked to a tendency to isolate phenomena for analysis, to analyse them separately, and to seek definitions which are not dependent on a specific context. The possible problems connected with this practice were alluded to above: isolating the object of study, for example through a very restrictive definition, might not be conducive to understanding the object. As Bartelson (1993: 10-13) puts it, the practice of clarifying the meaning of a concept through ever more fine-grained qualitative differences, emphasising essential features and eliminating borderline cases is an attitude indebted to the codes of semantic conduct drawn up by post-Kantian empiricists: gradually, he argues, it became scientific common sense to see that the rational settling of disputes over truth necessitates clear-cut definitions.

This is also what Morin criticises: the conventional view, or the traditional Western scientific paradigm as he calls it, for particularly its experimental methodology and the ensuing manipulation of objects of study have not only led to new discoveries but also to regression. In Morin's view, the 'desecologisation', or isolation of the object of study in order to make it more easily controllable by the researcher has reduced the possibilities for understanding it as it means reducing or eliminating knowledge about how it relates to the environment.[11] The objects of research are, thus, moulded in some way or another to allow for the kind of results which are deemed scientific. The rationality of science seems to set specific requirements for the objects of study. As Lowi (1992: 3) points out, if one supposes that science must be rational, it must follow a prescribed method and must concern itself with orderly, repeatable, and predictable phenomena. This is why, for Lowi, it analyses small, even microscopic units: the smaller the unit, the more units we have, and large numbers of units behave conveniently according to the regularities of mathematical probability.

Conventional research practice involves also a certain view of progress. According to this, the scholar has a tool kit consisting of definitions, theories (in the role of hypotheses to be tested) and methods, such as a way of formulating questions of a specific type, analysing the material and eventually concluding on the basis of that empirical evidence – which is taken to be more or less given and exist independently of the researcher.[12] Progress can be equated with the accumulation of knowledge or development of cumulative theory; this is seen to require consensus on the meanings of the central terms used, such as 'the state'. (Cf. Ferguson and Mansbach 1989, esp. pages 2-3, 68, 82.)

A central feature in conventional research practice is thus reflected in the wrangling over definitions considered above. On the surface, discussions on both 'state' and 'integration' seem to be concerned with progress, and therefore with shared definitions; on a deeper level, however, there are considerable differences in theoretical commitments which make it difficult to renounce a particular view in favour of this objective. Central concepts must be defined; they cannot have several meanings, although an explicit definition is not always required, and the scholar has to adhere to the definition throughout the research for the sake of coherence. This seems quite clear: one cannot understand the study, and its results have no relevance if one does not know what has been meant by the terms used. Moreover, in social sciences characterised by conceptual twists, is it not the task of the scholar to contribute with clear and precise, well-justified understandings? A large part of the research process consists of implicit or explicit concept definition: this is how the scholar renders the complex reality explicable or understandable.[13]

Thus, it is only natural if the scholar agrees without any particular need for reflection with the categorical warning Umberto Eco gives in his vademecum of how to do research. He is even against trying to write about something one does not succeed in defining. Terms one cannot define should be avoided; and should a difficult term happen to be central to one's study, adds Eco, it would be better to abandon the research altogether. (Eco 1995: 167-168.)

The normal practice of starting from a definition is not as such somehow wrong; rather, it directs research in a fairly uniform or narrow way. Much effort is put into finding the proper meaning and a sufficiently precise definition of the terms, one which, in addition, the scientific community could agree on. These aims reflect the need for explanation, generalisation and accumulation. However, it is not clear whether a definition should be *a priori* or based on the case in question. The disputes between different views also tend to be inconclusive as there is no agreement on the criteria for comparing them. Furthermore, despite the aim of defining, the same terms often appear in research without any explicit elucidation, as presumed basic building blocks of a conceptual apparatus used in the analysis.

While it is easy to justify an unambiguous use of concepts as being at the heart of scientific analysis, it could also be asked whether this in the long run could also be counterproductive. In the context of integration studies, defining both 'state' and 'integration' from the outset may be a precondition for a meaningful analysis, and a fixed understanding of the former may help understand the process of the latter. However, it could also be thought that the absence of the problematisation of the state may, in this case, actually turn out to be a stumbling block rather than a useful simplification. The variety of meanings can be seen as an important and integral characteristic of the two terms, and their reduction could impede explanation or constrain research.

On the other hand, the significance of universal, placeless and timeless definitions can also be questioned. They can be seen as a necessary basis for generalisations. However, one might argue that 'contextualised' definitions are more valid. Contextuality, in turn, can be seen as involving two aspects. First, a specific definition always serves a certain purpose in the theoretical context in which it has been put, and the adequacy of a definition depends on the purpose. Second, one could emphasise in Morin's way that the objects of research cannot be fully comprehended if abstracted from their environment, the links to the environment being an integral part of the object itself. In this case, for example, one could argue that the state cannot be understood as a separate unit, but only in relation to its environment, composed of phenomena such as integration.

Applied to the context of the study of the state and integration, the conventional research practice would, thus, mean that research would seek one (right) answer to the questions it poses, for example, one explanation or theory, through adapting one definition for each term, and with the view of eliminating rival views. This logic of research practice seems above all to make both the theoretical past and alternative answers disappear, and with them, it could be argued, the possibilities for dealing with the plural interpretations. The study of European integration seems, in fact, to illustrate this feature. Integration studies as a field, like many others, seems more concerned with its present shortcomings and future development than with its past, although it obviously would not be what it is without this past. The usual procedure in the study of integration starts from a review of existing theories; their comparison often leads to the conclusion that they are not enough and that new theories should be sought. The emphasis is on progress; existing theories are seldom seen as adequate, which has to do with the manner they are looked at: criticising theories often becomes an end in itself.

Criticism for its own sake is not a very demanding activity. Compared with the task of constructing something solid and new, it might even be fairly easy. After all, it is simple to criticise theories in that they themselves offer plenty of material for criticism, both by omitting factors and by being built on a specific view as to what is a good explanation. Therefore, a pertinent criticism can always be constructed on either the question of which factors can be linked to the question, or the question of what is a good theory. In short, one asks for more factors to be taken into account when the explanation is simple and for simplicity when the explanation becomes too multifaceted.[14] Further, the new contribution, or the solution offered after the critical review of existing literature, may often be just a new concept, new name or typology which in reality changes little if anything (cf. Strange 1988). It also happens that one simply keeps reinventing the wheel – or even something less useful – through details that were actually already present. The search for newness requires a considerable knowledge of the past and may still not succeed. A final pitfall, then, seems to be that the links between theories are not perceived to be important: a theory is criticised for its undue emphasis on certain factors, which is as such a valid procedure, but which loses meaning when one takes into consideration that the theory is an answer to another theory which, in turn, did not take that factor into consideration. Research, thus, seems to have the best intentions of improving our understanding of, for example, European integration, though not necessarily with the best means for doing so. Rather, it produces unduly incoherent and conflictual knowledge, without giving the tools for understanding it.

The hypotheses which conduct this analysis could be summarised as follows. First, a special research practice is an important factor in determining how a specific question is studied and what kinds of results are achieved. Secondly, research always involves choice. As regards in particular the definitions used, there are always several possibilities from among which one can choose; this leads to the question of interests, power and purpose. On the other hand, however, the scholar also has to choose one of these. In a way, the scholar has the ability and power to define, but also the unfortunate obligation to define, to choose among the definitions. Thirdly, an essential part of research practice is the way it affects choice. In the analysis of what has been chosen from what by whom, it might well be intuited that mechanisms internal to research, that is the research practice, affect the choice made to a considerable extent.

In brief, the basic consequence of choice, the exclusion of some views, together with the generally wary attitude towards choice in research practice, result in diminished consideration of alternative views and thereby also make the relations between different views more nebulous. Indeed, one might think that the various points in research where a choice is made are also points in which different views are related to each other. Concentrating on choices could therefore increase the transparency of research and thereby increase the capacities to evaluate it, perhaps even to improve its quality.

Further, it is supposed here that the normal analysis of the relationship between the state and integration avoids letting both terms 'float' but proceeds, instead, by holding one of the two constant and explaining in terms of the other. Conceptual problems can be avoided through making a certain concept an assumption. Indeed, if the state is studied, integration is 'stable', and vice versa – perhaps for the simple reason, pointed out by Bartelson (1993: 19-20), that every scientific practice has to start somewhere, taking something for granted. In the study of the relationship between integration and the state, this implies a contradiction between the existence of clear answers and the vague character of both terms considered separately: the uncertainty about the meaning of both terms hardens into firm views of their essence when research on their relationship is concerned as the problem is made into a remarkably neat research task. In the explanations of integration, most solid understandings of the state can be found, and likewise, integration appears unquestioned in contexts where the state is focused on. Further, one of the two terms may actually be the key to understanding the discussion. For example, the difference between various views on integration can be seen in the understanding of the state, and vice versa.

Finally, there seems to be inadequate consideration of the way in which both definitions and theories are linked to each other and among themselves, something that can be seen as a result of undermining the role of choice in research. As regards the links between concepts, one can interpret the wish to find a generally valid definition for each term as a factor contributing to seeing the concepts in isolation. Theories link concepts, both intentionally and unintentionally; on the other hand, theories are linked to each other through conceptual choices. In sum, conventional research practice discourages dealing with questions of plural interpretations, normativity, and relativity understood in the sense of relations between theories and concepts. Thus, its own plural outcome becomes a problem with which research practice is unable to deal.

Depicting plurality

This book aims to depict and understand the plurality of truth in integration theories, a plurality which tends to remain a problem due to some specific features of conventional research practice. Thus, it does not try to determine the relationship between the state and integration but to analyse and understand how and why various existing answers have been reached. In fact, it could be argued that still another study on the relation between the state and integration based on normal research practice would not necessarily add much. On the one hand, following one particular definition would obviously narrow the scope of investigation and hinder the analysis of what different definitions imply for research (cf. Bartelson 1993). Nor is it the intention here to make the usual dash across well-established stepping stones – a presentation and criticism of 'isms' – towards something new. The 'new', in fact, might not be very different from previous knowledge. Instead, this study proposes to take some steps back, to look at the origins and backgrounds of views. It is a critical study of research, of some internal mechanisms through which knowledge is created, transformed, criticised and transferred. The purpose is to arrive at a better understanding of how theories work and how scholars work with theories in the particular field in question.

In a way, the method of this study could be characterised as being horizontal in contrast to more vertical or chronological studies. Instead of reaching for a single best view or theory, attention is directed towards pointing out the relations between theories. This book analyses the choice of meanings, and in particular three aspects of these choices: the restrictions and consequences of choice and the function of choice as a link between apparently very different views. It also tries to see meanings in their specific contexts rather than starting with blank definitions, taking into account the mutual influence between the object, be it the state or integration, and its environment.

The historical evolution of the meanings or the conceptual history of the two terms is given relatively less attention. Conceptual history would obviously increase awareness of past development and existing, or previously existing, alternative views. In the case of the 'state' in particular, the importance of the historical variation of its meaning is easy to perceive. However, these aspects have been amply studied.[15] On the other hand, writing a conceptual history would bring with it the same problems related to normal research practice. Ferguson and Mansbach (1989: 17-18) comment on the conceptual history of the state by noting that the historical origins of the state cannot be pinpointed without an identification and definition of the object; the problem, therefore, is that in history, there is no good basic model to serve as a general definition and, instead, there is a risk of being too abstract. The problem, however, could rather be the opposite: there are many possibilities with which to start analysis and therefore many different versions of its conceptual history. In the analysis of the different views on the state and integration, this book takes a course somewhat similar to a genealogical analysis in explaining the formation of the present views in terms of their past. As Bartelson puts it, a genealogical analysis does not tell what actually happened in the past but how the present became logically possible. (Bartelson 1993: 6, 51; for a more thorough discussion, pp. 64ff.)

At the same time, however, the book stresses the co-existence of plural views and the importance of their interrelations for their development.

This study involves a view of scientific progress that is not necessarily shared by what has been called here the normal research practice. For normal research practice, progress in science implies a consolidation of a certain view and increasing consensus about the object. Here, progress is viewed in a different way. It is assumed that the ability to relate different results to each other is lost without knowledge of why different results emerge in the first place; therefore, undermining the non-objective characteristics of research actually constitutes a hindrance towards its development. In a sense, the study comes close to that of Feyerabend who emphasises the harmful effects of claiming that there is only one possible method, or, in general, certain given rules for scientific activity. For Feyerabend, progress lies not in the gradual consolidation of existing views but in different views, in the very falsification of theories by finding facts which contradict them. The requirement of consistency is not reasonable as it tends to conserve the old, he argues, pointing out the common tendency to see a theory as better not because of its superior quality but because of its age and familiarity (Feyerabend 1975: 35-36).

A final methodological point which the book makes in relation to normal research practice is also linked to the views on progress and concerns the relationship between theory and reality. Theories are often seen to be the aim of research; they are understood as solutions or explanations of problems, usually of causal type, to be tested by empirical evidence. Explanation is usually juxtaposed with description; the logic of explanation requires the singling out of the relevant, important determinants (cf. Allison 1971: 4). Progress, thus, would consist in increasing correspondence between facts and theory. It is, however, not necessarily possible to make a clear difference between facts and theory – indeed, they are not separate realms (cf. Feyerabend 1975: 66). As with a theory, a description involves choosing relevant elements, facts and phenomena, as well as ways of linking them together, or drafting causes and reasons – thus, essentially theoretical elements (cf. Hanson 1965, esp. 54, 70). On the other hand, if theory is seen as an explanation, it is still a relative explanation as its adequacy can be contested.[16] A theory, in fact, could be seen as essentially an understanding of how different elements are linked to each other, both at the level of events and at that of concepts. In a theory, concepts are not defined in isolation, one at a time, but are always interrelated so that the stand taken on one concept has bearing on the understanding of the other concepts. Therefore, relations between concepts influence single definitions in an important way. This makes the analysis of choice even more pertinent. The way concepts are used is a result of a choice, or a series of choices; their use is grounded in different interests or aims, be they theoretical or practical. The necessity of choosing and the expected coherence in following the choice made has wide repercussions: it is easy to see that this kind of a conceptual pre-understanding of the questions shapes the answers given, just as it shapes the framing of the concrete research problems.

Drawing on these considerations, this book begins by depicting in chapter two the different views on the relationship between the state and integration. It does not pretend to offer a complete overview of the state and integration in the literature, which is vast, but instead a broadly divided variety of views which enables us to investigate the reasons for the adoption of a particular view and to reflect upon its consequences for further research.

Three important branches or perspectives can be discerned in the study of this relationship. For the first, there is, evidently, the branch of integration studies, or the study of the process of integration and the theories of integration. There, the relationship between the state and integration constitutes an important fork in the debate – and also a perpetual source of contention. Thus, major differences appear in the answers to the questions of what happens to the state in the process of integration and what the role of the state in that process is. Put bluntly, a certain 'cartellisation' of views into two groups can often be discerned, represented by the claims that integration either weakens or strengthens the state (statements usually connected to neofunctional and intergovernmental theories, respectively).

Secondly, the relationship between the state and integration also appears elsewhere in the discipline of international relations. Questions such as how integration changes the role of the state, the meaning of sovereignty and the nature of inter-state relations are seen as increasingly important subjects of study on which to take a stand. On the other hand, the future of the state is in some sense even a classical theme of research in the field of international politics. A variety of factors influencing its role and position have been examined, including the process of integration together with phenomena such as technological development, nationalism or economic internationalisation.

Third, within comparative politics or political science proper, the study of national political and administrative systems increasingly takes into account the effects of integration which seem to strengthen the importance of widening the frame of analysis from a purely national one and to call into question the understanding of basic concepts such as democracy, political participation, rights and duties, and citizenship.

Chapter two, thus, presents *what* has been achieved in the field in terms of views on the relationship between the state and integration, and *how* different views have emerged, taking into consideration also *when* they emerge in relation to each other. The analysis of the views is also aimed at elucidating the kind of research practice adopted in the field. Whether or not it actually appears conform to that outlined above, it certainly affects the emergence of the views in an important way.

Chapter three, then, examines *why* these particular views have been attained rather than other ones. The reasons found for adopting a certain position are grouped together, emphasising particularly the domains of disciplinary factors, perspectives on methodology and theory, and values.

Similarities and differences between the stances and the specific relevance of what could be seen as a theoretical debate emerge when they are applied to definite cases. This application is made in chapters four and five. While the views are similar in their applicability to the cases, the consequences of their exercise are widely different, and significant in practice. This brings the study back to why precisely the answer to the question about the relationship between the state and integration is so important.

In practical politics, the problem can be translated into a question about the repercussions of membership of the European Union for a country or for other integrative processes and institutions. Clearly, these consequences can only be assumed on the basis of existing knowledge; yet, their role in decision-making about membership is decisive.

For this study, two cases are chosen which are particularly illustrative from this point of view: Nordic cooperation and Finnish integration policy. Finnish integration policy serves as an example of the importance the evaluation of the effects EU membership has for a state's decision on whether or not to join. This evaluation depends on how both integration and the state are understood, and therefore rather different interpretations may appear. The chapter on Nordic cooperation evaluates somewhat similarly the possibilities and future prospects of Nordic cooperation when several Nordic countries are EU members. Again, the evaluation depends on how integration is understood, that is, whether it is seen as impeding or making practically ineffectual the continuation of parallel Nordic cooperation. At the same time, the contents of integration and cooperation are compared. The perspective on the prospects of Nordic cooperation does not only depend on the understanding of integration: equally central is the way Nordic cooperation itself is understood. Often, in fact, Nordic cooperation seems to fall somewhere between cooperation and integration, while it has also been argued that it is more an extension of the state than integration. A common question in the literature is whether or not Nordic cooperation is integration, as well as whether it is important for the individual Nordic countries, and if so, in what ways.

In order to exemplify the array of possible interpretations and, thus, of choices, two versions are presented of both cases. These comprise alternative interpretations of past, present and future at the time when Finnish EU membership was being decided. The interpretations are examples of how different ways of understanding the relations between concepts and facts result in different representations. The method of presenting different versions underlines not only that they can be divergent but exact, but also that they are, in fact, quite far from each other in terms of their results and implications. In addition to showing the rather customary fact that 'reality' can be given very different theoretical interpretations and that evidence can be found for contrary claims about Nordic cooperation and Finnish integration policy, this book aims to illustrate that the activity of research entails a *version*, normally *one* version, of reality being rendered. The result is an interpretation, which in turn implies the existence of others.

This procedure might recall the well-known study of Allison about the Cuban missile crisis in which the author aims to explore the influence of unrecognised assumptions upon thinking about an event and the alternative perspectives available. Applying three different 'conceptual lenses' or frames of reference to the same material, he aims at uncovering additional facts but also underlining how the different lenses highlight different aspects of the same event. (Allison 1971: v-vi.) Allison's lenses give different explanations of what happened: in the rational actor model, a particular event is seen as a result of governmental choice based on national goals, while in the model of organisational process, what happens is seen as outputs explained by organisational features; finally, in that of governmental or bureaucratic politics, what happens is neither a choice, nor an output, but 'resultant' of various bargaining games among different players in the national government. (*Idem:* esp. 4-6, 67, 79.)

While Allison's study offers some important insights to the present study, it nevertheless leaves open some crucial questions which this book, in turn, aims to tackle. Firstly, Allison is in the end rather unclear as to whether his different versions are compatible with each other or are alternatives. In fact, Allison's versions can be seen as a mere accumulation of details which are compatible and actually only reveal more information about the same facts. He also calls the second and third model as improvements of the first and alludes to the possibility of having a grand model or working synthesis incorporating them all. At the same time, he notes that more attention should be paid to the points in which the explanations are compatible or incompatible. (Allison 1971: 5, 246-257, 257-259; see also pages 274-277.) This study differs from Allison's in that here, the 'results' are not the same. Where Allison presents three ways of arriving at the same point, at what happened in reality, this study presents three ways of arriving at three different interpretations of what actually happened. Here, therefore, the versions are not compatible.

Secondly, Allison does not fully reflect on the upshot of using his models. He alludes to how the lenses could yield different prescriptions for action and affect behaviour through influencing the interpretation of which factors matter most in a given situation. Yet, these allusions call for a further elaboration of how different these prescriptions can be when wholly incompatible views are juxtaposed.

There are, however, three essential points in Allison's study which have a direct bearing on this book. First, he approaches the question of why a certain view is adopted, even though he does not elaborate on anything like research practice more in general. Allison shows how such a simple question as technical feasibility – indeed, certainly one among the internal constraints in research – may to a surprising extent affect the choice of framework. The models are not in practice equally easy to put into practice. It might well happen that the scholar uses different models and different standards for analysing different actors, for instance governments; in particular, there might be a tendency to analyse the more familiar government of one's own state with sophisticated data on perceptions and priorities, while analysing that of another, in absence of such data, on the basis of rational calculations. (Cf. Allison 1971: 181, 251.) If these constraints were spelled out, the analysis would obviously not appear rigorously scientific.

Allison's second point related to the explanation of different views is the role of the scholar's understanding of theory, or the question of incompatibility of the standards for adequate explanation, their theoretical acceptability. The compatibility of facts notwithstanding, it might be impossible for someone committed to one of these models to accept the premises of the others. Allison illustrates this by noting that even if the information needed by model III were easy to acquire, those adhering to model I would consider the information needed by model III as an undue concern with subtlety, gossip and anecdotes, not as evidence. There is, in other words, an important difference between what is seen as relevant evidence and what is taken to be an adequate explanation. Similarly, models II and III held model I to be inadequate, since it neglects important factors; it is rather a shorthand, not itself a full analysis or explanation (*idem:* 254-255).

Thirdly, as to the effects of different views, Allison notes a simple consequence that might easily be disregarded: the existence of other models actually reveals that each model is but an alternative or a version. In the presence of models II and III, it is no longer possible to treat model I as a simple description: it is a *model*. While model I could alone be seen as a considerable contribution to the understanding and explanation of foreign affairs, the existence of models II and III shed another light on it and on the difficulties of applying it.

A version, or a result of research, however good, is always only one version as it is an effect of a series of choices and a selection of facts made in preparing it. The comparison of different versions, theories and definitions is problematic. This seems to suggest renouncing the aim of arriving at one version, and developing, instead, a thinking based on the existence of a variety of different versions. These, however, could be seen as linked to each other in that they result from the same situations of choice (crossroads, as it were). Together, they would seem to form the most adequate basis for evaluating each of them singularly and the matter in its totality. With the help of alternative versions on case studies, this book aims to show why plurality is so important in the interpretation of reality.

All in all, this study aims to bring together the conceptual constraints and possibilities of research on the state and integration with wider implications about the limits of research practice, the way in which an academic account emerges and how reality is presented through conceptual tools, and ending with considerations about the significance of plural and contradictory interpretation of reality. In emphasising the context-dependency or context relativity of definitions and theories, a certain relativism seems to characterise this book: there is no single right story about the cases chosen. The existence of several true versions is certainly not new, but, in fact, the starting point and the *raison d'être* of a normal scientific enterprise: one has to find out which one is correct, to evaluate, to compare. Therefore, this book does not in the first place aim to show that different versions are possible. It rather tries to tackle the problem of relativity in the sense of explaining theory construction or scientific analysis through its vertical and horizontal relations, origins and consequences. The validity of results depends on internal, vertical relations between assumptions and definitions which not only guarantee the coherence of the piece of research, but also imply that the final result can be neither the whole truth, nor 'more correct' than another version. In fact, horizontal relations between versions could be equally important in understanding why the final results actually emerge.

Finally, in its conclusions, the book is drawn into the question of interpreting what is the domain of the objective in comparison with that of the relative, what theory is, and how matters tend to become objective with the development of the discipline, or, how knowledge about facts is constructed.

Notes

1. In *Economy and Society*, edited by Gunther Roth and Claus W. High, 1968 (vol. 2, chapter 9; vol. 3, chapters 10-13).
2. The treaty concerning the rights and duties of states, made in a conference preceding the establishment of the Organization of American States (OAS) in Montevideo 1933, first formulated these classical criteria of statehood, a definition of the state as a subject of international law. See, e.g., Crawford, James, *The Creation of States in International Law,* Oxford University Press, New York 1979: 36, and Brownlie, Ian, *Principles of Public International Law,* Clarendon Press, Oxford, 4th ed. 1990: 72.
3. For example, C.H. Titus found in what he called 'a cursory examination of the term "state"' no less than 145 different meanings (an article entitled 'A nomenklature of political science', *American Political Science Review*, 25 (1) 1931: 45, 615; quoted by Ferguson and Mansbach 1989: 41 and by Cassese 1986: 120).
4. The main reason is that due to the development of military technology it can no longer guarantee the security and welfare of its citizens (E.H. Carr, *Nationalism and after,* MacMillan, New York 1945, esp. chapter 2; quoted by J. Ann Tickner, 'Re-visioning Security', in Booth and Smith 1995: 175); see also Herz 1957.
5. One could discern a tide carrying integration 'in' from late 1950s, culminating in the early to mid-1970s, and another from mid-1980s. Interestingly, Ferguson and Mansbach (1989: 13-14) observe that the state was 'out' in the same period, from the late 1950s to mid-1970s: a successful resurrection occurred when Krasner, among others, defended the state from the scholars who had 'multinationalized, transnationalized, bureaucratized, and transgovernmentalized the state until it has virtually ceased to exist as

	an analytic construct' (see Krasner in *Comparative Politics*, vol. 28, 3/1976, p. 317).
6.	See Milward, Alan S., *The Reconstruction of Western Europe 1945-51*, Methuen & Co, London 1984; af Malmborg (1994: 19-20).
7.	Niiniluoto calls these concepts *'primitive'* and gives as example the concept of 'point' in geometry. See Niiniluoto, Ilkka, *Johdatus tieteenfilosofiaan*, Otava (1980, pp. 164-166).
8.	W. B. Gallie, 'Essentially Contested Concepts', in *Proceedings of the Aristotelian Society*, vol. 56, London, 1955-1956 (reprinted in Max Black (ed.), *The Importance of Language*, Englewood Cliffs, N.J., Prentice-Hall 1962); quoted in Connolly 1974: 10.
9.	Thus, it is narrower than the well-known ideas of 'paradigm' by Kuhn, 'research programme' by Lakatos or 'research tradition' by Laudan. For Laudan, to exemplify the matter, a research tradition means a set of guidelines for the development of theories, which itself is not explanatory nor predictive or testable and does not give precise answers to specific questions. It involves an ontology delineating the types of fundamental entities that exist in the domain and to which theories reduce empirical problems when explaining them. It also outlines the different modes by which these entities can interact and often also the legitimate methods to analyse them; it may also define partially the problems and their importance. (Laudan 1977: 79-86.) Laudan's 'research tradition' acts negatively as a constraint on the types of theories which can be developed and justifies them (*idem:* 89, 93). Laudan argues that theories are never self-authenticating: they invariably make assumptions for which they provide no rationale (*idem:* 94). – Laudan also remarks that in an historical analysis (of science or of ideas), the basic units should be research traditions rather than individual concepts: change in the former explains changes in the latter. For him, concepts ('the state', 'space') do not have an historical autonomy which allows one to explain their historical transformation independently of the broader patterns of belief. (*Idem:* 183-184.)
10.	Cf. Morin's (1982: 78) understanding of what science is: 'scientific' has perhaps to be defined as what the majority of scholars understands as scientific; cf. Carr's (1961: 78) quote of a physicist defining a scientific truth as a statement which has been publicly accepted by the experts.
11.	Morin (1982: 64-66, 97, 112, 194; also 310 and 316); cf. Morin, 'Pour une nouvelle conscience planétaire', *Le Monde Diplomatique* 427, Oct. 1989.
12.	However, it should be noted that this does not mean that scholars think this way. Rather, conventional research practice is constructed as if that was really true, although the scholars know that the interpretation of reality is not objective and uniform.

13. Through the definitions, research could be said to create its object of study. In the evaluation of the truth value of results (theories), the importance of the definitions used can therefore even be seen to outweigh that of 'direct' empirical evidence. Conversely, it is questionable whether transferring the final answers into the realm of empirical research actually helps to circumvent the importance of conceptual choices.

14. Theory links factors and puts them into some order of importance; by definition, then, different theories have different orders and no one can have all factors included. This can result in an eternal debate between different emphases even though the discourse is constructed so that it seems to have an end, or all aim at an end which would be *the* theory, or a better one. These are aims which cannot be achieved, but which at the same time sustain research as activity, making it even some sort of *perpetuum mobile*.

15. For an introduction on the origins of the notion of state and classical literature (Bodin, Hobbes, Suarez, Grotius, Machiavelli), see Skinner (1989); also Poggi (1990). For conceptual change more in general (e.g., constitution, state, democracy, public interest, revolution), see Ball, Terence - Farr, James - Hanson, Russell L. (eds.), *Political innovation and conceptual change* (Cambridge University Press, 1989).

16. One could see, as Morin does, that theory is not knowledge, but something which makes knowledge possible: it is not an arrival or solution, but the possibility to address a problem. Pointing to Popper's view on the difference between theory and doctrine as the fact that theory accepts its own fallibility or the possibility that it is falsified, Morin argues that the very scientificity of theories lies in their 'mortality' - even though theories have, in his view, a tendency to degenerate into doctrines. (Morin 1982: 35-36, 314.) - Feyerabend (1975: 307) seems to be quite close to Morin in arguing that claims to the only right method or the only acceptable theory belong rather to ideology than to science.

2 Approaches to the relationship between the state and integration

This chapter identifies the different responses presented in the literature[1] to the question of the relationship between the state and integration. The aim is not merely to list the various views but to show *how* these views have emerged. This latter question of how different views or theories are reached is mostly absent from the usual accounts of approaches to integration. Often, in fact, different theories are presented as separate and autonomous, perhaps with a comparison of their relative strengths and shortcomings. Such a division into traditional 'isms' – neofunctionalism and the like – is not appropriate for several reasons. First, this division is not necessarily relevant when seeking answers to the precise question of the relationship between the state and integration. Secondly, labels such as 'neofunctionalism' tend to obfuscate the analysis in that there is seldom agreement on what ideas and what authors belong to which category (several examples of these difficulties will emerge later in this chapter).

This traditional mode of presentation may suit the purpose of criticism in that the shortcomings of the theories become particularly visible when the theories are presented out of context. However, this critical approach has obvious pitfalls. The object of criticism, a particular theory, is often depicted in a simplified way when speaking at an aggregate level about 'isms' and referring to secondary sources instead of the origins of a theory: a certain image of a theory is gradually created, and with it also a common way of criticising it. Certain criticisms become archetypical, repeated, and still there might not be a single author or work which would clearly represent the theory in question.

Thirdly, and most importantly, these categorisations miss an essential element needed to make the views understandable, that is, their succession or chronological order, how they are related to each other. Two exceptions confirm the rule that chronology is very seldom taken into account in the evaluation of different theories. On the one hand, some see theories as time-bound in the sense that they reflect the events of a particular period in time, therefore applying in such conditions but not others. An example of this type of presentation is given by Harrison (1974).[2] On the other, there is also an example in the previous literature in which chronological order is taken into account in the sense understood here, that is, aiming to show not only the influence between events in reality and theorising but also, and mainly, how the different theories influence each other. This example is Pentland's article (1981), a review of the sequence of integration theories where not only succession, but also a dialectical mode of development is identified. In his view, the prevalent theory at a given time comes to be challenged by a new one and from this confrontation a synthesis emerges as a new prevailing theory, to be, in turn, eventually challenged by a still newer one.[3]

This study presents a more systematic application of the chronological mode of presentation to theories concerning the relations between the state and integration. It is argued here that a proper evaluation and criticism of theories and research results must be based on first making them understandable. The variety of views concerning the state and integration cannot be fully understood if the views are analysed in abstract, one by one. It is important to note how central a role *other views* play in the development of a particular view on the question. Therefore, this chapter draws a path through the various views, showing how the ideas and theories have developed in relation to each other. This done, it will also be easier to explain the bends along the path, or *why* the views have emerged – something permitting an evaluation of the results and an overview of some general features of research practice, undertaken in chapter three.

Integration as a solution to the problems of the state and the system of states

The presentation of different views on the relationship between the state and integration can suitably begin by a view predating the establishment of the European Communities and which could be depicted as an inherently problem-solving approach. In simple terms, this view is that integration is a solution to some of the problems of the state and the system of states.

The background of this view is the immediacy of the problem of war and the problem of the post-war organisation of international relations. The likelihood of war is the main problem in the system of states. The state is a problematic entity, the main organisational unit (a rather closed one but not really self-sufficient or undisputed) and the relations between states tend to be conflictual, even war-prone. Thus, the relations between states should be made more peaceful. In this search for suitable ways of doing this, integration appears as one possibility, a way of transforming the relations between states.

Different variations are presented as to what 'integration' is seen to mean here. However, they all share the general belief in the positive consequences of pulling the states somehow closer to each other and increasing the linkages between them. Three of them have become particularly relevant for the development of integration studies: Mitrany's functional cooperation, Deutsch's transnational links, and the federalists' proposal to bring the states together as parts of a large federal state. They all share some elements with the larger theoretical frameworks of solutions to the problem of war through, e.g., a Kantian world government or through the League of Nations' approach to world organisation, as well as with literature on the formation of new political communities or regional unions, and with that on the inadequacy of the state as a form of political organisation. Characteristic for them all is that they are essentially prescriptions and proposals concerning possible ways of shaping interstate relations, not analyses of something already taking place.

In the context of early integration literature, federalism can be seen as an institutional or constitutional solution to the problem of war: in order to secure peace, something more is needed than mere international organisation between sovereign states, namely, strong common institutions which gather the states in one legal and political system. Federalist theory therefore examines the functioning of federal states and the advantages of this organisational form in comparison to a unitary state – as well as the possibilities for previously sovereign states intentionally to choose a common central authority and constitution. The example of how a federal state – the United States, Germany, Switzerland – is organised, the division of competencies between the central federal authority and the states (*Länder*, cantons), is to serve as a basis for the organisation of relations between the European states; a federal structure with a common central authority is seen to be a model which renders the otherwise bellicose interstate relations equally peaceful and organised as the relations between the parts of a federal state.

While federalism was a significant political movement of the post-war years in Europe – although perhaps not a particularly coherent one[4] – and inspired writings with titles such as *Will There Be a United States of Scandinavia?* (Franzén 1944) and *The United States of Europe* (Haas 1948) its internal variety has caused notable problems of classification. Even though federalism is usually seen as one of the cornerstones in the theory construction on integration, there is some hesitation as to what federalism actually means and whether some particular authors could be classified as federalists. For instance, Pentland (1973) seems to have difficulty identifying exponents of this tradition, pointing, hesitatingly, to Etzioni as being closest to federalism among the theorists.[5]

Nevertheless, functionalism played an important role in shaping the writings of David Mitrany. His contribution is, in fact, grounded on using the idea of functional cooperation[6] as criticism of the federalist ideas. Mitrany published in 1943 a short, pamphlet-like reflection entitled *A Working Peace System. An Argument for the Functional Development of International Organization*. The essay was presented by the publisher as 'one possible approach to the problem of post-war organisation'. It attained an influential role in integration studies, its author being commonly identified as the founder of functionalist integration theory. For Mitrany, the central question was how to avoid a new war, or how to alter the relations between the states and abolish reasons for waging war. In essence, he proposes the method of functional organisation, that is, conferring the management of an increasing amount of practical tasks, previously the functions of states, to common institutions, expressly created functional organisations. In practice, governments would transfer the executive authority and resources needed for the fulfilment of these tasks to the organisations.

Mitrany's approach is cautious: the territorial and ideological divides of the system of states should be surmounted, albeit gradually and unobtrusively. In the presence of war and hostile ideologies, one should not endeavour to unite states by what divides them, that is through building unions based on the shaky grounds of geographical or ideological proximity, but through what already unites them, that is, the specific, common functions. (Mitrany 1943: esp. 7, 10-14, 23.) Instead of an abrupt surrender of sovereignty, there would be inconspicuous and partial transfers of authority. National agencies would not be displaced; on the contrary, they might, indeed, derive fresh life and scope from wide functional co-ordination with the outside world. It is important that unity should grow freely, and the functional method is conducive to that goal: being endowed with 'the virtue of technical self-determination', logical and natural in character, it is naturally expansive, leading to further coordination within similar functions. (*Idem:* 35, 37, 53.)

The state is a problematic construction for Mitrany. In particular, he sees the division of the international system into states as an 'artificial amputation' of social relations and links. He deplores the way social actions are arbitrarily cut at the boundary of the state with only uncertain ways of linking them across the borders. Harmful for people, this division can be seen as unsatisfactory also for the states themselves, to judge from their inclination to become involved in conflicts over territory – the location of these borders – and to be concerned about their authority. Integrating the states' means and authority to perform specific, common functions diminishes both the authority of a state and its integrity in a more concrete sense: the development of functional cooperation leads to a gradual fading off of frontiers. The continuous development of common interests and activities across the frontiers makes these meaningless and brings an end to the 'artificial amputations'; hence, also changes of frontiers become unnecessary and causes of conflict therefore diminish. In this sense, Mitrany sees in functional cooperation a way to peaceful change and international society. (Mitrany 1943: 26, 42.) It is important, however, that this development be realised in a way that does not overtly go against the wishes of states, but, instead, through steps which the states can see as beneficial.

When associating Mitrany with integration studies, it is not sufficient to take into consideration only his view on the possibilities of increasing technico-functional cooperation in shaping interstate relations – as he seems to be linked to subsequent integration theories by, for example Haas. One has also to take into account his view that integration has certain limits. This becomes clear when analysing Mitrany's criticism of federalism. In his view, the aspirations of the federalists are both unrealistic and potentially injurious.[7] One should not try to unite states according to a pre-established general framework or theoretical pattern, as federalists envisaged. The unsuccessful example of the League of Nations as the first international organisation with (in principle) universal membership and the task to promote international cooperation and achieve international peace and security shows for Mitrany that it is better not to begin with constitutional forms. As such, though, functional organisation is not incompatible with a general constitutional framework nor precludes its coming into being (Mitrany 1943: 20-21).

On the one hand, plans of this kind would require considerable political will on behalf of the state, which Mitrany deems improbable.[8] On the other, a framework of that kind would not be needed, either: for Mitrany, the greatest common needs, peace and social advance, do not require overall political authority but are best advanced through functional cooperation at different fields. Furthermore, a union or federation of states, if formed, would not solve the problem of war. On the contrary, being 'mere change from the rivalry of powers and alliances to the rivalry of whole continents', it would only exacerbate the problem by reproducing the logic of political exclusion and the system of national states and, in reality, would only threaten security. Mitrany's ideal of unification differs fundamentally from that of the federalists in that he emphasises the importance of *universal* peace and cooperation over narrow regional arrangements. In his view, a close continental union could rather differentiate than integrate, implying even dangerous antagonism with the outside world, either as a result of the close internal cooperation or since the stimulation of internal unity could imply the need to invent extraneous dangers.[9] (*Idem:* 12, 34, 38, 53-54.)

A fruitful comparison can be here made between the writings of Mitrany and Karl W. Deutsch, in particular *Political Community and the North Atlantic Area* (Deutsch et al.1957). Both see in the increasing transborder or transnational activities a way towards more peaceful relations between states. Both are universalistic or general in outlook, and for both, the process of integration helps to overcome the intrinsically conflictual relations between the states, without, for that matter, replacing the system of states as such. Their views are also problem-solving in intention. What differentiates the two, however, is that Deutsch's study presents results of concrete research on different historical cases and is based on a different methodology. In fact, it can be seen to open a new type of research on unification or integration, a type which in the 1960s got a rather strong footing. Its central characteristics – rigorous definition, objective and precise hypotheses, testing – will be returned to in chapter three.

The point of departure in Deutsch *et al.* (1957) is the elimination of war and the building to that effect of a wider political community, the purpose being to find out general conditions for security communities to emerge or to exist.[10] 'Political community' is defined as a social group with a process of political communication, some enforcement machinery and some popular habits of compliance. 'Security community', in turn, is an integrated group of people, either pluralistic, if their governments remain separate, or amalgamated, if they merge formally. 'Integration', within a territory, is the attainment of a 'sense of community' and of institutions and practices which are strong and widespread enough to assure, for a long time, dependable expectations of peaceful change and settlement of disputes in lieu of resorting to large-scale physical violence. (Deutsch *et al.* 1957: 5-7.)

The authors first identify the conditions for the existence of security communities in the realms of social communication, interaction, values and expectations.[11] Subsequently, they examine the stage of integration, or the degree to which these conditions exist, in different subareas of what they call the 'North Atlantic Community'.[12] Deutsch thus aims at generalisable knowledge about the formation and existence of these communities, generating also prescriptions as to what could be done in the form of policy implications.

Deutsch's subsequent writings add a consequential element to his understanding of integration, namely, a rather negative view of the state. This appears in particular through Deutsch's characterisation of foreign policy. In his view, the foreign policy of every country deals, first, with the preservation of independence and security, and, second, with the pursuit and protection of its economic interests, particularly those of its most influential interest groups. Foreign policy consists of resisting penetration and manipulation by foreign countries and ideologies while aiming at accomplishing active penetration and manipulation of its own and spreading its own national and ideological propaganda. (Deutsch 1968: 87-88.) This being the case, integration is needed: mankind is unlikely to survive for long without a new political climate, greater international openness, understanding and compassion, which help to achieve integrated political communities in the long term. However, this is not necessarily easy to achieve: most governments and people prefer, in Deutsch's view, sovereignty or pluralism to supranationalism or integration, which would involve a loss of capacity and prestige. (*Idem:* 202.)

In sum, the three variants of the first view on the relationship between the state and integration present three different interpretations of integration as a solution to problems of the system of states: federalists see it as the establishment of common political institutions; Mitrany as the development of international organisations; and Deutsch as the development of relations between societies or people.[13] Together, these theories – labelled subsequently as federalist, functionalist and transactionalist or pluralist integration theory – serve an important function in the development of integration theories. Indeed, it is difficult to find studies of integration where at least one of these would not feature as a foundation for subsequent theoretical constructions. In general terms, one could argue that these views have contributed to the development of subsequent theorising particularly through fostering an approach in which the state is taken as the 'known', not in need of analysis but rather a background factor which justifies integration, and integration as the 'unknown' to be investigated. As will be seen below, these elements appeared linked in particular to a methodological stand close to that of Deutsch's.

Integration as a process in which the state is weakened or replaced

In part, the second view on the relationship between the state and integration can be seen as a direct continuation and further specification of the first. It assumes what was prescribed before; in other words, if integration previously was seen as a process which *could* have certain effects on the system of states, it is now analysed as a process which *does* indeed have these effects, and the thrust of the analysis is shifted to more specific questions on how this takes place. The crucial difference between the two views is that the proponents of the second interpret the events they are observing as instances of the phenomenon envisaged by the first.

Thus, according to this view, integration and the formation of a new political community is taking place, and it can be directly observed, first in the case of the European Coal and Steel Community (ECSC), then in the European Economic Communities (EEC). This is the starting point of Ernst B. Haas' studies on integration, paramount in directing the development in the field. In particular, Haas' definition of integration in *The Uniting of Europe* (1958) forms the basis of this second view on the state-integration relationship: for Haas, integration equals the formation of a new political community.[14] In the process of integration, national political actors are persuaded to shift their loyalties, expectations and political activities towards a new centre whose institutions possess or demand jurisdiction over the national states. A new political community is subsequently formed, superimposed over the existing ones (Haas 1958: 4-5, 16). Integration is seen as a two-way process in which the central institutions affect and are affected by the subject groups (*idem:* xxxii-xxxiii) and in which the actors' values and interests are redefined. While in the beginning, the national values held by the groups direct the decisions to join in or to abstain from the proposed steps of integration, these values gradually change towards a geographically larger, regional orientation and towards new 'nationalism'. (*Idem:* 13-14, 19.)

Haas builds partly on a criticism of the works of both Deutsch and Mitrany. In addition, federalism plays a role as a theoretical stand against which Haas examines his findings. Like Deutsch, he analyses the formation of political communities. However, he seems to criticise Deutsch's methodology and particularly his definitions. Direct reference to Mitrany does not appear before Haas' *Beyond the Nation-State* of 1964. In Haas' view, although dynamism and comprehensiveness make the functional approach better than other approaches (Haas 1964: x), he criticises, in particular, the proposition that the political can in an unproblematic way be separated from the technical. He also aims at refining functionalism with the help of qualifications and specifications concerning learning and unintended consequences.[15]

Haas' aim is to present a theory or generalisations about the processes by which political communities are formed among sovereign states, and also an account of the adaptive ability of actors (Haas 1958, preface of 1968: xi). There is, for Haas, one concrete example of this kind of integration in contemporary Europe, namely the ECSC, of which Haas analyses the first five years of activities.[16] Specifically, he asks whether the ECSC is intergovernmental, federal or *sui generis* in nature (*idem:* 34) and answers the question through studying the change in behaviour (comparing the years 1952 and 1957) by national political parties, trade associations and trade unions, national governments, supranational trade associations, supranational trade unions, supranational political parties, and the High Authority, the independent decision-making body of the ECSC. Haas concludes that the ECSC is not quite federal but rather 'supranational': it is a hybrid with plainly federating consequences. In his view, the ECSC has been a motor in a sectorially and geographically expanding process of integration in which interests are defined anew and new forms of behaviour emerge. (*Idem:* 526-527.)[17]

The results of this analysis concern the conditions for and the motors or mechanisms of integration. They are presented as what Haas calls a functional[18] theory of integration – further developed in *Beyond the Nation-State* of 1964 and the new preface to *The Uniting of Europe*, written in 1968. In short, the theory claims that the initiation of political unification does not require majority support or identical aims by all key groups, that the acceptance of unification will be facilitated if the state units are already ideologically or socially fragmented and if there is a tradition of mutual consultation and rudimentary value sharing, and that also an external threat is helpful. Once established, central institutions affect integration if they cause strong positive or negative expectations. What Haas calls his 'perhaps most salient conclusion' is that major interest groups and politicians determine their support or opposition to central institutions and policies on the basis of a calculation of advantage. In Haas' view, the process is dominated by nationally constituted groups with specific interests and aims, willing and able to adjust their aspirations by turning to supranational means when this course appears profitable. (*Idem:* xxxii-xxxv.)

Haas' approach is characterised above all by the aim at generalisable knowledge and theory formation and by the centrality of the idea of something new replacing the old, the new political community replacing the states – a development, moreover, which he seems to welcome, judging from the criticism against the state presented in Haas (1964). Haas sees the object he is observing and explaining – integration in the ECSC, the only existing supranational organisation – as something new and unique. He notes that what is interesting for him as a political scientist is to see voluntary 'integration' taking place before his eyes. He describes the object of study as one of the very few current situations in which the decomposition of old nations can be systematically analysed within the framework of the evolution of a larger polity, perhaps destined to develop into a nation of its own (Haas 1958: xxxi). This aspect of observability is most consequential for Haas' understanding of integration. Basing research explicitly on observation is, in his terms, preferable both to the prescriptive traditional theories where reality is analysed through a model of how it should be and to the ultra-scientific theories where reality is analysed through pre-established, abstract theoretical models.

The aim of theory formation, the view of the state and other factors which clarify Haas' understanding of integration appear particularly in Haas 1964. In this study, Haas combines his considerations on integration with a wider view of the international context seen as an international system, identifying the process of integration with a process which transforms this system or leads to an altogether different international system, from *Gesellschaft* to *Gemeinschaft*. Integration thus refers to a process which 'links a given concrete international system with a dimly discernible future concrete system', a process of increasing the interaction and mingling of national environments so as to obscure the boundaries between the system of international organisations and the environment provided by their nation-state members, a process beyond the nation-state (Haas 1964: 29). Particularly, he examines the role of international organisations in this change, seeking an effectiveness model in which the criterion of success of the organisation is its contribution to the transformation of the international system to a higher level of integration. The organisation analysed is the International Labour Organisation (ILO) and the author asks whether it is an organisation capable of maximising the process of integration. (*Idem:* vii, 76-77, 81, 92.)[19]

Haas underlines the importance of developing an explanatory and projective theory, aiming at predictions on, among other things, the capacity of collective decisions to transform the beliefs of the actors and on the capacity of an organisation to be a transformatory actor. To do that, Haas examines both theories of organisational efficiency, particularly the prerequisites for an organisation to be effective and grow, and systems theory (Haas 1964: 95-96, 101-102, 115). Haas maintains that systems theory – one of the novelties of the time characterised by 'immoderate theorising' – provides the opportunity of both explanation and prediction. He aims at elaborating functional theory 'in the light of social science theory and contemporary empirical studies', mainly in a system theoretical framework using the method of contextual analysis (*idem:* 23-24, 47-50), and underlines the role of scientific accumulation.

Developments within the view

In Haas' footsteps, a vast literature developed in the 1960s and early 1970s on integration which, remaining within the second view outlined above, added to it further specifications and at times also a rather technical outlook. Seemingly, the various authors concerned share merely a deep disagreement about what should be studied and how. In fact, the literature is characterised by constant quarrels about what integration is, followed by anxiety about the consequences of this disagreement for integration theory and the absent signs of progress or growth of knowledge. Nevertheless, the disagreements are rather superficial. Below the surface, there is, in fact, a solid common ground, a consensus as to the main questions to be asked and the type of research to be conducted.

Central in this common ground is the understanding of integration. It is viewed as a new and unforeseen process that has its driving forces in influential social groups and implies a gradual transferral of the state's functions and authority to the common, supranational institutions. Together with functions and authority, these institutions also garner the loyalty of the people, becoming a new centre not only of political activities but also of identification. Integration transcends the state; it offers a more effective way of political and economic organisation than the states and makes governments gradually accept and comply with the fact of their diminishing authority.

This understanding of the relation between the state and integration functions as the common premise of this group of analyses, to the extent that the question is not explicitly taken up at all. Indeed, the very entity 'state' does not necessarily appear in these studies, nor is the concept much used. Thus, the studies follow the example set in Haas (1958) where no such entity is involved in the process of integration. The only occasions in which the state appears in the analysis are rather fleeting in nature: on the one hand, the ECSC is accepted to consist of states; on the other, states and political communities are held to be, for the time being, practically the same. However, there is no such collective actor as the state which would have its interests in the process of integration. The actors considered are not states but political parties, interest groups and governments. In fact, in rejecting collective actors, Haas is moved to justify even his choice to see governments as actors: they have to be observed since their attitudes cannot be simply reduced to those of the leading party in a multi-party government (Haas 1958: 240).

The governments, then, have to adjust their behaviour to the new situation in which their own authority is increasingly limited. Haas actually observes clear changes: novel procedures and codes of conduct emerge in the relations between governments, even a supranational attitude comprising consensus and an atmosphere of cooperation, compromise formulas and concessions by all (Haas 1958: 489-491, 498, 512, 515-520).[20] France, for instance, behaves, according to Haas, in a different way in the ECSC and the OEEC, being more cooperative in the former because of the greater engagement and identification with the purpose of the organisation (*idem:* 520-523). Interests change, and national interests are always compromised. Governments seek to secure a maximal position but without obstructing the process, thus making possible the evolution of more integrated decision-making over time. In the long run, they defer to federal decisions as they recognise a point beyond which attempts to sidestep, ignore or sabotage them are unprofitable (*idem:* xxxiv, 240ff, esp. 279-280).

Later, Puchala (1972: 277-282) describes integration as involving procedures which facilitate cooperation and allow for efficient problem-solving and regulation of conflict. In this system, the states find it possible consistently to harmonise their interests and compromise their differences. Conflicts between the actors follow from divergent views about ways to cooperate rather than from incompatible interests. In the relations between the states, bargaining prevails over coercion and confrontation, which are considered illegitimate and occur infrequently. The system is also characterised by open communication, high mutual sensitivity and responsiveness.

Building on this understanding, there has evolved a growing body of literature which reflects the increasing popularity of the phenomenon as a central research object. It shares a research programme in describing, explaining and predicting the process of integration through the construction and refinement of theories and models. The main research questions concern the necessary or helpful background conditions for the process of integration to start, the indicators of the level of integration at a given time, the possibilities of measuring the speed of the process, and the explanatory value of single variables which affect the process.

While the contribution of this branch of research might not be impressive in terms of new findings or conceptual innovations, it does have an important role in directing subsequent research on integration. By its cohesion and accumulative research agenda, it succeeded in making some theoretical lacunae increasingly apparent, something that is later successfully used by those representing an opposite view on integration and the state.

Three such influential developments within this second view can be discerned. In the first, the literature comes to reject the possibility of comparison in integration studies, concentrating increasingly on the study of the European Community and depicting it in terms which cannot be applied to other organisations. Secondly, the theories used in the analysis of integration tend also to become more specialised and the early uses of theories of systems and organisations are replaced by the evolving theories on integration. Thirdly, the central objects of debate become what concepts and definitions should be used, what variables and indicators would be most suitable, and how the explanatory power of the theories could be improved.

Initially, a comparative approach seemed to gain popularity. It had an evident justification in that the aim of theory building and the nature of the claims presented about integration were such as to require applicability in several cases, for example in other geographical regions. The aim of testing the theories required material which was not the same on which they were based. In fact, the comparative approach characterised much of the writings in the late 1960s (cf. Hansen 1969: 242). On the one hand, the European Communities were compared with other European organisations; on the other, there were comparisons between the European integration process and similar efforts in other regions, in particular in Latin America and Africa.[21] Amitai Etzioni's *Political Unification* (1965) remains perhaps the most extensive comparative study of integration or the process of unification. He constructs a research setting which enables a comparison between four unions, the EEC ('growing union'), the Nordic union ('stable union') and two other contemporary but failed unions, the United Arab Republic (1958-61) and the federation of the West Indies (1958-62).

However, the approach soon encountered strong criticism. The comparisons were found problematic in that, for instance, the differences between less developed and industrialised countries were not adequately taken into consideration (e.g., Hansen 1969). At the same time, the authors themselves tended to conclude that the European experience was not really comparable: the comparisons mainly highlighted the special features of the European Communities. Haas (1961) pointed out the particularity of European Communities in respect to European institutions in that when different modes of conflict resolution in the organisations were used as indicators for integration, the European Communities emerged as the most successful institution availing itself of all the modes presented, and having, in addition, contributed by that of 'upgrading common interests' which emerged in no other organisation (Haas 1961: 367-370). In addition, Haas concluded that the European processes could not be reproduced in other contexts because the necessary preconditions existed to a much lesser degree, even though he acknowledged the possibility of different functional pursuits also yielding integration (*idem:* 389-392). Similarly, Etzioni's comparison rather ended than started comparative analyses on European Communities and other unificatory processes: his study presents the European Communities as different from the others, mainly because of the role of strong central institutions.

As a result, it was increasingly perceived that the terminology and theories developed actually applied only to the EC, which set it as a *sui generis* phenomenon apart from other endeavours. The very term 'integration' was increasingly limited to the EC so that, for instance, EFTA and Nordic cooperation gradually no longer qualified as instances. It was also argued that concentration on the EC instead of comparisons was conducive to more effective theory building and more powerful explanations (Lindberg and Scheingold 1970: 107). In the background, however, the basic problem of reconciling the unique nature of the object and the aim of generalisation remained, and integration studies continued to display a rather uneasy attitude to comparison.

The second main development concerned the limitation of theories applicable in the study of integration. Earlier on, theoretical inspiration had been searched for in different fields of research, and particularly the different variations of systems theory were applied to the study of integration.[22] As was seen above, even organisational theory was applied in Haas (1964). Soon, however, these ways of making integration part of some more general phenomenon come to be replaced by expressly created integration theories. In fact, in this mainstream of theorising, an article such as Galtung's (1967) emphasising the need for a more general conception of integration based on a structural approach appears rather unusual.

In the ensuing contest between the different integration theories, these scholars – who were closest to (neo)functionalism – found evidence for discrediting their opponents. Federalism, in particular, was seen as falsified by the events both in Europe and in Africa which effectively contradicted its descriptions and explanations; in Haas' view, none of its assertions-predictions had proven to be true (Haas 1970: 624-625, 629; cf. Puchala 1972).[23] At the same time, they also had to improve theirs to counter the same type of criticism from others. Notably, the mid-1960s crisis in the process of integration made them adjust their view on the subject.

Haas' second preface to *The Uniting of Europe*, written in 1968, is a good example of theoretical adjustment in which an unforeseen event threatening a theory, in this case the functional approach, is made to conform to it and even transformed into supportive evidence. The events between 1958 and 1968 seemed for the most part to confirm Haas' theory: it applied equally well to the EEC, which had inherited the role, spill-over potential and unique supranational style of the ECSC. Moreover, great developments had taken place; in Haas' view, integration had proceeded with a considerable speed after 1958. In its first five years, the EEC had attained astonishing results, coming close to voiding the power of the national state in all realms other than defence, education and foreign policy. Particularly striking for Haas were supranational decision-making and the definition of rights of individuals, enforceable by the Community. This development had not been planned or approved by the governments when establishing the EEC; it was more or less automatic.

Against this background, the abrupt deceleration of the process in the mid-1960s was surprising. The crisis was caused by a new attitude adopted by France, that was less enthusiastic about supranationalism and more based on furthering its own interests.[24] That a 'single charismatic Frenchman' [de Gaulle] could stop the process, as Haas put it, did not, however, undermine the validity of the functional explanation.[25] On the contrary, it demonstrated that functionalism, being gradual, was the only usable strategy. However, the theory had to be reformulated: it had exaggerated the automaticity of the process and did not sufficiently distinguish between the causative role of temporarily differentiated sets of conditions (background conditions, conditions prevailing at set up, and those prevailing after). Further, it assumed too strongly the end of ideology, particularly nationalism,[26] and gave too little weight to the different stimuli coming from the external environment. (Haas 1958, preface 1968: xiii, xx-xxv.)

This general aim of improving theory is also the common denominator of the third general development within the view. Essentially, it was seen that resolving the problems concerning the concepts used, as well as the choice of variables and indicators, would advance both theory and integration studies in general. As to the concepts and definitions used, there was a general agreement on the need for arriving at shared definitions in order to ascertain that all shared the same object of research, and, thus, to allow for accumulation, progress and more accurate results.[27] Although a specific terminology started to emerge based on considerable similarities in the choice of concepts to be used, there were also gaping differences in how the terms were actually defined. For instance, a comparison of Haas (1958) and Etzioni (1965) shows that both use the term 'political community' instead of the term 'state', which, like 'sovereignty', does not appear, whereas their definitions of 'integration' are quite different.[28]

Several authors reproached the unproductiveness of the studies thus far conducted. In fact, they were unanimously disappointed as to the achievements. Dougherty and Pfaltzgraff (1981: 453, 459) pointed out that integration theory has not been sufficiently advanced to arrive at either a commonly accepted definition or a general agreement on the relevant indicators of integration; Harrison (1974: 115) criticised the inadequate consensus particularly as to background conditions, arguing that they have neither been established as absolute impediments, nor as sufficient or indispensable for integration. (Similarly, e.g., Haas 1970: 607, Puchala 1972: 267, Caporaso 1971: 228, Nye 1968.)

Caporaso (1971: 228) noted a widespread controversy 'even on the simplest of issues' in integration studies, on the entities to be studied, definitions, concepts and indicators, and the lack of common standards for evaluating knowledge, interpreting evidence and measuring progress. Haas and Puchala were surprised at the fact that fifteen years of studies had not been enough to achieve a clear consensus on the delimitation of the field, and that the dependent variable still caused problems (Haas 1970: 607; Puchala 1972: 267).[29] Some advocated remaining within the core meaning the words commonly have, preferring simplicity to absolute precision (Harrison 1974), while others aimed at more exact and technical terminology. Nye, for example, wanted sharper analytical tools and a clarification and strengthening of the foundations of causal theory through conceptual clarifications. In his view, as the common usage of 'integration' was often confusing, scholars should agree on a common or easily translatable vocabulary. To this effect, he sought to relate some of the major definitions and formulate falsifiable hypotheses by disaggregating the concept of integration into different types – political, social, economic – and subtypes, and developing specific indices for the subtypes. (Nye 1968: 856, 858-859.)

It became quite common to find that the old terms of traditional political science were not applicable and that new ones should be invented. Several authors maintained that old concepts and models of the social sciences were not enough to describe the peculiar character of integration and the European Communities (e.g., Lindberg and Scheingold 1970: 306-307). For Puchala, the main problem was that although contemporary international integration was an essentially new, unfamiliar and rather unconventional phenomenon, scholars insisted upon analysing it as instances of more familiar patterns, as federalism, nationalism, functionalism or power politics. In his view, conventional models did not satisfactorily describe or explain this phenomenon, nor did they raise very productive questions about it. (Puchala 1972: 267-269.) Here, he followed Haas, who – true to his methodological stance – came to see that the main problem in the integration theories developed thus far was that they analysed integration as a process towards a 'federal union', 'security community' or 'political community', all 'lamentably unspecific and inconsistent' as dependent variables since they could not yet be observed or measured in nature (Haas 1970: 630-631). In all, the theories – federalism, communications or transactionalist approach and neofunctionalism – were no more than pretheories or empirical generalisations which did not meet any of the criteria of description, explanation and prediction. (*Idem:* 609-610, 613, 619.)

In Haas' view, the solution to the problem of scarce theoretical quality was to replace these dependent variables with new ones, namely 'regional state', 'regional community' and 'asymmetrical regional overlap'. Admittedly, these were also heuristic, without any real-life counterparts, but they provided 'orienting provisional points in the future', being illustrations of possible temporary results of the integration processes. (Haas 1970: 607, 634-635.) Apart from the labels chosen, a very similar proposal is made by Kaiser (1972: 227-231) who proposes 'super state', 'functional region' and 'regional conglomerate'. Similarly, Puchala argues that the problem of the conventional frameworks has been that they test the present in terms of progress or regression in relation to a hypothetical future instead of basing the analysis on what integration is at present in different regions. He proposes instead that integration be best thought of as a set of processes which produce and sustain a 'concordance system' at the international level. This model describes, in Puchala's view, Western European integration better than any of the models 'currently in vogue'. Essentially, it is a complex and highly institutionalised international system in which there are different types of interdependent and quasi-autonomous actors, the states being the main units. The relations between the actors are characterised by cooperation, mutual sensitivity and effective problem-solving. (Puchala 1972: 269-276, 283.)

As later examples of the perceived need for new concepts, one could mention Alger (1981: 136-137) who criticises Haas' new variables for not succeeding in really liberating the analysis from the hold of the nation-state model – which, in fact, was used as a point of comparison in that it was said to be 'the opposite of a regional state'. Similarly Schmitter sees that the essential problem of theorising about integration has been that all the theories have seen the end-state of integration as being either an international organisation, a nation, or a state. In his view, recourse to these traditional terms has impeded the understanding of the specific nature of European integration. Therefore he suggests seeing the European Community as a 'new form of political domination' in order to capture its long-term dynamic and different evolutionary possibilities. (Schmitter 1991: 2-3.) Other new concepts to describe the qualitatively different multi-layered European governance could be such ideal types as *condominio, consortio, confederatio* and *stato/federatio* (Schmitter 1996: 132-134).

In addition to concepts and definitions, the debate on the development of theory dwelled on the choice of variables and indicators and their measurement. Different authors tended to use different indicators, both quantitative and qualitative, but it was noted that even when the same indicators were used, the results could be different.[30] Indicators pose the problem not only of a certain arbitrariness, but also of possible confusion with the consequences of integration, as Scheingold (1970: 978-980) points out: what researchers study as indicators of integration – that is, different changes which are used to determine whether or not integration is taking place – can actually be seen to be the consequences of integration.

The variables used to explain integration tended to multiply. From the early Haasian conditions for integration such as value sharing, external threat or social fragmentation and Etzioni's (1965) emphasis on common institutions as explanatory variables of the level and scope of integration, research continued discovering more and more major relevant variables (cf. Hansen 1969). What were seen as the intervening variables between economic and political union in Western Europe, or the conditions in which an economic union will be transformed into a political union, namely, the internal logic of industrialism, pluralism and democracy, could in other regions be replaced by other cultural or stylistic attributes serving as 'functional equivalents'.[31] Dougherty and Pfaltzgraff (1981: 453, 459) deduced from the difficulties in arriving at agreements on definitions and indicators that the theories could lack emphasis on factors in the international environment and the role of coercion. Pentland, in turn, acknowledged the need for analysing an impressive amount of independent variables: being a complex, multi-dimensional phenomenon, integration necessitates taking into account several background variables, such as threat from the external political environment, structure of the international system, support of powerful outside states, convergence of interests, common institutions, patterns and habits of cooperation and consultations or conflict resolution, and geographical factors. (Pentland 1973: 211-212, 216-217.) Lindberg, indeed, gave his article in 1970 the telling title 'Political Integration as a Multidimensional Phenomenon Requiring Multivariate Measurement'.

At the same time, the snowball-like tendency of integration theories to include all kinds of elements provoked considerable indignation. Instead of theories, the outcomes were seen as accounts of all that integration involves, as Puchala referred to Nye's article of 1970. The results did not much resemble scientific theories in a strict sense, that is, being deductive-nomological and structured in a special way, as De Vree noted in his criticism of integration theories by Haas, Deutsch, Etzioni and Lindberg. In his view, the attempts at theory formation had been loose and informal. The theories presented a mixture of historical narrative and description of minute details, being characterised by undisciplined concept formation, impressionistic judgement on the basis of empirical propositions rather than precise observation, and were close to everyday language. (De Vree 1972: 3-5, 316-319.) Haas, too, criticised the amount of indeterminate variables and the tendency to add 'fudge variables' whenever the standard ones were not enough, including such 'mythical animals' as 'functional equivalents', 'catalysts', 'federalizers', 'compellingness' or 'high politics'. (Haas 1970: 630-631, footnote 28.) Hansen noted that the more comprehensive the scope of theories became, the more apparent it was that all aspects of international and regional change were a part of a 'seamless web' of social reality that defies exhaustive treatment (Hansen 1969: 253, 271). An intricate confrontation between different standards for adequate explanation was, thus, unavoidable. The more parsimonious versions which explained the process of integration with a few variables were criticised for disregarding important factors, while the more extensive versions were criticised for putting together too many disparate elements and thereby losing the explanatory power altogether.

Still, integration studies acquired in the early 1970s a rather technical outlook. Already in Deutsch *et al.* (1957) and Etzioni (1965), fairly scientific language was used. Particularly Etzioni's study was explicitly constructed as theory-led, consisting of the examining of precise propositions or hypotheses. The aim of testing models and hypotheses against reality was present in many studies. For instance, Puchala's 'concordance system' was such a model to be 'tested' through 'stepping out into the empirical world' (Puchala 1972: 283-284). Traces of simulating experimental methodology were not difficult to find. For instance, Haas and Schmitter (1964) explicitly used terminology related to experimental methodology stating that other regions may have functional equivalents for the important traits 'isolated' in Western Europe. Similarly, Lindberg and Scheingold (1970) wish to take advantage of the 'unique social laboratory that the Community offers for the study of integration processes', and for Haas (1970: 608-609), the units and actions studied provide a 'living laboratory' for observing the peaceful creation of possible new types of human communities.

Questions of quantification and measurement obviously surged[32] and Haas welcomed approaches which allowed for mathematical manipulation. In fact, his new dependent variables (see above, page 14) suggested by organisation theory, had specific value in this sense: allowing for mathematical manipulation, they contributed to a promising way of improving the theories, that is, systematic comparison with the help of computer simulation.[33] Haas is, however, optimistic about the development of theory. Referring to the work of Nye, Schmitter and Puchala, he maintains that the specification of independent variables, their operationalisation and the establishment of clear links between them, is advancing rapidly (Haas 1970: 637).

Although the development of more strictly defined research agendas can in some sense be seen as a requirement for progress in the studies, it also implies a certain one-sidedness and creates new lacunae in the form of questions which are not posed. Such was certainly the question of the consequences of integration, which Scheingold pointed out as having been neglected by the scholars who had mainly analysed the process of integration itself, describing, measuring, explaining and forecasting its course. Moreover, he pointed out that integration was seen as good by definition, which contributed to limited research interest in the consequences of integration or its costs and benefits. Posing the question of consequences involves, he argues, a change of perspective and sensitivity to value questions. It leads us to ask what difference it makes whether Europe integrates, without taking for granted either the merit of integration or the desirability of the Communities' initial goals. (Scheingold 1970: 979-981, 1002.)[34]

Even more visibly, the concentration on certain questions, terms and methods, encouraged by this branch of integration research, exposed a flank for the critics by leaving aside the state or depicting it as taken-for-granted, while integration was the 'unknown' to be analysed. Thus, to Lindberg and Scheingold (1970: 66) among others, the EC appeared as constantly shifting scope and amorphous in character when mirrored in a familiarly stable and clear nation-state, a fact which led them to conclude that the EC was only partially comparable to a nation-state as a decision-making system. Quite obviously, critics could point out that a similar view of the state showed inadequate consideration of the concept and was a major shortcoming of this view.

The state which strengthens itself through integration

The third approach to the relationship between the state and integration has in its background two important factors. On the one hand, it develops on the basis of a realist view of international relations. Integration is viewed as an instance of what are seen to be normal international relations. In the first and second views, it might be recalled, integration was a way – hoped for or effective – towards more consensual and less state-centric international relations. In the third one, it does not constitute an exception to the rules of the state-led and at times conflictual international relations; thus, it is also explainable as such. On the other hand, it develops as a criticism of the view considered above, at a time when this has a rather prominent position.

An early illustration of the differences between the second and third view can be found in Graubard (1963), represented by Haas and Raymond Aron. The main difference concerns the perception of change: quite clearly, Aron's framework is such as to make the possibility of integration constituting a notable change in international relations rather improbable.

Aron, eminent representative of the realist school of international relations, is sceptical about the possibility of the emergence of a 'new Europe' and the desirability of a European state, doubting the kind of objectives it might have. Central to Aron's understanding of integration is that it is not automatic; there is no inevitable, smooth progression from economic unity to political unity, and neither are there necessary linkages between different domains.[35] The governments, each with different views, have a central role in the process, and unification does not proceed if the governments do not wish to reach agreement. Nor does Aron see traces of a process towards community-building: the relations between the member states – outside the economic field – are not basically different from those in the past. Aron also stresses the importance of security and defence: without the capacity to defend itself (or at least a relative autonomy in the Atlantic Alliance), there will not be a federation. In all, Aron sees neither wish, nor ability nor capability in the states to form something of the kind including, for example, common diplomacy. (Aron 1963: 40-41, 46, 50-51, 60-61.) Thus, Aron emphasises the role of governments and sees that considerations of politics, history and security are fundamental for their policies, even more so than economy.

Haas, on the contrary, sees the question in terms of rational progress, even feeling. He observes important changes taking place and applauds them, in particular the new supranational method. In fact, while for Aron things continue to be as they have been, for Haas, almost everything has changed and the 'new Europe' is in fact a reality. The new Europe is a pluralist and industrial society where politics is less ideological, where there is more value agreement, and where the national state no longer 'feels capable' of realising welfare within its borders and which has made its peace with interdependence. Supranationalism is the appropriate method to secure maximal welfare, including military security, for a post-capitalist state in the new Europe. It represents the victory of economy over politics and over nationalism. (Haas 1963: 67-73.)

Haas stresses that the new method does not necessarily mean that the governments would only experience a loss of power; in fact, they are quite content with the process. The state itself sees its interests in a different way, understanding that isolation is possible only at the expense of welfare. It is true that governments can brake the process: spill-over is far from automatic. However, the integrative logic operates, and the process indeed advances. There is a cumulative pattern of accommodation in which the countries refrain from veto and seek compromises, upgrading their common interests. If difficulties in some area emerge, concessions are made in related fields. The European executive's ability to gain power does not alarm the governments, since there is no 'community point of view' or general interests which would subordinate the national criteria and the governments feel that concessions are rewarded by gains. The final compromise includes a feeling of commitment, creativity and gain. (*Idem:* 65-66, 77-78; cf. Haas 1958, preface of 1968.)

The second important background feature of the third view is that it receives an important confirmation and a spark from the difficulties encountered by the second in explaining the halting of the process of integration in the mid-1960s. In fact, events leading to the Luxembourg compromise are seen to falsify the second view, while from the point of view of the third, they appear only logical. In essence, they confirm the fact that the state has not succumbed to integration, constituting evidence for the realist view of the state as the main actor and the common institutions as subordinated to them.

Thus, Stanley Hoffmann, a central figure in the third view, argued in 1966 that integration in Western Europe was hampered or made impossible by the resistance of the nation-state. The failure of unification was caused by several features of the international system: differences in national situations, or the diversity among the units of the system (domestic context, geo-historical situation, outside aims), the globality of the system which means that regional subsystems have only a reduced autonomy, and the stability of the bipolar world which supports and expands the operations of national diversity. Integration would require both internal integration within the units, absence of domestic cleavages,[36] and subjective similarity, that is, policy-makers' conviction. (Hoffmann 1966: 904-905.)

For Hoffmann, the system is profoundly conservative with respect to the diversity of nation-states, and their very existence is a formidable obstacle to their replacement. Even though they are 'often inchoate, economically absurd, administratively ramshackle, and impotent yet dangerous in international politics', they remain the basic units because there is no agreement on what could replace them. The nation-state is the highest possessor of power, the main focus of expectations, initiator, pace-setter, supervisor and often destroyer of the larger entity. It survives, although *transformed* as regards national sovereignty and in that the states now resemble each other more (Hoffmann 1966: 863, 866, 889-890, 908-911). In Hoffmann's view, there is a race between the logic or necessity of integration and the logic of diversity or autonomy of governmental action. The former, functional integration, could win if it promised a permanent excess of gains over losses, but it cannot: while, theoretically, this could be true of economic integration, it is not true of political integration and 'high politics', where there is no common agreement on goals and methods. (*Idem:* 881-883.)

Thus, the state, or its resilience and the recovery of national distinctiveness (cf. Wallace 1982: 64), served in explaining why the process of integration did not advance as projected by the neofunctionalists: after all, the governments retained the power to block the process if it went against their interests.[37] In other words, the claim that there is an automatic process towards increasing unification, something that was seen as a central feature in previous theories, proved to be wrong. As the states are the central actors in international relations, they are such also in integration, and lead the process according to their interests, having also the power to suspend it, as was shown by France. Where the neofunctionalists saw the process of integration as a continuum, here appeared the idea of a pendulum between two different logics, one functional, having to do with economic and technological transformation, the other political, linked to statehood, sovereignty, national identity and political accountability (Wallace 1996: 440-441).

Typically, the characterisation of the second view by the representatives of the third reorders the polemics described above into an approach more coherent than was actually the case. Moreover, there were also similarities between the views. In fact, both depicted integration in a sense as a means of problem solution, with Haas (1958, 1963) pointing to different gains from integration and later (1975) seeing integration as an answer to various challenges from the environment, and the proponents of the third view increasingly viewed integration as a way to increase the states' possibilities to regain power.

In essence, the third view of the relationship between the state and integration can thus be depicted as a state-driven view on integration. Integration is seen as a way of improving states' capacities to solve their common problems through joint decision-making, common policies and a sharing of resources. It is also an efficient means or tool for a single state in pursuing its particular interests or increasing its power. As such, it may also imply elements of competition between the participating states. The states are the motors of the process of integration: having decided to start it, they subsequently control its development, which follows the logic of the states' interests. Integration is, thus, explained by the concrete preferences, needs and interests of the states, for example concrete economic gains. The states calculate the costs and benefits of different policies and outcomes, having also to weigh economic gain against loss of authority (cf. Morgan 1994b: 131). In Lindberg's terms, the states do not need to share the same reasons for supporting integration. What is necessary for integration, however, is that their interests converge and that their goals are interdependent. (Lindberg 1963: 289, 293.)

The state becomes thus a unit inseparable from the study and explanation of integration. Being introduced in explaining why integration had not progressed as foreseen by the previous theories, it was soon seen as a factor which also explained why integration took place and why it progressed in a certain way. The logic of the state is, in fact, not limited in its application only to difficulties in the process. It also allows for seeing integration as a real and significant process which effectively has an impact on the states. This impact, however, is seen as beneficial for and aimed at by the states. They might have to compromise on some questions, but, after all, these compromises are a normal part of interstate practices, having to do with differences between the states' goals and capabilities.

In this view, the research agenda for the analysis and explanation of integration consists of analysing state interests and policies. Characteristically, the conceptual apparatus also involves elements which were absent in the previous views. Particularly central are the concepts of 'high politics' and 'national interest'. This is clearly visible in Hoffmann's criticism of Haas' theories. Hoffmann criticises the 1950s and 1960s 'explosion' of theories about depoliticised progress in integration for overlooking the difference between low politics, issues linked to the aim of maximising common good, and high politics, issues of vital importance and zero-sum nature. The realm of high politics is not open to incremental spill-over of integration from economy and welfare. Integration in high politics is more difficult to achieve, and this may also explain difficulties in integration in the realm of low politics, as some degree of high political coordination seems to be a prerequisite for progress in economic integration (cf. Harrison 1974).

Further, Hoffmann criticises the theories for underestimating the power of the main actors to stop or to slow down the process of integration and the ability of national bureaucracies to resist the transfer of power. Moreover, these theories did not consider the differential impact of external countries on different members. For Hoffmann, a state-centred, pluralistic and structured approach is needed that takes into account the autonomy of both politics and the state, the diversities within and among states and societies, and the fact that each has its own dynamics, due to its own interests, social forces and institutions. In his view, integration theory should consider the domestic priorities and goals of the states, the compatibility of the goals and the possibility of achieving them by cooperation, the impact of environment on separate actors and the institutional interplay between community organs and states. (Hoffmann 1982: 26, 29-30.)

Parallel to the distinction between low and high politics, also international and domestic politics are seen to differ in crucial respects. In contrast, a major premise for Haas was their similarity. For Haas, as Harrison points out, the ends of foreign policy are qualitatively similar to ends implicit in any other field of politics; therefore, the 'laws' of political behaviour identifiable in the domestic field are applicable to the international field as well.[38]

In addition to the different concepts used, the methodological stand adopted in the third view also sets it apart from the second. To some extent, the third view is based on a methodological criticism of the previous one. It builds on a long tradition of explaining international relations through the state actor, leaning on traditional methods of foreign policy analysis: attention to single events prevails over the aim of rigorous theory-building. Still, constructing a theory is by no means excluded. As will be seen below, this approach involves several possibilities for developing state-based theories, such as assessing the relative importance of particular states, interest calculations, and, most importantly, the possibility of using comparison. While the second view faced a problem in that it had defined integration as a unique phenomenon and thus limited the possibilities of comparison, the third view makes comparison an obvious method: as a tool of the state or a form of international relations, integration is comparable to the other tools and forms available, such as international cooperation and organisations.

An example of such analysis of integration is provided by Twitchett and Twitchett (1981) for whom the EC is a framework for diplomacy. In their view, the states use the EC as a vehicle for promoting national goals. If there are sufficient shared interests and if benefits and a general strengthening effect on all participants are expected, even a common foreign policy may emerge. Understandably, then, attention turns toward the different aims and aspirations of the member states in their relations to the EC: the questions asked by the authors include the reasons for each state to opt for membership, the attitudes of successive governments on issues such as common foreign policy, the extent to which the EC is perceived to further specific national interests, and the differences of opinion within the state on membership and the future direction of integration. (Twitchett and Twitchett 1981: xv, 1, 15.)

As was seen above, the third view sees the state both as the founder of the process of integration and as its controller. The first aspect – how the states chose to create the integrative forms of cooperation and subsequently shape them according to their interests – is well exemplified by Milward's writings.[39] Milward argues that historical research suggests a theory of integration totally different from those presented by political scientists and economists, essentially one not based on the assumption of the decline of the state (Milward 1990: 262, 269). The EC is an international framework constructed by the state for the completion of its own domestic policy objectives, which, in turn, are shaped almost entirely by domestic political pressures and economic resources. (Milward and Sørensen 1993: 20-21.) In other words, integration is a strategy for the state in the pursuit of its interests, chosen among the possible strategies as the most advantageous. Basically, there are two alternative strategies or international frameworks for advancing national policy choices, intergovernmental cooperation and integration, which differ in that integration is more durable and binding, and therefore also more efficient.[40]

Against this background, the decision to launch the integration process was understandable: after the years 1929-1945, the European states were weakened, and there was a need to reassert, or rescue, the nation-state as the fundamental organisational unit of political life. Economic growth was the goal, and some policies – those with direct implications on international relations, such as industrialisation and agriculture – were seen as better advanced through integration than through individual action or cooperation. (Milward and Sørensen 1993: 5-6.) Thus, the Communities were not established because of commitment to the idea of European unity, but because of the need to solve certain domestic economic problems and to reassert the nation-state as the basic organisational unit (Milward 1992: 437; similarly in Baker and Kolinsky 1991; cf. Morgan 1994b: 132).[41]

Thus, a clear rationale or motivation was pointed out for the process – something that in Puchala's (1981: 157) view was actually missing in earlier theories: he criticises Deutsch for the missing motivational dynamics, for giving no answer to the questions of who opts for amalgamation, when and why. Moreover, the same logic of state strengthening also explains the subsequent developments. As Milward (1992: 447) puts it, the future of the integration process depends on national policy choices. The argument that the Community actually helps preserve the nation-states – far more than it forces them to wither away – was notoriously advanced by Hoffmann who saw that although traditional sovereignty had become clearly obsolete, it was not likely that the state would be superseded in the process of integration. In fact, the EC even regenerated the state, adapting it to the present world. (Hoffmann 1982: 21, 23, 33-35.) Similarly, Taylor (1978: 229) had argued that supranational elements help states to survive rather than tend to replace them.

From this view, only a small step was needed to argue that integration might even be necessary for the survival of the states, something alluded to already by Puchala (1972). Puchala encouraged analysing to what extent participation in integration actually enhances rather than undermines national sovereignty, and to what extent it preserves rather than supersedes an international state system. In fact, for him integration – or the 'concordance system' – is characterised by cooperation instead of coercion and confrontation and by a less egoistic definition of self-interest because of the perception of interdependence or national inadequacy as the affirmation that nation-states can be preserved as distinct entities only through the international pooling of resources to confront problems which challenge their separate existence. (Puchala 1972: 269-271, 277-282 and footnote 22.)

The necessity of integration notwithstanding, the states still remain in control of the process. This aspect is best illustrated in Taylor's analysis of the process of integration. Taylor's central idea is that the states control the process by setting limits beyond which integration cannot be allowed to proceed, and he examines where these limits are, or where the states choose to defend their sovereignty, locating the mechanisms and contexts of the imposing of limits. He observes that in the 1970s and early 1980s, the state remained on the whole intact: coordination prevailed over supranationalism and contradictions among preferences over spillover. In fact, intergovernmentalism was strengthened in the 1970s at the expense of supranational tendencies, and the states were becoming clearer about the limits of integration. (Taylor 1983: 29-56, 115.)[42] For Taylor, too, the *acquis communautaire* has become a vital precondition of national autonomy in that the success of negative integration[43] has become essential for the effective use of the governments' policy instruments. At the same time, negative integration has helped prevent positive integration: measures taken by the Communities tend to alert the governments who then take countermeasures, and economic costs are also a powerful disincentive for further integrative measures. (*Idem:* 187-188.)[44]

For both the aspects of shaping the common institutions and of controlling the process, the third view draws attention, again, to differences between states. Put simply, the relative strength and importance of the states varies, and major states may have more say than the minor ones. Thus, the positions of the large member states have acquired special importance in the explanation of integration. For instance, while Morgan (1972) saw the political structure of Western Europe as shaped by the interaction between national systems and supranational institutions, he singled out France and

Germany as the most important single actors. More straightforwardly, Keohane and Hoffmann (1991: 295) conclude that what matters most are the bargains struck between the major players. Typically, the analyses have concerned questions such as preference-convergence between the major states, the role of Germany and whether the states' influence is directly proportional to their relative strength.

A final important feature linked to viewing integration as controlled by the states is that it adds a further point of difference between the second and third views. In the second, the inherent dynamism of the process is stressed, and a certain automatic development appears (through the interests of the common institutions or through being necessary for carrying out the previous steps). In emphasising the states' control over the process, the third view thus implies that the process is reversible, at least more clearly so than the second. The basic condition of integration is that the member states must see their interests as consistent with the enterprise (cf. Lindberg 1963: 293).

Development across the views

To understand the subsequent development of the third view, and, at the same time, that of the second, it is important to take into consideration the emerging dialogue or contest between these two approaches that shapes both, and which increasingly takes the place of overviews of several theories as the central axis in the literature. From the 1970s on, a typical feature of integration literature was the aim to give an overview and evaluation of the whole field of integration theories, its 'isms', as it were, organising them according to the main differencies. Typically, Pentland divides integration theories into two groups as to what they see as the result of integration and to whether that result is compatible with the nation-state system, as well as according to their views on how integration is achieved or of what its causes are, and their assumptions about international politics. (Pentland 1973: 21-23, 189; cf. the divisions in Lindberg and Scheingold 1970 and De Vree 1972.)

Above all, these overviews revealed a considerable confusion as to the understanding of the theories. Apart from the generally shared conclusion that none of them was particularly good, the overviews were surprisingly different. It was not clear exactly how many different approaches had been presented and what the main contents of each of these were. While Haas (1970) analyses federalism, communications approach and neofunctionalism, Puchala (1972) evaluates federalism, nationalism, functionalism and power politics, Pentland (1973) federalism, pluralism, neofunctionalism and functionalism, and Harrison (1974) functionalism, federalism and neofunctionalism. As later examples, one might mention Webb (1983) comparing neofunctionalism, intergovernmentalism and interdependence, or Schmitter (1991) comparing functionalism, neofunctionalism, transactionalism, realism and intergovernmentalism. The state-oriented view is variably called traditionalist, pluralist, realist or intergovernmentalist, the label 'pluralist' being particularly ambiguous, as it is also used of the pluralists who see the state and society as consisting of different groups (thus, for example Haas).

The question of where to place a particular author was also difficult. For instance, while Pentland points to Deutsch as representing the pluralist integration theory, which is close to realist views, Lijphart (1981: 247) argues that he represents the opposite camp; Etzioni, in turn, is a federalist for Pentland and a neofunctionalist for Harrison (1974). There were also different conceptions of the differences between functionalism and neofunctionalism (see, e.g., Lindberg and Scheingold 1970: 7; Taylor 1983: 4). In fact, for some, the different approaches were, in the end, not so different: De Vree notes that, contrary to his expectations, the theories of Haas, Deutsch, Etzioni and Lindberg were not alternative, but rather variations of a common theme (De Vree 1972: 326; on the common theoretical core, pp. 328-344). Pentland, on the contrary, gives a picture of integration theories which unwillingly, it seems, minimises the points they might have in common.

However, an essential dividing line was emerging, corresponding largely to the distinction between the second and third views analysed here. Their mutual criticism became increasingly the central theoretical debate. Writings such as Hansen 1969 and Harrison 1974 are among the clear, early examples of how the two views are evaluated in comparison with each other. Both attack, in essence, the second view, basing their criticism on insights of the third. They criticise neofunctionalists for overestimating the expansiveness of functional integration in underlining automatic spillover. For Harrison, there is much greater likelihood that integration will set in motion conservative, equilibrium-restoring reactions. Spill-over or *'engrenage'*[45] is likely to be limited in scope and does not assume a continuing progress. Harrison sees that the political factor, involvement of national governments, is crucial in the process of integration: political integration depends upon acts of political will rather than upon any known dynamic process (Harrison 1974: 242-243, 247). Moreover, even though there was the political will to integrate, the states' capacity for integration cannot be taken for granted. This capacity is related to conditions of consensus formation and control in member units which are rarely found in practice (*idem:* 14-15, 95, also 100-101). Indeed, Hansen argues that the pace of European integration has actually slowed. For both, neofunctionalism failed to relate the process of integration closely enough to the international system and take into account the interaction between endogenous and exogenous variables, or the factors in the environment which affect the process. In addition, they denied the distinction between high and low politics and overestimated the role of institutions, while downplaying differences between states. (Hansen 1969: 247-249; Harrison 1974, *passim.*)

In all, both authors point to the lack of the explanatory and predictive power of neofunctionalism. In Hansen's view, it is illustrative that an event such as de Gaulle's effective deceleration of the process remains a mystery for Haas, while for Hoffmann, such 'deviance' is inevitable as perceptions change (Hansen 1969: 252, quotation marks original). The claim of the extending involvement and importance of institutions has also been subject to reappraisal in the light of the history of the EEC, its validity being limited to cases where certain necessary background conditions pertain and especially to pluralistic, complex societies (Harrison 1974: 75, 77-79, 81, 86). Harrison goes on to argue that neofunctionalism dominates by criteria of scholarly reputation, numbers, resources and volume, but not by quality (*idem:* 232-234), suggesting that its attraction resulted from the 'mesmeric effect of behaviouralism taken to the point of neglect of the authoritative element in decision-making', that is, the crucial role of government leaders (*idem:* 89-90). Harrison also sees a bias in integration studies deriving from a historicist view that there is something inevitable about the demise of the nation-state in a world shrunken and exposed to new terrors of war by the technological revolution, and that functional cooperation is the only rational transformation response (*idem:* 22).

Indeed, Harrison sees neofunctionalism as a systematic misapplication of a fruitful but imperfect model of domestic politics to relations between sovereign states. Though appropriate for the study of the United States, neofunctionalism is less useful as a theory of integration. This is because integration is governed by the same rules as international behaviour in general, being to a considerable extent system dominated, or determined by factors such as relative power, numbers, economic dependency and geographical position. In regional integration, as in international relations, all actors attempt in the long run to maximise security, prosperity and influence. Integration is a function of threat, leadership and crisis, and in its analysis, also the coercive power of the state has to be taken into account. (Harrison

1974: 238.) In all, Harrison sees that power-oriented conflict models of international society, where consideration is given to the perception of relative power in influencing decision-making structures and coalition formation, has considerable explanatory value and appear most relevant to the study of integration[46] (*idem:* 239-240).

Obviously, the criticism of neofunctionalism was met with countercriticism, as when Haas pointed out that Hansen downgrades too much the importance of 'expansive' bargaining styles and the institutions in which the styles take shape (Haas 1970: 619, footnote 18). Often, however, the critics seem to bark up the wrong tree; on both sides, the criticisms are based on rather simplified understandings of the opponent and may also contain evident misunderstandings. A typical case is the criticism of neofunctionalism for its assumption of automaticity in the integration process. For Haas, for instance, spillover was far from automatic, although, admittedly, he presented rather dissimilar views about it. Similarly, seeing the inadequacy of Haas' theory in its disregard for the interaction between exogenous and endogenous variables (Hansen 1969: 250) is misleading (see Haas 1958, preface of 1968). Rather curious is also the view which Keohane and Hoffmann (1991: 12) express on the older theories when maintaining that the emerging European entity barely resembles the entity foreseen by the most enthusiastic functionalists and federalists, who envisaged a transfer of powers to institutions whose authority *would not derive from the governments* (italics added). It is, in fact, easy to see that it was precisely the functionalists (Mitrany) and federalists who saw that the governments would decide either case by case or all at once the transfer of their powers.

A closer look at the original texts also shows that the 'new' ideas proposed by the critics are not always thoroughly new. This applies even to the centrality of the state in integration: Mitrany (1943) saw that states could derive fresh life and scope from coordination, and, indeed, Haas claimed that integration was dominated by nationally constituted groups, which turned to supranational means when this appeared profitable (Haas 1958: xxxii-xxxv; cf. later Milward, see above). Thus, the distinction between the opponents, which they themselves highlight, seems at times to disappear, as in the case of Harrison's and Haas' view on the role of the state or government. While the latter would argue that governments can be persuaded not to obstruct integration, the former holds that there will be no integration if not through the political will of the states.

Importantly, both views progressed by absorbing the criticism. The proponents of the second approach increasingly accommodated the state actor in their frameworks; Haas came to redefine integration as a process whereby states voluntarily 'mingle, merge and mix' with their neighbours, losing thereby the factual attributes of sovereignty but acquiring new techniques for resolving conflict between themselves (Haas 1970: 610-611). It was promptly noticed that this was a significant transformation in that the new definition embraces one of the central concepts of the political or federalist approach, sovereignty, which Haas had previously denounced as alien to neofunctionalist theory.[47] Haas (1975: 72) also agreed with the validity of the distinction between high and low politics, although he points out that it refers to attitudes, and not to fixed objects of politics and that the same issue may shift on the spectrum between 'low' and 'high' according to the specific circumstances, in time and between different countries[48] (cf. Harrison 1974: 199; Hansen 1969: 252).

In a way, the two came to share a common research question in finding a rationale for the state to integrate. This became the main problem for the third view, which could be criticised by pointing out that integration had not completely halted in the late 1960s, but continued, and that it indeed acquired new emphasis and efficiency. Particularly in the mid-1980s, the third view was challenged by the project of a common market by 1992 and the Single European Act of 1987. Finding an explanation for the states' voluntary integration became more difficult when this integration implied increasing the transfer of power away from the states. However, the logic of the third view could be extended: the answer was to show that the states preferred integration to non-integration because of its (still, overwhelmingly) beneficial consequences. After all, had integration weakened them, it would not have been rational at all to join in the process.

What is seen as beneficial for the states is somewhat altered. It is acknowledged that integration does comport some loss of power, but that, summing up, the final outcome is still positive. An example of this type of calculation, influenced by a neoinstitutionalist analysis of state behaviour, is provided by Milward. He sees that transactions, integration included, naturally imply that the weaker party has to sacrifice something to maximise its national advantage. At the same time, extending the range and complexity of transactions with others and formalising them may be beneficial in reducing the vulnerability of the actor to interdependence (Milward 1992: esp. 18-20). Integration in particular does imply some sacrifices in terms of concessions of the state powers or a partial loss of sovereignty; these sacrifices are, however, compensated by other elements of integration which make it, in all, preferable for the states.[49] Moreover, being able to structure the central institutions, the states are able to preserve the balance of power within the integrationist framework in their favour. (Milward and Sørensen 1993: 12-20.)

Similarly, Grieco depicts integration as a possible and advantageous strategy for the state as an explanation of why states not only cooperate through institutions but may also wish to strengthen them. He proposes that relatively weaker states may wish to institutionalise the coalition's activities in order to avoid being dominated by the group's strongest member. This is called collective binding strategy. The strongest member, in turn, has its reason to integrate in that it may prefer the institutionalisation as a vehicle for exercising limited leadership of its coalition partners. (Grieco 1991: 9-21.) Further, in the common institutions and cooperative arrangements, the weaker states will seek rules which provide sufficient opportunities for them to voice their interests and possibly prevent their domination by stronger parties (Grieco 1995: 34).

Emphasising the compensation of losses by the diverse benefits from institutionalised integration was not the only way of explaining why the undeniable loss of decision-making power by the states was not totally negative. Another consisted in arguing that the states were actually not transferring or renouncing sovereignty, but sharing or 'pooling' it. Therefore, nothing was really lost. This idea is visible in Keohane's and Hoffmann's (1991: 7-8) formulation: for them, the puzzle to be solved is how to account for the pooling of sovereignty and the unexpected set of institutional changes accompanying this process. They remark that the governments have sacrificed their legal freedom of action, 'sovereignty in the operational sense', to a remarkable extent. In issues where the decision-making authority is removed from the states, it is shared among governments, through a process of qualified majority rule. Thus, sovereignty is pooled.[50] Moreover, they stress that an interstate body – the Council of Ministers – has the crucial decision-making role, and that the decisions are implemented by governments or through national courts enforcing Community law. Baker and Kolinsky (1991: 119), in turn, argue that sovereignty has not been lost to the Community or some supranational institution, but to the executive branch of each state and to the Council of Ministers.

The 'threats' of integration are, thus, minimised; gradually, integration comes to be seen as absolutely necessary for the state. The idea of an obligatory surrender of a degree of national sovereignty (cf. Morgan 1994b: 133) appears. First, it is seen necessary to guarantee or achieve something else, notably welfare. Here, the surrender is clearly voluntary, comparable to, e.g., the willingness to accept limitations of national sovereignty for the goal of international peace and justice, as manifest in the late 1940s constitutions of France, Italy and Germany (cf. Baker and Kolinsky 1991: 102).

Soon, however, it comes to be seen that even sovereignty itself, or what remains of it, can be secured through its partial relinquishment. As Wessels puts it, the only way the state can secure not only welfare but also sovereignty is participation in the decision-making in interstate level and efficient (read: sovereignty-cutting) forms of cooperation (Wessels 1992: 43; cf. Pinder 1986). The growing demands on the state and the fact that it is increasingly evaluated by its performance make it rational for the state to resort to interstate mechanisms. These, in turn, induce a development towards a more open state or a self-induced erosion of the closed state organisation, towards a fusion between the participating states (Wessels 1992: 40-43). Indeed, it can even be seen that it is in the interests of states to abandon their own interests: as Wessels puts it, while the states are still able to place boundaries to the incremental development, increased efficiency takes precedence over the protection of self-interests which, finally, are counterproductive (*idem:* 48, 51).

Towards a synthesis

From the late 1980s on, the question of state-integration relationship emerges as an increasingly central division in the analysis of integration. The theoretical debate concentrates around this question, and around the two, by now familiar, positions. They present themselves as quite different, even mutually exclusive. On the one hand, states are seen pushed into the process of integration through forces in the international and domestic environment, being then profoundly influenced by the common institutions and increasingly unable to influence the process. On the other, integration is seen as a result of political will, as process started and led by states which also control the common institutions. It is typical, however, that the 'pure' positions which correspond to the second and third views become less common. Both sides make concessions to each other, coming – perhaps unwillingly – also closer to each other's positions. While giving different answers, they tend to become sweeping, and well aware of the pitfalls pointed out by critiques.

A look at Matlary's and Moravcsik's writings illustrates this reformulation of the views – the second and third respectively – based on mutual criticism. Moravcsik (1991) compares, on the basis of empirical evidence, the intergovernmental and supranational[51] explanations for the success of the Single European Act. Comparing the relative role of the Community institutions with that of the member states, he concludes that the states are more important. Thus, the intergovernmental approach, based on the relative power of member states and the convergence of their national policy preferences, has more explanatory value. In his view, the 'historical record' does not confirm the importance of international and transnational factors in integration. (Moravcsik 1991: 44, 49-50.) However, as a concession to the supranational view, Moravcsik argues that his 'intergovernmental institutionalism' also accords an important role to supranational institutions in cementing existing interstate bargains as the foundation for renewed integration (*idem:* 56).

Subsequently, Moravcsik examines in more detail the question of why states aim at integration. As the state-based explanation of integration is criticised for a too generic understanding of the state which can see anything the state does as being in its interests, further specification seems needed in order to make the claim convincing. Thus, he does not simply argue that integration and even supranationalism can benefit the state, but specifies the argument through defining 'the state' more precisely. Instead of viewing the state as the traditional 'black box' – a typical criticism of the realist view – he sees it as an entity entrusted to governments, which themselves are responsible to domestic constituencies (Moravcsik 1991: 21-27). In his view, supranationalism strengthens the governments' control over domestic affairs, permitting them to attain goals which are otherwise unattainable. Thus, supranationalism is acceptable insofar as it strengthens the state through strengthening the position of the national executive. (Moravcsik 1993b: 507.)[52] This argument about the EC increasing the power of the executive – both national and the Council of Ministers – has been forwarded by Baker and Kolinsky (1991: 119); also Lindberg and Scheingold (1970: 86) noted the strong position of the executive. For them, executive power is virtually autonomous of the legislatures when it comes to determining national positions on Community problems. In fact, the parliaments were pointed out as the main losers already by Lindberg (1963: 295) and Cox (1965: 114).

On the other side of the division, Matlary gives a different answer to the question of why states choose to maintain a supranational institution which *de facto* and *de jure* implies a transfer of sovereignty and which can and does act against the interests of the member states on particular occasions. She criticises the intergovernmentalist explanation, based on state interests, for inability to assess whether the state really has succeeded in pursuing its interests. This inability is due to the intergovernmentalist conception of the state. The state is a 'black box', assumed rather than examined; it is seen to be a rational, unitary and egotistic actor; its behaviour and interests are static and given. Both the interests and identities are seen as exogenous to interaction. Therefore, in this framework, there can be no change of interests or strategy. (Matlary 1994: 21, 23.)[53]

At the same time, Matlary observes, intergovernmentalism denies the uniqueness of the EC, reducing it to multilateral cooperation which leaves the state unchanged as the pivotal actor. As the EC is not seen as an independent actor – if not in the sense of being a 'neutral', technical actor which facilitates agreement – it cannot have own strategies; therefore, it does not make sense either to assume that the EC could impose rules on a recalcitrant government. Thus, integration can only strengthen the state. For Matlary, on the contrary, integration should be seen as more than cooperation, a change and possibly the creation of new units or political entities. It may strengthen the state, but the effect can also be the opposite. (Matlary 1994: 9-11, 17-18.)

Matlary agrees that states do further their interests, and that they can benefit from integration, as their interests can coincide with those of the Commission. The state can benefit from the ability of EC to deal with issues of an international scope which need multilateral solutions. It may also favour integration where there appears to be a transferral of power to the EC when it can make use of EC rules to deal with a domestic problem which it cannot resolve alone. In that sense, states do not 'pool' their powers in the EC arena but rather *create* power. (Matlary 1993a: 188-192.) However, what makes the EC unique compared to other international organisations is the specific interplay of formal and informal aspects; one particular feature is the commitment to the EC on the part of an inner core of members which is not explicable in terms of instrumental interest but which must be accounted for on historical grounds (Matlary 1994: 7).

For Matlary, to understand integration, one must take into account both formal variables – states, institutions, interests groups and the internal market programme[54] – and informal ones, comprising the regime of deregulatory politics and transnational policy networks which identify and modify the interests of the formal actors. Informal integration, or the intended but indirect effect of agenda-building by the EC or the expansion of an issue-area through linking to other areas, is important in explaining formal integration: it is less visible and thus more easily accepted, and it causes pressures for more formal integration. Therefore, the framework for analysing the role of the state has to include an emphasis on domestic politics and a processual view of interests as modified by institutions in interaction with the EC, taking into account also the less egoistic needs to arrive at a common interest and posit a sense of common identity and objectives, also transcending own interests. (Matlary 1993a: 182, 185, 193-196, 198-201; see also Matlary 1993b.)

In all, both the second and the third view make direct references to each other, even concessions. For instance, Keohane and Hoffmann (1991: 10) start their third view type examination of European institutions by explicitly stating their intention to take neofunctional theory seriously, and, in fact, refer extensively to Haas.[55] They also deny that a state-centric perspective would provide a satisfactory explanation of the SEA. However, they still remain within that view, noting that such an explanation must begin with governmental actions, as these are what they observe as leading directly to the Act. When explaining institutional change in the EC, therefore, they stress the 'preference-convergence hypothesis' holding that the convergence of governments' preferences is necessary for widening or deepening integration. Yet, the spillover model, explaining change through the role of the institutions of the Community, and explaining them by the political economy hypothesis as adaptation to pressures from the world political economy, also contain some elements of truth. (*Idem:* 17-25.) Later, Hoffmann (1995: 5-6) admits not only that institutions often have 'more than a superficial effect' on interest definition and calculations of gains and losses, but also that the European unity *has* made progress, and that the EU has, in fact, become a necessary and permanent part of the European political landscape and thus a subtle, if often shaky, international actor.[56]

Neofunctionalists' concessions are not less visible. In addition to the shifts, noticed above, towards less determinism or automatism in spillover and an allowance for the inclusion of political will as an important element (see also Mutimer 1989: 80), the proponents of the second view seem able to accept the basic claims of the third with the help of some alleviating conditions. For the first, state interests can be deemed important, if understood not as given but affected by, for example, the common institutions. In this connection, it is also acceptable to explain the process on the basis of state actions, when these are also seen as having unintended consequences: the process itself and the functioning of common institutions may be such as to make seemingly inconspicuous decisions lead to an unintended factual decline in the position of the states. The states may have an important role in controlling integration, but it is not necessarily under total control by the states or any one of them, nor is it based on the conscious following of clearly defined objectives (cf. Wallace 1977: 322). As Morgan

(1994b: 129) points out, there is also a difference between arguing that the Community was developed in order to enhance the sovereignty of its member states (as Milward does) and that the member states can (still) act from a position of strength in determining the future of the Community (as Hoffmann 1982 does).

In taking into account the criticisms and formulating answers also to questions originating from the other approach, trying thus to explain all that is explained by the rival and even some more, the two views show a certain tendency to 'inflate' and become complete mirror-image explanations of integration. The mutual tendency to come closer to the opponent is facilitated by the various possible interpretations of the central concepts, such as 'supranational'. As a result, the theoretical discussion is close to an impasse: criticism becomes predictable, as it without exception leans on either one or the other,[57] and the differences between the views become increasingly theoretical, with no clear evidence for the preferability of one answer. There is the choice between two very general modes of explanation which both can be criticised but which do not seem to have alternatives.

The intergovernmental view, as noted, can be criticised for its notion of the state, too generic and self-validating to serve as a basis for explanation. It is claimed that the state matters, but it seems, at the same time, to be altogether lost; it disappears or becomes a convention. On the other hand, the neofunctionalist line of argumentation stresses that the state is no longer central or sovereign; in doing this, it *creates* a rather formidable state which plausibly never has existed.

The generalisations of the state seem to have equally problematic consequences for the two views on integration. For intergovernmentalism, the exaggerated generality of the state makes it nearly eternal and universal, a highly flexible arrangement which adapts to all changes. At this very general level where the particular characteristics of the state do not matter and therefore may alter, changes are interpreted as adaptation to the environment and policies as rational for survival. In this view, the ultimate character of the state is also manifest in that it is the state that ultimately defines its own characteristics, such as population, and measures the efficiency of its government. Similarly, 'sovereignty' can have many meanings, to the point of none at all. For the purposes of research, this implies the irritating fact that as the state adapts to circumstances, its meaning has to be constantly updated or recomposed; in addition, the tautological validity of the arguments diminishes their credibility. Accordingly, the state becomes, in a way, immune to integration: its essential features cannot be threatened, since they are constantly redefined. Adopting the logic of the state also implies that integration can only strengthen the state, as it otherwise would not be undertaken.

In the second view, then, the state is analysed against a fixed picture of what the states have previously been. With a clear view of what the state is or has been, it is possible to formulate quite precise appraisals: for instance, having proceeded to a certain level or point, European integration has deprived the member states of the attributes of statehood, such as decision-making competence in economic or commercial policy, the supremacy of national legislation, or, more generally, sovereignty. The insinuating assumption that states actually have sometimes been really sovereign and supreme authorities may well be needed for the formulation of precise hypotheses or statements. Different indicators and criteria seem, however, to succumb to the particular resilience and tenacity of states: the latter are more resilient and tolerant towards integration than a theoretical point of view might indicate. Absolute autonomy is, in fact, not vital for the state. Abstractions or 'ultimate' features such as 'being in control of the people and territory' or 'being sovereign' can in practice be understood as nominal rather than as real features. Moreover, states seem to be rather ill-suited to generalisations, since being a state does not seem to require being similar to other states. It seems, in fact, that an important feature of states is some kind of right of being different. In all, statehood seems to be a convention, but it is also a convention which entails the idea that statehood is not objective, not to be decided by others. One could argue that the essence of statehood is that states have the right to be different, to refuse intrusion in their internal affairs, even to decide for themselves what constitutes an 'internal affair'.

The consequences of these generalised concepts for the study of integration are quite puzzling. In fact, the views do not seem to lead very far if not to two dead-ends, diametrically opposed. It could be said that while in the first view, integration is held constant while the meaning of the state is variable, in the second, the state is the constant which explains integration. Both views, however, practically remove the state from the central concerns in integration studies. In fact, the result may be a certain marginalisation of the central research question about the relationship between the state and integration. Firstly, the 'dismantled' character of the state impedes the analysis of concrete questions or the taking into account of empirical variations. The view of the state affects the way the impact of, for instance, different consequences of integration is evaluated: what is an important change depends on what is important for the state, that is what is seen to be the core of the state, and therefore many empirical facts are seen not to affect the state. Secondly, the questions about the basic character of the state, in turn, are impossible to answer as empirical problems, as what is said to be common to all states and important for statehood either changes limitlessly, which ultimately means that it becomes immune to change, or becomes meaningless in that the states do not in practice care very much about fixed meanings or general characteristics.

Against this background, it is easy to see why conclusive evidence for any of the views is hard to find. The example of ascertaining the truly supranational character of the EU and the indisputable weakening of the position of states illustrates this problem. The legal argumentation on the development of European law or the process of constitutionalisation with federative elements – supremacy of Community law over national law, irrevocability, development of enforcement – does not succeed in conclusively ruling out the intergovernmental interpretation.

Weiler, Burley and Mattli could here exemplify the argumentation in favour of supranationalism and constitutionalisation. Weiler sees that a constitutionalisation of the Community has indeed taken place, transforming the relationship between itself and its member states; the nature of the Community has changed from an international organisation into a truly self-contained legal regime. Central components of this constitutionalisation are the doctrine of direct effect and the doctrine of supremacy of Community law in relation to national law. Even more important, however, is the doctrine of implied powers. While in international law, treaties must be interpreted in a manner which minimises their encroachment on state sovereignty, in the EC the Court of Justice has adopted a teleological, purposive rule according to which powers are implied in favour of the Community where they are necessary to serve the legitimate ends it pursues.[58] (Weiler 1991: 2406-2407, 2413-2417.)

In practice, this has meant a significant diminution of the states' possibilities of 'exit', or of avoiding their obligations under the treaty.[59] The particular system of judicial remedies and enforcement of the Communities places them apart from traditional international organisations. National courts and the European Court are integrated into a unitary system of judicial review as regards the treaty, and therefore, even though a member state could disregard the European Court, it cannot disregard the decision of its own court. For Weiler, the combination of constitutionalisation and the system of judicial remedies have to a large extent nationalised the Community obligations and introduced on the Community level a habit of obedience and respect for the rule of law which is traditionally more associated with national obligations than international ones. (*Idem:* 2418-2422.)

Somewhat similarly, Burley and Mattli (1993) argue that legal integration – the gradual penetration of EC law into the domestic law of its member states – makes it difficult to maintain that the member states really are able to further their interests through integration.[60] In their view, those claiming that integration serves the interests of the states through asserting that a particular decision was in the interests of a particular state, do so with the luxury of hindsight and by manipulating the analysis at a very high level of generality. If one assumes that states will comply with the judicial decisions only if they are in their interests, there is an obvious incentive to deduce interest-compatibility from compliance. The authors note that the rulings of the Court are not consistent with the preferences of (some) member states which the Court would attempt to track. In reality, many cases show that governments have strongly disagreed on the outcome of a particular case and have also strongly argued against the ultimate position of the Court, which, however, has followed the lead of the Commission. Over time, the member states tend to accept the Court's position and regard the path chosen as inevitable. Explained in neofunctionalist terms, the primary players in the process of integration are above and below the state (government), which, circumvented, may either choose to or feel constrained to yield to the pressures of converging supra- and subnational interests. (Burley and Mattli 1993: 51, 54-56, 60-65.)[61] There is a structural logic of law which favours integration rather than the protection of state interests (*idem:* 73-74).

Yet, what constitutes evidence in one context is not necessarily evidence in another.[62] In fact, representatives of a more intergovernmental approach interpret the situation described above in a different way. For instance, Taylor, for whom 'the continuous assertion by a distinguished group of lawyers that Community law is superior may also be seen as part of a political process of realising that possibility' (Taylor 1983: 280), concludes that the Communities are not a federation and that the position of the member states therefore is clearly stronger; the states' system prevails, and they are also those who are ultimately responsible (*idem:* 292, 301). Taylor underlines the voluntary aspects of integration, seeing that measures agreed to by the member states cannot be against them; he finds support for this view in the general idea that an international commitment by the state which restrains its behaviour is not evidence for a loss of sovereignty, but for the effective use of that sovereignty (for applications, see Taylor 1983: 281 and Taylor 1991a: 78).

For Taylor, a sovereign state is by virtue of its sovereignty entitled to decide upon those laws which shall apply within its territory – though members of the EC may be sometimes disinclined or lack the capacity to do this. Governments remain 'masters of the treaty' since they are not bound by any amendments they do not consent to; a withdrawal is also a feasible alternative to accepting amendments. That Community law is effective in the member states does not automatically imply its superiority. Its effectiveness can also be grounded in it having been introduced as an international treaty, a decision taken according to national constitutional norms, which therefore remain superior to the Communities' constitutional norms. In sum, the Communities' system is an extension of the judicial arm of the state. (*Idem:* 276-281.)

Moreover, Taylor sees a tendency in the Community to use sparingly the supranational measures available as the use of these could have disintegrative effects. Although the interpretation of Community law and its application is the exclusive right of the Court, the latter has tended to avoid policy issues where there is a chance of sharp dissent. Similarly, the possibility of sanctions and counter-measures by other countries against a state, for example in the case of unfair competition, cannot be used too often; otherwise, the Community would be enforcing at the cost of its own disintegration. (*Idem:* 287-291.)

Interestingly, Taylor's argumentation is, in the end, not totally discredited by Weiler. In all, the effects of the supranational characteristics of the Community on the position of the member states are difficult to estimate, and Weiler remarks that they are not necessarily negative at all. The differences between the Community legal system and traditional international law might not be that important in practice: the intergovernmental character of the procedure of judicial review and the consequent limitations on its efficacy are clear and, most importantly, no real enforcement exists (Weiler 1991: 2419-2420). On the other hand, the states have also defended their position. As the possibility for the member states to evade their obligations has diminished, the Community law has become binding inside them, and effective legal remedies to enforce the law have been adopted, the states have strengthened their hold on decision-making.[63] Thus, an equilibrium emerged in that the member states could accept the constitutionalisation because they took the real control of the decision-making process, minimising the threats to their position. Actually, Weiler argues, the closure of exit was in the interests of the states. It contributed to the strengthening of the Community, but also in fact bolstered the member states. All could attain decisive power of influence that was elusive in more traditional fora of international relations: the small states increased their general weight and power, while the larger states had particular interests they could effectively vindicate through the Community (e.g., agriculture for France and relegitimation for Germany). (*Idem:* 2429-2430.) A somewhat similar conclusion is presented by MacCormick (1993) who argues that the relationship between the states and the Community cannot be seen as a simple 'zero-sum game'; states are not mere delegates of the Community, nor is the Community a delegate of the states. Actually, no state is any longer in a position whereby all power exercised internally in it derives from purely internal sources, but neither has the Community such a plenitude of powers.

These mutual concessions and more or less successful efforts at reaching consensus between rather different views lead the scholars to two conclusions and two ensuing strategies for further studies. One group of scholars tend to conclude that neither of the contradictory and equally imperfect views can be adopted, and therefore seek new openings in other realms, leaving aside the explicit question of integration. Others welcome the achieved consensus and attempt to refine it, building on the elements both views share.

The first position, thus, is that the development towards some kind of synthesis of the two contradictory views involves the risk of finding oneself in a theoretical impasse between them. The only solution is to search for new problem formulations. Haas, as a notable example, quitted integration studies in 1975 referring to the argument that he wanted to study questions which were more timely and relevant.[64] He declared that integration studies were no longer interesting or important and that a further development of integration theories was 'probably not worth our while'. Instead, one should study more important and recent phenomena, systems change, interdependence and turbulence.[65] Interdependence is a condition in which governments are so vulnerable that unilateral action is (seen as) unwise to survival; turbulence, then, denotes a setting of great social complexity and uncertainty in which actors have confused perceptions, incompatible objectives and in which they are interdependent. Taken in this framework, integration can be understood as an effort towards the management of turbulence or 'control of turbulent fields'. (Haas 1975, *passim.*)

In fact, Haas' 'exit' is a criticism of all integration theories – once again put into one bundle – using arguments presented by intergovernmentalists against neofunctionalism and transnationalist criticism of state-centred analyses of international relations. Thus, in particular, he remarks that the theories did not take into consideration the obstinate character of the state and that the national capability to resolve problems might recover. Moreover, they depicted the process of integration as too orderly, unambiguous and rational a process. (*Idem:* 12, 14-20.)[66]

Hoffmann (1982: 33-35), in turn, concluded from what he saw as the 'paradox' of integration, that it simultaneously curtailed states' capacities for unilateral action and served to preserve the state as the basic unit, that an explanation could be found by analysing the whole as a 'regime'. Other promising new research focuses have been identified in such phenomena as globalisation (e.g., Rosamond 1995, Anderson 1995).

Others, however, saw that as both views were well-developed and events seem to confirm that what both foresee can take place simultaneously, a theoretical synthesis of the two was a natural solution. While it seems that integration theory has in the 1990s increasingly adopted a common research agenda in the form of explaining why and how it is possible that both views can be true at the same time, efforts at a synthesis appeared much earlier.

In the 1970s, there was a search for a synthesis of the many approaches and definitions used in the literature. Puchala (1972) compared integration scholars to blind men examining each a different part of an elephant and failing to agree on what it actually was, and Lindberg and Scheingold (1970) expressed the need for an overall perspective in the 'vast outpouring' of theories and analyses of integration. Advocating some kind of synthesis, they maintained that the seemingly contradictory theories actually focus on different aspects of a larger whole.

Notably, the idea of synthesis appeared in the literature which claimed that integration simultaneously strengthens both the states and the central institutions, and that there is thus no necessary opposition between the state and integration. The idea of symbiosis between the state and integration was presented by Lindberg and Scheingold in 1970. They saw that it was no longer appropriate to think of the integration process in terms of the Community's capacity to accumulate the power to impose decisions on the nation-states, since both the states and the Community thrived: instead, integration should be seen as a kind of symbiosis between the systems, a merging of systems which results in the actors' increasing tendency to define their roles in terms of joint problem-solving rather than as agents of one or another system.[67] The authors also ask whether the Community has really contributed to the reconsolidation of the nation-state and whether its existence can be seen a precondition to the long-term viability of the nation-state. In their view, the most convincing case for the relevance of the Community for the nation-state can be made with respect to economic matters. As regards the political reconsolidation of the members, the authors see that increases in political capacity at the national and supranational levels are likely to be mutually reinforcing rather than mutually exclusive. (Lindberg and Scheingold 1970: 32, 35-37.)

Later, Taylor also suggests that in the EC, the organisation and the state are mutually reinforcing, and that the relationship between the state and the Community is symbiotic. Both are strengthened in integration; it is even possible that the subnational entities are strengthened as well. States are pushed to accept some constraints in their struggle to promote their own interests. However, they have also reason to promote the common system because of its benefits, such as an increase in economic and military or strategic security. A convincing potential of common action helps preserve the capacity for individual action; at the same time, the strengthening of the common system can reinforce the distinctiveness of the participating units.[68] Instead of a linear and progressive view on integration involving increasing accord among the participants and gradual strengthening of the community level, Taylor proposes a consociationalist view which does not expect a reconciliation of regional differences but identifies the built-in pressures in the EC that tend to consolidate the sub-units (the states). (Taylor 1991b: 109, 119, 121-122, 125.)

Matlary proposes similar ideas of both the states and the Community being simultaneously strengthened. She sees that the emergence of an issue of international scope requiring multilateral solution is a precipitant for a period of integration; the EC receives legitimacy, which is needed for the Commission to increase its own institutional role. In periods of rapidly progressing integration, therefore, both the states and EC institutions gain in influence and, through the attention paid to the institutions, also the profiles of the states and the pursuits of their national interests receive much more attention. The reverse applies for periods of less integration. The Commission may pursue a strategy of its own provided that the states are able to satisfy theirs. (Matlary 1993a: 193-194.) In addition, Matlary points to the need to conceptualise the state as semi-integrated, not a unit totally distinct from the EC. Interaction between the state and integration varies from area to area, and their divide is not clear-cut. (Matlary 1994: 12-13, 23; see Kelstrup 1992.)

One could even see that the theories of multilevel governance are, in a sense, syntheses between the two approaches. They also seem to share the method of appealing to the ambiguous and complex nature of reality for justifying the need for applying elements from different theories. This is particularly visible in Marks (1995). He presents multilevel governance as a model between the state-centric one and a purely supranational system where common institutions have autonomous coercive power. In this model, states remain 'immensely strong institutions'. However, the increase in the scope and depth of institutionalised, collective decision-making dilutes sovereignty, and transforms the relation between the state and its domestic constituency. In addition to their monopoly position in decision-making, states' control of individuals in their territories is diminishing. They are losing their grip on interest aggregation and the mediation of domestic interest representation in international relations. Political interests and pressures are not nested within each state, nor are states separate arenas providing the sole channel for domestic political interests to the European level. Instead, the political arenas are interconnected, and subnational actors act directly in both national and supranational arenas. (Marks 1995: 1, 3-5.)[69]

Integration which transforms the state

In the fourth view of the relationship between the state and integration, the latter is seen as a process which transforms the former. The state is not seen to disappear, nor necessarily to be weakened or strengthened in the process. It remains, although it is changed in different ways. These changes may concern its functions, policy-making processes, administrative apparatus and power relations between the different state organs, but also such features as political culture or identity. The extent and nature of the changes depends on the particular features of the state in question; the focus is therefore on a single state rather than states in general.

The appearance of this view can be explained by two main phenomena having to do with the previous development of integration theory. The first is the tendency towards a synthesis of the views considered above; the second is the new centrality of domestic politics in the study of integration. In a way, the tendency towards synthesis creates a special 'niche' in which this approach can be based. It is seen that integration effectively influences the state, even though the state is not replaced, and it is also seen that the previous views, when remaining concentrated on the puzzle of whether or not states control the process and benefit from it, risk overlooking the central question of how the state is influenced in concrete terms. Thus, the view also takes into account the criticism directed against the third view for analysing some general conception of state, or *the* state, without taking into consideration the differences between states. After a considerable expedition in other questions, thus, the fourth view brings the discussion back to Hoffmann's (1966) state which 'survives, although transformed' (see above), building its research agenda on analysing these transformations closer.

The second background factor, the centrality of domestic politics, is also underlined in the fourth view as an important criticism of the former views, and, thus, as a step forward in comparison to them. Bulmer (1983) proposes the domestic politics approach as an alternative to those used thus far in integration studies. His central idea is that domestic politics may have a vital impact on the policy-making output of the EC. He therefore aims at an approach in which domestic politics, the domestic policy-making structures and attitudes within a member state regarding the EC are synthesised to explain the behaviour and positions of a member state in the Community. Consideration of domestic politics had, in Bulmer's view, been pushed into the background by two factors. On the one hand, interest had turned from developing integration theories to examining how policies are made in the EC as a result of the deceleration of integration in the 1970s and 1980s. On the other, domestic politics, or some important findings concerning policy-making in the member states, was overshadowed by the evolving debate between supranationalism and intergovernmentalism – the second and third view in this study. (Bulmer 1983: 349.)

In this debate, Bulmer takes the side of intergovernmentalism, which, in his view, is based on actual developments in contrast to neofunctionalism which is merely based on theoretical predictions and assumptions, moreover, on assumptions which have not stood up to developments in the real world. He adopts the intergovernmentalist postulates of retention of power by governments and of comparability of the EC to other international organisations.[70] Thus the policy-making analysts, such as Wallace, Wallace and Webb, are right, in Bulmer's view, in identifying the national governments as central in the EC. However, they did not fully explore the linkages between domestic and EC tiers. Neither is intergovernmentalism sufficient for the study of the member states' attitudes towards the EC, because it sees the governments as omnipotent, monolithic structures. The disaggregation of the governments' positions is essential in Bulmer's approach. Another essential difference is that while intergovernmentalism focuses on the EC as an international organisation, Bulmer sees that since the same actors – political organisations, parties, interest groups, parliaments – are involved both in the EC and national politics, EC policy-making should be examined in the same way as domestic politics. (Bulmer 1983: 349-351, 355-356.)

Integration, or perhaps better EC policy-making, is thus seen as government-led and nationally anchored: the national polity is the basic unit in the EC. As Bulmer puts it, the domestic policy-making process does not follow the logic of integration, as assumed in integration theories; instead, integration follows the logic of decision-making processes. However, although governments formally are in a key position between national politics and Community politics, it is important to note that the power of the governments varies from case to case. A government may be captured by domestic interests or transnational forces, but it may also have power to impose policies on domestic interests. (Bulmer 1983: 353-354.)

Thus, Bulmer's approach deviates further from the intergovernmentalist position in that the member states are seen as essentially different with respect to policy structures and instruments, internal conditions, interests, degree of centralisation and relationship to the outside world. Their policy-making styles and political cultures differ, which is seen, for instance, in the relations between government and other political actors; whether the government develops policy through consensus building or imposition depends on its strength and political culture. Thus, EC policy, as any other domestic policy, is formulated differently within the different member states. In addition to differences in the domestic policy environments, there are also important differences between different policy areas. For Bulmer, the domestic policy-making structures together with the attitudes held within the member states regarding the EC explain why a particular state adopts a certain policy or negotiating position in the EC. The national positions together, then, explain the final outcome of EC policies. (Bulmer 1983: 350, 353, 357, 361.)

Against the background of the development of integration theories, it is perhaps only predictable for Bulmer to remark that the domestic politics approach is 'arguably more embracing and/or more realistic as a device explaining Community negotiations than the alternatives on offer' (Bulmer 1983: 363). What is interesting, however, is that the approach is presented as a novelty by criticising the former contributions for having been dominated by international relations approaches. This is pointed out by Bulmer also in 1993 as he notes that the study of integration has been mainly conducted within international relations theory, using their 'toolkit'. Hix (1994) goes on to specify that the EC has been mainly studied as an example of supranational integration or of intergovernmental cooperation between nation-states, using, consequently, approaches of international relations, such as neofunctionalism and intergovernmentalism. In other words, the previous views now appear reorganised in a somewhat peculiar way, stressing their shared origins in international relations. For neofunctionalism in particular, this categorisation is surprising,[71] and seems to affirm the factual rapprochement between the originally very dissimilar second and third views.

The novelty of the approach is in fact relative, especially as regards both the emphasis on the differences between states and on the importance of disaggregating the position of the government instead of treating it as unproblematic and coherent. Both seem rather to have only temporarily disappeared from the analysis. For Haas (1958) this disaggregation was the very starting point; only subsequently does there seem to have been an aggregation. A similar circularity appears also in the way of introducing domestic approaches to balance the international approaches, as these were introduced as an alternative to the previous dominance of the domestic ones (see, e.g., Harrison 1974).

Domestic politics has often played an important role in explaining state behaviour in the EC context. In parallel to Bulmer's work, state policies and preferences have been studied in the framework of analysing decision-making in the Community in terms of the member states' capacity and resources, domestic constraints, extra-national constraints, goals and strategies (e.g., Helen Wallace) and in the framework of foreign policy analysis.[72]

However, Bulmer also introduces the domestic politics approach for a another reason, that of analysing the EC as a political system. What makes it important, in Bulmer's view, to use a comparative public policy perspective instead of international relations approaches is that the EU can be seen as a multi-tiered system of government in the process of becoming a state. Again, a circle seems to have been completed: Bulmer chooses the path of comparison with the state unaware of or indifferent of where it took his predecessors, those who concluded that the two were not really comparable or that 'state' was an old and inadequate concept for analysing integration.

Leaning on new institutionalism, by basically emphasising the role of institutions as constraints on behaviour but also as shaping goals, Bulmer undertakes the task of examining the nature of policy processes in the EU through its governance structures, institutions, instruments, procedures and rules. Further, he remarks, as empirical studies have shown that the EU represents governance without government, a certain regulatory governance regime, it is appropriate to study it according to policy subsystems, taking into account the differences in national patterns of governance in different policy areas (Bulmer 1993: 351-356, 371).

Similarly for Hix, theories of international politics are of limited use in the analysis of the Community which has developed as an internal political arena, becoming something more than an international organisation. In fact, Hix claims that politics in the EC is not inherently different from politics in any democratic system: it is dominated by questions of representation, participation, distribution, allocation, and political and administrative efficiency. As the EC begins to address 'positive' integration issues such as social policy or questions of allocation and distribution of resources, the international approaches become insufficient. By contrast, comparative analysis – for Hix, the study of the internal politics of political systems or politics within rather than among nations – suggests that there are two fundamental dimensions of politics in the Community: in addition to the dimension of national versus supranational, identified also by the international approaches, there emerges also a socio-economic conflict along the party-political left-right dimension. (Hix 1994: 1-2, 6, 24, footnote 2.)[73]

Thus, Hix argues that the more fruitful comparative approach to the analysis of the EC should challenge the still dominant international approaches which simply describe it as unique (Hix 1994: 20-22).[74] Again, the earlier discussions for and against comparability seem to be forgotten. In fact, the analysis of the EC as a political system, based on a comparison between the EC and the state, is one of the basic approaches to the EC. For instance, for Wallace (1977: 303, 322) conventional models of domestic policy-making are one source for understanding the Community process, or 'the partial political system' as he calls the EC. Thus, questions such as how policies are made in the EC or who participates in the decision-making are amply reflected on by, e.g., Lindberg and Scheingold (1970) – closely resembling Bulmer (1993) – and in detailed comparisons of different policy-making areas.

This lengthy discussion on domestic politics approaches serves to make understandable the appearance of the fourth view which is evolving from these elements. It can be seen as based on still a new, third, application of the domestic politics approach to examine the influence of integration on the domestic scene, on the state. With a slight change of perspective, the domestic politics approach thus gives substance to a mirror image of the Bulmerian (1983: 353, above) perception of integration following the logic of domestic decision-making processes, namely, to the analysis of how domestic policy-making changes as a result of integration, based on the assumption that national decision-making processes, structures and policies are influenced or transformed by integration, if not altogether follow it. While the idea that the process of integration changes the state is by no means a new contribution of this view, it differs from the previous views by the conceptualisation of that change. On the one hand, the changes are seen to be the empirical question to be examined on the basis of the study of concrete, single states; and yet, even a deep transformation is expected to occur instead of a generic 'strengthening' or 'weakening' effect. In addition, 'integration' is partly seen as covering both formal and informal processes. In comparison to the preceding ones, the fourth view seems, however, to be more a view under formation, albeit an increasingly popular one.

An important part of the studies on how national political processes have changed under the influence of integration appears under the notion of 'Europeanisation'. As an example of the use of the label, it is useful to examine closer the contribution of Andersen and Eliassen (1993) – a study which seems to be situated in between the study of the EC policy-making and its effects on the national system. What these authors deplore is the fact that most studies of policy-making – including comparative studies – have retained a national bias: the unit of analysis has been the national system, which has been looked at as relatively closed. The EC has mainly been regarded as external to it, almost as a distraction. Further, they also see that EC policy-making has often been studied from the perspective of international politics, as extension of foreign policy or an arena of international cooperation,[75] or as a formal legal politico-administrative system, as a legal entity, an orderly system with a common body of law at its core. Andersen and Eliassen stress the need for studying policy-making in a new way because of the important changes that have occurred (or will occur, or even will have to occur) in its nature, that is, because of the Europeanisation, or 'Europeification' as they call it, of policy-making. The European political system has to be made the unit of analysis; the authors see that their approach differs from the above in 'emphasising the totality of the EC institutions and the national political system'. (Andersen and Eliassen 1993: v, 10-12, 255.)

In their view, there is 'a complex game around the policy-making process'. The increased importance of central EC institutions has mobilised a variety of interests which seek to influence the process, and this has further strengthened the role of the central institutions in relation to member countries (Andersen and Eliassen 1993: v, 17). Their – by now hardly surpising – conclusion is that one has to take into account the enlarged scope of national policy-making and increase the number and types of actors to be considered. A fundamental aspect of the conceptual model describing the EC as a new type of political system, which the authors claim to introduce, is the tension between the member states and the emerging transnational authority at the EC level. The key question is how policy-making is affected; the authors examine conditions in which national traditions prevail and in which attempts to structure policy from above succeed. In particular, they study EC decision-making and various areas of EC policy-making (but also implementation), looking at the degree of institutionalisation of policies at EC and national levels and the distribution of interests, their complementarity, possible alliances and conflicts. They aim at locating the driving forces in the decision-making levels and showing the relative importance and role of different actors in the process, taking into account actor strategies, coalitions and dependencies. (*Idem:* 11-17, 19-, 256-257, 261.)

Nevertheless, the authors have problems to locate what it actually is they propose as a novelty. A mere centrality of the EC and its political processes, instead of a focus on the state, is obviously quite common in research, as is the study of how EC policy-making can be influenced. Attempting perhaps to see the EC and the state as intertwined, they still remain, as to their results, in the realm of some well-known features of the EC policy-making process.

A possible reason may lie in the very concept of 'Europeification' which is, indeed, somewhat confusing, and appears more as a substitute for 'integration' used by others in similar contexts. In some respects, the authors seem to examine the Europeification of the national policy-making – which, indeed, is the title of the book – arguing, for instance, that almost all policy areas will in the future have an EC dimension. In others, they also speak about 'the Europeification of the EC system of policy-making'. While the need for this new approach is first motivated by referring to Europeification as a fact, the authors subsequently argue that Europeification is needed as a reaction to the increasing complexity of the European policy-making context or that it can be necessary in certain sectors to deal with the effects of a Europe without frontiers, they later turn the argument again by noting that the Europeification of EC policy-making leads to increased complexity. (Andersen and Eliassen 1993: v, 10, 12-13, 255.)

Actually, Andersen's and Eliassen's contribution is more about EC policy-making in different fields than about national policy-making. It points out differences between various policy areas concerning both the policy-making in the EC and whether there is European policy-making at all. It also points out how different new and partly unconventional actors, such as large enterprises, get involved in the regulatory activities, a fact which certainly has implications for the functions of the state in interest representation and aggregation. However, it does not consider the tangible changes in the national sphere as a result of Europeanisation, or the situation in which policies implemented in the member states are no longer made in the states, but at the EU level, and in which the national policy-making adapts to its new position as a part of a larger process.

A further step towards the analysis of the changes in the states is made by Héritier *et al.* (1994), based on the view that the extending rule- and policy-making at the European level induces changes in the member states or in their very statehood. The change in statehood is examined with the help of a particular case, a comparison between France, Germany and the United Kingdom as to their policies in the EC environmental policy-making, especially clean air regulation, and how the rule-making in this field has influenced their statehood.[76] The theoretical framework is that of policy network analysis, linked among other things to rational choice, symbolic interaction theory, new institutionalism and policy analysis; a series of in-depth interviews constitute the research material. (Héritier *et al.* 1994: 4, 7-8, 25-26.)

The dimensions of statehood which integration is seen to influence are the central organisational features of the state (degree of centralisation or decentralisation, administrative competencies and practices, distribution of financial resources between different administrative realms), the instruments of governance and juridical rules, the dominant problem-solving philosophy or ideology (e.g., justification of state intervention), the borderline between the state and society, and, finally, the societal interest aggregation by political parties and their position in the system. (Héritier *et al.* 1994: 1, 3-5.) Two features of these changes deserve particular attention. First, while some of the changes are not only easy to notice but, indeed, striking, there are also important incremental changes which are close to being indiscernible. Secondly, integration does not influence all member states in the same way: while some need no particular adaptation, others need only formal changes, the substance of regulations remaining the same; some, however, have to make even major substantial changes.[77]

The changes in statehood could be divided in general and particular. On the one hand, the authors conclude that in general, the national governments and executives have lost influence in policy formulation as the Communitarian law-making replaces the national. The borderline between the state and society has moved; patterns of interest mediation and representation have changed; the state is 'opened up' and the quality and form of direct contacts between the state and private actors has changed. Local actors are strengthened, and national actors increasingly have direct contacts with the Commission; political parties lose power as policy formulation is increasingly carried out in the Community, and as the European parties are weak. On the other hand, the countries examined experience different changes, such as the requirement for Britain to open its administration to public scrutiny as a result of converging domestic and European goals of increased transparency, and its changed problem-solving philosophy. (Héritier *et al.* 1994: 391-394.)

In the end, the authors see that the overall change in statehood is significant, but not subversive. Some old patterns of statehood are changed or substituted; more often, however, what takes place is an addition: new elements – institutions, measures – are added to the old patterns. In all three states studied only very partial substitution has taken place. This is made understandable by pointing out that the states attempt to resist change. First, the influence between integration and the state is not one-sided: the starting point of the analysis is that there is an ongoing process of mutual transformation between the European institutions and the member states. While the European regulations influence statehood, the states influence the European policy-making. In addition, there is also a mutual influence horizontally between the member states. (Héritier *et al.* 1994: 1, 3.)

Second, European policy-making is seen as a regulatory competition – *'ein regulativer Wettbewerb'* – between the member states, a contest for putting their own imprint on Community policies and legislation, or transferring their own regulatory culture, practices and regulations on to the European level. All states share the aim of influencing the common policies and regulations in order to minimise the pressure for change emanating from the process, and, consequently, the scope of specific changes they have to realise. They attempt this for both institutional and economic reasons: on the one hand, they aim at preserving their own traditions and institutions, the changing of which is costly; on the other, they also aim at preserving or increasing the competitiveness of national industry by avoiding increases in production costs not shared by others or by selling own products or innovations to other member countries. (*Idem:* 2, 13-14.) This being the goal of the states, the authors proceed to answer how they attempt this and in what conditions they are likely to succeed.

The outcome of the contest does not depend solely on the states: subnational and sectoral actors inside a member state and supranational ones also participate. Especially the strategies, structures and traditions of the Commission have to be taken into account. To answer why the Commission strives for certain regulatory solutions, what strategies it adopts and what conditions are helpful are, in fact, part of the authors' research agenda. (Héritier *et al.* 1994: 4, 12, 15-18.)

All in all, the authors' approach is perhaps less state-changing than state-conserving. They balance changes against influence, and underline that the transfer of competencies is not a zero-sum game. Even when sovereignty is lost, national identity and the representation of national interests are not, and the state still has the tasks of implementation – particularly so because of subsidiarity – and of being the caretaker of democracy in that it is the only existing infrastructure for democracy. (Héritier *et al.* 1994: 388-390, 393.)

In sum, the analyses based on the fourth view on the relationship between the state and integration seem to point to the continuing, if not increasing, relevance of the basic questions of the state and integration, rather than yielding any essentially new answers. The studies of the transformation of a particular state open the question of what the cause of this transformation actually is, that is what integration or Europeanisation represents. Integration is now made to explain, while it was previously explained; on the other hand, the transformations observed may come to be seen as an explanation of integration. Two aspects seem to make it more difficult to define: on the one hand, the 'European' influence could be part of some larger phenomena; on the other, the process influences the state both through its formal and its informal parts.

Among the scholars examining the transformation of the state, these aspects are brought forward especially by Olsen and Matlary. For Olsen, the question is about the way political processes transform political actors and structures. Europeanisation not only influences institutions, but also identity and perceptions of reality.[78] He points out the difficulty in isolating the effects of Europeanisation on the nation state from other influences and sees Europeanisation as a result of global processes, economic, technological, demographic and cultural development which make the nation-state in many respects too small to be functional. (Olsen 1994: 11-12, 14-15.) For Matlary, Europeanisation means increasing the importance of political processes at the European level; for this, the EU itself is, however, only one reason, economic changes being among other possible reasons. For her, the central question of how states change as a result has to be analysed with tools which make the division between the state and the EU disappear. Such tools are, for example, comparative policy, network analysis and policy diffusion. (Matlary in Humlebæk, May 30, 1996.)

The transformation of the state can without doubt be seen as a development in the direction of a fusion between the state and the EU.

Complete Europeanisation, as was seen above, would imply the disappearance of the 'national' from the political processes and decision-making. Wessels's 'fusion thesis' comes perhaps closest to describing this development. Instead of a transfer of loyalty, Wessels observes a new system of shared government, a significant trend towards *engrenage,* or the interlocking of the national and the communitarian. While national civil servants participate in EC decision-making, they gain access to and influence on this decision-making and implementation, but gain also more weight in their own national systems. The same applies for Community officials, ministers and interest groups. (Wessels 1990: 230.) As noted above, Wessels also argues that in resorting to interstate mechanisms in order to cope with the growing demands, the state induces a development towards a more open state or a self-induced erosion of the closed state organisation, towards a fusion between the participating states (Wessels 1992: 40-43).

All in all, the fourth view on the relationship between the state and integration seems both complex and attractive as a basis for further research. It might well develop into a prominent branch of integration studies, in a way similar to the development of the second view in the early 1970s. After all, the empirical material which can be analysed from this perspective is nearly limitless. The question of how integration transforms the state can be translated into a variety of different research problems regarding different countries, time spans, policy areas, procedures or state functions.

At the same time, the premises remain ambiguous. The process of transformation is clearly double-sided: while the state is changed, it also changes or influences the process of integration and the common institutions. What can be seen as a Europeanisation of national policy-making can also be seen as nationalisation of European policy-making. As a result of the transformation, the state might virtually 'disappear' in a fusion with the larger community, and so disappear also as a research subject. Still, the state as a unit is also seen as recomposed and strengthened by the same process. Not surprisingly, the view that the EU maintains the state appears anew in the context of Europeanisation, for instance as the 'lobbyification' at the central EU level is seen to require a higher degree of coordination at the national level (cf. Andersen and Eliassen 1993: 14-15, 257, 261). Further, perceiving transformation requires some stable point of comparison, a view on what the object of transformation actually is. This implies dissension on definitions as well as on methods. Changes in the state cannot be observed without focusing on it, with the ensuing problem that the more one focuses on the state, the more permanent it becomes. This may again further the perceived need to make it vanish from analysis. The fourth view, thus, does not give a definitive answer to the initial question. Rather, it reminds of its importance and sustains the basic debate on the state and integration.

Notes

1. The literature examined consists of research on integration in the field of political science and international relations, with only very limited reference to integration studies in other disciplines such as law, and leaving aside material such as memoirs of persons closely involved with the development of the European Communities.
2. Harrison argues that functionalism, the least politically ambitious theory, was in vogue between the wars, at a high point of European nationalism. Federalism, the most ambitious one, came next in the post-war disruption and disillusion. Finally, neofunctionalism, a compromise, emerged in conditions of recovery and improving political atmosphere (Harrison 1974: 66).
3. Pentland saw two of these circles already completed: the confrontation between federalism and functionalism (until 1950) was replaced by a neofunctionalist synthesis, which was then challenged by pluralist or confederalist theory; these were again synthesised into a policy-making approach, which came to be challenged by structuralist views. Importantly, however, the old theories have continued to exist, increasingly 'populating the intellectual landscape' in the field.
4. Note, in particular, the European Union of Federalists (later European Federalist Movement) which was established in 1946, convening in the Hague in 1948 and 1953, and the Congress of European People, established in 1956 and aiming at a common constitution, universal suffrage, etc. (see, e.g., Harrison 1974: 44-52). – In analysing the Hague conference of 1948, Haas notes the wide range of views represented and the disagreement on anything beyond the common denominator of the will to create a united Europe, e.g., on whether a European state structure was needed, on its functions, degree of centralisation and form of government to be adopted (Haas 1948: esp. 550).
5. Reference is often made to Richard Coudenhove-Kalergi, notably to his *Pan Europe* (Alfred A. Knopf, Inc., New York 1923), Carl J. Friedrich, *Trends of Federalism in Theory and Practice* (Frederick A. Praeger, New York 1968), Arthur W. Macmahon (ed.), *Federalism: Mature and Emergent* (Doubleday, Garden City, New York 1955) and William H. Riker, *Federalism: Origin, Operation, Significance* (Little, Brown, Boston 1964) but also to Proudhon, *Du Principe Fédératif* (1863).

6. A wide literature on international functional organisations developed as a result of the period of unprecedented efforts in planning and creating new organisations both at a universal (UN) and regional level after the second world war. Particularly in Western Europe, the organisational activities of the early post-war years were such as to prompt an observer to claim that "during the years 1947 and 1948, the ideal of a united Europe has been pushed closer to realisation than ever since the breakdown of the universal church and the universal empire" (Haas 1948: 528; Haas had in mind Bulgaria's call for a formal federation of the communist-controlled parts of the Balkan peninsula, the customs union between Benelux countries, the Franco-Italian customs union, the Organisation for European Economic Cooperation (OEEC) and the Western Union or the Treaty of Brussels). (See Taylor and Groom 1978; also Abi-Saab 1981.)

7. In a sense, then, Mitrany is not an integration theorist at all; cf. Harrison (1974: 27-28) who notes that the functionalist thesis was not originally related to the question of integration, unless in *opposition* to it. For Mitrany, it was important to break away from the link between authority and territory.

8. This pessimism about the prospects of resolving political differences through constitutional arrangements which involve limitation of sovereignty suggests that Mitrany's political observations have much in common with the realist school of international politics (cf. Harrison 1974: 31, 34; note also Morgenthau's 'brilliant and enthusiastic' introduction to a collection of Mitrany's essays, published in 1966 with the title of *A Working Peace System*; cf. Taylor 1975).

9. For Mitrany, it is useless to hope or to prescribe that relations between these kinds of unions or a union and other states should be liberal and co-operative: finance, production, defence and the like cannot be organised tightly in a sectional unit, and at the same time be open on equal terms to other units. The closer the organisation of the sectional unions, the sharper will be their division from other similar unions, and the more tenuous their links with any universal body. (Mitrany 1943: 17-19; cf. Mitrany 1975: 154 and Mitrany 1963.)

10. The book deepens the analysis of Deutsch's *Political Community at the International Level* (Doubleday, New York 1954) and leans on case studies by historians who, in separate volumes, have studied four cases, the relations between Norway and Sweden at the time of writing, the United States, the relations between the United States and the Soviet Union, and the Habsburg Empire in 1914.

11. An important condition for an amalgamated security-community to exist or emerge is found to be the mutual compatibility of main values. Other essential conditions include a distinctive way of life, expectations of stronger economic ties or gains, a marked increase in political and administrative

capabilities of at least some particular units, superior economic growth for at least some of the participating units, unbroken links of social communication between territorial and social strata, a broadening of the political elite, a mobilisation of persons (at least the politically relevant strata) and a multiplicity of ranges of communication and transaction. (Deutsch *et al.* 1957: 58, 123-159.)

12. The area comprises 19 countries in Europe and North America. The result of the analysis is that the highest degree of community is found to exist between the United States and Canada; this core is followed by a triad with Ireland. The third highest degree of community exists between these three together with the Scandinavian countries and the Benelux, after which there is a considerably larger leap in the degree of integration. (Deutsch *et al.* 1957: 10, 156-157.)

13. The differences can be striking; in comparison to federalists, Deutsch's way of examining people rather than institutions is particular. No new common institutions are envisaged in his political communities, and the existing institutions disappear in the background as institutional affiliations and various integrative efforts do not seem to influence much the results (for instance, as the United States, Canada, Ireland and the Scandinavian countries together show signs of remarkable integration).

14. 'Political community', for Haas, is a condition in which specific groups and individuals show more loyalty to their central political institutions than to any other political authority, in a specific period of time and in a definable geographical space. In Western Europe, the existing national states are such political communities.

15. For Haas' criticism of functionalism, see Haas (1964: 6, 13, 21-22); for more specific criticism of Mitrany based on, e.g., organisation theory, especially the role of experts v. politicians in the process of integration, pp. 95-96, 101-102, 115.

16. The Treaty of Paris establishing the ECSC was signed in 1951 by France, the Federal Republic of Germany, Italy, Belgium, the Netherlands and Luxembourg and came into operation in 1952. The ECSC was planned as one side of a triangle together with the European Defence Community (EDC) and European Political Cooperation (EPC) (Haas 1958: 29-30).

17. In particular, Haas refers here to the 'strikingly federal' powers of the ECSC regarding the routine regulation of the common market of coal and steel (part. pages 29-30, 38-48, but see also pages 51-58 for the limits of its power in questions not directly related to these domains), but also to its expansive nature, both regarding a spill-over of its powers into sectors other than coal and steel (e.g., to labour policy) and geographical spill-over or attractiveness. (*Idem:* 49-50, 301, 313-315.)

18. Although Haas is often presented as the *neo*functionalist *par excellence*, he in fact calls his theory 'functional'; nor does Haas later place himself in the category of neofunctionalism (see, e.g., Haas 1970).
19. The analysis of the ILO might appear largely a digression from the analysis of European integration (especially since the results of the analysis show that in the end, the ILO was not particularly successful in the task of transforming the international system), were it not for the fact that it has an important role in further developing Haas' view on integration.
20. Haas' supranational method of decision-making corresponds to the 'community method' identified by Lindberg and Scheingold (1970: 96-97) as emerging in the Council, characterised by the governments frequently showing commitment and accepting the Community as an active and valid partner, by a spirit of problem solving, responsiveness, will to compromise, long-term thinking, common interests, issue-linkages, and the achievement of unanimous agreements in the end. (Later, different interpretations of 'community method' have been given. For instance, Baker and Kolinsky (1991: 108) interpret it as meaning that the Commission, the 'European element', can identify sectors for inclusion in integration, which implies its widening.)
21. For example, Haas (1958: xxxvi) saw that his findings on the ECSC could be generalised to apply also to NATO, Scandinavian cooperation, OEEC and the relations between Canada and the United States, although not so much to other regions, such as Latin America. In Haas (1961), the question is whether the successful technique of integration in Europe can be imitated elsewhere, as it presumably would contribute to peace (Haas 1961: 366); Haas examines the various European efforts – more or less as parts of the same integrative process – and applies the findings to the Soviet bloc, Latin America, Arab states and United Nations. For examples of further comparisons with Latin America, Africa and Asia, see Haas and Schmitter, 'Economics and Differential Patterns of Political Integration: Projections about Unity in Latin America' in *International Organization*, vol. XVIII (4) 1964, pp. 705-737 (revised in *International Political Communities: An Anthology*, New York 1966); Haas, 'The 'Uniting of Europe' and the Uniting of Latin America' in *Journal of Common Market Studies* 1967; Nye, 'Comparing Common Markets: A Revised Neo-Functional Model' in *International Organization*, vol. 24 (4), 1970, and Haas (1975) in which 30 regional organisations are compared. For literature on socialist integration, see Muoser (1986).
22. E.g., Haas (1964), Lindberg and Scheingold (1970), Lindberg's article in *International Organization* 1970, based on systems analysis and decision-making theory, and Karl Kaiser, 'The U.S. and the EEC in the Atlantic System: the Problem of Theory' in *Journal of Common Market Studies*, vol.

V (3) 1967. However, Lindberg and Scheingold adopt quite different aspects of systems theory than does Haas: they do not, like him, consider integration as a transformation of the international system but analyse the EC as a political system of its own. In addition, they consider the EC in terms of system equilibrium, something abandoned by Haas for a more dynamic view of system transformation. (Seen as a further development of (neo)functionalism, this is a modification almost by reversal: integration does not necessarily lead 'forward' or mean continuous, automatic progress, but can evolve towards equilibrium and persist as such.)

23. Remarkably, although federalism first was not identified with a specific author or as a specific theory, it comes to be pointed out as the only clear case of falsified theory. The critics point out that federalism, based on rather disparate historical examples and not having specified any integration dynamism, is not conducive to scientific study about how the conversion might take place. (For further interpretations of federalism, see, e.g., Nye 1968: 875-876; Lindberg and Scheingold 1970: 11-12; Harrison 1974: 42-43, 55-58, 235-236.)

24. Between 1964 and 1966, France stayed outside the Community decision-making and created a crisis in the financing of the agricultural policy, objecting the proposals for 'own' revenues for the Commission and the use of qualified majority voting. The problem was resolved in January 1966 with the Luxembourg compromise which recommends unanimity and gives the possibility of vetoing the decisions on the basis of vital national interest of the member states. (See, e.g., Baker and Kolinsky 1991: 115; Miriam Camps, *European Unification in the Sixties: From Veto to the Crisis*, McGraw-Hill, New York 1966.)

25. The importance of the integration already achieved in influencing the perception of interests was confirmed. Haas mentions the integration threshold, a condition by which the beneficiaries of earlier integration steps have achieved such vested position in the new system as not to permit a return to an earlier mode of action: e.g., expectations which the politicians do not dare to disappoint, or regional enmeshment of administrative ties and practices with the consequence that national and supranational agencies cannot perceive themselves as functioning except in terms of ongoing cooperative patterns. (Haas 1958, preface 1968, xxix-xxx.)

26. Haas proceeds to explain that in certain conditions, supranationalism is likely to be substituted for nationalism, while in others, nationalism prevails. Supranationalism prevails over nationalism in conditions such as those of the 1950s: pessimism and frustration prevailed, national self-identity was not highly valued, and the nation-state seemed unable to guarantee welfare, security, democracy and human rights. These conditions, the trauma of war, need for reconstruction and the perceived threat of communism favoured the

search for regional unification as the remedy, the acceptable shared goal being economic advantage (not federalism or cultural unity). (Haas 1958, preface 1968: xviii-xx.) At that time, the situation was very different in Britain and the Scandinavian countries; it was also very different in 1967 (*idem:* xvi-xvii).

27. It is striking how many researchers seem to arrive at a personal conclusion that a particular term does not have a single, commonly agreed definition. In a way, the researcher seems to expect there to be a single definition in the literature, being surprised when, instead, a whole variety can be found. Similarly, those worrying over inadequate definitions of 'integration' seem to believe that some other notions (such as the state) would present a considerably higher degree of development in this aspect.

28. Etzioni defines 'political community' as efficient control of means of violence, decision-making centre capable of altering significantly the resource allocation and the dominant focus of political identification. 'Integration' for him is the ability of a unit or system to maintain itself in the face of internal or external challenges, while 'unification' is a process by which the bonds among the units of a system are strengthened (see the glossary in Etzioni 1965: 329-332).

29. Despite the claims that the very understanding of what integration was and how it was to be studied had not yet been achieved, there were also quite sophisticated analyses based on apparently unquestioned assumptions. Above all, those arguing that the earlier efforts of theorising were not relevant were quite positive that what had been studied as integration was not integration, or at least should be called by some other terms. For instance, when Haas brings integration studies to a rather abrupt end in 1975, the meaning of integration is definitively taken for granted, coinciding with its dismissal as an interesting and important object of research.

30. Dougherty and Pfaltzgraff find that Deutsch and Haas use transaction flows as an indicator, while Lindberg uses the delegation of decision-making power and Inglehart the survey of opinions towards integration. In addition, sentiments and contacts, loyalty and legitimacy have also been employed (cf. Caporaso 1971: 228-229). Even diametrically opposite results have been achieved with the same indicators so that while for Deutsch, integration has stopped or reached a plateau since 1957-58, Lindberg sees substantial progress in the five years after 1958 (cf. Haas 1958, preface 1968), and for Inglehart, integration never halted after 1958. (Dougherty and Pfaltzgraff 1981: 454-455.)

31. While this term was used in Haas and Schmitter (1964), Nye proposed instead the concept of 'catalyst' (an accidental historical factor which decisively influences integration) which for him was better than the 'functional equivalence' (see Nye, 'Patterns and Catalysts in Regional

Integration', *International Organization* 19, 1965; see also Harrison 1974: 108).

32. See, e.g., the use of the index of relative acceptance (RA index) in showing that integration has slowed down; the index [$RA_{ij} = (A_{ij} - E_{ij}) \div E_{ij}$, in which $-1 < RA_{ij} < \infty$, A_{ij} = actual trade between two countries, and E_{ij} = expected trade between two countries] is developed by Deutsch and I. Richard Savage to assess the preferences of the members of the Community for internal transactions as opposed to transactions with third countries (see Deutsch *et al.*, *France, Germany and the Western Alliance: A Study of Elite Attitudes on European Integration and World Politics*, Charles Scribener's Sons, New York 1967; Lindberg and Scheingold 1970, page 38 *et passim;* see also the test made in Fisher, William E., 'An Analysis of the Deutsch Sociocausal Paradigm of Political Integration', *International Organization*, vol. 23 (2), 1969, pp. 259-290, and Caporaso 1971). – Caporaso writes about the problems of measurement and scoring, the relation between theory and measurement, and proposes criteria by which to assess the state of integration examining convergence between scoring procedures, differential predictive and explanatory capacity of a variety of different scoring procedures, average interindicator correlation and factor analysis. (*Idem:* 233-253.) For integration as an object of formal reasoning, multiequation causal models, flow charts and computer simulations, see, e.g., Alker, Hayward R., Jr.: 'Integration Logics: A Review, Extension, and Critique', in *International Organization*, vol. 24 (4) 1970, pp. 869-914.

33. For Haas, computer simulation is one of the most exciting possibilities open to students of regional integration, having both a 'sobering and an intellectually explosive impact': it demands standardisation of variables, links and measures, and requires subordination to concepts which seem to summarise observed processes and which can thus 'become branching points on the flow chart'. The most exciting possibility is the chance to go beyond the very limited number of actual historical cases. Progress in theorising depends on the acceptance of the discipline which computer simulation implies, although computer simulation, in turn, depends on further progress in theorising. (Haas 1970: 644-645; also footnote 33, p. 634.)

34. In Scheingold's view, there is little understanding about the extent to which integration actually has the impact it was expected to have, such as altering dramatically the relationships between the nation-states in Europe, or of how integration affects the distribution of influence and material welfare. For him, it seems just as reasonable to expect the changes that the Community was supposed to generate to breed dislocation, discontent and instability, at least in the short run (he points to, e.g., nonparticipatory tendencies as possible costs of regional integration, suspect materialistic orientations of the communities and the probability that certain groups will be disadvantaged,

Approaches to the state and integration 97

as well as the disruptive international consequences of integration). (Scheingold 1970: 991-997.)

35. Aron maintains that those arguing for the smooth advancement from economy to politics are more Marxist than they realise; for him, it is 'pure fantasy' to imagine that identical foreign policy emerges on the day there is free circulation. (Cf. also Harrison 1974: 185-186, 197.)

36. On the contrary, Haas argued that the acceptance of unification will be facilitated if the state units are in fact already ideologically or socially fragmented (see Haas 1958: xxxii-xxxv).

37. Obviously, a different explanation was forwarded by Haas who attributed the failures to increasing interdependence with the United States, Japan and other industrial countries, which had overwhelmed the integrative forces (cf. Grieco 1991: 5).

38. Harrison (1974: 237-238) confronts Haas' neofunctionalist integration model based on pluralism and mutual adjusting behaviour with Hoffmann who distinguishes domestic and international politics by the relative centralisation of decision-making in the former and the relative decentralisation (lack of supranational authority) in the latter, basing the analysis on *Dynamics in International Relations* by Haas and A.S. Whiting (McGraw Hill, New York 1956) and Hoffmann's *Contemporary Theory in International Politics* (Prentice-Hall, Englewood Cliffs, New Jersey 1960).

39. Yet, one has also to observe that Milward argues that it is wrong to claim (as does the elitist historiographical tradition) that it is states and institutions which mould events; the true origins of the EC are economic and social (Milward 1992: xi).

40. Actually, Milward uses the word 'interdependence' for the first strategy, and defines it as international cooperation. This is quite confusing, since 'interdependence' is commonly used in many other ways; for instance for Keohane and Nye (1977: 8-11), it denotes mutual, often asymmetric dependence or a situation characterised by reciprocal effects among countries or among actors in different countries. (For the definition of interdependence, see also Milward *et al.* 1993.)

41. Cf. Lindberg and Scheingold (1970: 3-6, 24) who argue that the Community was a result of balancing different interests and reconciliating different forces: after the war, the viability of the state was questioned, but it was difficult to say whether the weakening of the state was a cause or a result of war and whether, consequently, the state should be strengthened or not. Those favouring the decline or demise of the nation-state had, in Lindberg's and Scheingold's view, more weight in this process.

42. As indicators of supranationalism, Taylor weighs the extent of majority voting, financial autonomy and right of initiative of the Commission and the challenges posed to the exclusive competence of the member states. In his

view, although integration was wide in scope, its level was low due to the low level of independence of central institutions. (Taylor 1983: 80, 106, 110.) Factors such as the fragmentation of the idea of national interest and the undermining of a hierarchy of interests admittedly undermined the status of governments in the political system of the Community (*idem:* 107-108), but several factors such as the establishment of COREPER and the summits or the membership of Denmark and the United Kingdom served the intergovernmental side, helping to impose limits upon the incursions of the Communities into the actions and structures of the states (*idem:* 96-97, 101-102, 214).

43. Negative integration means measures aimed at abolishing different barriers, e.g., to trade or free movement, while positive integration, seen as more difficult to achieve, denotes merging of authority and the creation of new, common regulations (see also Harrison 1974: 242-244, 247).

44. Referring to Lindberg (in *International Political Communities,* 1966, and in 'Integration as a source of stress on the EC system', *International Organization,* vol. 20, 1966) Harrison also refers to the evidence that the governments can avoid the logical consequences of integration for an 'unexpectedly long time', and that the success of an integrative step causes stress and raises barriers to further integration (Harrison 1974: 87).

45. The enmeshment of units and 'locking-in' of the achieved steps, making the costs of opting out of the joint policies higher than those of continued involvement.

46. With the help of Kaplan's models (used also by Haas 1964) of behavioral regularities based on the number and powerfulness of actors and on a balance of power, Harrison analyses integration as a factor of Western strength confronting the Soviet Union, while the Europeans are also keen on more power towards the United States; a bipolar system provides impetus towards integration among bloc actors, while its effect on the uncommitted is divisive (Harrison 1974: 132, 137-138, also 149).

47. Kaiser (1972: 210, also footnote 11) points out that Haas had previously (*Journal of Common Market Studies,* vol. 8, p. 70) argued that it is misleading to say that neofunctionalists share with federalists a strong reliance on the concept of sovereignty and that he himself does not see any need for using the concept.

48. Thus, in opposition to Hoffmann for whom certain values (particularly the control of diplomatic influence and military security) always have primacy, Haas sees that there is no permanency or dichotomy given by nature between the low and the high, but that it is an empirical question.

49. Milward presents three such elements: the irreversibility of integration, which means certitude of bargaining results, the possibility of reducing the number of members, which simplifies the agenda, increases efficiency and

reduces potential conflicts, and the central system of law, which implies compliance. Thus, the very features pointed out as evidence for the effective undermining of state authority in the process are converted into benefits.

50. On page 30, however, they see sovereignty as both pooled and *shrunk*. Cf. Held's 'divided' and 'limited' sovereignty in Held (1989: 237-239).

51. Actually, however, he labels the two explanations 'supranational institutionalism' and 'intergovernmental institutionalism'. The labels seem to underline that the author has taken into account criticism against the views and does not aim at comparing already discredited versions.

52. In specifying this influence, Moravcsik uses neoinstitutionalist terms, as Milward above. The EC institutions strengthen the power of governments in two ways, through reducing transaction costs and the costs of identifying, making and keeping agreements, and through strengthening the autonomy of national political leaders *vis-à-vis* particularistic social groups within their domestic polity. In general, international cooperation redistributes control over important domestic political resources (initiative, institutions, information and ideology), and such shifts tend to benefit those who control access to international negotiations and institutions, generally the national executives (Moravcsik 1994). Moreover, turning domestic issues into international ones means less transparency and more possibilities of government manipulation. The government is also able to use the EC as a scapegoat for unpleasant domestic policies. (Moravcsik at the EUI, October 19, 1993.) Similarly, Marks (1995: 5-6) claims that as states tend to be more autonomous in matters of foreign policy and as a variety of ex-domestic issues is lifted to the EU level, state dominance is consolidated. - Cf. the idea the government leaders playing a 'two-level game' simultaneously in international and domestic 'game boards'; Putnam (1988), Evans *et al.* (1993).

53. This seems, again, a somewhat simplistic characterisation of the adversary. One could also see that the peculiar self-validating nature of the realist view is based exactly on the mutability of these interests (precisely because the interests of the participants change during negotiations, the result, whatever it might be, can be seen as being in their interests). - Note also for Matlary, intergovernmentalism is less a theoretical approach to integration than a set of assumptions about the role of the state in multilateral cooperation, attractive perhaps because of its simplicity.

54. Matlary notes that the internal market programme, as a formal regime which sets limits to specific areas and serves as justification of policies, is a powerful basis for arguing against individual state interests; it has made a policy which goes against the 'four freedoms' virtually impossible. (Cf. Haas' notion of 'upgrading the common interest'.)

55. For the authors, the EC is best characterised as a network involving the pooling of sovereignty, and by the term 'supranational'. They note that this characterisation might be surprising, taking into account their position on the intergovernmental side of the debate. As a matter of fact, the authors aptly welcome Haas' view on supranationality from 1958, a view which, for them, depicts it as a mere style of political behaviour, a cooperative strategy in interstate relations (seeking to attain agreement by means of compromises upgrading common interests). Although the process of policy-making in the EC is supranational, it takes place in the context of agreements between governments; also successful spillover requires prior agreement among governments. (Keohane and Hoffmann 1991: 10, 15, 17.)

56. His formulations are, however, cautious, and underline continuity. For Hoffmann, the relation between the state and the EC is not a zero-sum game; the European entity has helped the restoration and consolidation of the former. Further steps envisaged (losing sovereignty, the enhancing position of the executive) have, on the other hand, alerted citizens and parliamentarians. (*Idem:* 3-4.)

57. When, for instance, Harrison (1974) maintains that the neofunctional view has neglected the role of political actors and political will, a certain deadlock is approaching: while it is not very productive to criticise a theory for not having taken into account everything, Harrison's criticism is particularly unproductive in that neofunctionalism developed as a criticism of approaches in which political will was particularly stressed (especially federalism). – A search of the faithful understanding of the neofunctional approach – or any other approach – in integration studies is as unavailing as the search for the real definition of the state. However, for a large part, literature evolves in terms of theories, assuming a consensus on their contents and representatives which stems perhaps more from the evaluative discussion itself than from the original contributions.

58. Further means of constitutionalisation have been exclusivity (total prohibition of own action by the states, e.g., the common commercial policy) and preemption (in some areas, only positive Community legislation preempts the action by the member states).

59. Weiler adopts Hirschman's concepts of exit and voice (in Hirschman, Albert, *Exit, Voice and Loyalty – Responses to Decline in Firms, Organizations, and States*, Harvard University Press, Cambridge, Mass., 1970), that is, the mechanism of organisational abandonment in the face of unsatisfactory performance and the mechanism of intraorganisational correction and recuperation (put simply, less exit means more voice and less voice more exit, the possibility of exit leading to the question of loyalty for the organisation). Thus, the constitutionalisation of the Community and the system of legal/judicial guarantees mean that the possibility of 'selective exit'

60. has been at least partially closed. (*Idem:* 2411-2412.)
The authors argue that neofunctionalism (in Haas' formulation) provides a convincing and parsimonious explanation of legal integration in the Community, driven by supranational and subnational actors pursuing their own interests; law, mostly perceived as 'technical', takes here the role of mask for politics, originally forecast for economics (Burley and Mattli 1993: 43-44).

61. The authors see that legal integration expands integration incrementally through, e.g., the method of upgrading common interests: the *modus operandi* of 'teleological method of interpretation' means that the Court justifies its decisions in light of the common interests of the members as enshrined in the objectives of the Treaty of Rome. Referring to concepts such as customs union, freedom of movement, non-discrimination or mutual solidarity shifts the analysis to a more general level on which it is possible to assert common interests and long-term interest over short-term interest. (*Idem:* 68-69.)

62. A clear example of how evidence for state power can also seem evidence for the power of institutions is the problem of whether the relative strength of states v. institutions can be resolved by looking at the power relations between the Commission and the Council. Usually, it is seen that the Commission represents the supranational forces while the Council represents the states; their relations have, however, been seen as difficult to estimate. E.g., Lindberg and Scheingold (1970: 92) hold that if power is defined traditionally as formal authority, ability to impose sanctions and possession of monopoly of legitimate force, the Council is all-powerful; if, however, power is defined in a 'positive' way, as participation in decision-making and objective success in getting one's preferences accepted by others, the Commission wields substantial power (power of initiative, European perspective, technical knowledge). (Cf. Marks 1995.)

63. In other words, if 'exit' if foreclosed, the need for 'voice' increases. In Weiler's view, this took place in the formative period of the Communities. While the Rome Treaty's original decision-making process had strong supranational elements by virtue of the central role of the Commission and the intended development towards decision by majority voting, the Luxembourg Accord meant that each member state could veto the legislation proposed by the Community. In fact, all other supranational features of Community decision-making collapsed, and a new organ, the European Council of Ministers, assumed a central role. (Weiler 1991: 2411-2412; 2423-2427.)

64. Cf. Haas, 'Turbulent Fields and the Theory of Regional Integration', *International Organization*, vol. 30 (2) 1976, pp. 172-212; *The Web of Interdependence*, 1970.

65. One cannot fail to observe the influence of, e.g., management and game theories and of the development of the conceptual apparatus of social sciences: a series of 'new' concepts appear, ranging from 'interdependence' and 'turbulence' to other typical terms of the 1970s, such as 'spaceship earth' or 'global village'. (See esp. Haas 1975: 83.)

66. Actually, Haas extends his criticism so far as to indirectly accuse himself of something he did not do: in Haas' view, a shortcoming was that the theories did not allow for the possibility that actors' motives, interests and values change (*idem:* 8-9) – something very basic in his own early writings (e.g., Haas 1958).

67. In the book, however, the idea of symbiosis seems to be abandoned quite soon, the Community and the states being analysed as separate realms; it reappears in the end when the authors conclude that the EC and the states are *becoming* more and more subtly intertwined and that some symbiosis between the state and the EC might be the most flexible and adequate form [of system] (*idem:* 308-310).

68. In fact, Taylor argues, states can even join the Community in order to develop their distinctive identity, as in the case of Spain, Portugal, Western Germany, and arguably even Britain.

69. Marks notes that the model of multilevel governance presents (only) an indirect challenge to state sovereignty and is as such 'infinitely more attractive to state executives than a purely supranational system where European institutions would have autonomous coercive power'. Ambiguous and complex in nature, it is unlikely to be a stable equilibrium; especially the larger states press hard to reinforce intergovernmental safeguards (in the form of voting weights, etc.). (*Idem:* 23-25.)

70. Bulmer argues that the state has the ability to decide at which level it defends its interests, to choose between the national level, the EC or that of other international regimes. The domestic political tier has an important function in determining whether the EC is seen as the most appropriate level of action for responding to the international challenges (Bulmer 1983: 353, 356; cf. later Milward, above); note also Webb (1983: 2, 37-38) remarking that the EC can be seen as a forum for the pursuit of important interests, and that the question of relevance is central.

71. As Webb (1983: 17-18) points out, the contribution of neofunctionalism has actually been to point out the political nature of policy-making in the EC, the specific bargaining and consensus-producing mechanisms and strategies, and the comparability to domestic politics.

72. Bulmer's analysis of governments as in a key position between national politics and Community politics, sometimes captured by domestic interests or transnational forces and sometimes in the position to impose policies on domestic interests, deriving power both from their domestic and EC position,

is also close to Moravcsik's position (see above).

73. Hix distinguishes between the analysis of European integration, for which the international relations approaches may still be valid, and the analysis of European Community politics, for which comparative politics approaches are more appropriate. For him, particularly neofunctionalism and intergovernmentalism give only a unidimensional view on the political conflict in the EC, seeing the situation as one in which the actors (states or interest groups) either support or oppose further supranational integration. Functionalism and federalism, in turn, both sought to deliberately prescribe systems which would minimise political conflict, which makes them perhaps the least useful of all international relations theories for the study of EC politics.

74. Hix refers here to Sbragia, A.M. (ed.), *Euro-Politics: Institutions and Policymaking in the 'New' European Community*, Brookings Institute, Washington 1992.

75. Here, the authors rather sloppily mention the 'integrationist' perspective of neofunctionalism as represented by Keohane and Moravcsik (and not by, e.g., Haas), and definitively blur the distinction between previously emerged views.

76. The three are chosen as 'high-regulating' countries (countries with specified domestic regulation on the issue and a suitable implementation machinery) which, accordingly, are assumed to strive for similarity between own and EC rules and to have interest in extending the common rule-making (Héritier *et al.* 1994: 12-13). For analyses on specific states, see Knill on France and the European Union in *French Politics and Society*, vol. 11 (1) 1993, and on the United Kingdom in *Politische Vierteljahresschrift*, vol. 36 (4) 1995.

77. Similar analyses have earlier been conducted by H. Wallace (1973) who examines the patterns of national administrative inputs into the Community process and the effects of this involvement on the national institutions of the member states, and Webb (1983) who also sees transformational effects on the states.

78. Olsen pays attention to differences between countries and between policy-areas; he also notes the close links to basic questions in political analysis, such as how political identity is changed or created, how institutions and rules are changed and how the allocation of values is changed.

3 Causes and consequences

The state of the art in integration studies: a self-portrait with some corrective remarks

In the preceding chapter, four quite different views on the relationship between the state and integration were identified. According to the first, integration is a remedy for some inherent weaknesses of the state and the state system: pulling states closer together in some form or another would make interstate relations more accommodating and peaceful, in addition to improving the states' capacities to fulfil their functions. In the second view, states are eventually altogether replaced in the process of integration. The superiority of integrative solutions compared to what separate states can achieve is compelling; a dynamic process of integration is put in motion, and states have to adapt themselves to its consequences, that is to their diminishing role and power. The third view, by contrast, sees states as the real driving forces of the integration process, which in essence is a series of measures aimed at strengthening them. The states set the direction and limits of the process, halting or accelerating it as needed. Finally, in the fourth view, integration is a process which causes consequential changes inside the state, transforming its policies and policy-making procedures, and influencing gradually also its administrative, judicial and political systems.

A similar plurality of views usually leads one to look for ways to find out which of the views is the correct one, given that they contradict each other. Could it be that the latest one is perhaps the most accurate? Could all the views be correct, simply suiting different time periods? Such a simple answer would free us from further reflection on the issue of plurality. Yet, it is difficult to find convincing evidence for such a solution. To sustain the idea of progress from one view to another, or that each view would apply in some specific circumstances, would require that the views be simply based on reality at a certain time and on a specific scientific standard, thus, that there was only one reality and one scientific standard which could be used as a yardstick. Yet, when looking at *how* and *why* the views, and just these views, have emerged, one cannot really argue that some of them were based on false assumptions about reality or were reached in an unscientific way. An analysis of the *causes* of these views shows that factors having to do with how research is conducted tend to outweigh the influence of how things are in reality as their immediate cause or origin.

These causes are here identified in the *choices* made by the scholar in the course of research. Conversely, the four views can be seen as *consequences* of certain basic choices that have been made. In analysing *how* the views have been reached, one sees first the role of succession, or theoretical accumulation. Indeed, succession showed its importance in chapter two where the views were presented chronologically. It was shown how the scholars explicitly referred to views presented before, finding evidence for their view in the manifest accuracy of previous views, when the authors concurred – or in their equally manifest inaccuracy, when the authors disagreed. In addition to evidence, however, they also took on board elements which they were perhaps less aware of, namely concepts, assumptions, beliefs and standards of adequate explanation. Thus to a notable extent, the views emerged as outcomes of what had been reached earlier on.

Chapter two delineates a path through the various views, showing how the four have succeeded one another. As such, it is not the only possible path or *the* history of integration studies; yet, it reveals an essential interdependence between the views. In particular, the role of succession was found to be paramount in that theories and conceptual frameworks were seen to rest heavily on previous research. Some general conclusions can thus be drawn. First, the views are not single or isolated, but relate to each other either through criticising previous views or through building on previous findings and conceptualisations, that is through accumulation. This also implies that none of the views is alone definitive or exhaustive. Secondly, the different views also make each other understandable in that they constitute a part of their explanation in being the background from which successive conceptions emerge. None of them, therefore, is irrelevant to the whole picture.

This, however, is not how the study of integration depicts itself. In the self-portrait which emerges from the ways in which the scholars themselves explain what they do, the succession of views and theories admittedly constitutes a central part of that portrait. The authors examined in chapter two frequently referred to other scholars' results as an immediate reason for what they argued; they would emphasise a specific feature in their own explanation either because it was traditionally seen as important or because it had been neglected by previous research. However, in these works, succession is understood in somewhat more straightforward terms. Succession is closely linked to the evaluation of previous theories, something that plays a crucial role in research. This evaluation is done in the light of real world developments: the succession of theories is seen as progress towards a better understanding of reality. Research is, thus, seen to produce improved results through the comparison and criticism of previous research, rejection of the disproved elements and accumulation or synthesis of the elements that have been verified.

Accordingly, in fact, all new theories developed in the literature are invariably presented as better than the earlier ones. Also the grounds on which the theories are seen to be better are the same for all, namely the superior explanatory capacity or better correspondence with reality. This correspondence, then, is understood to be self-evident rather than questionable, and is indicated *en passant*. Thus, for instance, Puchala (1972: 283) argues that his 'concordance system' describes Western European integration better than any of the current models, being based on actual reality or the current situation instead of projections of the future; Moravcsik (1991) sees the historical record confirming one theoretical view and disproving another; Bulmer (1983: 363) maintains that the domestic politics approach is 'arguably more embracing and/or more realistic as a device explaining Community negotiations than the alternatives on offer'. In leaning on this type of reasoning, integration theorists hardly differ from other social scientists who rather sporadically reflect on the problems in the evaluation of theories and their development.[1] Indeed, it is not uncommon to find overviews of existing theories in which all of them are shown to be defective – at times magnifying their defects through a simplification of their contents. Often, the scholars also depict the field of research as consisting of two extreme views or positions which have both to be rejected and present their own contribution as a superior alternative.[2]

Importantly, however, this self-portrait seems not to reach beyond some kind of pseudo-metatheoretical discussion. The role of empirical reality as the arbitrator in theoretical debates appears exaggerated: the definite empirical events are roughly the same for all. On the contrary, the differences between views stem much more from assumptions which cannot be empirically grounded and which, moreover, often seem to be taken for granted rather than deliberately chosen. The picture which emerges from the previous analysis of the literature suggests, indeed, that scholars do not necessarily work in the way they themselves describe. Instead of being progressive, the actual development of research seems often circular, based on standardised criticisms of previous views. Moreover, research seems to remain silent on the influence of background factors other than reality. A rare exception is Pentland (1981: 545), who suggests that theories have been influenced not only by reality, or the 'checkered fortunes' of the EC, but also by changing norms, interests and methods. These kinds of background factors would typically be less objective and less easily evaluated: they would concern values, attitudes, understandings of science, and so forth; indeed, were the differences between views based on such factors, it would be difficult to see some of them as better than others in absolute terms.

This chapter elaborates on the significance of these findings or of the internal logic of research and its assumptions. It questions, first, the assumed progression in terms of the explanatory power and proceeds to an analysis of the essential assumptions and their backgrounds in the study of integration. In other words, this chapter exposes the crucial choices made in research and offers elements for understanding why certain choices have been made.

Some problematic effects of research practice

The examination of literature in chapter two shows the crucial role of existing academic research in any analysis. However, it does not show that this necessarily entails any progress or, indeed, a replacement of old views by new ones. In general, scholars seem to be unaware of or underestimate the factual influence of previous research. Obviously, all agree that research builds – in some way or another – on existing inquiry. Indeed, the very aim of research is to improve the previous results through the correction and accumulation of established knowledge. Existing research, however, has also less perceptible effects. First, through 'vertical' accumulation, it acts as a powerful constraint by leaving a legacy of conceptualisations and research problems to subsequent research. Second, more 'horizontally', the opposing theories also have their influence. Mutual criticism or competition between different theories is a central motive for their development. In taking into account the criticisms from and achievements of rival views they develop by reflecting each other. Several instances of this reflection were seen in the preceding overview where particular views were usually justified by juxtaposing them to the existing ones and showing their relative merits.

As a whole, it could be argued that the development of the study of integration manifests more signs of circularity than of actual progress. It was repeatedly observed that arguments introduced as new had, in reality, already been presented in previous research; instead of views giving place to new and better ones, one could find strikingly resistant and durable views. This durability has been noticed before – notably Pentland (1981) observes how old approaches to integration continue to exist alongside newer ones. Yet, he does not expand on the possible reasons. The present analysis, then, points to some of the reasons which lay in the research practice itself: it seems that the inherent necessity of taking into account previous theories takes the lead, forging the discussion into rather complicated theoretical answers to the question of whether different theories are compatible.

Three tendencies in reconciling different views appear in the literature, all of them actually conservative as to the existing theoretical frameworks. The first is one which rather openly acts to defend all the different views by claiming some sort of consensual 'division of labour' between them. The second is the development of two main rivalling views into mirror images, perfect opposites, through the need to (better) answer all the questions the rival succeeds in tackling. The result is a predictable, never ending debate with the same arguments re-emerging. A third tendency is to develop the views towards an all-embracing synthesis by explaining away their differences.

The first of these could be seen as the least theoretically ambitious in that it circumvents the problem of making different views compatible. It is argued that different theories describe and explain different aspects of reality: the existence of each theory is justified by mutual complementarity. Puchala (1972) compared integration theorists to blind men each examining a different part of an elephant and incapable of arriving at a consensus on its description; subsequently, many integration theorists have adopted the notion that each scholar, or theory, may well have a part or a question which they explain better than the others. For instance, it has been argued that neofunctionalism explains everyday integration while intergovernmentalism is better at explaining the 'big decisions' such as those concerning the extension of integration to new areas (Moravcsik 1991: 48), or that a similar division applies to different historical phases, to the distinction between high and low politics or to that between formal and informal integration (Hoffmann, Harrison).[3]

A similar development has been observed also in international relations theory. Wæver argues that the different schools of thought, after having gone through both a period of incommensurability and of synthesis, relate to each other in the 1990s through this kind of compatibility or division of labour. They do not explain the same but, instead, 'do different jobs'. They have different explanatory sources in different areas, and, instead of modifying each other, may be mutually serviceable. (Wæver 1994: 21-22.)[4]

Conventional in nature, this understanding leaves aside the problem that the assignment of proper fields and questions is somewhat arbitrary. It is impossible to see from an empirical case which view applies to it and which does not. Moreover, the basic argument that there are essential differences between areas, periods or domains (such as domestic and international politics) that justify the application of different theories is itself a rather problematic assumption to take as given and even more problematic to prove.

The second tendency, the development of different views in contact with each other towards increasing opposition, leads to a situation in which there are two equally established and equally problematic views to be chosen. In particular, the debate between neofunctionalism and intergovernmentalism has acquired these characteristics as both have developed complete and quite established understandings of integration. They can be seen to exclude each other as integration is seen to work against the state in the one and to favour the state in the other. However, neither is groundless; they simply build on different conceptualisations in that in the first, the state is seen through, directed and formed by integration, while in the other the state is the motor of integration, with integration being defined through the state.

This development can lead to a paralysis or impasse in the theoretical discussion: the two views cannot be combined – having become exact mirror images – but, at the same time, neither of them is alone a convincing basis for understanding integration. Again, rather than being typical of integration studies only, this problem is encountered in several contexts which address the conceptualisation of the state. Two analogous examples from other fields of research might illustrate the question on a more general level.

In his analysis of legal argumentation, Koskenniemi (1989) has identified two exhaustive and mutually exclusive ways of arguing about order and norms in international law. On the one hand, it is argued that norms are based on factors such as common interests or the nature of the system which makes them prior or superior to the state: there is a set of norms which not only effectively regulates the behaviour of states, but also dictates what their legitimate interests can be. On the other hand, it is argued that norms are based on the (factual) behaviour, will or interests of the states; in this case, the states are taken as given, and they are prior to the international system. What is essential is that neither of these views can be definitively or systematically chosen as the basis for argumentation. The proponents of either of them cannot accept the other view as it appears too 'political' and subjective. The first, 'descending' or normative model seems subjective as it assumes that there exists some kind of natural moral; it cannot demonstrate the content of its aprioristic norms in a reliable manner. The second, 'ascending' or concrete model is subjective because it privileges state will and interest over objectively binding norms; it cannot bind the state behaviour at all. Thus, the one leads to utopia, the other to apology. Koskenniemi sees that as the international legal discourse cannot fully accept either of these justificatory patterns, it works so as to make them seem compatible: the result is an incoherent argument that shifts between the two and remains open to challenge from the opposite – providing also the dynamics for international legal argument. (Koskenniemi 1989: 40-46, *passim.*)

Similarly, Bartelson juxtaposes two views on the relationship between the state and the international system represented by international politics and macrosociology of state formation. The two fields understand this relation in opposite ways, taking for granted what the other seeks to explain. Being state-centric, international politics[5] takes, in Bartelson's view, sovereignty, the defining property of the state, as given: it is ontologically and historically prior to the system of states and therefore explains the presence of the international system. The second view, in turn, problematises both state and sovereignty and explains state formation and consolidation with reference to external anarchy and conflict. The presence of the state is accounted for in terms of generative structural features of a sphere of social action that is thought to exist prior to the state. (Bartelson 1993: 16, 19-20, 31-33.)

It is understandable, then, that the debate between integration scholars from opposing camps can be exhausting. In attempting to defend a view on the basis of empirical evidence or analytical superiority, these scholars are constantly exposed to criticism from the opposite, equally developed camp. The same arguments for and against tend to return, and new openings or alternative viewpoints are rather *déjà-vus* than real novelties. In the examination of the literature, it was seen, for example, how those critical of earlier theories that neglected the role of the state were subsequently criticised for overemphasising the same factor and being exaggeratedly state-centred. Similarly, the suggested originality of the proposal to disaggregate the position of a government was lost when noticing that the opposite (and preceding) idea of aggregation had, in its turn, been offered as an alternative to an anterior view based on disaggregation. The factual impossibility of rejecting either one out of hand is obviously problematic and if the choice is reduced to two completely opposite and equally impossible views, it is more appealing to avoid the whole question.

The imminent risk of circularity and the slim hope of conclusion notwithstanding, a vigorous debate between the two views continues. It could be argued that the reason for this vitality lies in the benefit both get from the debate: it could be the debate itself, and thus the existence of the opponent, which sustains them. Again, a markedly similar case can be seen in international relations theory. Indeed, the usual self-image of the discipline in textbooks is a succession of important debates between different views.[6] It has been pointed out that these debates might not necessarily be 'real' in the sense of aiming at verifying and falsifying views, but that they can also have a conservative function.[7] In Guzzini's view (quoted in Wæver 1994: 9), the 'inter-paradigm debate', or the debate between the different schools of thought, can constitute a barrier against critique and legitimise scientific routines, when the other theories or paradigms are taken to speak a different language and therefore be both beyond criticism from the others and themselves unable to criticise in turn.

On the other hand, the vitality of the debate between two different views may also be seen as evidence that the views are perhaps not so different but, instead, share important elements. Attempts to synthesise the different conceptions can be seen as an important contribution, a possibility of progress through collecting the elements of truth which they have been amply shown to contain. A synthesis saves the trouble of accepting either view in its totality and brings the debate between the two to an elegant conclusion. It is, in fact, the third main tendency in reconciling the different views on integration. To judge from the literature, synthesising even such opposites as neofunctionalism and intergovernmentalism is not at all an exercise in the class of squaring the circle: merging the two seems simple. To extend Pentland's (1981) reasoning about the dialectical development of the field, this particular synthesis would only be the next in a series consisting of syntheses of the main rivalling approaches which then come to be challenged by new ones, a series which started from neofunctionalism as a synthesis of functionalism and federalism.

This kind of merger has been visible both within the two views themselves – partly through the deliberate accommodation of mutual criticism, partly unconsciously through preparing for criticism from the other side – and on a more abstract metatheoretical level. It was seen in the previous chapter how those advocating the view that states lead the process of integration have also felt compelled to give credit to the influence of common institutions and to specify what they mean by the state. The proponents of the other view, in turn, have acknowledged that national interests and political will may indeed play a role in the process, although one has to take into account that these very interests are shaped by the process itself or by the common institutions, and that even though the state may indeed have a powerful role in the process, its actions can have unintended consequences which actually work against them. Once again, these efforts could be compared with what Wæver has identified as the 'neo-neo-synthesis', that is, the tendency of the mainstream of international relations theory to converge around a synthesis of neorealism and neoliberalism.[8] (Wæver 1994: 13, also Wæver 1992.) In this case at least, the synthesis has not only become a popular research programme but also allowed for cumulative research. Yet, a similar convergence may also render research less interesting and even harm it by narrowing the topics to be considered. (Cf. Wæver 1994: 16-17 and Smith 1995: 23-24.)

On a more metatheoretical level, a synthesis has emerged in the context of structurationism, an answer to the problem of how to balance or combine structuralist and agency-oriented explanations, that is to take into account the influence of structures on the behaviour of an actor together with the influence of the actor on these structures. Structurationism would depict the state in relational terms as constituted by relations to others and conceivable as a state only in the structure (Wendt 1987: 357); in the analysis of the relationship between the state and integration, it would emphasise the mutual influence between the common institutions and the state.

An example of structurationism as a solution to the opposing interpretations of integration – and also an example of abstract synthesis – is provided by Wind (1996) who aims at explaining the simultaneous existence of two opposite tendencies, intergovernmentalisation and constitutionalisation, in the development of the European Community, and solving the puzzle of why states, if they genuinely want to preserve their autonomy, nevertheless accept measures which considerably limit this autonomy. The proposed answer lies in understanding that the outcome, or what actually takes place in the process of integration, does not depend solely on the actors, their preferences and goals, nor on the pressure by the structures or the constraining influence of common institutions. While the outcome has usually been explained in terms of either the one or the other, neither one will do alone. In short, Wind links the explanatory factors across the two into a circle-like pattern. The goals and interests of the actors do matter, but they are shaped by institutional dynamics. These institutional dynamics, or the structures in general, have their own autonomy in the sense that the actors are not fully capable of controlling them. The actors attempt to modify the structures according to their preferences, but their actions also have consequences which were not originally intended or anticipated; therefore, they can indeed cause institutional dynamics which go against their self-interests – albeit, to close the circle, these institutional dynamics simultaneously shape these interests. (Cf. also Matlary 1994.)

This type of synthesis is, however, perhaps more a *deus ex machina* than an authentic solution to the problem. The elements it brings to the discussion, such as unintended consequences, are not new, but have been present from the beginning (Haas; see also Navari 1991b). More importantly, it does not lead very far, as it does not eliminate the problem. Put simply, the question of whether integration strengthens or weakens the state is answered by saying that both are possible, leaving the matter at that. As an effort, it greatly resembles the attempt to resolve the problem of the contemporary discourse of sovereignty and its two contrasting views, an attempt which merely restates the original problem. In fact, having identified the two views on sovereignty, the one in which sovereignty is a defining property of the state and exists prior to it, and the other in which the state and sovereignty are both seen as generated by structures existing prior to them, Bartelson examines a third, dual view, which combines the two. This third model, structuration theory,[9] blends structures and agents which the two others try to keep ontologically and epistemologically distinct – international relations adopting ontological individualism and macrosociology adopting structuralism. Sovereignty now becomes a link between the two; it constitutes both. The irony, as Bartelson puts it, in this answer is that the original problem is restored. The attempted synthesis tries to overcome the same ontological difference that nourishes it: sovereignty is made either into an agency that structures or a structure that acts; in both, the problem is restored, now beyond the reach of critical concepts. (Bartelson 1993: 39-42.)

Finally, synthesis does not escape a more general problem of scientific accumulation: that it may actually work too much for the conservation of particular understandings. Accumulation is inherently problematic in that although it is necessary and rational to build on existing bases, the ensuing sedimentation of certain assumptions makes it increasingly difficult to question them. Accumulation tends to confine assumptions and research questions to those that can be met within these assumptions. In a way, one could see a debate such as that between integration strengthening or weakening the state as a pseudo debate: the important background assumptions on the state remain unquestioned.

What is most problematic in this development is that the very question of the relationship between the state and integration may fall outside the central research concerns, becoming, instead, a background assumption. This is a possibility if it comes to be judged totally uninteresting or impossible to analyse, either because the efforts at answering it end up in repetition or an all-encompassing synthesis, or because both terms have so many meanings that they cannot be meaningfully used in research, or because there are seen to be no grounds for comparing the different views. The only possibility of posing the original problem again is through analysing *why* particular assumptions on the state and integration have been made.

In the development of the studies of integration, the 'whys' seem, indeed, to have gradually disappeared. It also seems that new reasons are invented subsequently to justify the original choices, as when empirical reality or some objective scientific standards are presented as the reasons for different claims. This chapter concentrates on these 'whys'. After having shown the assumptions behind the different views on the relationship between the state and integration, the chapter continues with an analysis of the crucial and complicated questions to which these assumptions are answers, identifying the alternative assumptions among which the scholar in principle can choose. Finally, several constraints on this choice are identified. These are, then, the 'whys' of the assumptions. These factors – the methodological stand of the scholar, the notion of the aims of theory and science, disciplinary divisions, and values, linked to time and place – are argued to be not only more stable than the rather shaky points of reference in empirical reality, but also more important, and even more productive, when spelled out, in increasing the value of scientific analysis.

The crucial assumptions and questions

Assumptions make research coherent in forming the basis that is accepted as true; in contrast to hypotheses, their validity is not at stake in the investigation. At times, assumptions that are widely approved may lose their 'assumed' character: they come to be seen as shared background knowledge instead of being explicitly stated. Thus, identifying the underlying assumptions in a given piece of research is not necessarily simple.

In the overview of integration studies, the variety of assumptions is, however, easily observable. For instance, when Burley and Mattli (1993) propose to study the role of the Court in the Community, they assume that it does or can have a role; when Moravcsik (1994) asks why the European Community strengthens the state, he assumes that it does strengthen it; when Weiler (1991) asks how to conceptualise the transformation in the relationship between the member states and the Community, he supposes that it has been transformed; when Bulmer (1983) asks how domestic politics may have a vital impact on the policy-making output of the EC, he assumes it can have; when Taylor (1983) asks where the states choose to defend their sovereignty, he assumes they can and do choose; when Grieco (1991) poses the question of why states integrate, he sees this behaviour as somehow anomalous, due to certain assumptions about how states normally conduct their relations.

That these assumptions indeed are assumptions can be shown by linking them to wider questions and theoretical debates which, particularly in the case of state and integration, appear intricate. Systematically speaking, one could discern the following chain of influence as the explanation of a given understanding:

state-integration view ← assumption ← theoretical question ← constraint

Thus, each view is based on specific assumptions, which are related to wider theoretical questions. Why these questions come to be answered in the way they do depends on particular constraining factors. The assumptions and their theoretical contexts are first presented here case by case.

The first view on the state and integration – seeing integration as a remedy for some inherent weaknesses of the state and the state system – involves the assumption that these weaknesses exist, in other words, that the state is not (or is no longer) capable of fulfilling its functions and that interstate relations are inherently conflictual, due to the adverse nature of the state. These assumptions obviously prompt wider questions about whether or not the state is an adequate or appropriate form of political organisation, what its functions should be, how its effectiveness should be assessed and whether its position has changed as a result of certain challenges. A further basic question is what the nature of the state and interstate relations actually is and whether something like the inherent nature of the state actually exists.

The second view stresses the role of the interests of certain societal groups or the common institutions in the process of integration which is also seen to have its own driving force in some functional logic of expansion. The state is seen to be replaced by a more appropriate framework. It is thus assumed that integration is not in the interests of the state but actually works against it, diminishing the actual decision-making power of the member states. On the other hand, the state is seen to have only a minor role in the process, if it is at all conceived as an actor of its own. On the contrary, common institutions are seen to have an important role both as structures and as actors. Finally, the nature of the integration process is seen as relatively difficult to foresee or control.

The third view assumes that the state is a rational actor and that integration can essentially be explained as international politics in general. States are the motors of the process and they also control it, being capable of countermeasures in case of adverse effects. Integration is in the states' interests: it consists of measures which increase the states' capacity to solve different problems. The common institutions, then, are created by and subordinated to states, and therefore they are not independent actors.

The assumptions of the second and third view can be seen as instances of the same background problems. Is the state an actor, and if it is, is it a unitary and rational one? Are institutions independent actors? Whose interests are the state interests, and how are they formed? Is the state autonomous from its society and/or international system? Are states central in international relations? Is the process of integration controllable? Is it reversible?

The fourth view, finally, assumes that integration causes some particular, definable changes in the state which can be given such labels as Europeanisation. These changes, which are not necessarily beneficial nor necessarily foreseeable, affect not only the capacities or capabilities of the state but also its inner structures and identity. In the background of these assumptions the main questions are how to conceptualise the kind of influence integration can have, and, above all, whether states are similar or not, whether they have the same interests and whether integration thus influences them in a similar way.

The different background questions can be grouped into six major problems to which each view implies some stand. The first is the nature of the state, including its behaviour and interstate relations. This is an issue which might not seem to be worth considering because it is too metaphysical, but important statements in the literature are based on assumptions concerning the nature of the state, and have a direct influence on how the nature of integration is seen. The second problem concerns the efficiency of the state in fulfilling its functions. This involves how to measure efficiency, who should measure it, what the state functions are or should be, whether they change in time and if so, why.

The third problem is the actor capacity of the state and/or institutions. This comprises matters concerning the possibility to constitute a unitary and/or rational actor, with the ensuing question of what is understood by rationality (a rationality based on the analysis of costs and benefits or one based on a pursuit of relative gains), the way its interests are defined and formed and the groups or parties comprised in this formation. This last question is further linked to the question of the autonomy of the state, which, together with the question of state functions, is tied to the question of legitimacy. Autonomy is also an aspect of the question of what are the relations between the state and (other) institutions. In addition, actor capacity has to do with the question of whether and how institutions, including the state, alter, and whether they can adapt themselves to changes in the environment.

The fourth problem is whether states are to be seen as essentially similar, and this can be added to all the other questions. It appears not only in the form of whether states are similar in their nature and interests or their conception of what is political or not political, 'high' or 'low', but also in the question of whether the state is the same in international and domestic contexts. This leads to the fifth problem: the nature of international relations, whether states are central and whether integration is a part of international relations, with implications for understanding the role of the state in the process of integration. Finally, the sixth problem concerns the conceptualisation of integration as a process, the possibility of seeing it as an instance of a more general phenomenon, its controllability and reversibility, its dynamics and motivations – and, indeed, whether some actors matter – as well as the question of what integration actually causes among the participating entities.

The most complex questions concerning the state and integration are thus implicitly answered in the assumptions behind the four different views. All share a basic duality in that they can be answered in both ways, 'yes' and 'no', as it were: like coins, they seem inherently to have two indispensable sides. The whole question of the relationship between the state and integration changes shape depending on the answer. Yet it does not seem that there is, in fact, a perfectly free choice among the alternative answers; neither does the academic community seem to be particularly aware of why these questions are answered as they are, unnoticed.

Next, four crucial factors which lead to the adoption of a particular answer, or constrain the choice among the possible answers, are analysed with the aim of showing how they have influenced the study of the relationship between the state and integration. They are, first, methodological considerations, second, explanatory standards and aims of research, which influence the definition and formulation of concepts, research objects and questions, third, disciplinary divisions and peculiarities, which influence the conceptualisation of different phenomena, and fourth, values, which enter when evaluating the nature and appropriateness of the state.

Origins of the assumptions

Methodological considerations

It is impossible to point out any single research method which would be the suitable one for studying integration. Since there are many ways of understanding the nature of integration, there are also plenty of different methods that can be used in its investigation – methods that, in turn, influence the results obtained. It seems that the general methodological stand of the scholar, together with a strong hold on a specific understanding of the aims of research, explains much about the emergence of different views on the relationship between the state and integration. Similarly, the debates about the suitability of particular methods reflect the understandings of integration. While the general debate between what could be called a traditional and a modern, scientific stand on research will be the subject of the next section, the present one concentrates on the influence of certain methodological views on the research on integration and on the discussion about the suitability of these methods.

One can discern three crucial methods or methodological choices which have formed integration studies in a particularly profound way: recourse to observation, use of comparison and the application of different assumptions of rationality. It could be argued that in general, the discussion about these methods has been insufficient, if not altogether absent, and even evaded, with the possible exception of comparative methodology. In some cases, methodological statements have been made explicitly, while others give the impression of an obliviousness to the importance of methodology. Then again in some cases, certain methodological ideals are espoused superficially, and there may also be a discrepancy between the statements on methodology and the actual methods used.

Observing integration

One could with good reason ask whether integration is something that can be observed or whether it is, on the contrary, something intangible or invisible. One might also want to recall of the problems of subjectivity and credibility involved in observation. In the early phases of integration theories, however, these questions were not posed: Haas adopted observation as his prime method, and this choice of his left a clear mark on integration studies.

For Haas (1958), observation represents the most appropriate and reliable method for the study of integration. Indeed, to instill more credibility in his conclusions he underlines that they have been attained exclusively by using observation as method. Observation, in his words, is preferable both to the prescriptive traditional theories where reality is analysed through a model of how it should be and to the 'ultra-scientific' theories where reality is analysed through pre-established, abstract theoretical models.

Haas followed quite closely the change in methodological and scientific thinking introduced by the new behaviourism in social sciences of the 1950s and 1960s. The goal was to explain behaviour, and this was done through empirical demonstration rather than, for instance, by referring to the general rules which in principle could be said to govern it. It was also important to strengthen the argument quantitatively through collecting data on many cases and many variables, which is why statistical methods and computing were introduced. What was observed, in turn, was prescribed by the pluralist view of politics as a contestation between different interest groups or political forces in the society. As Krasner puts it, observation was peculiarly compatible with a pluralistic view of the political universe as heterogeneous and atomistic (Krasner 1984: 229-230).

Haas' study, thus, is based on the observation of behaviour by different groups. Importantly, also his widely quoted definitions are based on observation. At least, Haas underlines that he has defined the central terms of 'political community' and 'political integration' on the basis of observation and description of behaviour. The preferability of this method, for Haas, lies in the ensuing political relevance of the definitions. Haas is distancing himself from what he sees as unsuitable objective definitions, definitions which rely on some objective criteria superimposed by the observer upon the social scene – such as the volume of economic transactions and similar criteria used by Deutsch. Instead, Haas relies on the assessment of the actual conduct or habitual behaviour patterns and the perception of interests and values by the major groups involved, for example, ECSC officials or trade associations, as the only politically relevant method. (Haas 1958: 11-13, 32-33, footnote 5.) For example, Haas' definition of the term 'supranational' – the vague and novel term sadly in need of precise definition, as he puts it – is based on observation of the ECSC and of the behaviour towards it of other actors. It is defined as the existence of governmental authorities closer to the archetype of federation than any past international organisation but not identical with it, verifiable through a certain behaviour of men and groups. (*Idem:* 9, 32, 59; observations on pages 29-58.)

For Haas, thus, observation connects the scholar in an unproblematic way to reality. That his observations are similarly 'imposed' on reality as those he criticises is, however, quite clear; the theoretical preconceptions involved are simply not mentioned. *What* he actually chooses to observe – political parties, trade associations and trade unions at the national and the supranational levels, governments and the High Authority – is given by previous research. For Haas, it is enough to note without more specification that what he studies has already been demonstrated 'to act as unifying agents in political systems clearly "integrated" by any applicable standards and the one organisation *a priori* capable of redirecting the loyalties and expectations of political actors, namely the ECSC' (*idem:* xxxii). This last expression alludes to the circularity involved in the method: that these actors behave in a certain way in the context of integration becomes more a matter of definition than of any candid observation.

Therefore, a rather basic but fundamental consequence of observational methodology is that Haas studies what is already there instead of, for instance, envisioning future arrangements. Haas (1958) is about what already exists and aims to explain and generalise the processes observed. The theoretical framework and the observations become fused: Haas is observing integration, and thus what he is able to see becomes integration. Observability, the possibility of pointing out definite behaviour, is an evidence of the actuality of integration; at the same time, integration is defined as what could be observed in a certain situation.

Secondly, the method contributes to the notorious absence of the state. Seen from a pluralist point of view, the state is incompatible with observation: as the state is not a unitary actor and does not as such behave, it is unobservable. In Haas (1958), the only occasions in which the state appears are rather fleeting in character: on the one hand, the ECSC admittedly consists of states; on the other, states and political communities are seen to be, for the time being, practically the same. However, there is no such collective actor as the state which could have interests in the process of integration. The actors considered are not states, but political parties, interest groups and governments. In fact, the rejection of collective actors goes even further: Haas sees a need to justify even his choice to see governments as collective, unified actors instead of going directly to the different interests influencing the governments' position. Haas' reason for observing governments is that their attitudes cannot be reduced to those of the leading party in a multi-party government (Haas 1958: 240). Accordingly, there seems to be no single 'national interest' involved.

The dilemma of comparison

The discussion on the suitability of comparative methods, or whether integration can be studied by comparison, has followed the study of integration throughout. The question is fundamental in that the choice is between seeing integration or the EC/EU as unique, and therefore not comparable to other phenomena, or as in some sense similar to other phenomenon and thereby comparable. How the term 'integration' is understood has implications not only for whether the process of European integration can be compared, but also with what exactly this comparison is made - if it is possible - and about whether integration studies can be seen as a discipline of its own (cf. below).

Uneasiness on the issue of comparability was already present in Haas' work. On the one hand, he underlined the novelty and unique nature of the process of integration he was observing: his designation in 1958 of the ECSC as the only existing supranational organisation restricted the domain to be studied under the heading of integration. Similarly, he later draws a distinction between integration studies, limited to the EC, and studies of other regional cooperative phenomena (Haas 1970: 616; but note Haas 1963: 78-79). On the other hand, Haas also aimed at generalisations about the phenomenon in order to construct a theory of integration. For this aim, Haas urged comparison, which he saw as a promising path towards the improvement of theories (Haas 1970).

Explicitly or implicitly, several possible points of comparison have been proposed and used in the literature, usually with the effect of excluding each other. International relations scholars tended to see integration as normal interstate relations or foreign policy, or compare the EC to other international organisations or regimes. As seen in chapter two, there was a general tendency in the 1960s to study integration as a general phenomenon, comparing different regional integrative endeavours. Gradually, the EEC/EC came to be seen as the sole object of analysis sufficiently dissimilar to any other regional groupings. As a reconciliation of this unique or *sui generis* nature of the object with comparative methodology, it was proposed that if the EEC in all its features was not comparable to others, it could be compared with itself, across different areas or different points in time, seeing the EEC as a variety of decisions, actions and series of processes (Harrison 1974: 22-

23; similarly, Anderson 1995: 453-454). It was also proposed that integration was to be seen as an instance of more general phenomena such as interdependence (Haas 1975) or domestic politics (Bulmer 1983).

Without doubt the most problematic comparative setting has been to compare the evolving Community and its institutions to the state: the possibility and appropriateness of this was among the first main research debates in integration studies, and has remained one ever since. From the beginning, integration theorists (Haas, Deutsch) were studying the formation of a new political community, alluding by 'political community' to something thus far represented by the state. The state was a suitable point of comparison: in order to perceive both the novelty and the proceeding nature of integration, some stable point was needed for comparison. At the same time, the traditional importance of the state gave integration additional relevance as it was seen to create a new centre for political activity and loyalty.

A thorough analysis of this kind is provided by Lindberg and Scheingold 1970.[10] They see the EC as a political entity or system, a 'would-be polity', and aim at analytic models which would help understand how and why changes in this political system occur, or what accounts for the growth, stabilisation or decline of an enterprise like the EC, and, in essence, whether the EEC will continue to exist as it is now (Lindberg and Scheingold 1970: v). In their study, states compose the environment of the EC, while the state also functions as the suitable political system for comparison with the EC. Even though the authors maintain that integration is a 'substantially unprecedented phenomenon', and that 'the constantly shifting scope and amorphous character' of the EC make it only partially comparable to a nation-state as a decision-making system, they evaluate the Community system on the basis of standards for the evaluation of political systems or states in general, their support and efficiency (*idem:* iv, 25, 66). Taking as a starting point a list of the functions commonly attributed to a government, they compare the scope and intensity of Community decision-making process with national processes in the different areas to find out the relative importance of the former.[11]

At the same time, the idea of using the state as a point of comparison and as a tool of analysis in integration studies was strongly criticised. For many, it was precisely the way of adhering to the state, or using such an obsolete term, which impeded the integration scholars from perceiving the real, different nature of integration and the EC. The comparison to the state, thus, was seen as a burden for these studies (cf. chapter 1).

These criticisms notwithstanding, approaches rather similar to that of Lindberg and Scheingold have subsequently been reintroduced that either refer to the character of the EC/EU which increasingly resembles the state (Bulmer 1993) or stress the fruitfulness of comparison as a method in relation to simply describing the EU as unique (Hix 1994: 20-22). Thus, the Community has been seen as a political system and decision-making in this system has been compared to that of domestic politics.

In the end, however, the uneasiness with comparison cannot be erased. The similarities and differences which form the basis of a comparative setting are definitely relative, as is the novelty and uniqueness of the phenomena. Taking into account examples such as Zimmern (1939), who sees the League of Nations as something unique and new in international relations, one could argue that, in some sense, everything new is unique for some time. This uniqueness can be a construction which impedes the real understanding of the phenomenon, but equally, the claim that integration does not have any unique features can be a misunderstanding, a position which impedes the scholars from seeing its peculiar features. Obviously, the understanding of the consequences of integration for the state depend on how the question is regarded: a unique integration is dramatically different from integration as a part of normal politics or international relations as it can have consequences for the state that go beyond the 'normal', constraining and moulding the states in a more profound way, or even dissolving them. The dilemma with comparison, thus, is that both incomparability and comparability alone are untenable; even the unique and new has to be made understandable through something already known, and the unique, in fact, only becomes discernable through comparison.

The assumption of rationality

Referring to actors of some type in the process of integration and aiming to explain their behaviour necessarily leads to the assumption of a form of rationality governing that behaviour, since locating the causes of certain actions also makes them rational. If the motives cannot be found, the behaviour is irrational and thereby also inexplicable. Where the explanations differ is therefore not the assumption of rationality as such but the nature or type of the rationality in question, especially whether one refers to an objective rationality shared by all actors or to individual rationalities, and to which extent the rational action is seen as predictable on the base of calculations. Thus, one can differentiate between moderate rationalists, those who refer to rationality in the explanation of behaviour in the general sense of pondering the costs and benefits of alternative actions, and more pronounced rationalists who make rational choice an explicit basis of explanation, analysing negotiations with the help of models and game theories, shading the calculation to different degrees with different constraints of the situation and of the actor itself (so-called bounded rationality).[12]

The first, general use of rationality is clearly recognisable in the view that integration is in the interests of the state which, accordingly, furthers integration as long as it can benefit from the process. However, this is not limited to realist or state-centred views. Rational calculation was actually the basis of Haas' functional theory of integration. As he himself put it, his 'perhaps most salient conclusion' was that major interest groups and politicians determine their support or opposition to central institutions and policies on the basis of a calculation of advantage. As a matter of fact, Haas came even closer to the realist explanation in arguing that the process is dominated by nationally constituted groups with specific interests and aims, willing and able to adjust their aspirations by turning to supranational means when this course appears profitable. (Haas 1958: xxxii-xxxv.)

Haas concluded that no government habitually sought to hinder or to advance integration, and no one consistently 'won' or 'lost' in the process (*idem:* 524-525). Governments sought to secure a maximal position but without obstructing the evolution of more integrated decision-making over time (*idem:* 240ff, esp. 279-280). Indeed, they recognised a point beyond which attempts to sidestep, ignore or sabotage the federal authority's decisions were unprofitable: in the long run, governments defer to federal decisions in order not to set a precedent for other governments (*idem:* xxxiv). From the point of view of the formation of a political community, it is rational that governments give way in negotiations when in minority; they should not make themselves 'constantly and invariably the spokesmen of national interest groups' or insist on formal veto, thereby obstructing the process (*idem:* 9-10).

Haas' assumption of a utilitarian rationality was clearly expressed also later, such as when he remarked that 'as long as political actors are sufficiently rational to calculate their interests and seek accommodations on that basis, our ingenuity ought to be great enough to devise observational techniques, concepts, and indicators to catch the interregional variation in their modes of calculation' (Haas 1970: 642).

The assumption of rationality seems to be most convincing when it is understood that different actors assess rationality in different ways, that their values and aims differ. The problem of the assumption is, however, that it is almost too convincing. Once adopted, every action appears in the interests of the actor: since it chose a certain action, it must have perceived it to be in its interests. In integration theories, the problem is constantly close by that integration is always interpreted as in the interests of states.

Taken to its logical end, this view assumes there is some general interest behind all actions which make even the decisions which might have disadvantageous consequences somehow beneficial in the long term. If only the benefits of integration in the end outweigh its costs (cf. Grieco), the logic of state action may also include moves which limit its powers (cf. Navari 1991b) or its sovereignty to some extent; in other words, participation and limitation of sovereignty and renouncing one's own interests can actually be in the interest of a state. As Wessels (1992) remarks, 'own interest' remains as long as there is an actor. Not even sovereignty, thus, is a steadfast principle with which to assess rationality. States may indeed stress the importance of preserving sovereignty, but the actual contents of the term vary. In Milward's words, 'national sovereignty and the state itself have been a legal and administrative convenience, not an absolute irreducible entity'. He argues that to define an inviolable core of the state, which must be preserved against any future trend of integration, or to define the 'surrenders' of sovereignty in advance, would have been to negate the process of integration as a solution to the national problem, for it was inherent in the process that surrenders would be accepted whenever necessary, as the need for them emerged. (Milward 1992: 344, 446.) Finally, then, the state is made eternal and immune to anything that might challenge its position.

Some critics maintain that one cannot treat the state as an actor with clear, unambiguous aims, since it is not a unitary actor, but that its acts – if it 'acts' at all – are based on different, competing interests. Others observe that the state, while acting as rationally as possibly, is evidently also weakened in the process of integration. As a compromise accepting both state rationality and the possibility that the state cannot always maximise its interests, the idea of unintended consequences has been referred to. This, however, does not solve the main problem connected to the question of rationality, namely the difficulty of finding out whether an action was intentional and what the intentions actually were.

As Burley and Mattli point out, the conclusion that a specific outcome has been in the interests of the state and that it has succeeded in the pursuit of its objectives may well be accomplished deductively: if it is assumed that states will only comply with judicial decisions if in fact those decisions are in their interests, they have an obvious incentive to deduce interest-compatibility from compliance. It is, they point out, easy to assert that a particular decision was 'in the interests' of a particular state with the luxury of hindsight and the ability to manipulate the analysis at a very high level of generality. (Burley and Mattli 1993: 51.) The same result is achieved, one could argue, by referring to the general goals of integration – such as economic well-being or peaceful interstate relations – as justifying decisions taken in domains not directly connected to the aim, that is, by the method of upgrading common interests, or referring to the general goals of the state, as has been done, among others, by Milward.

The task of evaluating whether a state has been able to influence integration according to its interests is, in fact, a matter of interpretation to which the way preferences are formed is obviously a central key. There is an apparent division between theorists who argue that preferences are formed prior to a negotiation, and those who contend that interests are constantly revised in the course of the negotiations or any other types of interaction (cf. Matlary 1994). Actually, none argue that states would not revise their interests – after all, it is only rational to adapt them to the situation. In reality, it is precisely the changing nature of the national interests that makes the realist position so impermeable: since the state modifies its interests according to its possibilities, it can always be said to have secured them.

It could even be argued that it is once again the critics of a realist view of interstate relations who commit the error of assuming fixed interests, not the realists themselves. As was seen in chapter two, Haas emphasised that the tendency of interests to change in the process and the use of compromises and mediation were the characteristic novelties in the relations between states in the ECSC, later carried over to the negotiations for Euratom and EEC treaties. He observed that new codes of conduct were emerging, implying an atmosphere of cooperation and concessions by all: simple intergovernmental bargaining from fixed positions was abandoned in favour of delegation of power to experts and mediation (Haas 1958: 515-520). Seeing these as a novelty implies, however, that in Haas' view, states did not behave like that before.

Clearly, no state is able to choose, without any constraints, any action, or to control all of its consequences. Rational state action quite understandably involves not only an adjustment of interests according to the situation, but also a more general alignment of policies according to the environment. It is therefore equally difficult to say whether a state should be deemed vulnerable to external changes or as rather prudently adapting its policies to them, as it is to assess whether a state has attained its objectives in the context of integration or whether it has experienced a serious decline. As Wendt (1994) notes, there always exists the possibility of counteractions to compensate for the possible losses.

The essential question, therefore, is whose aims and whose rationality are taken as the starting point in the analysis. Those criticising an overtly state-centred interpretation of integration and the ensuing way of seeing integration as rational for the state seem easily to overlook this question, referring instead to some kind of inherent rationality in the process itself. This kind of teleological interpretation of the process was typical of early integration theories which emphasised rationality and intentional action motivated by the need to improve the functioning of the system, but it has been present also later. Rationality, however, necessarily resides in some actor. Therefore, the first choice which has to be made is that between the actors – the state, the common institutions, firms, individuals, or the executive – for which the process of integration might or might not be rational, also explaining why. Secondly, one also has to choose between two alternative ways to analyse the question of rationality from the point of view of a given actor: either following the way the actor, e.g., the state, itself depicts its interests and successfulness – which easily becomes a story of endless successes – or constructing external, objective standards of measurement, with the risk of having to use very general arguments. If these choices are disregarded, a rather superficial use of the rationality assumption follows with logical problems, e.g., when the common institutions (the Court, the Commission) are described as capable of having their own interests and strategies and successfully pursuing these interests while maintaining that the state is not capable of similar behaviour in that it is not a unitary and rational actor.

Views on science and theory

Continuing debate

As the previous section already suggested, the basic debate between two methodological stands of the 1950s and 1960s, one 'traditional', the other 'modern', played an important role in integration studies, as it did in international relations or social sciences more generally. It would be misleading, however, to think about that debate as associated with a specific period of time or limited to strictly methodological questions. Instead, one could speak about a continuing debate between two different understandings of science and theory which has appeared in different forms in the discussion about research.

In international relations literature, the debate is known as the second 'grand debate' of the field, the one between traditionalists and behaviouralists, and it could be seen as a debate between the descriptive and the explanatory, or between idiosyncratic and nomothetic explanations. It partly reappears in the juxtaposition of understanding and explaining (cf. Hollis and Smith 1990) and in the debate between reflectivists and rationalists (as labelled by Keohane 1988), or constructivists and positivists. The first emphasise the particular, intuition and reasoning, and the traditional methodology of history and philosophy. The second position, in turn, holds to objective reality, the general, and, to differing degrees, the aims of theory construction, explanation and prediction. Together with new methods, the behaviouralist 'theoretical revolution' (cf. Lijphart 1974) introduced new links across disciplinary boundaries, emphasising the possibility of sharing the same methodology in different fields (cf. Smith 1987: 195).

Reading the contributions to this debate by Bull and Kaplan (1966) gives a vivid picture not only of the character of the debate as a contest between two irreconcilable views trying to defeat the other, with a serious commitment from both sides, but also of the difficulty in arriving at any results due to the different standards employed on both sides, and thus of its endless and always timely nature.

In integration studies, the debate could be personified by Mitrany and Haas, or, in Taylor's way, between functionalism and neofunctionalism. For Taylor, in fact, neofunctionalism was a scientific restatement of functionalism, developed by such American scholars as Haas and Lindberg for whom behaviouralism became by the 1950s a backdrop to the discovery of functionalism (Taylor 1975: xii-xiii).

As was seen in chapter two, a voluminous branch of integration research based on the new, scientific methods evolved in the 1960s, aiming at explaining why and in which conditions integration took place, how exactly it proceeded and what types of consequences it had. An early manifestation of this direction was the way in which Deutsch *et al.* (1957) used an apparatus of explicitly defined concepts, induction and comparison in order to achieve generalisable knowledge on security communities. It was characterised by the wish to formulate objective and precise hypotheses which could be operationalised and measured, allowing for subsequent testing and verification, with the overall aim of theory building. Models were constructed and tested through 'stepping out into the empirical world' (Puchala 1972:

283), and several authors explicitly referred to 'laboratory conditions' in their studies. The aims of formulating falsifiable hypotheses and arriving at clarification and strengthening of the foundations of causal theory were advanced by, for example, disaggregating the concept of integration into different types and developing specific indices for the subtypes (Nye 1968: 856). The wave of 'scientism' oriented the study on integration towards more specificity, locating, as it were, the laws which govern the process of integration in its background conditions, phases and pace. This required shared definitions, measurability, operationalisability, and verifiability. The call for shared or 'translatable' vocabulary led partly to an increasingly technical language, partly to desperate attempts to abolish the old terms unsuitable for that aim, including, in the end, the term 'integration' itself. The ideal of measurability, in turn, was followed sometimes despite the fierce resistance of the material to the attempts at quantification.[13]

Haas, with some hesitancy, led the scientists. His own view on integration cannot be understood without taking into account the intentionally 'scientific' character of his studies, but also the meaning attributed to 'scientific', which, indeed, has changed somewhat from study to study. Characteristic of Haas'study of 1958 were the aspiration to accumulative knowledge and an at least metaphoric use of 'laboratory conditions'; his theory was based on existing, demonstrated facts and concluded as substantiating what pluralists had argued earlier on. Sometimes, though, the ideals of accumulation and verifiability seemed to render the study somewhat circular.[14] In 1964, Haas dissociated himself from what in his view were 'unscientific' studies, that is, mere descriptions and prescriptions. Haas argued that theories had previously often been given normative or descriptive, even propagandistic tasks: a major tradition in international relations consisted in applying some doctrine, such as Hobbes's, to description and prescription, and theories were merely judged as correct or incorrect, true or false. In Haas' view, theories had to be judged according to their usefulness and capacity to 'rise above advocacy, order phenomena, explain relationships, isolate trends, and thereby project the future rather than prescribe for it'; thus he underlined the importance of developing an explanatory and projective theory. (Haas 1964: 51-52.)

In particular, Haas saw that systems theory[15] – for him, one of the novelties of the time characterised by 'immoderate theorising' but still in its infancy in its application to international relations – provided the opportunity for both explanation and prediction; it forced a re-examination of traditional tenets and involved a new way of seeing the role of theory. The system theoretical framework, together with the method of contextual analysis, were the suitable tools for elaborating functional theory. (Haas 1964: 23-24, 47-50.) As the virtues of systems theory Haas saw its close relationship to functional analysis: it involves considerations on the proper operationing of the system and the assessment of the functionality or disfunctionality of the parts of a system for the whole. The systemic approach also helps in avoiding the erratic separability doctrines of the functionalists; it does not imply automaticity or inevitability, projecting, instead, probable evolutionary patterns. (*Idem:* 82.) In addition, the actor-oriented variety of systems theory seeks to combine international and domestic political relationships (*idem:* 59-60).

At the same time, however, Haas also underlines that he is distancing himself from the boldest aims of scientific analysis and quantitative behaviourism in general systems theory. On the one hand, he sees systems as analytical devices rather than real entities; he himself concentrates on a level of concrete activities of observable social units. Systems theory is useful, in his view, only when it 'facilitates projective thinking based on important abstractions that group and categorize important recurrent events'. On the other hand, although he aims at projection, he confines the goal to a relatively short-term prediction – 'perhaps for the next decade, but not more'. (Haas 1964: 52-53.) Still, the issues he projects on are rather large: he examines questions such as whether plurality at the national level will increase or decrease and where national movements will occur (*idem:* 464ff).

Similarly, his own method, 'contextual analysis', is for him more ambitious than historical narration but more modest than deductive science: it aims at generalisation within a confined context of a given historical, regional or functional setting, seeing the context, or the 'whole' of which the phenomenon under investigation is part in 'relatively modest and easily observable terms' (Haas 1964: viii). Haas underlines the need for historical sociology in which systems are always concrete and defined by the concerns of the epoch's actors (*idem:* 29), characterising himself as 'historical-clinical' rather than quantitative (*idem:* 82-83). As he explains, he does not present a theory, model or case study, assuring prominence to 'pre-behavioral political theory' (*idem:* vii). In the end, he sees his own functional approach as hardly exhaustive and certainly not a self-sufficient explanation: its utility is largely heuristic (*idem:* 458).

In 1970, Haas' view on theories becomes stricter and he deems what integration studies had thus far achieved as 'empirical generalisations' with a doubtful theoretical status; they explain successfully some outcomes but are not justified in terms of a more comprehensive intellectual structure. For Haas, the three achievements – federalism, communications approach and neofunctionalism – are three pretheories or 'theoretical conventions', which all have their own methodology; they do not 'provide an explanation of a recurring series of events made up of dimensions of activity causally linked to one another'. (Haas 1970: 619, 622-623.) Although only the federal approach has been falsified in the sense that none of its assertions-predictions have proven to be true, Haas argues, the two others have neither been falsified nor have they demonstrated positive predictive power outside Western Europe; they have been better in predicting failures. They cannot be easily compared since they address different levels of abstraction, and the axioms are loose. Moreover, the ideal types and terminal conditions they have developed – federal union, security community, political community or union – are, for Haas, not true dependent variables, since they cannot *yet* be observed or measured in nature (*idem:* 629-631, emphasis added).

Mitrany disapproved of the 'scientific' study of integration claiming that his own functionalism not only was more useful in practice, but that it also was more scientific in that it was more realistic: born of realities and dealing with them, Mitrany argued, it could be said to be more scientific than the would-be ones. In fact, Mitrany argued that '[I]n the flood of international methodology, with most practitioners tending to use a contrived idiom of their own, there is a fair presumption that the more "scientific" the less relevant it all becomes.' According to Mitrany, the international political theory – unlike natural sciences – has seen almost as many approaches as performers, and, thus, no solid basis has developed; neither is there evidence of any of these would-be scientific notions having had any effect on practitioners and their policies. The scientific theorists dismiss the old national limits without, however, being able to break away from the old territorial conception. (Mitrany 1975: 248, 259-260, 262-266; cf. Bull 1966.)

One of the main sources of criticism towards the 'scientific' scholars has been their inability to maintain their promises to be able to use the theories for prediction. The problem with the predictions, however, is not so much that they would altogether fail; it is rather that they are rather vague and could well be achieved with no more advanced scientific method than logical reasoning. In fact, what emerges as the typical predictions are either that integration proceeds as it does now, following from the point where it seems to be now,[16] or that integration either proceeds forwards, goes backwards or remains static. As an example of the latter, Lindberg and Scheingold (1970: 279) 'perceive' three possible future outcomes for the EC, the first being that it continues to grow, but at decreasing rate, eventually approaching overall equilibrium state, the second that growth pressures mount, leading to a series of forward linkages which could eventually transform its system and capacities into federal or quasi-federal pattern, and the third that a cumulation of crises leads to a general spill-back and reconfirmation of national decision-making patterns.

Perhaps as a result of this criticism, a certain 'science of the short run' appears, characterised by projections cautiously limited to 'the foreseeable future', or 'the short to medium run' (as Haas 1975: 84-85). Thus, Lindberg and Scheingold (1970: 277) conclude that '[I]n the short run, there is no reason to expect dramatic variations in the level of support available to the EC.' At the same time, however, the authors qualify their conclusions as being reached 'on the basis of the evidence presently available' (*idem:* 279). They also stress that 'prognostication' or predictions are possible only on the basis of orderly assumptions, in conditions of 'all other things being equal'; if events prove us wrong, they say, it should be possible to pinpoint the errors in facts, assumptions or theory (*idem:* 281).[17] That the style and problems of prognostication have not considerably changed in time is not difficult to see; as a later example, one could quote Wessels' (1992: 55) three scenarios for the development of the state in Western Europe – towards the fused federal state, back to decentralisation, or, by a qualitative leap, to common constitution – which, moreover, can also happen all simultaneously, or Wallace's (1994: 68) remark that despite the loss of national economic autonomy, the national abilities to shape the balance of advantage within European and global markets remains and 'is likely to remain for some years to come'.

Together with the aim of prediction, the scientific approach to concepts has been a constant bone of contention. Operationalism, linked to positivism, stresses that each concept must be associated with a precise and definite testing operation which specifies the conditions of its application. As Connolly remarked (cf. chapter 1), this doctrine is often advanced both as a vehicle for specifying more closely the criteria of concepts and as a standard against which competing interpretations of concepts can be appraised. To actually apply operationalism was found to be laborious; moreover, it might not be particularly useful. Even if it were established that one proposed definition of politics was the most operational, this would not in itself suffice to establish it as the preferred definition. As Connolly argued, the more operational definition might drop out some elements which are central to, for instance, our idea of the concepts.

In fact, Connolly notes that authors advocating operationalism cannot always themselves deliver on their promises. As an example, Connolly criticises Deutsch's endorsement of this doctrine.[18] Deutsch claims that each concept in his study is defined in terms of some operation that can be repeated and tested by different people regardless of their preferences; yet, Connolly remarks that none of his definitions is translatable either into a single operation or a small set of invariantly associated, simple operations. Indeed, he notes that the doctrine is most often invoked by political scientists when they criticise the work of others, less so that the author explicitly claims to conform to the doctrine himself. (Connolly 1974: 15-16, footnote 5.)

In part, however, the scientific approach has been misperceived, and it has been accused of a rigidity and aims actually remote to many of the practitioners in question (cf. the arguments in Kaplan 1966), constructing what could be called a strawman of positivism to which no one actually subscribes in the real world (cf. Oppenheim 1981: 190). Both the scientific and the traditional approaches evidently have their own standards of evaluation. They provide the common frameworks which make it possible to perceive the results of research as results and which also make a certain type of progress possible and visible; however, that it is 'progress' might not be clear for those in the other approach.

In particular, the logic of falsification of the scientific approach is ambiguous as it factually produces falsification of the views presented. This has sometimes been interpreted as a failure, for example by Taylor (1975: xix) who suggests that the 1960s attempt to subject functionalism to the discipline of modern social science was in fact felt as a relative failure also by its main architects. Taylor argues that as neofunctionalists were seeking scientific rigour in the sense of modern social sciences, they were vulnerable to the short-term challenge of events; their propositions were deliberately constructed so that they could be falsified, and that is what also happened. The falsification, however, can also be interpreted as a sign of progress unattainable for those whose arguments cannot be falsified (cf. Kaplan 1966).[19]

Middle-of-the-road theorising and its consequences

Contemporary integration studies are in some form still characterised by the basic debate between scientists and traditionalists, with perhaps the additional step that moderately positivist 'rationalists' would now be seen as the traditionalists, while the challenge would come from the reflectivist or constructivist side, those seeing reality as socially constructed and subjectivity as constructed through values, norms and practices. Even this debate shows, however, signs of compromise. One cannot fail to remark a certain convergence of the two towards a moderate, middle-of-the-way view on science and theory.[20]

This moderate understanding could be summarised as the current generally accepted research practice, the general view on the aims and nature of the study. It consists of those features usually associated with 'scientific' which are shared by all. In part, it consists of a mere adoption of certain terms without necessarily espousing all their implications.[21] In part, however, this shared conception is rather influential for the results, perhaps even more so because of its presumed nature. In particular, these influential components of the middle-way view are the aims of accumulation, generalisation, explanation and the improvement of theories and the state of knowledge.

The influence of the ideal of accumulation, for the first, is ambiguous. It is easy to see that research does not necessarily get very far if nothing can be taken as already established knowledge, as it also is understandable that common definitions and concepts, if attained, facilitate communication. At the same time, accumulation both helps and hinders: shared definitions as well as shared assumptions might, despite their worthy purpose, also restrict and mislead research, becoming an insuperable sedimentation of facts rather than assumptions, as was seen in the cases of the decline of the state or the spill-over of integration. Generalisation, in turn, may similarly be an implicit ideal, when knowledge overtly based on one case only is valued less than one apparently applicable to all cases. A main problem of generalisation in integration studies can be seen to be the difficulty of choosing whether to stress the similarity or the differences between states. Both choices, again, may lead to exaggerations, as when the progress of integration is implicitly based on the assumption that states are similar as to their interests (and, thus, also functions and nature) or their conception of the distinction between low and high politics or the political and the technical.

The aim of explaining phenomena causally, for instance, of identifying causes and dynamisms of integration, requires an evaluation of the relative importance of different possible causes. This has interesting consequences for the question of whether integration is automatic or irreversible. If the incentives to or forces behind integration are seen to be on the level of general phenomena such as technological development or security, the reversibility of integration might appear less probable than if they are identified as more time and place-specific conditions. Lindberg and Scheingold (1970: 22-23), for instance, see that many original incentives to integrate have disappeared; the historical point of time in which the Communities were established was a time when co-operation was universally recognised as necessary in every problem-solving programme. Seen from the present, however, it was perhaps a period of transitory weakening of a fundamentally healthy system.

The most intricate problem related to explanation is, however, the question of how to evaluate the adequacy of explanations, reflected in the aim of improvement through criticism and comparison of different views. Mostly, it is understood that theories can be compared and that this is also an appropriate way of presenting one's own contribution as superior to others'. The cautious approaches to comparison are fewer: for example, Webb remarks that the existing choice of theories might not be the best possible (indeed, she sees the available choice as reduced by 'market forces') and argues that each image of EC policy-making is imperfect and distorting, discussing whether it is, in the end, possible to choose satisfactorily between various theories (Webb 1983: 9, 37). As all theories have their problems, it might be mistaken to look for one model or theory only (Wallace 1977: 321); yet, theories also develop or transform and may correct themselves, thereby becoming less vulnerable to criticism (Webb 1983: 20-21).

The discussion on the adequacy of explanations can, in broad terms, be characterised as a discussion which proceeds as if there really were some objective criteria for their evaluation.[22] By far, the most popular criteria for the superiority of some explanation or theory to other seem to be the ability to reflect reality, preferably, moreover, with the ability to explain change. In the above, various examples were seen of authors referring to events in the 'real world' as evidence for the validity of their theories. Mitrany (1975), for instance, presents functionalism as more realistic than neofunctionalism. For him, this realism was manifest in the serviceable character of the theory: it presented a pragmatic and usable way to a peaceful change and to viable non-coercive authority, practical in that sensible to the 'size' of the problems (*idem:* 252-256, 264-265).

The virtue of being able to explain change is popular, not only in integration studies but in political science and international relations more generally.[23] At the same time, the constant change which characterises integration, or the evolving nature of the EU and the increasing complexity of the modern world are referred to as an excuse for the shortcomings of the theories, for not being able wholly to explain the phenomenon under consideration, or for not *yet* being able fully to comprehend it – with the optimistic conviction that this problem is only temporary in character.[24]

In fact, 'reality' and 'change' are only apparently reassuring points of orientation for scientificity or research practice. They are taken to be such when correspondence with reality and capability to explain change are referred to as the goals and yardsticks of research. Nevertheless, they are rather intricate for such a function. Both 'reality' and 'change' involve endless problems of perception, explanation and interpretation. The observation of change requires a stable *a priori* view or definition, compared to which change becomes visible; the example of 'the state' reveals, however, the risks involved in defining the state *a priori*. On the other hand, if integration is seen as constantly changing, one could also expect the state to be similarly perceived. In the end, what 'scientific' implies can simply be seen in different terms, as shown in the examples of the debates between Haas and Mitrany, or Kaplan and Bull, debates between the representatives of two different views not really speaking the same language.

The effects of disciplinary divisions and idiosyncrasies

It is not difficult to see the importance of disciplinary divisions for the emergence of different views on the state and integration: almost by definition, different academic disciplines could be said to contribute to the study each with its particular perspective. Each discipline has its own research problems or objects and particular ways or methods in approaching the problem; equally, it has its own theories, concepts and underlying assumptions. Both the state and integration belong to the objects of research in several different fields; put together, the different perspectives can be both contradictory and complimentary.

At the same time, drawing the boundaries of a particular discipline is not a straightforward task. Indeed, defining an academic discipline is always controversial, as is the very question of what is required of a field of study or a branch of knowledge in order to be considered a discipline. There are, however, some clear marks the disciplines such as international relations have left on the study of integration; these disciplinary inheritances will be closer examined below.

Before the examination of these idiosyncrasies, it is important to consider some more general aspects of disciplines which the review of integration studies brings into light. They are linked to the very idea and structure of disciplinary divisions, to how the disciplines actually function and how they lean on each other. A discipline bestows on the scholar a certain array of theories and approaches; thus, it also – efficiently though often unnoticed –

limits this array. Typically, a discipline also has its blind spots and tactical strategies for avoiding or explaining away certain questions and for justifying their solution in a certain way rather than another. In fact, an academic discipline is essentially defined by the difference, by what distinguishes it from other disciplines, and therefore the different disciplines actually justify each other.

Two aspects of this structure of disciplines emerge as having particular importance for understanding why and how the different views of the state and integration have been attained. The first is the construction of disciplines, the other is their tenacity. The study of integration, in fact, is a fitting example of the efforts of creating a new discipline and of the consequences of such discipline construction, while it also suggests how the established disciplines might react when faced with a new object of study.

Discipline construction

It is important to understand disciplines as intentional constructions and a continuous construction of new disciplines as an integral part of research practice. The need for a new discipline stems from the inadequacy of the existing ones in answering certain new questions, from new approaches and methods. At the same time, however, discipline creation may also involve certain opportunism because of the attraction of the advantages and status of an established discipline, and it certainly involves a complex interplay between the importance of the research object and that of the academic status. Obviously, becoming an object of study of a particular discipline also greatly affects the way the object is understood.

In the case of integration studies, one might legitimately ask whether integration studies could or should be seen as a separate discipline and whether they at any time have been such. The answer, however, has only limited importance. Yet, the question itself is crucial: whether or not the study of integration constitutes a special discipline is a question of the nature of integration, whether integration is something particular, perhaps unique, or rather something 'normal', an instance of a more general phenomenon, something that can be explained through the already existing frameworks of the established disciplines – for instance, interest group politics or international relations.

In order to justify the need for a special discipline of integration studies, one has to prove that integration is in some way 'new' and 'different', a procedure which involves a degree of artificiality. The novelty of integration is obviously relative and has to do with how both it and the existing frameworks are understood rather than with, for example, specific events or the state of the process in the period in question. Indeed, the review of integration studies points to a continuous alteration of claims for its novelty and for its adaptability to existing frameworks, exemplified below by the 'accommodation' of integration by realist international relations study.

It is easy to see how the early deliberate efforts at discipline creation considerably affected the way integration was subsequently understood. For Haas in particular, it seems to have been essential to underline the novelty of what he was studying, the process of integration; it was actually this newness that made the phenomenon so important as a research object.[25] Yet, this novelty was not purely a conclusion from Haas' observations on integration; it was also a basic assumption in his early studies. Thus, on the one hand, Haas observed factual changes in the behaviour of political actors which justified the particularity of integration, while on the other, he took these changes as given: integration in the ECSC was new since the ECSC was the first and only existing supranational organisation which provided – in Haas' words – one of the very few current possibilities systematically to analyse the decomposition of old nations within the framework of the evolution of a larger polity, perhaps a nation of its own (Haas 1958: xxxi).

In a way, integration studies was built on and justified by the shortcomings of existing frameworks in dealing with and explaining the peculiar and unexpected elements which integration involved. Haas himself used his findings both to discredit traditional approaches to international relations and to search for a distinct identity for integration studies if not as a specific discipline, then at least as a 'significant field of study', elaborating on its particularity compared not only to international relations but also to other studies of political unification and regional cooperation. Haas argued that while the study of regional cooperation or regional organisations simply furnishes material on the beliefs and important activities of the actors, the study of regional integration is concerned with the *outcomes* or *consequences* of such activities and with their impact on members. As to the difference between the study of regional integration and the traditional study of international relations, then, they had quite different concerns: the former was concerned with tasks, transactions, perceptions and learning, the latter with sovereignty, military capability and balances of power. Moreover, integration studies had a particular justification in that they were not constrained by the dichotomies between 'high' political and 'low' functional concerns or between the domestic and the international. Indeed, for Haas integration studies were particularly valuable in that they advanced the empirical theory of international relations by clearly delineating and establishing recurrent practices and allowed for comparative studies (Haas 1970: 608-609).[26]

The important consequences of the assumption of novelty and particularity were twofold. In the first place, a logical corollary to this assumption was that integration cannot be studied as an instance of something already seen or by using old conceptual devices: a new *corpus* of concepts and methods was needed. Partly because of Haas' influentiality, partly because of the inherent appeal of novelty, this idea came to be widely accepted. Claims about the inadequacy of old concepts and theories in the study of integration were subsequently made by a considerable number of authors (e.g., Lindberg and Scheingold 1970, Haas 1970, Puchala 1972, Alger 1981, Schmitter 1991), becoming close to a permanent feature of integration studies. In particular, the use of the concept 'state' was discouraged as it was seen to hinder the understanding of integration; this obviously contributed to the difficulty of analysing the state in the context of integration. At the same time, the assumed novelty of integration also had methodological consequences. Notably, as was seen above, the possibility of studying it through comparison was put into question as there was, by definition, nothing comparable to it. In all, the tendency of the late 1960s and early 1970s to build up integration studies as a field of its own was an important long-term factor that influenced the understanding of integration, and was particularly visible in the efforts to limit the research objects and the theories that were seen as applicable, specifying a set of particular research interests, theories and methods.

Later, a new particularity of integration was introduced by Haas as a motivation for the search for a theory of the subject. While the study of integration had, in his view, previously been motivated by (or, 'we were stimulated by') 'two otherwise unrelated trends, the flowering in the United States of systematic social science and the blooming in Europe of political efforts to build a united continent, to "integrate" Western Europe at least' (Haas 1970: 607), it was now impossible to abandon the study because 'the stakes are too high'. Approaching a Mitranian viewpoint, in fact, Haas had come to see that integration was an important object of study because of its possible adverse effects. (*Idem:* 645.) Moreover, he argued that one major normative utility of the study of regional integration was its contribution as a conceptual, empirical and methodological link between work on the future of the international system and the future of the nation-states whose interrelationships make up the system.

In all, no decisive steps in the direction of an accepted disciplinary status or into that of its denial seem to have been taken in the case of integration studies. Rather, there is a continuous process of discipline construction with temporary halts and new openings. The measure of artificiality involved in this construction is manifest in the fact that it was Haas himself who in 1975 quite successfully argued that integration was no longer a field distinctive or important enough to be studied separately. On the other hand, others have maintained that while the phenomenon really is particular and worth a field of its own, the concept of 'integration' is no longer a suitable term for analysing it – having thus come to share the reputation of the state. Finally, periods in which integration studies seem to have had a relatively firm identity – perhaps linked to the overall changes in the popularity of integration studies[27] – have given rise to doubts about the reverse of this identity, a relative isolation, being possibly disadvantageous (Scheingold 1970: 1001-1002).

Discipline tenacity

While the formation of new disciplines helps to explain some features of the emerging theories, it also contributes to the tenacity of existing disciplines: new theories challenge older ones, making them develop and strengthen themselves. In fact, old frameworks do not seem to succumb easily to new, unexpected events. Instead, the existing frameworks and perspectives form the new event as an object of study through their ways of posing problems and their assumptions; indeed, they make the object of study an illustration of what they are studying, denying its suggested novelty. This tenacity is the second aspect of disciplines which has considerably shaped the study of the state and integration: several established disciplines have effectively 'appropriated' integration into their frameworks.

A particularly impressive example of how this has been done is the case of the realist international relations paradigm converting integration from an anomaly into additional evidence confirming the validity of the approach. At first, integration and its study were seen to be quite antithetical to and, in fact, greeted as a useful criticism of the realist paradigm. Integration studies were seen as providing an alternative to the traditional realist view on international, or interstate, relations, closer to an idealist background of collective security or world government (Alger 1981: 126), even to the extent that integration theory was seen as having a prominent position among the contemporary approaches to the study of international relations (Hansen 1969: 242).

Theories of integration were above all seen to challenge the realist 'power politics' paradigm by bringing to light patterns of behaviour and events which were either not supposed to happen or which were not supposed to be especially consequential if they did. Such contradictory findings included the important role of cooperation in interstate relations – for Puchala, integration theorists were in the 1950s and early 1960s virtually alone in holding that international collaboration for welfare ends was an important aspect of contemporary international relations – the role of actors other than the state such as international organisations, including the nongovernmental ones, the different linkages between states in such forms as transgovernmental links between bureaucracies or interdependence, and the connections between foreign and domestic politics.

Integration studies were seen to free the analysis of international relations from the state-centred paradigm of international anarchy in that they allowed for new ways of treating the state, not as a unique entity or something impermeable and autonomous, but as an entity influenced by its environment and also amenable to analysis by new methods and analogies from other social sciences. Thus, integration studies also contributed with new methodological and conceptual alternatives; they enriched the study with, among others, international political economy, bargaining theory and attention to the social context or processes of organisational growth. This, in turn, increased the possibilities of integration studies to, in Alger's words, 'inquire into the dynamics of change'. (Lijphart 1981: 233, 240; Pentland 1973: 240; Puchala 1981: 147-148, Alger 1981: 123, 125.)

Taking into account these evaluations of the influence of integration studies, one could expect that the traditional realist approach to international relations would have been seriously threatened. As integration was observed to change state behaviour and the nature of interstate relations, and particularly because it was seen to blur the distinction between foreign and domestic politics, it could have made the previous approach – if not the very discipline – redundant in its traditional form. What happened, however, was that international relations scholars turned integration into something to suit their own views, showing the appropriateness of the traditional paradigm and, respectively, questioning the validity of alternative views.

In broad terms, this turn can be described as proceeding through four different phases. A first reaction of realist scholars to the early integration theories was to deny the possibility that any real integration, as defined by these theories, could actually take place, as it was completely contrary to the real behaviour and nature of the states. Realist explanations of international relations are based on the assumption of international anarchy, a situation in which cooperation is too risky, or costly, to be rational. Cooperation, thus, needs explanation, and its explanation is particularly difficult, except for allusions to some form of alliance formation (cf. Grieco 1991). While integration was seen and studied as nation-building, realists like Aron (1963) doubted the very existence of such a process. Aron tended to minimise the relevance of the integrative measures taken, stressing not only that the transfer of sovereignty was very limited, concerning mostly technical and economic functions, but also that these measures and the common market in general did not necessarily lead to more advanced forms of unity, such as a federation. On the contrary, he saw that the significance of national independence was increased by the widening of the functions of the state, the rules of international law impeding open intervention in the internal affairs of another state, and the nationalisation of culture. (Aron 1962: 713-734.)[28]

To the integration scholars' argument that integration could be a solution to many intricate problems the states faced, then, it was answered that there were other, less ambitious but equally efficient methods of solving the problems and receiving the same benefits. Hoffmann (1966: 892-894) argued that what the state can no longer provide by itself, it can provide through cooperation, or the citizens can go and find it across borders, without any need to transfer their allegiance (cf. Harrison 1974: 11-12). Similarly, Hansen (1969: 256) saw that a mere common market *coordinated* by sovereign states would give sizeable benefits without any need for management by ceaselessly expanding supranational authorities.[29]

The first phase of the realist 'appropriation' of integration could perhaps be described as a phase in which it is seen that integration does not in any fundamental way change the logic of power politics or the international order. For Aron, the necessity of the logic of having enemies and friends is constitutive of politics and, in a way, also of integration itself. In the background of the efforts towards unification, there was the common threat from the Soviet Union and the wish to obtain some measure of independence of the great powers. Thus, if the conflict between the two blocs were to disappear, not much would remain of European integration either. (Aron 1962: 740-741.)[30]

In a second phase, it was admitted that integration could, indeed, take place, albeit as a mere geographically limited exception which does not challenge the principles of international relations. As late as 1979, Waltz – in difficulties with integration (the subject is practically impossible in the light of his assumptions about the nature of the international system) – argues that 'although the integration of nations is often talked about, it seldom takes place', even if it could be mutually enriching. This is because the structure of international politics sets limits to cooperation in the form of inequality in the expected distribution of the increased production, the uncertainty about the others' intentions, and the fear of dependency through cooperation and exchange. (Waltz 1979: 104-106.) In Waltz's view, the system would change if all chose not to have interest in preserving themselves, preferring amalgamation; however, if only some do, the system as such remains unaltered (*idem:* 118).[31]

Subsequently, realist scholars developed the view according to which integration in its contemporary form served the interests of the states. As a concession to the supranationalist theorists who argued that integration gradually weakened the state, they admitted that there were certain limits beyond which integration could not go without having a considerable impact on the state and cutting its powers. These thresholds, however, were chosen so as to make it unlikely, even impossible, to attain them.

Taylor's early writings show how particularly demanding criteria can be used to refute the opposing approach. He argues that for the supranationalist view to be correct, the EC should be an actor in international relations or a federation – both conditions it cannot fulfil. *Why* it cannot fulfil them, in turn, stems from Taylor's view on what an actor or a federation is: he equates actorship with exclusive role of representation or foreign competence and deems the EC's competence occasional rather than typical or incremental (Taylor 1983: 120ff, esp. 131-132, 156.)[32] Federation, in turn, involves the superiority of federal law in relation to national law and the existence of an independent sphere of central authority. Further, a federation has constitutional immunity against dissolution by secession of its constituent regions, the central government controls exclusively foreign relations and defence, and the federal constitution can be amended without the consent of all constituent regions (*idem:* 270). In the light of these features, the Community is not a federation.

Further examples of setting conditions for integration to be 'real' or effective include Hoffmann's defence issues: contrary to economic and monetary regimes, defence issues were of a zero-sum game nature, and therefore the formation of a defence community would be the decisive change which would solely weaken the state[33] (Hoffmann 1982: 36-37). For James, then, the threshold is the existence of a common constitution and a factual irrevocability of the process of integration. As the European Community does not have the ultimate legislative power but only limited competencies, the member states are not part of a common constitutional arrangement and remain, thus, sovereign.³⁴ (James 1986: 246-253.) Similarly, Taylor claims that the Treaty of Rome is a treaty and not a constitution: as long as the basis of the Community rests upon a treaty, there is, in his view, no decisive legal loss of sovereignty; he also rejects the claims that a monetary union would be a decisive threat to sovereignty (Taylor 1991a: 73-74 and 1991b: 123).

A final step in the 'appropriation' of integration by the realist scholars was completed when it was noted that integration in any case was in the interests of the states, even when seemingly going against it. Otherwise, in fact, it would not have been embarked on. It was a strategy deliberately chosen by the states, defensible in terms of efficiency and benefits; the process of integration increased both the possibilities of states to regain their otherwise diminishing power, or to extend their ability to manage international issues. W. Wallace (1977: 322), for instance, noted that the EC was an institutional framework which served the interests of governments better than alternatives, partly as a defence against interdependence (cf. Hoffmann 1982). In sum, it was seen that there was no antagonism between the state and integration (Milward and Sørensen 1993).

Among the most coherent realist explanations of integration, one could cite Grieco's systematic examination of the challenges posed by supranational integration to (neo)realist thinking – an examination which also shows the elasticity, or tenacity, of realism.³⁵ Grieco points out that the simple introduction of calculation of costs and benefits, which well fits the premises of a rational (and egotistic) actor-state, is enough to explain the establishment of institutions and cooperative frameworks, and thereby also integration, which is seen essentially as a framework for cooperation: cooperation may be profitable, but it is costly, and institutions are seen to lower these costs. (Cf. Grieco 1988.)³⁶ For Grieco, European integration shows how states may cooperate through institutions and actually seek to strengthen them. Institutionalisation of the coalition's activities may help the weaker states to avoid being dominated by the group's strongest member; they will also strive for such common rules which will best guarantee the possibility of voicing their interests. The strongest member, in turn, may prefer institutionalisation as a vehicle for exercising some leadership over its coalition partners. (Grieco 1991: 9-21 and 1995: 34.)

Thus, the realist international relations theorists have made integration not only perfectly explainable as normal international relations or normal state behaviour – analysing it as cooperation or a way to facilitate cooperation, as well as adaptation, a security mechanism (cf. Wæver 1995) or foreign policy – but also as evidence for their own framework. In fact, the assumption that cooperation is difficult, or that transaction costs are high particularly outside institutions, makes integration rational. This turn of interpretation, facilitated by the notable flexibility of central concepts such as 'cooperation' or 'sovereignty',[37] could be compared to translation: the EC comes to be seen through a certain conventional terminology. Thus, integration can be analysed through the concept of 'hegemony' (e.g., in Keohane and Hoffmann 1991: 32); it can be seen as an international organisation, as when Taylor (1983: 24) defines integration as a process whereby the international organisation acquires responsibility for taking decisions in areas previously reserved for the state, or as an international regime, as by Hoffmann 1982. As a regime – a set of norms, rules, policies and the like – the EC both restrains states' actions by imposing costs and limiting the freedom of unilateral action, and provides them with new opportunities through burden sharing, external support, etc. Thus, Hoffmann proposes that integration theory should be built on the domestic goals and priorities of the states, thereby resembling foreign policy analysis. Essentially, both regime theory and the framework of international organisation withdraw the specificity or unique nature of the EC.

It is also interesting to see how Hoffmann introduces his approach as a new and better one. Instead of taking the road explained above of claiming that integration cannot become a threat to the state, he argues that this outcome was originally possible but has since become less likely. Therefore, when he starts by remarking – by now in a rather predictable way – that integration should no longer be seen in traditional terms, he means that one should not assume an engagement in the formation of a new entity which supersedes nations and a zero-sum game between the state and the EC. Actually, integration simultaneously curtails the state's capacities for unilateral action and serves to preserve it as the basic unit. The regime approach, then, not only helps explain this state of affairs which otherwise would remain a paradox, but allows also for an explanation of change: simply, the process of integration halts if the restraints outweigh the opportunities. (Hoffmann 1982: 33-35).

The 'appropriation' of integration by the field of domestic or comparative politics, then, rests in a similar way on the novelty and superiority of the approach in the study of integration. In essence, it was a conquest of integration from the international politics approach, based on the understanding that integration thus far had been studied mainly as international relations, and that 'politics' had been virtually absent from the study. The 'appropriation', thus, was a question of showing that integration was not something special, nor an instance of normal international relations, but normal domestic politics.

The domestic politics approach could be seen to involve three different perspectives. First, there are the explanations of state behaviour in the context of integration by domestic factors and the variation in the internal situations of each state – for example, policy making structures and attitudes held within a state on the EC. Next, the EU is analysed as a political system which comprises primarily the same actors as the national political systems, such as political parties and interest groups, even as a new or evolving state, the aim being an understanding of policy-making and power relations in this system (e.g., Bulmer 1993). Thirdly, there are analyses of national political systems and political decision-making procedures in terms of the changes and challenges caused by integration, the EU membership or more generally 'Europeanisation' (e.g., Héritier *et al.* 1994).

The novelty and superiority of these perspectives is quite obviously relative. As was seen in chapter two, the domestic politics approach was introduced by Bulmer (1983) as a new, alternative way of analysing the behaviour and position of the member states in the EC. Thus far, it was claimed, the analysis had been unduly dominated by international relations approaches which were deemed inadequate for the understanding of the process, particularly in its more recent phases, and had to be completed or replaced (Bulmer 1993; similarly Hix 1994). Bulmer characterised the domestic politics approach as 'arguably more embracing and/or more realistic as a device explaining Community negotiations than the alternatives on offer' (Bulmer 1983: 363), while the use of a comparative public policy perspective was (more) appropriate, in his view, because the EU had increasingly come to resemble a multi-tiered state (Bulmer 1993). Hix, in turn, emphasised the inability of the international politics approaches to deal with the actual substance of politics, or the 'normal' issues of political conflict on a left-right axis (Hix 1994: 10-11; chapter 2).

It is somewhat surprising to see the claim that the field of comparative politics has 'only recently woken up to the possibility of applying its theories and principles to political behaviour and action in the Community' (Hix 1994: 12) in that if the approach literally was something new, one would have to conclude that political scientists thus far had somehow naively ignored integration. Not taking into account that integration could have effects on the states' administrative systems and policies, or concepts such as democracy, implies a negation of integration comparable to that by the early international relations realists. One could, in fact, sketch an itinerary similar to the realists in appropriating integration gradually into the study of political systems through links such as a new resemblance between the state and the Union or the increasingly important changes in the state caused by integration.

Rather, the appeal of novel approaches might have led to a somewhat cursory consideration of the preceding ones. Above all, to place Haas among the neofunctionalists on the side of international relations approaches is to overlook the fundamental way in which pluralistic political science formed his study of integration and, consequently, integration study in general, through providing a certain understanding of its causes, participants and mechanisms. As a matter of fact, Haas (1970) argues that integration studies must rely on the study of comparative politics and economics. Considered more closely, though, several 'novelties' are already familiar from previous research. Several examples emerged in chapter two: when Bulmer (1983) claims that it is important to disaggregate the government's position instead of treating it, like international relations approaches do, as monolithic and non-contradictory, he actually adopts Haas' original pluralist position. Further, when Bulmer (1993) sets himself the task of examining the governance structures, institutions, instruments, rules and procedures of the EU in order to get to know the nature of its policy processes, he comes close to what Lindberg and Scheingold did in 1970. Finally, introducing the analysis of the domestic environment as an important and so far neglected part of the explanation of integration and state policies in that context (e.g., Moravcsik) quite interestingly illustrates the 'tactics' of paving the way to important openings through a selective view of the achievements gained.

Novel or not, the domestic politics approach is certainly different from that of the international relations approach, and its specific bequests to the study of integration are of particular interest here. Most importantly, seeing the EU as domestic politics rather than international (interstate) relations allows for a different conceptualisation of the mutual influence between the state and integration. While the position and behaviour of states influence integration and the common institutions, these in turn influence the states, their institutions and practices. Changes have been identified in policies and policy-making as well as in the political system as a whole, for example through changes in power relations between its different components (e.g., Moravcsik and the growing importance of the executive). Finally, also the conceptualisation of citizenship, political participation, democracy or identity can change. One could argue, in fact, that analysing these changes is an important step forward, perhaps unduly delayed by the tenacity of the traditional research frameworks which do not allow for recognising the possibility of such changes.

Analogously, changes in the national juridical systems – and not only in laws and law-making – as well as changes in the administrative systems and procedures can be seen as an extension of integration to law and administrative sciences, giving rise to a similar 'appropriation' of integration by these branches. Notably, administrative science literature on integration – the studying of the internationalisation of national administration and the features of international (communitarian) administration – is rapidly growing.

It is important, however, to avoid simplifying domestic politics or international relations by disregarding their internal variation. Both include an abundance of approaches. Therefore, delineating the inheritance of the different disciplines in terms of generalised differences between the two would only repeat the mistake of those who ground the superiority of some particular approach on a simplified view of the others. Some of the approaches have been particularly consequential in influencing the way the questions are posed, pointing out what does and what does not need to be explained. A primary example is without doubt the need to explain why states cooperate, stemming from the realist international relations assumption that states do not normally do so. Nonetheless, not all international relations theory sees cooperation as a problem, neither is the state always seen as the central actor, a 'black box' or inherently egoistic; similarly, domestic politics also includes a range of different conceptions of the state.

Therefore, it is more accurate to describe what integration theories have inherited from these disciplines in terms of certain debates rather than assumptions. Thus, integration studies have not inherited from international relations the problem of cooperation but rather the debate on whether cooperation is a problem; not the assumption of state centrality but the debate on whether or not the state is to be considered central. Accordingly, a closer look at these debates helps to understand the development of integration studies.

In the study of international relations, the debate on whether the state is or should be central is almost classical, eternal. In its most familiar form, this debate is between the archetypal realist view, consciously centred on the state, and its different critiques. In the realist view, international relations are, in essence, interstate relations; other actors have only a subordinate position *vis-à-vis* the state, and as a result explanations are based on state behaviour and state interests. Institutions are seen as secondary entities which are created and controlled by the states and derive their power from them. They are essentially tools of the states, aimed mainly at facilitating cooperation, as was seen in the case of the realist view of integration. (See, e.g., Abi-Saab 1981: 12.)

This realist position is often cast as the dominant approach to international relations. However, in terms of popularity and perhaps also of quantity, the position which criticises realism seems to be prevalent. Notably, the theorists of interdependence or transnationalism of the 1970s – particularly Keohane and Nye (1973 and 1977), Haas (1975) – criticised the traditional analyses of international relations for the exaggerated importance given to the state and the consequent neglect of new actors. However, the state had been pointed out as an anachronism well before that (cf. chapter one), and the argument appeared subsequently in other forms. The many sides and meanings and the broad scope of the state seem to make it susceptible for as many challenges from various directions, challenges which are seen to undermine the relative importance of the state in theory and practice. In fact, virtually all major changes in the contemporary world, technological as well as cultural, have been seen as potential challenges to the state as an autonomous and primary actor in international relations, including, obviously, integration (cf. the discussion on values below).

One of the main targets of criticism has been the realist – or in the context of integration, intergovernmentalist – view of institutions which follows from the emphasis on the state and its ability to appear as a unitary actor above or beyond any profound influence by other institutions. For instance, Hix (1994: 6-8) criticises intergovernmentalism for not taking into account the institutional dynamics and the influence of institutions in shaping not only the behaviour of national actors, but also their preferences, for seeing the integration process as a strict zero-sum game and for defining the notion of national interest in too monolithic terms, while it should be seen as incorporating competing views on what is vital for a particular state.[38]

Judging from those who brought institutions 'in' with new vigour under 'new institutionalism' (see notably Bulmer 1993 for integration), the prevalence of realism and the ensuing neglect of institutions has been quite comprehensive. The critical discussion, in fact, seems often to stay at the level of general problems, presented in rather 'black and white' terms. As such, the question of whether institutions matter or not much resembles the argumentation between those who claim that governmental preferences are formed prior to interaction, such as international negotiations, and those claiming that preferences are formed by that interaction. These problems are apparent in that they conceal the central assumptions used; at the same time, research practice seems to give the tools for responding to these, while the more profound questions remain outside its reach.

The problem of institutions is, however, slightly more complicated in that the divisions are not necessarily clear: a distinction has to be made between the ways in which they are seen to matter and what, indeed, the institutions are. In addition, the views hardly exist in pure forms. In international relations, a large literature exists on the autonomy or 'individual will' of international organisations (cf. Virally 1981: 53) and on the ways of measuring their relative strength. While the influence of European institutions on the member states has been underestimated by realists, others have certainly taken it into account. The view that institutions shape the behaviour and preferences of actors, in the precise sense of European institutions shaping the preferences of governments, featured in Haas' early contributions. It is also difficult to find in the literature any total rejection of the possibility that institutions could influence actors' behaviour. Although some game theorists and advocates of the rational actor model are sometimes accused of committing this error, these approaches also mostly take into account the institutional context of the actor.

Actually, the question of how institutions should be understood is a part of the discussion of state centrality, which, in turn, is a permanent feature both of international relations and of domestic politics. Both international relations and domestic politics involve the same debates on state actorship or autonomy versus the importance of structures; indeed, there is an agent-structure division within both disciplines, not between the two (for a useful categorisation, see Hix 1994: 9-10).

In the study of domestic politics, the question of state centrality takes the form of whether the state is an appropriate unit of analysis, or whether it should be reduced to some other, more important forces or actors. Going back in time, one might note how formal legalism, an approach that dominated political sciences in the United States till the 1950s and identified political life with the state and emphasised formal rules in the explanation of behaviour, was challenged by pluralism, a counterreaction against this understanding developing in association with the methodological views of the 'behavioral revolution' of the late 1950s and 1960s. According to the pluralist view, public actors and institutions such as the state can be virtually ignored: they are not seen to have an identity or existence separate from the society. Instead, they are depicted as constrained by societal forces and pressures, which, consequently, become the focus of analysis. Society is seen to consist of diverse groupings, each attempting to maximise their own self-interests, struggling for them in arena such as the government, or the state. For a seminal pluralist author such as Dahl,[39] the state is equated with the government, that is, a collection of individuals occupying particular roles; it is not an administrative apparatus or a legal order. (Krasner 1984: 226-230.)

It can reasonably be argued that the development of integration studies cannot fully be understood without taking into account the pronounced influence this pluralist research setting had in the most influential early work of Haas. In the beginning, 'the state' was notoriously absent from studies. Subsequently, it was disaggregated into a variety of different actors, disappearing from the analysis as an entity, while integration was rather seen as politics in general, a competition between different interests. Even the government's position was disaggregated into the different competing background interests.

Drawing these disciplinary inheritances together, one can easily see a convergence of the pluralist approach to domestic politics and the well-developed criticism of state-centrism in international relations theory towards something close to a fully-fledged apprehension for any overemphasis of the state. In fact, to counterweigh the realism-oriented view, there developed a 'non-state-centred' understanding of integration, equally problematic because it was avaricious of possibilities of analysing the state – something reflected also in the debate of whether it was appropriate to depict the end result of integration as a state, or whether this altogether hampered analysis.

Clearly, one cannot overlook the problems of straightforward state-centrism.[40] It was seen in chapter two how the lack of the problematisation of the state turns out to be a stumbling block rather than a useful simplification: the state comes to define itself,[41] placing itself outside the reach of any 'objective' measures of its relative power. In particular, 'sovereignty' – a central feature for all, and a clear indicator of the influence of integration on the state for the supranationalists – comes to be seen as defined by the state itself. This implies that sovereignty cannot diminish, since it is constantly redefined: when constraints emerge, the limits are simply changed. Taylor provides a good example of this way of thinking. He argues that sovereignty has never been untrammelled; it has always been subject to the 'givens' of international economic and political circumstances. In order to be accepted as members of international society, states have always recognised that they must acknowledge the prevailing rules and codes of behaviour. There is a general sense of what sovereignty entails at a particular time. The outer limits of freedom of action are *conventionally* defined and sovereignty is the right to act within those limits. Sovereignty, thus, is conventionally defined, and therefore its perceived aspects change over time.⁴² (Taylor 1991a: 76.) The ultimate result of this reasoning is actually that the state is immune to integration; the argumentation about sovereignty which simply changes meaning in time and place is close to self-validation, implying that nothing really can be said.

Similarly, the previous analysis pointed out problems also in the non-state-centred view. Statements about the factual decline or non-centrality of the position of the state require firm definitions of integration – or Europeanisation, or internationalisation – in terms of the nature of the 'European', of the changes this development causes or requires from the participants, as well as clear views of the situation of departure in the state studied. The demands on the state easily become unrealistic, or else the state cannot be dealt with at all due to the apprehension of excessive state-centrism. 'Integration' becomes loaded with explanatory tasks, something that leads away from the question and explanation of what integration actually is (cf. Bartelson and chapter 1). In a way, one could even see the framework as a mental disposition for observing certain changes and indicating integration, not something else, as their cause.⁴³

Firm opposition to state-centrism faces a particular dilemma especially because of its assumptions about the autonomy of the state – that the state is not autonomous (enough) to be the main actor – and the similarity of states, or that all states can be considered similar in this respect. Both the questions of state autonomy and state similarity might be, in fact, too complicated to function as a solid basis for a framework.

The critics of pluralism emphasise that the state is much more autonomous and that the state preferences are at least as important as those of the civil society in accounting for what a state does; state autonomy is reflected in the translation of state preferences into public policy and the existence of autonomously adopted policies.⁴⁴ (Nordlinger 1981: 26.) In other words, the pluralists simplify in explaining public policy by societal constraints, as a response to the expectations and demands particularly of those who control the most important resources, and in making the state little more than an arena for social conflicts or interest mediation, dependent even to its existence from societal forces. (*Idem:* 1-3, 5.) They see politics more as a question of rule and control than one of allocation, as in pluralism, and the state as an actor in its own right which cannot be understood as a reflection of societal characteristics or preferences (Krasner 1984: 224-229).

Two assumptions strengthen this view. First, an important factor which contributes to Nordlinger's conclusions is his way of seeing the state as a defined group of individuals. Nordlinger argues that public officials can act on their preferences not only in absence of opposition but also despite opposition. They have different ways to free themselves from the control of private actors. The state, then, can affect the societal preferences and direct them, freeing itself from opposition or constrain. It can also bring about a shift in the alignments of societal resources or reinforce societal convergence. In fact, Krasner specifies a wide array of resources that public officials can use to strengthen their own position and secure their preferences or in arguing for their autonomy – for instance, limiting resources or masking decision-making procedures. (Nordlinger 1981: 9-11, 209-210; Krasner 1984: 230-231.)[45]

The second assumption concerns institutions, their nature and what the category of institutions actually comprises. When Krasner claims that a greater emphasis should be put on institutional constraints on individual behaviour in that structures limit, even determine, both the actors' conceptions of their own interests and their political resources, he seems to come close to the non-state-centred view. In reality, however, he is underlining the importance of the state as an institution, including certain administrative apparatus, legal order and political beliefs or ideology, which coordinates expectations, delineates legitimate modes of interaction between state and society and serves as a basic source of identity. Krasner draws on some (assumed) characteristics of institutions, in particular the idea that institutional change is difficult, episodic and dramatic rather than continuous and incremental. The influence of institutions is, thus, magnified by their unresponsiveness to the environment. Krasner claims that institutions respond more to their own needs than to those of their domestic society or the international environment. The state as administrative apparatus and legal order does not adjust smoothly to changes in its domestic environment. Once in place, institutions will perpetuate themselves, not least since the cost of maintaining existing institutions may be less than the cost of creating and maintaining new ones, implying a possibly growing incongruence between the state and its environment. (Krasner 1984: 234-235 and 1989: 84-86.)

In the end, the autonomy of the state is not an empirical variable in that it could somehow be measured. As Nordlinger (1981: 21) argues, state autonomy is not the same as state capacities, powers or strength; their relationship may even be inverse: a state with wide-ranging capacities is also confronted with great demands and pressures. Rather, the question is linked to the choice of assumptions, especially the already familiar twist over whether the state should be seen as an actor, a structure, or both – the last alternative being the most presumable and also the most complicated in practice. (Cf. Skocpol 1985: 9, 14-17, 21.)

Analogously, then, the question of whether the states are essentially similar to each other is a question of theoretical assumptions, in this case perhaps more clearly also one which depends on the discipline in question. In much of the realist international relations literature, particularly following from Waltz 1979, states are essentially seen as similar to each other; their differences do not count, except for some strategic variations in capabilities. It has been commonplace to use the stand on whether or not states are similar as a crucial divide between the disciplines of political science and international politics, the former focusing on the differences, the latter assuming that there are no differences.[46] Thus, for instance Nettl (1968), for whom states are so different that in some of them, there actually is no 'state' at all, argues that this does not apply for international relations; Ferguson and Mansbach (1989: 2, 83) observe that a certain concept of state defines in practice the boundaries of the discipline of international relations. However, it is not only the realists who maintain that states are similar; the same assumption is clear in the critics' argumentation that states – without distinction – are not central.

The essential problem is that in order somehow to verify the assumptions of state centrality and state similarity, if that is needed, one has to take the variety of states into consideration, and thus analyse the state, instead of making it something unanalysable, as the extreme positions tend to do. The dilemma behind this kind of verification is illustrated in Nordlinger's problem of how to show that the state is not autonomous. He sees that the imminent problem of theories of the pluralist type is that as they fail to differentiate state and society, they do not have any possibility of validating their own assumptions either: only if state and society are distinguished does it become possible to make a case for the autonomy [but also non-autonomy] of the state (Nordlinger 1981: 4-5). In other words, although any distinction between the state and society is a simplification, it has to be drawn in order to validate the thesis of non-autonomy or to show the existence of a trend in which the state has become less and less distinctive (*idem:* 12-13). The same is true for state similarity: the possibility of arguing like Halliday (1994: 95) that international pressure makes states increasingly compelled to conform to each other in their internal arrangements, requires an analytical starting point in seeing the states as dissimilar.

The argumentation about the non-centrality of the state, far from decreasing the need for studying the state, even increases it. The position of the state in the analysis is, in fact, ambivalent: on the one hand, it is needed for comparison and verification, on the other, it is seen to hamper analysis. Moreover, if used, it is easily attributed unrealistic characteristics. One might recall Alger remarking that the way in which neofunctionalists [!] use the state as a yardstick in the analysis of integration inhibits them from seeing anything new or different. Furthermore, Alger notes, the characteristics of states thus used are exaggerated: they are assumed to have single centres of authority, co-ordination and planning, and a clear hierarchical organisation. (Alger 1981: 136-137, 140.)[47] Similarly demanding criteria appeared above in Taylor's features of federation (read: statehood): the superiority of federal law, an independent sphere of central authority, constitutional immunity against dissolution by secession of the constituent regions, exclusive control of foreign relations and defence by the central government, and the possibility to amend the federal constitution without the consent of all constituent regions (Taylor 1983: 270). They appear also in Wallace (1996: 451) when he sees the EU as a quasi-state 'without the coherent articulation of interests and political preferences characteristic of a well-developed polity'. In other words, not only is the EC expected to have state-like characteristics, these characteristics are somehow imaginary, and it is not clear that they would fit the states, either. In fact, Keohane and Hoffmann (1991: 12) also remark that '[P]ortrayals of the state are often bedeviled by the image of an ideal-typical "state" whose authority is unquestioned and whose institutions work smoothly. No such state has ever existed (...).' These high demands obviously increase the 'immunity' considered above.

It is not strange, therefore, that the concept of the state disappears, then reappears in the studies of political science and international relations. The concept has in successive waves been thrown out and 'brought back in' both as an analytical concept and as a research focus. Its virtual absence from the professional academic lexicon in the 1950s and 1960s – as Krasner puts it – shaped the beginnings of integration studies. Pluralist and structural-functionalist approaches dominated both political science and sociology, replacing the 'old-fashioned' state by society-centred explanations of politics and governmental activities and the study of, for instance, government, interest groups and voting (cf. Skocpol 1985: 4). A contributing factor to its dismissal was perhaps the relatively 'stateless' environment in which the research took place, the United States. Nettl (1968: 561-562), for whom conceptual changes are both 'ideologically and geographically' conditioned, notes that the erosion of the concept of state coincided with the shift of the centre of gravity of social science to the United States; similarly, Nordlinger

(1981: 5) remarks that a concept of state has been barely thinkable in the United States. A geographical concentration of research facilitated, at least, a development of a methodologically and conceptually uniform research agenda.

Yet, the state did not disappear for a long time. Perhaps its 'skeletal, ghostly existence' has remained there all the time, as Nettl (1968: 559) put it, as 'for all the changes in emphasis and interest of research, the thing exists and no amount of conceptual restructuring can dissolve it.' In fact, the concept returned in the 1960s with the renewed success of Marxist state theories, which actually predict the crisis and dissolution of the state (Cassese 1986: 120) and in the mid-1970s with the questions of the extent of state autonomy and the relations between the state and its environment (Krasner 1984: 223-224). In integration studies, the 'introduction' of the domestic politics approach managed, in fact, to put the state in the focus of attention afresh. The state was vigorously reintroduced via three routes. First, through explaining EU policy outcomes on the basis of national positions, domestic environment and policy-making; secondly, it came through analysing EU policy-making with the help of the toolkit of domestic politics but, and here is an essential difference, by making the national level disappear from between (either by concentrating on the EU institutions, as in studying a particular state, or by linking relevant parts of the domestic political settings, political parties and the like, directly to these institutions). Thirdly, it was reintroduced when analysing the influence of the EU on a particular state, thereby reversing the first research setting.

To sum up, the tenacity of disciplinary frameworks faced with the domain of integration cannot go unnoticed. Instead of blurring their divisions, integration studies might do us a favour by locating and underlining the divide. Disciplines are, in a way, necessarily artificial; the basic reasons for maintaining disciplinary divisions, the interplay between different disciplines, the internal order of a particular discipline and debates on whether some field does or does not constitute a discipline do not necessarily have anything to do with any real qualities of the objects of study. Rather, the existence of disciplines requires an affirmation and protection of their dissimilarity; they need a consensus on that they actually are different and also all needed. One could assume, thus, that there is a 'conservative' debate on the disciplines similar to that on different schools of thought.

In the case of integration studies, one can clearly see that the disciplines have a stake in maintaining that they are distinctive: the difference between domestic politics and international relations can be presented in accentuated rather than opaque terms, as when both supranationalism and intergovernmentalism are seen as theories which focus on the characteristics of the EC as an international organisation instead of studying it as domestic politics (Bulmer 1993), or when Hix (1994) maintains that neofunctionalism too is an international relations approach. The practice of presenting a particular view as superior to the others also persists, as do, in fact, the reasons for why it is seen to be better. One can thus add Krasner (1984: 243) to the list of those who see as the assets of the particular approach ('new statism') the inclination to detect disjunctures and stress within any given political system and to take into account historical evolution; moreover, this is seen to allow for the study of the influence and change of political institutions and their adequate descriptions. (Krasner 1984: 226-230).

Indeed, whether or not one agrees that this particularly disciplinary division between international relations and domestic politics is appropriate, it is certainly necessary to admit the existence of basic theoretical problems which cannot be overcome by simply adhering to either the one or the other discipline, as is often done. That is, it is not possible simply to claim that one of them 'suits better' as both not only suit, but are also needed, as exemplified by the neglect of the state which, albeit avoiding the shortcomings of state-centrism, leads to problems which recall the necessity of looking at the state.

Values

Among the main factors influencing the views on the relationship between the state and integration, values play a fundamental role. Yet, their role is seldom recognised. The general idea that science could be completely value-free may no longer convince large audiences, but in the case of particular theories, the assumption of objectivity still seems to live on, and the theories are seldom, if at all, analysed as to the values they represent. Similarly, while 'the state' is easily recognised as a value-laden concept, the theoretical statements in which it is used are not necessarily seen to involve values. At the same time, in the case of integration theories, some of the most clearly value-laden statements on the state can be found in the writings that otherwise adhere to the ideal of objectivity and value-free science.

Not only does the understanding of the state often involve attitudes – inclination or aversion – in discord with the empirical character of the study; this understanding also tends to colour the understanding of integration and the whole question of the relationship between the two. The analysis of integration, in fact, seems at least partly to be based on views of the state which are value statements and therefore cannot be 'verified' or 'falsified' through empirical evidence. Further, statements of value and statements of empirical fact seem to get confused in that the former are accumulated and transmitted further in the guise of statements of empirical origin.

It is imperative, thus, to distinguish between facts and values in order to locate the consequences the latter has for research. This section is concerned with identifying the values involved in three particularly influential statements concerning the state and integration – without, for that reason, claiming that values would not play a role in other examples as well. The statements or assumptions are, first, that the state is not an adequate or appropriate form of political organisation, second, that it is no longer capable of fulfilling its functions, and third, that international relations are inherently conflictual due to the contentious character of the state. All three are actually implied in the first view of the state and integration, for instance, seeing integration as a remedy for the inherent weaknesses of the state and the state system. Concretely, statements on the value of the state or the estimate in which the state is held, are identified as positive or negative judgements, explicit or implicit, on its usefulness or importance.

The state is a value-laden concept *par excellence*, a concept with strong normative connotations that, at least below the surface, often carries a multitude of positive and negative beliefs and attitudes. Its value-laden character can actually be seen as an essential reason for the difficulties in finding a consensus about the proper meaning of the concept. As Grant points out, the concept of state is actually composed of two inherent and equally important parts, the one formal, the other ethical. Thus, even in the event of a shared understanding of the formal component or definition of the concept, one would still have a variety of different views on the second part of the concept, that is, on values concerning the nature and functions of the state. (Grant 1988: 691-692, 709; cf. chapter 1.)

Further, it is useful to divide the ethical or normative component by distinguishing between *instrumental* and *intrinsic* values: the state can be seen to be valuable as a means to something else, in which case it has instrumental value, or it can be seen as a value or an end in itself, which is the case of intrinsic value. The question of whether the state has instrumental or intrinsic value is actually among the most far-reaching divisions in political theories. On the one side, as proponents of instrumental value, one could mention Hobbes, for whom the state guarantees a minimum political subsistence and the only defence against anarchy, J.S. Mill, or Locke, for whom the purpose of the state is to protect private property and represent property interests.

Especially for Locke and Mill, the state is, as it were, a matter of choice, one instrument among others. On the other side, Hegel – together with, among others, Aristotle, Burke and Rousseau – represents those for whom the state has intrinsic value. For Hegel, individuals are constituted by the institutions and practice of which they are part; there are rights of the collective which are different from and more important than those of the individual. (Grant 1988: 693ff, esp. 704-708.)

This theoretical distinction is an integral part also of the discussion of the state in integration studies: statements on the diminishing or altogether nonexistent value of the state as such or as a means to something else form a central, although rarely explicit part of the understanding of integration. Thus, the distinction serves in the following as a device for classifying the value statements identified in the studies.

Intrinsic value, or the nature of the state

In view of all the disagreement on the proper understanding of the state, it is somewhat surprising to find a fair consensus about its intrinsic value, not only in integration studies but also in the international relations literature in general. Or rather, one might speak about a consensus on the lack of intrinsic value: mostly, in fact, the state is pointed out as the cause of different problems and injustices. In particular, it is said that states are by nature warprone, the relations between states being intrinsically conflictual, and that the state is an inadequate or ineffective form of political organisation. In Bull's words, we are constantly reminded that the state is an obstacle to the achievement of a viable world order, peace and security, that it stands in the way of the promotion of economic and social justice in world society and hampers efficient solutions to the problem of living in harmony with environment in that the division of mankind into states prevents tackling problems on a global scale (Bull 1979: 111). Statehood is seen as morally indefensible egotism either because it creates artificial distinctions among members of the human community or because state apparatuses are used for the oppression of individuals (Koskenniemi 1994: 23).

This view seems even to unite the critics and the criticised, to judge from Hoffmann, who despite his role of a state-centred realist portrays the nation states as 'often inchoate, economically absurd, administratively ramshackle, and impotent yet dangerous in international politics'. The problem for him is that states still remain the basic units as there is no agreement of what could replace them. As such, they are also central for the understanding of integration. As the highest possessor of power, the nation-state functions as initiator, pace-setter, supervisor, even destroyer in relation to the larger entity. The very existence of states is a formidable obstacle to their replacement; the system is, in fact, profoundly conservative of the diversity of nation-states. (Hoffmann 1966: 863, 866, 908-909; cf. Hoffmann 1982: 26, 30.)

In the early writings on integration, one can perceive a clear mistrust towards the state. In fact, they had focused on resolving the problem of war that stemmed from the system of separate, sovereign states. Thus, the federalists advocated a federal structure with a common central authority as a model which would render otherwise bellicose interstate relations equally peaceful and organised as between the parts of a federal state. Mitrany, also concerned with peace and security and the aim of finding new ways of organising the relations between states, argued, on the contrary, that federations would not solve the problem of war, only magnify it, reproducing the logic of political exclusion and the system of national states on a larger scale, and actually constituting a *threat* to security.

Similarly, Deutsch *et al.* (1957) wrote about the building of a wider political community in order to eliminate war. The rather negative view on the state which lies behind that effort becomes clear especially in Deutsch's work on international relations in his characterisation of foreign policy. It was noted in chapter two how Deutsch, in the best realist style, claimed that the foreign policy of every country deals, first, with the preservation of independence and security, and, second, with the pursuit and protection of its economic interests, particularly those of its most influential interest groups. This, in his view, implies that countries aim at resisting penetration and manipulation by foreign countries and ideologies, while simultaneously accomplishing active penetration and manipulation of their own, spreading their national and ideological propaganda, for example through economic aid or the support of cultural and scientific exchange missions. (Deutsch 1968: 87-88.)

This situation makes it understandable that integration is needed, although it is also difficult to achieve. In Deutsch's view, most governments and people prefer sovereignty to integration, which would diminish their capacities and prestige. Yet, Deutsch argues that mankind is unlikely to survive for long without a new political climate, greater international openness, understanding and compassion, which help to achieve integrated political communities in the long term. (Deutsch 1968: 202.) Later, he hopes that scientific and technological breakthroughs will shorten the time needed for dismantling the coercive state machineries.[48] (Deutsch 1986: 220-221.)

Similarly for Haas (1964), who also uses rather strong expressions, the adverse character of the state plays a role in the reasoning for functional organisation. Functional organisation, for him, is a way to overcome 'the distorting role of the modern state with respect to the possibilities of human fulfilment'. Haas goes on to notice that pre-industrial and pre-national primary occupational groups were the 'true focuses for human happiness' because they afforded a sense of participation in the solution of practical problems. The rise of the territorially bounded, omnicompetent national state led to the loss of group spontaneity and an end to the tendency to identify with occupational colleagues elsewhere, while the search for national security became the focus of life in the state. Even the administration of general welfare measures, such as social security legislation, took place within the depersonalised context of the state structure. 'The unnatural state' took the place of natural society. (Haas 1964: 9-10.)

Both Haas (1958) and Haas (1964) can be seen as presenting reasons for the preferability of integration to the previous state of affairs. Integration needs to be explained, since it involves new or unusual elements – characteristics which integration obviously assumes in juxtaposition to the classical view on the egoistic and competitive behaviour of sovereign states in international relations. In the case of the ECSC, Haas observes that a special code of conduct or supranational attitude emerges among the participants; the rule of simple intergovernmental bargaining from fixed positions is abandoned in favour of delegation of power to experts and mediation; collective action and review replace specific national demands (Haas 1958: xxxiv, 515-520). More generally, as functions create loyalties and the transfer of functions thus reorients them towards welfare agencies, the field of the non-controversial widens, and cooperation becomes possible, in the long run, in all interstate relations (Haas 1964: 6).

On the other hand, however, Haas also leaves space for the state to change. For him, supranationalism seems the appropriate regional counterpart to the national state which no longer 'feels capable' of realising welfare within its borders and which has 'made its peace with interdependence'. In the process of integration, the interests of the actors, including governments, change: the state itself comes to see its interests in a different way, for instance seeing supranationalism as the method to secure maximal welfare (Haas 1963: 67-73). Haas argues that governments are able to learn the art of revising their demands and seeking new ways of satisfying them without destroying themselves in the process (Haas 1964: 81) – although seeing this ability as a consequence of integration is odd as it presupposes that states did not previously have the capacity to revise their demands according to the environment.

What is seen as the essential core of the state is perhaps more often than not seen in negative terms also in that the functions of coercion and defence are emphasised at the expense of other functions. In all, the state is easily made a scapegoat for all kinds of failures, and its persistence a reason for pessimism and passivity concerning the possibilities of improvement. At the same time, as Bull (1979: 114-115) remarks, there is no reason to assume that any alternative order would not be associated with the same problems; in his view, abolishing the state system would not bring any alleviation, since the problems associated with the state, such as war or economic injustice, have deeper causes than those embodied in any particular form of political organisation.

The consequences of the view that the state has scarce intrinsic value are tangible both in the understanding of international relations and of integration. The egoistic character of the state is seen to make it war-prone, something that makes international relations inherently unstable and conflictual, and interstate cooperation so difficult. Perhaps as the utmost representative of this logic of state action, Tilly (1985: 181, 184-185) describes the activities which states carry on 'under the general heading of organised violence' as war making (elimination or neutralisation of outside rivals), state making (elimination or neutralisation of inside rivals), protection (elimination or neutralisation of the enemies of the states' clients) and extraction (acquiring the means of carrying out the first three activities). The consequence for international relations is that war becomes the normal condition; external competition creates internal state making.

In reality, the view involves an unavoidable circularity. The state is seen to behave necessarily in a specific way because of the nature of the system of states where it simply has to behave like that; the nature of the system, however, is not a real cause but only a logical consequence of the assumed nature of its composing units, the sovereign states.

Secondly, the view also contributes in rendering the concept of integration equally value-laden. Integration comes to be seen as something positive in that it is depicted as a solution to the problems of the system of states otherwise unattainable, not only because of an adherence to its own, valuable goals. Thus, a negative view on the state can be a ground for arguments in favour of integration; conversely, a positive view of the state may induce a negative view of integration, if the state and integration are seen as incompatible. This could even be presented in the form of a simple table concerning the values (positive and negative attitudes) towards integration, as explained by the view of the state and the understanding of the relation between the state and integration:

	Attitudes towards integration	
	Relation state – integration symbiotic	Relation state – integration antagonistic
View on the state positive	+	–
View on the state negative	–	+

Instrumental value, or the declining position of the state

As regards the instrumental value of the state, an argument comparable in popularity to that of the problematic nature of the state, concerns the decreasing importance, diminishing centrality or withering away of the state. Indeed, in speaking about the profession of international lawyers, Koskenniemi (1994: 23) notes that there is probably no general statement about the condition of the object of study that arouses more enthusiasm than the thesis of the 'withering away of the state'. In a similar vein, Navari (1991b) remarks that the thesis is advocated from a whole theoretical spectrum from systems theorists, realists and political economists to pluralists, socialists and marxists. The different reasons for seeing the state as *no longer* what it used to be, or no longer capable of fulfilling its functions, for seeing that the state gradually loses its ability to control or to govern what was called 'national economy' and the ability to influence its environment are often gathered in general statements about the crisis of the nation-state or that of the welfare state.[49] As a general consequence, it is seen that the state no longer is the central actor in international relations it once was.

Classifying these statements as reflecting values rather than facts may seem curious. Mostly, indeed, when an author claims that the state no longer is what it used to be, he is explicitly referring to empirical facts as the basis for that claim. Koskenniemi, too, discerns these arguments from the criticisms based on ethical or moral considerations; the state is seen to wither away because of factual developments in the international world, such as interdependence and globalisation of politics. As a result, states are no longer able to handle even their own external security, not to mention problems such as air pollution, without entering into forms of cooperation which entail the dissolution of their sovereignty. (Koskenniemi 1994: 23.) Nevertheless, these statements evidently concern the instrumental value of the state, not always clearly discernible from arguments on intrinsic value. They also tend to acquire the role of assumptions.

Various coinciding examples of reasons for the decline of the state can be found in the literature, and are usually similar also concerning the consequences of this decline in terms of the incapacity of the state to fulfil its functions. States are seen to be simultaneously threatened from different directions: the development of military technology renders traditional security policy and military alliances meaningless, transnational markets and multinational enterprises threaten national trade and social policies, and global environmental problems question the control of the state. Furthermore, also cultural challenges, the diminishing cultural differences, and growing sub-, supra- and transnationalism, challenge the state. Together, these factors make the state less able to fulfil its functions in security, welfare, and social justice. (Brown 1988: 41-43, 160, 193ff.)

Strange argues that although states collectively are not obsolete (indeed, they are still the most influential and therefore critical sources of authority in the world system), they are becoming defective: like old trees, they are hollow in the middle, even though they still grow new shoots. For Strange, authority over society and economy is becoming increasingly diffused after two or three centuries in which it became increasingly centralised in the institution of the state. She proposes that state authority – and, consequently, state legitimacy – has diminished partly because it has leaked away, both horizontally and vertically, partly because it seems to have just evaporated. State authority is undermined, first, as a result of its growing asymmetries, which make the notion of state sovereignty itself increasingly fictional. Second, some authority over less politically sensitive issues has shifted from national states to international authorities of various kinds – interstate, private and commercial. The authority of the state is increasingly either shared with, sustained or constrained by these authorities, and often also shared with local and regional authorities. (Strange 1995: esp. 55-57, 63, 66-67.)

In the background of this development, there is a profound structural change, determined by the increased pace and costs of technological development and changes in international financial structure, in particular increased capital mobility, a change which has severed the connection between the power of the state and its control over its territory. Power over production, security, credit, and ideas is now also exercised from outside its territory. Accelerating technological change suggests that the nature of the competition between states in the international system has changed, and so have the nature of the states and their behaviour towards one another. In this new situation, the state has growing difficulties in fulfilling its functions, such as progress in industrialisation and raising living standards. As industrial policy and trade policy become more important than defence and foreign policy, states are obliged to seek commercial rather than military allies; these might well be, e.g., foreign-owned firms. (Strange 1989: 169-170; Strange 1995: 58-60; Stopford and Strange 1991: 43-44, 49-50, 205.)

In the studies of integration, the arguments on the decline of the state appear at least in three versions. Firstly, integration is seen as one of the challenges to the state, as one reason for its withering away. Integration, thus, weakens the state, which makes irrelevant the frameworks where integration is explained as state policies, perhaps even the use of the term 'state' in the analysis. The fact that decision-making and rule-making is increasingly shifted to the European level and made collective, multilateral or supranational, or perhaps tied to a system of multilevel government, implies not only a dilution of sovereignty but also fundamental changes in the locus of political control: Marks points out that states are, in particular, losing their grip on the mediation of domestic interest representation in international relations. Although states remain 'immensely strong institutions', they have not sustained their former control of individuals in their territories. (Marks 1995: 1; cf. Matlary 1995.)

Among the factors diminishing the role of the state, the priority of European community law over domestic law in the areas of Community competence is obviously central. States are losing autonomy in the sphere of economy, but also over national defence and defence procurement. Wallace remarks that they are also beginning to lose autonomy over the central state functions of public order and maintenance of territorial boundaries. In his view, even though little has changed for the state as a focus for popular identity and a basis for legitimacy, the nation as a political and social community is disconnecting from the state as provider of security and welfare; both the state and the nation have lost coherence, and the European nation state is in retreat (Wallace 1994: 55, 74-76).

Others go on to claim that the position of the state is questioned also as to identity and legitimacy. Matlary (1995: 100-102) sees that the state is in decline as a political ordering principle and weakened as the source of democratic legitimacy, as tasks formerly undertaken by the state are now increasingly on the international and EU agenda. Therefore, she argues, a new type of democratic theory is needed, looking back to federalist ideas, where subsidiarity becomes a principle of determining the appropriate *locus* and participants in decision-making. Functional or corporate representation will become more important than territorial belonging and the scope for non-state actors will increase; factors such as ethnicity become more representative of identity than the state.

In the end, not much remains of the traditional state. As Schmitter (1991: 2-3) puts it, the state now least resembles its historic self: it has lost its capacity for unitary action, its unchallenged centrality in human existence, differentiation from civil society, boundedness and security stemming from territorial exclusivity, sovereignty which separated and protected it from other political units, and the monopoly of collective means of violence.

A second way of linking integration and the position of the state is to use the argument of the decreasing centrality of the state as a rationale for integration. The decline of the state can be seen not only as a widely accepted fact, but also as an irreversible, natural process: as Beloff (1963: 52, 55, 61) puts it, the middle-sized nation state is obsolete for many functions of modern government, and the need for larger political institutions 'is widely felt'. Examples of this thinking were seen above, for instance in Haas 1963. Finally, as a third interpretation of the situation, one might see the realist position that in order to recuperate and regain lost capabilities or to face new challenges, states choose to integrate. Integration, thus, is seen as a method of management of the states' problems (e.g., Milward). One can also see an incentive for integration in the widening of the functions of the state: governments are increasingly measured or evaluated through their performance, through the goods and services they now can provide only in cooperation with others (Wessels 1992: 42-43).

Nevertheless, the 'withering away' argument has some obvious problems linked, first, to its ubiquity, and, second, to its nature as a statement of values. The ubiquity, or the sheer volume of the argument may increase its plausibility, but it may also undermine it: the overt generality of the statements about the decreasing value of the state is actually among their main problems. They are not particularly time and space specific; they may have become more common in recent years, but this does not necessarily reflect a corresponding change in reality. Rather, it could evidence accumulation, an emerging consensus in seeing reality in these terms. It is, in fact, difficult to locate a starting point in time for these arguments; 1990s 'Europeanisation' is not such, neither is the 1970s discussion on transnationalism, interdependence and new actors.

Parallel to this discussion, counterarguments have also thrived. On the one hand, it has been argued that if the state is not always directly able to control changes, it can adapt, and often also benefit from them, increasing its power (e.g., Rosenau 1989, Thomson and Krasner 1989, Puchala 1993). For some, the role of the state has also dramatically grown through its geographical and functional spreading, even to the point of bringing an end to the autonomy of transnational relations (Bull 1979: 112-113). On the other hand, it has been emphasised that no unambiguous or definitive changes have actually taken place; it is noted that the state has never been the only central actor in international relations (Bull 1979: 112-113) or that the state has always been part of a system of competing and mutually involved states (Skocpol 1985: 8).

It is therefore not surprising that somewhat more cautious, balancing views appear which leave space for both interpretations. Some see that a more general *transformation* of the state takes place (e.g., Rosecrance 1996). It is also remarked that the changes notwithstanding, states still remain very powerful (Strange 1995, Marks 1995), or that the same types of changes may in different times have different effects. For example, Wallace notes that while economic integration, industrial modernisation and technological innovation have decreased national autonomy, they previously operated in an opposite way, to *reinforce* national political systems – something which explains that the 1960s were the high point of national consolidation and state management of economy and society. They might still give new possibilities for governments in pursuit of objectives they no longer can achieve on a national basis. (Wallace 1994: 61, 68.)

The 'withering away' arguments are rather problematic as regards the possibilities of answering whether they actually are true. Firstly, they are said to apply to all states, that is, to an abstract idea of the state rather than to a particular case. Arguments about states in general, however, are inconsistent with the obvious variations between the existing states. It is certainly true that 'different states manage differently', and that the divergences between countries are growing (Stopford and Strange 1991: 29). The question of the degree of similarity needed in order to claim that states in general, even a particular group of states, is 'withering away' is intricate. Secondly, an empirical verification of state power or position is obviously complicated not only because these might not be countable – indeed, how to weigh the losses in some sectors and the gains in others, or weigh the regionally differentiated influences? – but also because the assessment of the state's effectiveness depends on whose view is taken into account in the assessment.[50] Analogously, it is difficult to ascertain whether the role of other actors has increased at the expense of the state, as it is impossible to reduce the question to quantitative terms (Bull 1979: 112-113); the mere existence of nonstate actors in international relations does not prove that they are autonomous (Haass 1979: 131).

Shadowing these difficulties is the general problem that the assessment of the state's value is complicated by the tendency of empirical elements to get intertwined with value judgements: it is difficult not to find, at some stage, references to what the state *should* be. This is particularly visible in the question of the functions of the state. While there seems to be a broad agreement on the fact that the state cannot fulfil its functions, the views on what these functions are, or should be, seem to differ. Are the states' functions for instance security, welfare and social justice, or, as Wallace (1994: 64) puts it, the preservation of internal order, maintenance of national boundaries, defence of national territory, provision of legitimate government, services and welfare, and the promotion of national prosperity? Are the functions put in a specific order of importance? How is welfare interpreted – does it mean progress in industrialisation and raising living standards?

The discussion on state functions seems to involve, again, the problems of deciding whether states are essentially similar, the tendency to depict the state in a relatively negative manner, and the risk for creating a exaggerated image of what the state has been or should be. One might argue with Navari (1991b) that for those advocating the 'withering away' argument, the state has some integral functions which it no longer can fulfil or which are no longer needed, while one could also assume that there are no really indispensable functions. That these indispensable features are portrayed in negative terms is questionable and returns the discussion to views on the intrinsic value of the state – especially because of the apparently neutral terminology in which they are presented. The custom of referring to the Weberian conception of the state as some kind of basic, shared understanding illustrates this problem well: when Wallace, for example, uses this view in arguing that the 'irreducible minimum of the concept of a state' is a body which exercises an accepted monopoly of violence within its boundaries and a willingness to use violence against outsiders to defend those boundaries, frontier controls and rights of entry and residence being among the most basic tenets of the nation state (Wallace 1994: 61-62, 70), the state seems directed *against* someone more than it is meant to be *for* someone. (Cf. Tilly, p. 50.)

Finally, statements about the loss of attributes and capabilities by the state seem to create an understanding of the state as actually more powerful than has ever been the case. It often happens that the specific state under observation is compared to rather demanding definitions of what the state should be, or has been, in order really to be a state. For instance, Schmitter uses a rather sharp depiction of the state, referring to Tilly and Weber: the state is a 'political organisation which *uniquely* controls the concentrated means of coercion within a given contiguous territory, which *exclusively* claims the right to control the movement of peoples and goods across its boundaries and which is formally centralised and differentiated from society' (Schmitter 1991: 2-3, emphasis added). One can ask whether such exclusive control ever has existed and if it has at some point in time and in some particular state, whether this situation should be made a norm for what the state should be.

The subjective and the objective assessments, the values and the facts, thus tend to get mixed when evaluating the state, and, typically, those advocating a view opposite to their own are accused of employing subjective criteria. The 'withering away' school draws on what its members see as factual changes in reality. Their opponents, in turn, reproach them for replacing objective assessments by subjective analyses of the adequacy of the state – something that Haass (1979: 136), for example, sees as quite inconsistent with the 'modernism' implied in their emphasis on interdependence and non-state actors. Still, this tendency of mixing facts and values and the difficulty of constructing an objective view of the instrumental value of the state seem to be inherent in the concept itself.

As Koskenniemi (1994) points out, a valid criticism of the state cannot lean solely on facts or values: it has to appeal to both empirical and ethical arguments. Therefore, criticisms combine sociological rhetoric and ethical principles in order simultaneously to appear objective and to appeal to conscience. At the same time, the ethical component of the critique comprises contradictory evaluations: it is the Achilles' heel which makes the criticism in the end so feeble.

Koskenniemi illustrates this problem by going through no less than eight common criticisms of the state. His list reveals not only that the state has been criticised from all possible directions of political thought, but also that these criticisms can be played against each other. States are criticised for being either too large or too small to respond effectively to the recent challenges of economy, technology and legitimacy; they are also said to hamper the creation of efficient financial and commodity markets. A legacy of criticisms stem from the idea that the state in some way serves some groups or individuals more than others. The state is criticised for being a tool for the oppression of workers by the bourgeoisie, for being 'prisons of nations' hindering the realisation of self-determination and authentic communities, and for being an obstacle to the realisation of human rights and individual freedoms used as justification for overruling these rights. Further, the state is criticised for fostering artificial 'official' culture at the expense of spontaneous, indigenous cultural formations, or an equally artificial public-private distinction or boundary between the state and the household and a formalistic, patriarchal power structure against civil society. (Koskenniemi 1994: 24-26.)

The problem with these criticisms is revealed, in fact, when they are brought together. All appeal differently to the authentic in comparison to the artificiality of the state, and this makes them contradict each other. In other words, each posits a foundational principle outside statehood on which the ordering of human affairs should be based. Koskenniemi argues that the ideal of authenticity implies a naturalistic view of human society which further refers to a conception of unconditional, self-evident knowledge, used against the state. The problem is that none of these authenticities can sustain itself merely by appeal to its self-evidence. The criticisms are contradictory as the various authentic states of affairs cannot be realised simultaneously. For example, economic efficiency might well be inconsistent with individual rights. On the other hand, the criticisms are also indeterminate. Even if the 'real' principle were known, it would be impossible to reach it, to know how public life in practice should be organised to reflect it, without, for instance, creating conflicts between individual rights. In the end, Koskenniemi argues that the criticisms function as political ideologies in that they suggest the necessity of realising something that is already there and, consequently, they de-emphasise the decision processes needed to realise them. For example, to call for the replacement of the state structures by bundles of human rights takes these latter as given and fails to see their historical, context-dependent character and the need to decide what is required to attain them. (Koskenniemi 1994: 26-27.)

This discussion also shows how the question of state autonomy, addressed above, cannot be separated from values attached to the state. As Nordlinger remarks, the questions of whether the state is autonomous and whether this autonomy should be 'applauded, accepted or condemned' are two different, essential problems. His answer to the latter question, however, reveals the common inability to deal with values: he claims that the answer is, 'in a way', empirical (Nordlinger 1981: 211-212). Evidently, the autonomy of the state can be seen as inconsistent with democracy, for instance when the incongruence between state and the internal environment becomes too large as a result of excessive demands upon society, and threatens legitimacy (Krasner 1984: 238). Alternatively, one might also see autonomy as a precondition for effectiveness.

In conclusion, the discussion on values shows that the inadequate consideration of the ethical component of the concept of state – caused by obvious unease about the role of subjective assessments – risks taking statements based on values for factual statements, as developing consensual knowledge on the state. This has several problematic consequences. First, accepting the view that the state no longer is as important as it used to be as an assumption for further studies – something not at all uncommon – cannot be seen as an improvement in comparison to seeing the world as state-centred. Rather, it is a replacement of one type of consensual knowledge by another. An 'anti-realist' starting point as a new cornerstone could only become a new 'black box' on which research is built. It could hardly avoid the same type of criticism one can direct at realist assumptions: simply overriding the state by the argument of its invalidity can do it as much injustice as does the realist habit of explaining everything through the state.

The second problem is the combined influence of statements about the intrinsic and instrumental value of the state on the use of the concept itself as an analytical tool. The diminishing value of the state in the contemporary world is translated into a diminishing value of the state as a concept or an explanatory factor in research: 'the state', accordingly, should be abandoned or replaced by something else, e.g., 'form of political domination' (Schmitter 1991) or 'political process' (Palan 1990). (Cf. chapter 1.) It is concluded that much of Western social science is obsolescent, if not yet quite out-of-date, as it is based on tacit premises about the state as the most important unit of analysis, concentrating on issues within a state or comparison of two or more national systems or societies, but also because of the overemphasis of the violent conflict between states as the core problematique of the system (Strange 1995: 70). This certainly shows to what extent theoretical assumptions – in which also the withering away thesis has to be included – really direct research. As Haas puts it, the status of integration theories 'is of tremendous importance because it is they rather than the nature of things which lead students to postulate the relationships between variables; it is they, not the nature of things, which lead us to the specification of what is an independent and a dependent variable.' (Haas 1970: 623.)

In fact, not only are the possible positive functions of the state not given much consideration, even though statements about the decreasing value of the state do not as such necessarily imply there are none. States can also be seen as providing order in the international system. For Bull, the system of states is the form of universal political organisation most able to provide minimum order in a political society where there is not a broad enough consensus to sustain the acceptance of a common government, but in which there is a consensus that can sustain the coexistence of a plurality of separate governments. The state has provided order both internally and at an international level, limiting rivalry through cooperation, guides of conduct and common institutions. In some cases, there has been an additional need for the state, as in third world countries, where peoples have been able to take charge of their own destiny only by gaining control of states. (Bull 1979: 115-119, 121, 123.)

Similarly, Koskenniemi maintains that as long as there are no shared basic values or wide agreement on what constitutes good life, the formal-bureaucratic rationality of the state provides the best possible safeguard against the totalitarianism inherent in a commitment to substantive values, which forces those values on people not sharing them. In his view, there is also little reason to be confident that some subject-matters (peace, economy, environment) are authentically global and must be dealt with by globally uniform solutions. Therefore, statehood should continue to survive, if only in the absence of any better real alternative. (Koskenniemi 1991: 397, 401-402, 405, 407.)

In other words, Koskenniemi sees that the *raison d'être* of the state is its 'artificiality' or formality. The state provides a space for the ascertainment of the truth or the acceptability of the proposed forms of life of the various views on the state. In a way, it is the language through which to examine and compare the various jargons of authenticity, or to reconcile the various conceptions of justice, rights and effectiveness. This reconciliation is always subject to criticism and change, but the state is never simply the values it seems to espouse at any moment, nor only the interests it most closely reflects. As Koskenniemi expresses it, the *polis* has not existed for the fulfilment of passions ulterior to itself, it has not existed to *provide* us with well-being: it has instead defined to us – differently in different times and places – what well-being means. It has not existed to realise just principles:

it has encapsulated justice in itself. Thus, he sees that the thesis of the withering away of the state is a thesis about the uselessness or unrealistic character of the concept of the *polis*, and of law: '[I]t is a tragical thesis that has found us unable to rule our public lives through conscious choice and debate, just as we are unable to control forces that dictate our private wishes. It holds that we must surrender the *polis* to an exterior purpose, to some self-evident certainty in no need of public reflection.' (Koskenniemi 1994: 27-29.)

Finally, the exclusion of both the state and of values from the analysis effectively hinders research from dealing with some of the most central questions concerning the changes in the locus and nature of authority, such as those pointed out by Strange (1995) as the new, important questions facing social scientists – who, in her view, shirk their responsibilities if they fail to think about them. After problems of war and peace – removed with the state-centrism – the question becomes, she argues, how to deal with the asymmetry of structural power. Another important question is the emerging void of authority. As authority in general has diminished, and some necessary authority once exercised by states is now exercised by no one, one needs to assess how much authority actually is needed, or how much rules, supervision and intervention by political authority is necessary for the system's continued stability, equity and prosperity, and where the authority is to come from. (Strange 1995: 56, 69-72.)

The questions cannot be answered if the state is excluded from the analysis; on the contrary, they suggest more consideration to the state, for instance in the form of the classical debate on the limits of state action, on how and to what extent to limit state action *vis-à-vis* the individual, or the questions of how to justify coercive institutions, what the state should do and how, that is, what is the nature of the best type of political regime. These, again, are questions about values, the importance of which could, in the end, also be justified by reference to their function as a motor of change.[51] Why, after all, should one see the state as something stable by nailing it down with some definitive statements on its nature, if it actually constantly changes through reflection of its internal and external environment?

From theory to practice: the inherited theoretical ambiguity and its implications for empirical research

With this third chapter, the book has come half-way towards its aim to help evaluate the plurality of scholarly answers to the question of the relationship between the state and integration. In chapter one, the question was noted to be both difficult and important to answer: it is about two basic concepts which form a nexus of a variety of theoretical debates, while having, at the same time, very concrete implications in practical politics. The analysis started from the idea that the 'consumers' and the 'producers' of academic knowledge on the question might not be well equipped to deal with the plurality of answers this question entails.

Dealing with plurality, or its evaluation, requires an understanding of the background of these answers, of how they are achieved and why they emerge. These aspects, however, tend to remain invisible in most research, as if they were self-evident. Indeed, when delineating the development of integration studies in chapter two, it was found out that the prevailing research practice was not particularly conducive to an analysis of the background of the views. Rather, emphasis was put on the 'fact' that integration studies progress through continuous adjustment to reality and refinement of theoretical standards. New and better views were continuously presented with an ever-improving explanatory capacity or correspondence with reality. The plurality of answers, therefore, was seen more or less as a temporary shortcoming of research in the field.

Chapter three put forward four 'whys' of the answers, four internal reasons which fundamentally shape the view of the state and integration. These were the methodological standpoint, the view of the aims of research, disciplinary boundaries, and values. While these factors do not determine the scholar's understanding on the state and integration, they involve fundamental choices as to how the subject is examined and written about. Reality cannot be approached without a stand being taken on these questions. This is obvious in questions of methodology, where the decision, e.g., to approach integration as comparable or incomparable to other cooperative phenomena makes a profound difference, but it is equally present in questions concerning values. In each domain, it was seen, what was at stake was a choice between two alternatives: those of seeing the state as good or bad, as efficient or not, as unitary or not, as rational or not and as autonomous or not, but also between seeing states as similar or different and institutions as 'mattering' or not. Symptomatically invisible, these choices connected integration studies to broader debates in international relations and social sciences in general.

This state of affairs leaves us with two theoretical conclusions. First, one has to admit that adopting a specific view, for instance, maintaining that integration weakens the state, or placing the various views in some order of correctness, may imply an even unintended stand taken on normative issues. In other words, one has to recognise the role which values play in evaluation.

Second, one has to admit that the questions are inherently double-sided, and that plurality is therefore an inherent characteristic of research. There is a continuous oscillation between two possible views on the nature of the state and integration, and the results of a piece of research are bound to reflect at best one half of the question. Therefore, our picture of each view, as well as of integration research as a whole, becomes decisively more complete when we make the effort towards taking into consideration several possibilities at the same time. While we thus are, on the one hand, better able to analyse the different facets of reality, we also understand better the internal functions of the plural interpretations in research: the different views need each other, both for the support they can gain because of the shortcomings of the others and for the possibility of development through criticism – perhaps also to maintain a debate which constitutes the field of research.

At this stage, the reader might agree in principle that various theories exist on the state and integration, and that choosing one among them is not necessarily as simple as we perhaps would like it. Yet, this study has now come only half-way and achieved only the first part of its task. Its final conclusions could not be drawn without combining the *practice* of research to the question of what research appears to be like in principle. Empirical cases are needed for understanding how the background choices influence practical research. Questions of the evaluation and development of research have to be taken to the level of particular events and phenomena in order to see how, in reality, a case study is written, and to give the reader the possibility of evaluating 'normal' research with the help of the factors previously identified. Moreover, without definite cases, one would not be able to see how the analysis of the state-integration relationship may have clear relevance also for political decision-making.

Some words of explanation on the nature of the case studies in this book are, however, needed. The reader, in fact, might still want to see *one* result, one picture of reality emerging as a result of the analysis, instead of being reminded that reality is hardly less complex than the world of our theoretical interpretations. Here, however, no 'one result' emerges. The role and form of case studies is somewhat uncommon. Most often, they serve the purpose of testing (read: validating) a proposed theory: they tend to be reassuring, even with no decisive role of their own. Counterfactuals that would contradict the study are seldom taken up; in fact, the theoretical framework might shape the presentation of the cases to appear in any case in harmony with the theory.

Here, the cases do not 'test' a view, for the aim is not to show that a case supports one or several stances, or to show that they are equally applicable.

The four views do not need such support. In the end, writing case studies that show that the state is weakened or strengthened by the process of integration would obviously not be uninteresting, but it would not produce any additional knowledge in comparison to the already known. Therefore, the case studies will not be constructed in a schematic way to follow precisely the four views on the state and integration analysed above. Their aim is to show the plurality of truth 'in reality' and reflect on how plural interpretations contribute to the understanding of specific examples. Conventional cases tend to be unhelpful in such evaluations of the research itself: they are unable to reflect on the choices made. The choices become visible only if alternative views are presented, too: the existence of several versions makes each of them appear as *a version* (cf. Allison in chapter one).

Two versions are therefore presented on the two cases, Nordic cooperation and Finnish integration policy. In both, the context is the time period roughly from 1992 to 1995, a period of debates on possible Finnish, Norwegian and Swedish membership of the EU. The debates concentrate on the consequences of membership, both for Finland and for Nordic cooperation. In simple terms, the question for Finland is whether to join or not, and for Nordic cooperation if it will face a serious challenge from integration in the EU and could or should something be done to protect it. The answers depend on the consequences of EU membership. Now, what are they? What do we know about them? Following the previous analysis, it is easy to see that the issue of consequences is a question of how the two parties influence each other. Thus, it is our basic question of the relationship between the state and integration put in concrete terms: will Finland become a mightier member of the European system, will Nordic cooperation cease to exist? This study has amply shown that various views exist, and that they are to a great extent formed by theoretical oscillations that cannot be resolved on factual grounds in favour of any of them. Our knowledge about the consequences is thus constructed on the basis of assumptions.

This becomes clear in the specific studies. In chapter 4, Nordic cooperation is seen to succumb to the EU; in version 5, it is seen to manage, even thrive, if not altogether be an example for European integration. In chapter 6, Finnish EU membership is seen to imply the beginning of a profound and partly involuntary change in the Finnish state, while in 7, it is but a logical continuation of Finnish integration policy, its aims and nature. These results are based on different assumptions or views on the requirements for efficient cooperation, on the nature of integration and on that of Nordic cooperation, on integration's influence on the state and the nature of the state.

178 The Plurality of Truth

Individually, the case studies are examples of normal research based mainly on secondary sources. They are to be seen as independent pieces of research, out of the immediate context of the precedent theoretical analyses. As normal case studies without any particular theoretical ambitions, they are not directly connected to any of the four views analysed previously: in their *genre*, questions such as 'what is the relationship between the state and integration' are seldom posed overtly. There are no apparent theoretical differences between the versions: their assumptions are only partly visible and tend to be built-in rather than explicit. Similarly, the versions take for granted many problematic conceptualisations. Neither do the cases themselves much refer to supporting theoretical literature. They are mere descriptive analyses – something that, in the end, tells a lot about our conventional views on what 'description' is. Finally, normal case studies do not contain references to the fact that they are only *versions;* so, neither do these cases. In fact, without the previous analysis, one would not probably recognise the choices made in their writing. With its help, however, what should be visible are not only the choices, but also the 'mechanism' through which choices lead to other choices, how logical accounts emerge – for example how the story of Finnish integration policy comes to follow rather different paths in the two accounts.

The versions are written on purpose for this study, in order to have as complete and comparable versions as possible, versions which, moreover, take into account the same facts. Thus, the differences between the accounts do not stem from their analysing different facts, but from their *interpreting* the very same facts in different ways, each following their own logic. This implies a considerable amount of repetition in the accounts, which the reader might find disturbing, but the idea is that the very repetition makes the research practice transparent and allows the reader to notice the differences in interpretation.

Put together, the cases can be said to build a rather confusing whole: they are incompatible and contradictory. This is a tangible manifestation of the 'whole', or the plurality of truth. In the final analysis, it is up to the reader to see the cases as confusing and the inconclusiveness as disturbing, or, alternatively, to recognise the role of this confusion in leading to reflection on why the versions are like they are despite their same factual contents.

It is argued here that the contribution of the cases is even wider. What we are able to observe through them is, first, the firm link to real politics and decision-making, something that reveals why the capacity to evaluate research is so fundamental in practice. Secondly, we acquire a more clear understanding of the bases of our knowledge and of how it is constructed: the cases function as examples of how knowledge is constructed on the level of 'mere' description. This becomes evident when asking how to give, in concrete terms, different interpretations of Nordic cooperation. Description is not neutral: from the moment the description of Nordic cooperation starts, the first choices are made regarding its nature. In fact, they appear in the very titles of the chapters. These choices, then, as will be seen, are directly linked to the basic oscillations on the state and integration with which the reader has been able to familiarise himself. They, together with the assumptions, are more closely analysed in the concluding chapter.

Thirdly, being transparent, the cases give additional material for conclusions on the choices made, compatibility and links between different views. Moreover, they provide information on the possibilities and limits of analysis; these will be taken up in the final chapter. The cases show that much more can be achieved in research than would be thought. Still, not everything may be possible in practical terms. Scholarly reasoning tends to – or is forced to – take sides and find evidence for one of them as the 'right' way of seeing a question.

Notes

1. When the question of the evaluation of theories is addressed, it is usually done by referring to some general criteria which are themselves seen to be beyond criticism. For example, see Vasquez's criteria of good theories which he deems 'standard in philosophy of science' and which include, e.g., accuracy and greater explanatory power, but also falsifiability and consistency with what is known in other areas (John A. Vasquez: 'The Post-Positivist Debate: Reconstructing Scientific Enquiry and International Relations Theory After Enlightenment's Fall', in Booth and Smith (1995); p. 230 *et passim*); similarly Sørensen (1991: 92). However, although these criteria may serve in criticising others, they seem of scant help in constructing something not exposed to the same criticism.
2. Cf. Hannah Arendt, 'Lying in Politics: Reflections on the Pentagon Papers', in *Crisis of the Republic*, Harvest/HBJ, San Diego, New York, London; quoted in Wæver 1994: 22.
3. Further, Hix (1994) sees that neofunctionalism and intergovernmentalism may still be valid for the explanation of integration, while comparative politics approaches are more suitable for explaining Community politics. Pollack, in turn, suggests that while intergovernmentalism applies to redistributive policies, supranationalism characterises regulatory policies (see Pollack, Mark A. (1994): 'Creeping Competence: The Expanding Agenda of the European Community' in *Journal of Public Policy*, vol. 14

(2), pp. 95-145).
4. Examples of the idea of a division of labour are not difficult to find in any period. For instance, Grieco refers to this kind of division in explaining different forms of interstate relations in maintaining that realism is typically the form of analysis for relations between adversaries; except for military alliances, realism is not usually applied to relations among states which are on friendly terms (Grieco 1990: 14). He even uses this specialisation in testing the views against each other: for him, the superiority of realism is better demonstrated by applying it to a field where it has not usually been applied. (For Grieco, realism is 'analytically superior' to liberalism: 'from a logical viewpoint', it offers a more complete understanding of the effects of anarchy on states and the problem of international cooperation than liberalism does as it identifies one consequence of anarchy which liberalism does not, the fear for survival and problem of relative gains). (*Idem:* 29, 49.)
5. Seeing international relations theory as state-centric can be taken either as a misunderstanding or a tactical choice of representation; cf. the discussion on how a somewhat simplified image of international relations theory was used in justifying the preferability of domestic politics theories in the analysis of integration in chapter 2.
6. For examples as well as for a further elaboration on the theme, see Wæver (1994) and Guzzini (1992); for a different view on the self-images of the discipline, see Smith (1995).
7. For Wæver (1994: 11), the inter-paradigm debate was perhaps partly a real debate, partly a constructed one, invented for specific presentational purposes, teaching and self-reflection of the discipline.
8. More on the debate and its main themes see, e.g., editor's introduction in Baldwin, David (ed.), *Neorealism and Neoliberalism: The Contemporary Debate,* New York: Columbia University Press, 1993. Wæver maintains, thus, that a central debate between two opposite views turned into a synthesis which became the dominant research programme of the 1980s. The two became increasingly compatible; the participants of the debate were striving to set up a joint framework, a 'rationalist' research programme, and they came to share a conception of science, a shared willingness to operate on the premise of anarchy, shared interest in the evolution of cooperation, and shared research questions, such as whether institutions matter and why cooperation is possible despite the anarchy. Wæver maintains, thus, that a central debate between two opposite views turned into a synthesis which became the dominant research programme of the 1980s. The two became increasingly compatible; the participants of the debate were striving to set up a joint framework, a 'rationalist' research programme, and they came to share a conception of science, a shared willingness to operate on the premise of anarchy, shared interest in the evolution of cooperation, and shared

Causes and consequences 181

9. research questions, such as whether institutions matter and why cooperation is possible despite the anarchy.

9. Structure is thus reconceptualised as a set of rules which serves as both medium and outcome of state agency; the international system is conceptualised in terms of constitutive and regulative rules which condition the possibilities of state action and are reproduced and transformed as a combined result of its intended and unintended consequences. Thus, the international system is dependent on the actual practice of states, which is made possible by the system itself.

10. See also Lindberg, Leon N.: 'The European Community as a Political System: Notes toward the Construction of a Model', *Journal of Common Market Studies*, vol. 5 (4) 1967, pp. 344-387.

11. Basing the study on Easton's *'A Systems Analysis of Political Life'* (and using also the RA index, cf. above), they use data on attitudes and behaviour and achieve rather mixed results (*idem:* 60-62, 99-100).

12. See, e.g., Garrett, G., 'International Cooperation and Institutional Choice: The European Community's Internal Market' in *International Organization*, vol. 46, pp. 533-560, or Garrett and Weingast, *Ideas, Interests and Institutions: Constructing the EC's Internal Market* (paper presented at APSA annual meeting, Washington D.C., September 1991); for the analyses of voting power in the common institutions, Widgrén (1995); on rational choice approaches in general, Hix (1994: 12-20).

13. E.g., when Lindberg and Scheingold present an equation for explaining and predicting system change ($Ds=f[(S+Su)(Dd+Dl)]+e_n$), they actually do not accomplish more than a replacement of words with symbols, the meaning of the assumption thus clothed being that change in a system (Ds) is a function of the system (S), systemic support (Su), change in demand (Dd) and change in leadership (Dl), with the addition of the panacea of a general error term (e_n). The problem obviously is how to get further, how to operationalise the variables to give them countable values. Even though the authors are careful to specify the limits of their models and equations – in fact, the equation is not used in the book – and specify that '[T]he model cannot posit quantitative relationships among the variables [...]', they nevertheless see this shortcoming as temporary: '[...] since we do not *yet* have quantitative scales for their measurement. Hence, its use at this stage is essentially heuristic. More concrete applications implying efforts to operationalize and quantify are possible, however.' (Lindberg and Scheingold 1970: 114-115, footnote 18; emphasis added.)

14. In Haas (1958, preface 1968), the ECSC is found to be what it was defined in the first place. Integration is defined as a process whereby values and behaviour change, and the ECSC is defined as an instance of integration; thus, it is logical that values change – even though the brevity of the period

studied make value changes appear more surprising. Much is taken as given: both the nature of the ECSC as a special, supranational organisation and the identification of unifying agents are assumed, or taken as verified by previous studies. Cf. the introductory statement according to which Haas studies 'the selected groups, institutions and ideologies which have already been demonstrated to act as unifying agents in political systems clearly "integrated" by any applicable standards and the one organisation *a priori* capable of redirecting the loyalties and expectations of political actors, namely the ECSC.' (*Idem:* xxxii.)

15. Notably Morton A. Kaplan, *System and Process in International Politics* (New York, Wiley 1957); cf. also volume XIV of *World Politics* (1/1961) which contains a whole spectrum of system theoretical approaches, including optometry, and articles about the applications to integration, e.g., Lindberg, Leon N.: 'The European Community as a Political System: Notes toward the Construction of a Model', *Journal of Common Market Studies*, vol. 5 (4) 1967, pp. 344-387. Haas refers also to Talcott Parsons, *The Social System* (The Free Press, Glencoe, Ill., 1951, pp. 27 and 36), to Robert K. Merton, *Social Theory and Social Structure* (The Free Press, Glencoe, Ill., revised edition 1957, pp. 30-36) and to Alger's application of Easton, Almond and Riggs to integration studies in *American Political Science Review*, vol. LVII, 1963.

16. Haas exemplifies this on at least two occasions. In 1948, he saw that military cooperation was the first step towards integration; considering the general will or interest towards a (con)federation and the measures thus far taken, he concluded that 'the way toward European unity, in which sovereignty will inhere predominantly in the central authority, will apparently proceed through military alliance and economic integration to confederation, and then on to final full federation.' (Haas 1948: 550.) In 1964, he concluded that integration 'must be expected to proceed in line with the forces here outlined, without significant acceleration over the present rate'; it will come about in the same unplanned and almost accidental fashion that has dominated in the past. (Haas 1964: 484, 492, 496.)

17. The problem obviously is that one cannot know in which of these three the error lies.

18. In *Politics and Government: How People Decide Their Fate*, Houghton Mifflin, Boston 1970, p. ix.

19. The scientific approach is in fact characterised by remarkable optimism, either about the potential of the tools already constructed – as when Haas (1970: 638) asserts that '[T]he multiple dependent variable we have devised enables us to specify to whom the authority and legitimacy have been transferred' – or about the possibilities of continuous improvement, visible in Haas' statement that 'political community' cannot *yet* be observed or

measured in nature (similarly, Lindberg and Scheingold 1970 and Kaplan 1966).
20. Wæver argues that the clear polarisation between rationalists and reflectivists in the 1980s was turned in the 1990s into increasing rapprochement as regards, e.g., sovereignty. Rationalists have admitted the existence of 'deep conventions' and thereby moved towards acknowledging the role of constitutive principles like sovereignty, very close to the writings of some reflectivists, while both the extreme rationalists (rational choice) and the extreme 'anti-IR' approaches (deconstructivists) have been increasingly marginalised. (Wæver 1992: 178 and 1994: 14- 17.)
21. This is the case for, e.g., 'independent' and 'dependent' variables or hypotheses and their testing. Without necessarily implying that the hypotheses should or could somehow be tested, many scholars use the 'technique' of presenting their research first in the form of hypotheses and then in that of results. Hypotheses of this type can be found in both explicit and implicit forms. An example of a normal hypothesis testing could be Mutimer's (1989: 100) statement that if the removal of internal borders with the consequent need for a common immigration policy is effected but does not result in substantial centralisation of decision-making, it is reasonable to conclude that there are problems with the spillover hypothesis.
22. If the question of the criteria is posed at all, reference seems typically to be made to Lakatos, whose 'auxiliary hypotheses' seem appealing for the purpose of keeping the theory 'whole' while 'recognising various roads to salvation within it' (Haas 1970: 642; cf. references to Lakatos' views in Moravcsik 1993a, Matlary 1994 and Grieco 1995). As suitable auxiliary hypotheses, one might see the specifications concerning the applicability of the various theories through distinguishing between the nature of decisions, formal and informal integration, etc. described above as ways to reconcile the different theories.
23. In integration studies, e.g., Alger (1981). As an example of the discussion on whether or not a theory explains change, see the debate between Hoffmann and Strange on regime theory (*International Organization*, vol. 36).
24. While impressive pictures of this complexity are given in the literature (see, e.g., Wessels' [1992: 55] above mentioned three different scenarios for the development of the state in Western Europe which all take place simultaneously), one can hardly find a point in the past or in the future when reality was or would be less complex. Again, the problem is not limited to integration studies. Current circumstances seem invariably more complex than the past, irrespective of the field of study. In fact, even 'power' was once an uncomplicated term, if one is to believe Herz who suggests that in the past power was something measurable and calculable and served as a standard of comparison between units which were impermeable, and that it

made sense to consider the power units as politically independent and legally sovereign. Now, he argues, this can no longer be made due to changes in territoriality caused by economic, psychological and nuclear warfare – something that also leads to the conclusion that 'the state' is no longer a useful concept. (Herz 1957: 486-487, 473-475.)

25. Haas seems to have a special quest for the new and the (therefore) important. In 1948, he was fascinated by the unprecedented activities in establishing new international organisations; later, he shifted his analysis from integration to the new, more important phenomena of interdependence (Haas 1975).

26. The way in which Haas defined 'integration' served the purpose of differentiating between the fields of study. As was noted above, integration led in his view to specific new forms of interaction between states; this did not happen in other regional organisations. At the same time, when Haas claims that cooperative state behaviour is new and results from integration, he rather confirms than discredits the realist confidence on the fact that states never cooperate otherwise, or that they never learn, make concessions or sacrifice their purposes. (Haas 1970: 608, 611-612.) – For a comparable justification of the realist view as addressing a subject of its own, see James (1989).

27. The rises and falls of the popularity of integration have often been associated with the bursts and halts of the process of European integration itself. After having been relatively popular in the 1960s and early 1970s, integration studies became somewhat disregarded after mid-1970s, and regained energy from the mid-1980s.

28. In the index to *Paix et guerre entre les nations* (first but also the subsequent editions), words such as 'European Economic Community' or 'integration' cannot be found; the nearest would perhaps be 'Europe and the concept of state'. The phenomenon of integration can be found, finally, in the chapter 'Au-delà de la politique de puissance' the first part of which is on international law (paix par la loi) and the second (paix par l'empire) on sovereignty and federations.

29. Taylor, in turn, proposes that the conviction of statesmen about the virtual impossibility to act in Europe without further transfer of authority, or to increase the scope of integration without increasing its level was probably wrong, the statesmen being victims of their own rhetoric in euphoric moments and of a mistaken strategy by the Commission (Taylor 1983: 113).

30. In fact, integration would not necessarily contribute to peace; it might worsen the situation by magnifying conflicts: 'Croire que l'unité européenne serait pacifique alors que les nations étaient belliqueuses serait reproduire l'erreur de ceux qui croyaient que les nations seraient pacifiques alors que les rois avaient été belliqueux' (Aron 1962: 300).

31. Waltz also reserves the word 'integration' for the national realm and 'interdependence' – in the sense of a looser connection – for the international realm. As states are like units, interdependence among them is low as compared to the close integration of the parts in a domestic order. Further, the growing interdependence between states, caused by increased international activity, is for Waltz a unit level characteristic and thus it has no profound importance for the system as such. (Waltz 1979: 144-145, 204.)
32. Cf. notably Sjöstedt (1981) for an earlier, more thorough analysis of the actor capability of the EC and, more generally, the problem of how to define an actor and assess its autonomy as an actor.
33. However, Hoffmann also notes a paradox in that the absence of a defence community is, at the same time, a weakness of the state and of the integrated entity as a whole.
34. James also notes that reaching the point of 'no return' is neither likely, nor particularly important: even if this point was reached for the members, it would not challenge *sovereignty as such*, as other states would hardly follow the model.
35. For Grieco, adjustability is an asset to the theory: referring to Lakatos, he argues that a good theory has to be both adjustable and not less useful than its rivals (Grieco 1995: 26-27).
36. This way of thinking unites several different strains of theories: it makes new institutionalism and realism match quite well (see Keohane) and, indeed, connects Haas with realists; also for Haas, calculation on the basis of interests was the foremost motive for governmental action (see Haas 1958).
37. As to 'sovereignty', the question of how much transfer of sovereignty 'matters', what actually is lost when sovereignty diminishes, and, naturally, whether sovereignty is a countable which can exist in different degrees are all matters of viewpoint. The background problem is whether the 'common' (authority, institutions) increases or reduces the 'own' and whether the state can perish through its own actions, which is also a problem of rationality (cf. above).
38. For Hix, there are, however, two refinements of intergovernmentalism which attempt to address these drawbacks. The preference-convergence approach (Bulmer 1983) sees that integration proceeds as a result of converging policy preferences among the major member states, and that these preferences are results of domestic political factors. In the elite-bargaining approach, then, the state is not monolithic, but there is a rational zero-sum bargaining; also the two-level game between domestic and international elites is referred to (e.g., Sandholtz and Zysman, '1992: Recasting the European Bargain', *World Politics* 41 (1) 1989).
39. See, e.g., Robert Dahl, *Who Governs? Democracy and Power in an American City* (New Haven, Yale University Press, 1961).

40. On the other hand, state-centrism and realism often appear like the villainous strawmen of the story. Bull reminds that the term 'statist' is applied in a pejorative sense to describe those unable to free themselves from the bad old ways, while 'it is difficult to believe that anyone ever asserted the "states-centric" view of international politics that is today so knowingly rejected by those who seek to emphasise the role "the new international actors" ' (Bull 1979: 111-112).

41. When looking at Koskenniemi (above) on legal argumentation, one sees the dilemma in international law which results from the difficulty in deciding whether a state is a state because of some subjective criteria, that is, whether the state really defines itself, or because of some objective criteria, being defined collectively – i.e., what comes first, the system or the state? The criteria for statehood is seen as a question of 'sufficient' isolation, independence or sovereignty from other states and entities. On the other hand, the internal matters of a state are excluded from the intervention from the part of other states which makes the definition of the state an internal matter at the discretion of the states themselves.

42. As practical examples, Taylor points out that as constraints emerged on the independent ability of Britain to control its own economy, the British simply changed their view about the outer edges of sovereign action. He also refers to the example of military contingency planning, which used to be seen by the states as a matter of their exclusive sovereignty. In NATO, however, joint planning became the norm without creating the sense that sovereignty had been endangered. Precisely the opposite was the case: giving up an outmoded condition of sovereignty came to be seen as necessary in order to preserve sovereignty.

43. This is particularly visible in concrete empirical cases such as how to anticipate or evaluate the possible consequences of EU membership for a country in economic terms, cases in which it is clear that something will change, although the causes of the changes are very unclear and it is difficult to assess how significant they will be or when they will take place; cf. chapters four and five.

44. Whether or not these policies correspond to societal preferences is related to representativeness or, in Nordlinger's terms, how the public officials carry out, ignore and circumvent their representative responsibilities. In general terms, it is assumed that the goals of public officials comprise the realisation of both autonomy and societal support. (Nordlinger 1981: 206.)

45. This discussion can be directly linked to the views of integration as strengthening the state. Navari argues that the international element is used to resolve the problem presented by the state seen as free from society and capable of autonomous action, though still in some relation to society. She refers to Skocpol and Giddens, for whom the state's participation in an

international system of competition both frees the state elite and yet keeps it chained to some social 'reality'. (Navari 1991a: 10.) Skocpol notes that the state's involvement in an international network of states is a basis for potential autonomy of action over and against inside groups, also the dominant class (quoted in Nordlinger 1981: 23). Accordingly, integration is pointed out as one aspect of international relations which increases the autonomy of the state, either through the increased problem-solving capacity (Kahler 1987: 299-302) or through increasing independence from society (Halliday 1991: 196, 199-200). In fact, Halliday (1994: 78-80) argues that seeing how and why international participation strengthens the state requires distinguishing between the state and society and understanding the relation between the two as variable. Cerny (1990: 96-102), in turn, sees that the international system can help maintain the state as a structure.

46. A study of integration based on the assumption of state similarity obviously yields quite different results from those based on the assumption that states are different and that, accordingly, the relationship between the state and integration is also variable. In practice, assuming state similarity simplifies the analysis. Differentiating between states is not unproblematic: a mere distinction between large and small states (e.g., Aron [1963: 52] who notes that an integrated Europe gives better safeguards to the *small states* than a Europe composed of sovereign states) leads to endless discussions on what constitutes a small state.

47. In Alger's view, integration scholars have not differed from other scholars in international relations: 'they have rarely freed themselves from the outlooks of those whose actions they study. Rather, the hallmark of their craft has been legitimization of the operating theories of these officials by translating them into scholarly language. In the process they have also legitimized these practitioners in the eyes of the public at large by accepting their self-proclaimed roles in world affairs – an important part of their operating theories' (Alger 1981: 137).

48. Deutsch even estimates that these machineries will be needed – for national defence and for immigration control – until about 2200 A.D. Afterwards, only the provision of services and the production of goods will be left under the administration of the state.

49. Cf. the special issues of *Dædalus* (vol. 124 (2) 1995, 'What Future for the State'), *Political Studies* (vol. XLII, 1994, 'Contemporary Crisis of the Nation State?') and *West European Politics* (vol. 17 (3) 1994, 'The State in Western Europe – Retreat or Redefinition?').

50. The assessment may not only be influenced by diminishing capabilities and the growing gap between the causal capacities of states and the demands placed upon them (Dunn 1994: 5, 11), but also by the growing expectations of the state – Bull (1979: 119) notes how states are presumed to facilitate,

e.g., the management of world economy, the eradication of world poverty, the promotion of racial equality and women's rights, or the raising of literacy and labour standards.
51. Cf. Habermas *(Knowledge and human interests,* 1968), who objects to the exclusion of value judgements as this undermines critical opposition to existing structures of domination and drives the discussion on the 'good life' out of politics (cf. Lessnoff 1988: 800).

4 Opting for integration: the slow retreat of Nordic cooperation

EU enlargement: a push towards a necessary reappraisal of Nordic cooperation

Codified in the Helsinki Agreement of 1962 and institutionalised in the Nordic Council and the Nordic Council of Ministers, Nordic cooperation – between the five Nordic countries, Denmark, Finland, Iceland, Norway and Sweden – encompasses a wide variety of activities. In the Nordic countries, it has come to assume an imprint of something self-evident; it has for decades enjoyed unanimous popularity among both Nordic politicians and the public, being even above criticism or censure. Outside *Norden*, in turn, the Nordic[1] countries are commonly perceived and treated as a unit.

However, with the signing of the Treaty on the European Economic Area, the decisions by Finland, Norway and Sweden to apply for EU membership and, above all, the membership attained by Finland and Sweden, axiomatic Nordic cooperation has increasingly been called into question. Not only are three of the five countries now EU members; the EU has itself developed considerably from the EC Denmark joined in 1973. In this new situation, the political activities, time and resources of the member countries are increasingly concentrated on the EU. The same is true for the two countries outside the EU, Iceland and Norway, involved in the process of integration directly through the EEA and indirectly through the practical necessity of taking into account developments in the EU. The decisions and policies of the Union have nowadays a fundamental importance for the policies of the Nordic countries, whether members or not.

This new centrality of the EU for the Nordic countries implies a multiplication of the fields and forms of their participation in international collaboration, notably a new binding and supranational character of that participation. At the same time, it implies an unintentional duplication of work, as matters traditionally dealt with in Nordic institutions now appear also in the EU ones. This calls into question the appropriateness of a separate Nordic level of cooperation. Not only might Nordic cooperation now be less central and interesting for Nordic politicians; it might also be less needed. Moreover, it might become altogether impossible, either for the simple reason of feasibility, in view of the limited resources, or because of its incompatibility with the binding nature of EU membership. Therefore, a re-evaluation of the achievements and nature of Nordic cooperation is imperative in order to judge whether it still involves such specific features or extends to fields that justify a purely Nordic cooperation within the larger context of European integration, or whether one should recognise that it now has definitively become a second order issue for the Nordic countries.

The symptomatic failures of the grand designs in security and economy

In the long history of Nordic collaboration, far-reaching plans for cooperation between the Nordic countries have been presented. In particular, those in the fields of security policy and economy have even come close to the establishment of what could be called a Nordic union, or, to borrow Franzén's (1944) term, the United States of Scandinavia. Symptomatically, however, the wider European schemes of cooperation have always outweighed the purely Nordic plans in the vital fields of security and economy. The decisions of the Nordic countries to opt for the EEA and the EU are therefore not unforeseen but a continuation of this familiar pattern.

In security policy, the most far-reaching plans for cooperation were presented by Sweden in the late 1940s. Nordic cooperation in matters of security had before that been mainly limited to the joint declarations of neutrality by Denmark, Norway and Sweden during the two world wars. Other plans had not been particularly successful: the Stockholm plan on cooperation between Finland and Sweden for the defence of the Åland Islands, presented in 1939, was never implemented due to opposition from the Soviet Union (Wendt 1981: 25-26), and, well before that, the Danish initiative for a Scandinavian defence alliance in 1864 against the German threat collapsed as the other countries adopted a neutral position when Denmark was attacked.

The intensification of the cold war in the late 1940s, however, gave initial impetus towards increased Scandinavian defence cooperation, and Sweden presented an initiative to coordinate the defence policies of the Scandinavian countries as an alliance outside the two rival blocs. Negotiations with Denmark and Norway began in 1948. However, both countries were cautious about the capabilities of such an alliance. For them, access to Western strategic material was vital, and this also destroyed the foundation for a Scandinavian defence union. The United States, in response to the Danish request of arms for the Nordic Alliance, made arms deliveries conditional upon a Nordic membership of NATO, and, in fact, Norway and Denmark joined NATO in 1949. (Etzioni 1965: 198-199; Turner 1982: 113-115; Wendt 1981: 27-28.)

Iceland also joined NATO, and in 1951 it signed a defence agreement with the United States which led to the establishment of a military base in Keflavík (Turner 1982: 116-117; Jervell 1991a: 27). Finland had signed a pact on mutual friendship, cooperation and assistance with the Soviet Union in 1948 recognising in principle Finland's wish to remain neutral in conflicts between the blocs. At the same time, the pact forbade the signatories from entering into alliances directed against each other, something which for some years hampered Finland's participation even in Nordic cooperation, regarded by the Soviet Union as a camouflage for links to the West. Finally, Sweden remained neutral, bolstering its neutrality with a strong national defence.

Thus divided by their orientations in security policy in NATO allies[2] and neutrals, with the specific Finnish concern for not taking risks in its relations to the Soviet Union, it was clear that Nordic cooperation in the fields of foreign and defence policy was not appropriate. There were instances in which foreign affairs were discussed, such as the informal ministerial meetings related to common concerns in the United Nations, but in the formal context of the Nordic Council, it was understood to be natural that the Council refrain from considering problems related to defence or foreign policy. Although no formal reservations on this point were made, parliamentary debates in Sweden and Norway confirmed the view that Nordic cooperation did not include defence or foreign policy matters and that these matters were outside the competencies of the Nordic Council. (Wendt 1981: 343-344.)

This general agreement and the overall low profile of the Nordic Council notwithstanding, Finland could not join the Council from the beginning. The Finnish representatives could not accept the proposed statutes due to the highly critical attitude of the Soviet Union towards Nordic cooperation which saw the Council as a tool of forces behind NATO. Together with the general relaxation in international relations in 1955, however, this view changed; objections to Finnish membership were removed and Finland became member of the Council before the end of that year. To remove all uncertainties, Finland emphasised the non-political nature of the Council. Moreover, a reservation was made stating that the Finnish representatives should not participate in discussions if the Council, against accepted practice, were to discuss military questions or questions which would lead to adopting a position on conflicts of interest between the great powers. (Wendt 1981: 35-37, 343-344.)

In fact, international questions were until the 1990s rather marginal, if not totally absent from the agenda of the Nordic Council. To a large extent, discussions on foreign affairs revolved around the question of whether these kinds of issues could be discussed at all. Some regarded discussion as possible, without claiming, however, that the Nordic Council could attempt to interfere with the member states' attitudes concerning foreign affairs. For the majority, matters of foreign and security policy did not belong to the field of the Council; therefore, no explicit exclusion of these issues from the Council's work was considered necessary. (Wendt 1981: 249-250.)

The Finnish initiative on a Nordic nuclear weapon free zone has been one of the most persistent issues of discussion linked to foreign policy and security. For Wiberg (1986: 5), it is also one of the failed grand schemes for Nordic cooperation. Having been debated for the first time in 1964-1966, the issue returned on several occasions; only in the late 1980s, some measures were taken when a study group was established to investigate the issue. Other proposals of a similar nature, such as the proposal for a Nordic security and cooperation agreement to refrain from the use of force or the threat of it, were rejected without any support and, consequently, led to no action. Reference was also made to the need to avoid ill-considered changes in foreign policy issues and to the fact that the Nordic Council was not the right forum for their treatment. (For an extensive account, see Wendt 1981: 249, 347-348, 350-358; see also Joenniemi 1990: 212.)

Comments on international affairs outside the purely Nordic sphere were even more occasional. The Council was forced to consider a lengthy dispute between Iceland and the United Kingdom over Iceland's fishing limits which began in 1954 (see Wendt 1981: 356-367, 388-394). The cautious attitude of the Council was reflected particularly when, in 1964, a proposal was presented for a recommendation to support the United Nations' declaration of 1963 on the elimination of racial discrimination in South Africa. No action was taken: it was emphasised that it was not expedient for the Council to deal with matters of such an internationally controversial character in the light of the pre-judicial effect for the future which could result from an initiative from the Council. (*Idem:* 249.)

In the field of economy, a more concerted effort was made to achieve cooperation in the form of a Nordic customs union or common market. Economic cooperation between the Scandinavian countries also had deeper roots than political cooperation. In the 19th century, there had even been a Scandinavian Monetary Union between Denmark, Norway and Sweden (Wendt 1981: 92-100). The 19th century proposals for customs union had not, however, been realised. In the 1930s, the Scandinavian countries had collaborated as parties to the Oslo agreement together with the Benelux countries. The agreement aimed at common principles in foreign trade policy and prevention of increase in customs duties (Wallensteen et al. 1973: 50, 53). While planning for a purely Nordic arrangement, however, the Nordic countries kept an eye on developments in Europe – developments which, in the end, made these plans redundant.

The specific negotiations for a Nordic customs union started in 1947, originally as a response to pressure from the United States to form regional groupings to qualify for Marshall aid (e.g., Nielsson 1978: 288). Denmark, Iceland, Norway and Sweden formed in 1948 a Joint Nordic Committee for Economic Cooperation to plan for common tariffs and a customs union. The negotiations proceeded rather spasmodically: there were two waves of negotiations between 1947 and 1954 which both collapsed due to disaccord on the range of cooperation as well as to Norway's reluctance. Nevertheless, it was Norway who took the initiative for new discussions soon after the decision on NATO membership, prompting the second wave of negotiations in 1950. This initiative was, however, partly aimed to be a remedy or compensation for the ensuing new division between the Nordic countries regarding their security arrangements,[3] and, for Norway, perhaps more motivated by the need to make NATO politically acceptable than by the sake of customs union itself (Jervell 1991a: 27).

The final committee report of 1954 judged the customs union plan unacceptable both economically and politically. The economies of the three countries differed considerably. Free trade in agricultural products would have exposed Norwegian and Swedish agriculture to potentially destructive competition from Denmark, with the ensuing risks of a gradual depopulation of large rural areas. Moreover, Norway was against the proposed dismantling of tariffs and restrictions as they would not have benefited its industry, which was not export-oriented like those of Denmark and Sweden. (Wendt 1981: 102-104.)

This negative view notwithstanding, the plan persisted: the negotiations resumed and a third round was undertaken from 1954 to 1959. It was motivated by, on the one hand, the recovery of Norwegian industry, which gave greater confidence in the beneficial effects of a customs union. On the other, it was also thought that a Nordic customs union and industrial investments could be competitive with Germany; as the Marshall plan was ending, other investments were needed in order to guarantee economic growth.[4]

Meanwhile, the Nordic Council had been established; it encouraged the negotiations by recommending in 1954 that the governments prepare the conditions for a common Nordic market, with Finland also taking part in the ensuing governmental investigations. In 1957, a new committee report was issued, together with a draft convention for Nordic economic cooperation. (Wendt 1981: 104-105, 109.) Now, however, the plans were discussed in a new light. While 'the Six' - Belgium, the Netherlands, Luxembourg, France, Germany and Italy - meeting in Messina in 1955 and Venice in 1956, prepared a plan for an economic union, the United Kingdom, a major trading partner of the Nordic countries, had requested in 1956 the OEEC[5] to examine prospects for the creation of a European free trade area including the six, the United Kingdom and other interested countries. Thus, the question became whether or not a Nordic market should also be established; without doubt, the Nordic countries would follow the United Kingdom. An additional Nordic arrangement was induced by the fact that it would make it possible for the Nordic countries to form a united front in free trade negotiations; moreover, a Nordic common market would be useful for Finland, which otherwise might be isolated as it could not become a member of a Western European trade area. Some perceived the Nordic arrangement as useless, even harmful. Danish farmers began to think that the Nordic customs union would prevent Danish EEC membership, which they believed necessary. (Wendt 1981: 105-107.)

Despite the differences in the attitudes of the Scandinavian countries about the solution to be chosen,[6] the agreement on a Nordic common market was, indeed, very nearly achieved in 1959. Even Finland seemed to be ready for such a move, and when the Nordic prime ministers met in Kungälv that year, it was announced that the Finnish government was prepared to propose to parliament to join the Nordic common market. It soon became clear, however, that there was no such thing to join. Instead of approving the plan, the meeting conveyed a tacit understanding that it was to be abandoned. The Nordic option had lost ground faced with the parallel investigations the three Scandinavian countries had conducted together with the United Kingdom, Portugal, Switzerland and Austria about the possibilities of a free trade area

Opting for integration 195

among themselves. Already in July 1959, the seven signed the Stockholm Convention establishing the European Free Trade Agreement, EFTA, which came into effect in 1960.

As a result of EFTA, tariff barriers were removed in Scandinavia and trade increased. A specific Finnefta agreement (1961) gave Finland for practical purposes the status of a member state, and Finland could also benefit from this increase (see Turner 1982: 132-133). In short, as Sundelius and Wiklund note (1979: 64), what had been impossible to accomplish during twelve years of Nordic negotiations had suddenly been reached within a broader perspective in less than a year, from 1959 to 1960. Purely Nordic cooperation in economic matters continued in the form of meetings between the heads of the trade departments of the Nordic foreign ministries and a permanent committee of economic ministers (Wendt 1981: 111-115).

Plans for a Nordic common market had, however, not yet been completely forgotten. When the attempt of some EFTA members to join the EEC failed, the 'second-best' Nordic option once again became appealing. When in 1961 Britain announced its decision to apply for EEC membership, it was followed by Denmark and Norway, while Sweden applied for association allowing certain trade concessions without corresponding political involvement (Turner 1982: 136). The entry negotiations, however, were ended by France's veto in 1963. Roughly the same sequence of events was repeated in 1967; Sweden's renewed application for the closest possible association agreement in line with neutrality never got beyond the stage of formal submission (Turner 1982: 160; Wendt 1981: 123-124).[7]

Due to the delay in the EEC plans, Denmark was now particularly receptive to the idea of a Nordic economic community, and on its initiative at the 1968 session of the Nordic Council, an examination of common market interests and economic and trade cooperation was again undertaken. In the meantime, the Nordic countries – excluding Iceland – had successfully cooperated in the Kennedy Round of the GATT negotiations on tariff reductions (1966-1967) acting as a bloc through a joint negotiating delegation. This common front was perhaps not a unique phenomenon – this particular GATT round had also been reported to be a success for the EEC's common trade policy, as the EEC acted there as a unit. Nevertheless, the Nordic countries, the largest trading partner of the EEC, effectively counteracted the EEC and other countries seeking to exclude important Nordic exports from the offer of tariff reductions. (Wendt 1981: 122; Turner 1982: 139.) This success without doubt facilitated the agreement to take new steps in cooperation, the aim of which was, however, now more clearly to ease participation in an expanded European market.

This was the start of the negotiations on an organisation of Nordic economic cooperation, or NORDEK.[8] A draft treaty was promptly finished in 1969. The formation of a customs union was a required condition for GATT acceptance of mutual concessions exclusively between Nordic countries. It was also a prerequisite for effective common trade policy; it would prevent the distortion of imports in favour of Denmark and Norway which had lower tariffs for raw materials and semi-manufactured goods than Sweden. NORDEK was to give a push towards full coordination of the four economies – Iceland aimed to join the NORDEK later, after having joined EFTA (Turner 1982: 109).

The NORDEK plan was, in fact, extensive. It contained provisions on economic policy, capital movement, tariffs and trade policies, shipping, energy and industrial policy, agriculture and fisheries, land transport, labour market and social welfare, state supportive measures, public procurement, control of business methods hindering competition, right of establishment, harmonisation of legislation, education, research, development aid and financial assistance. It also contained the establishment of new organs for cooperation – notably the Nordic Council of Ministers and an independent NORDEK secretariat – and regulations on the introduction of common tariffs towards countries outside EFTA. (Wendt 1981: 119-121, 125-129; Solem 1977: 83.)

Public opinion being broadly favourable to NORDEK, the Nordic countries' views on what NORDEK actually would be differed considerably. For Finland, it was particularly important to know whether NORDEK would be permanent or transitional: it emphasised NORDEK's value in itself rather than as a launching pad for EEC membership. Sweden could perhaps have accepted NORDEK as an alternative to the EEC; Denmark and Norway, however, were in favour of Nordic cooperation only if it was not a hindrance to EEC membership. There were further differences as to the possible supranational features of NORDEK. Denmark, while preferring the EEC, was not opposed to a union-like NORDEK with, for example, a common agricultural policy and capable of exercising supranational authority. Norway, however, was hostile to supranationality, above all in defence policy. In fact, the preamble of the NORDEK treaty was to state, confirming the practice in the Nordic Council, that cooperation should not impinge on the foreign or security policies of the members; it should not be seen as an invitation to

NATO forces to extend their area of influence. (Wendt 1981: 128, 133-135; see also 346-347, 351.)

1969 was, however, also a turning point in the EEC enlargement process: after the resignation of de Gaulle, there were no obstacles to beginning the negotiations with the applicants. This obviously coloured the NORDEK negotiations. Finland became more cautious. It announced that it would be prepared to complete the talks only conditionally: it reserved itself the right to refrain from continuing the negotiations and from implementing the treaty in case any country initiated official negotiations aiming at a connection with the EEC, either before or after the NORDEK treaty came into force. It also required that a general provision be added to the treaty stating that all participants had the right to refrain from implementing it if any country reached a decision on a connection with the EEC after the NORDEK agreement was approved. These conditions being accepted, the Nordic Council approved the NORDEK proposal in February 1970, and the treaty was to come into force on 1 January 1971 with the establishment of institutions. The customs union was to take effect one year later. (Wendt 1981: 131-132.)

In March 1970, however, Finland announced that it was not prepared to sign the treaty, although, as it stated, it was satisfied with its contents and still supported the intensification of Nordic cooperation. The announcement, a surprise for the other Nordics, was motivated by reference to the reservation concerning possible negotiations on EEC membership by other signatories, particularly important due to the criticital Soviet attitude towards Nordic cooperation (see Turner 1982: 149). Henceforth, the NORDEK treaty had to be considered inescapably dead, and the twenty years of unsuccessful efforts to create a Nordic customs union had come to an end.

Very soon, the attention of the Nordic countries turned again to the wider European framework: they began initial meetings with the EEC already before the end of the year. Negotiations with Finland, Iceland, Sweden and the other EFTA countries concerning free trade arrangements for industrial goods started in December 1971. Norway and Denmark, in turn, signed the treaties on EEC membership in January 1972 together with the United Kingdom and Ireland, the last three becoming members from January 1, 1973. Norway's accession treaty was defeated by a referendum in September 1972. Instead, a free trade agreement was signed between Norway and the EEC in May 1973. (Wendt 1981: 136-145, 158; Turner 1982: 159.) After the failure of these grand designs, Nordic cooperation developed in a more informal and practical form in economic matters, trade policy, industrial policy and production. (See Wendt 1981: 148-153, 160-166, 181-182.)

In conclusion, the attempts to build a Nordic union both in the field of foreign and security policy and in economy have failed for two main reasons. Firstly, the interests and orientations of the countries have been too different to combine, and their views on what Nordic cooperation should be have differed too widely. Accordingly, the Nordic countries have come to be divided economically, politically and militarily both between NATO and neutrality and between EFTA and the EEC. Moreover, further discrepancies have appeared on a North-South and East-West axis regarding the relative importance of, respectively, the Arctic and the Atlantic interests for the different Nordic countries. (See Tunander 1991: 59; Hettne et al. 1991; Andrén 1991: 281.)

Secondly, even if sufficient agreement could be achieved, a purely Nordic arrangement would hardly be large enough to be independent from external forces or a viable alternative to wider European arrangements. That the three plans for Nordic governmental cooperation, defence union, customs union and common market, were all dependent on external incentives and developments, such as the Marshall plan, shows that there does not seem to be an independent impetus inside the Nordic countries towards Nordic cooperation (Stråth 1980: 104-106; Miljan 1977: 87).The influence of external political and economic long-term factors has been mainly centrifugal. They have, as a rule, exceeded the internal political factors which have occasionally worked for Nordic cooperation. In a long-term historical perspective, there has been no independent Nordic alternative to Europe (cf. Stråth 1980: 107, 113 and Jervell 1991a: 37-38). A purely Nordic solution has been resorted to only when better alternatives have not seemed available.

The low profile of Nordic achievements

In the shadow of the grand but unsuccessful Nordic union plans, Nordic cooperation has nevertheless been quite effective in areas of less immediate political and economic relevance. A wide array of achievements have emerged as a result of pragmatic, day-to-day work in the common institutions, themselves rather modest in character. To a large extent, cooperation has built on the agreements reached in the 'golden years' of Nordic cooperation, the 1950s.

As Jervell remarks, the political energy, central politicians and the attention of the mass media were in these golden years concentrated, or at least more involved than nowadays, on the Nordic context (Jervell 1991a: 33 and 1991b: 189). The main achievement of the 1950s, and, indeed, the basic foundation of Nordic cooperation was the common labour market, established by facilitating the movement of persons across frontiers and by harmonising legislation concerning social policy.

The work for a Nordic passport union began in the early 1950s. In 1954, the need for work and residence permits was abolished for citizens of other Nordic countries and an agreement on Nordic labour market principles was signed. In addition to the free movement of labour, this included the objective of full employment policy in each country. (Wendt 1981: 188-189; see also Wallmén 1966: 51.) These measures were accompanied in 1955 by a Nordic Social Security Convention (*idem:* 213-218) which has subsequently been revised on various occasions. The aim of the convention is to guarantee equal welfare for the citizens of other Nordic countries in such areas as sickness insurance, unemployment benefits and pensions.

Nordic citizens are also in a specially advantaged position in comparison to other foreigners with regard to the right to vote, eligibility to stand for posts in local councils and access to citizenship. Together with a number of 'infrastructural' facilities,[9] the Nordic conventions permit the Northerners to live and be active in all Nordic countries partly under the conditions applying to the nationals, partly under conditions similar to those in the home country.

In the background of these advantages, Nordic legislative cooperation has been particularly important. Stemming from the 19th century, it became more structured through the establishment of the Nordic committee for legislative cooperation in 1946. Subsequently, regular cooperation between the ministers of justice began in the form of long-range programmes of legislation. The areas of cooperation gradually widened from trade law to different aspects of private and criminal law, family law, traffic regulations and citizenship as well as commercial and business legislation. In 1932, a convention on the recognition and enforcement of judgements in civil trials was signed. (Wendt 1981: 258-261.) Legislative cooperation and harmonisation has subsequently concentrated on consumer policy, food control, environmental cooperation and working environment (see Working programme 1990: 71).

Legislative cooperation has been urged by the Helsinki Agreement which actually sees the greatest possible legal unity between the Nordic countries as a goal to be attained by continuous collaboration as well as harmonisation or, where possible, the uniform formulation of legislation or joint legislative measures. Harmonisation has not been interpreted as an objective in itself, but, instead, as a means to provide better conditions of life. (Wendt 1981:

264-265.) In fact, a large part of the aims of the Helsinki Agreement, especially uniformity in private law and juridical equality between a country's own citizens and the resident nationals of another Nordic country, are essentially measures that facilitate the functioning of the Nordic labour market.

In addition to the common labour market and legislative cooperation, a third cornerstone of Nordic cooperation has without doubt been culture. As early as 1946, a Nordic cultural commission was set up by the ministers of education to assist the governments. In 1966, a Nordic cultural fund was created to support private persons and organisations, while the Council of Ministers supports public bodies. An agreement on cultural cooperation was signed in 1971; it included a secretariat for cultural cooperation and, actually, the first joint Nordic budget. Cultural cooperation covers, among other things, education and research, arts and sport. A general aim and principle has been to preserve the Nordic cultures and languages and to promote their mutual understanding. For this purpose, a Nordic language secretariat was established in Oslo 1978. There are also councils for the protection of each language. The Council of Ministers supports literature translation, and a Nordic literary prize and music prize are awarded yearly. Radio and television have been seen as a central means in cultural cooperation, and programme exchange and joint productions have been encouraged. (Wendt 1981: 289-299, 317-328; see also *Verksamhetsberättelse* 1993.)

In all, the Nordic countries form without doubt a fairly coherent region as regards both culture and legislation. Effectively, there also exists a unique sense of community in the Nordic countries. In questions such as those concerning the free movement of people, culture and environment, Nordic cooperation has not met major obstacles; rather, it is considered self-evident. Public opinion is positive towards Nordic cooperation and tends even to attribute more fields and achievements to it than what is actually the case. For example, in a Nordic opinion poll of 1993, cooperation in foreign and security policy was seen as the most important field of Nordic cooperation after environmental questions, and when asked whether there should be more or less cooperation or whether the actual extension was suitable, a large majority welcomed more. While the contents of Nordic cooperation were not well known, practically no one had anything against it.[10] In fact, as Solem (1977) notes, Nordic cooperation resembles democracy in that nobody seems to be against it, or even to afford to question it (cf. Lange 1965: 164).[11]

To what extent the sense of community is due to deliberate efforts in that direction is difficult to assess. Some see the efforts as superfluous. Lidström and Wiklund, for instance, maintain that the Nordic countries would probably adopt coinciding positions in different international contexts even without consultations or other special efforts, simply because of the similarity of their basic attitudes (Lidström and Wiklund 1968:121; Wiklund 1968: 148). The Nordic countries have always resembled each other not only in being small and homogeneous, but also in their culture and political and judicial systems. Cooperation would not be so smooth without the suitable background of common traditions and history as parts of the same state formations under the same basic laws[12] or the parallel national structures which help to identify the right counterpart (Sundelius 1982: 182, 190-193). On the other hand, the natural bilateral relations between the Nordic countries have also brought them closer together.[13]

In any case, the sense of community encourages pragmatic and informal cooperation in all fields – to the extent that informal cooperation taking place outside the Nordic institutions is perhaps of greater extension than formal cooperation. Some informal Nordic cooperation actually takes place on all levels, from an indefinite list of private Nordic organisations and associations (see Wendt 1981: 90 *et passim)* to cooperation between political parties and interest organisations. In public administration, regular meetings and contacts occur from municipal level to that of the central administration, comprising the judicial, executive and legislative branches. Direct contacts and cooperation without special formalities between Nordic public bodies, organisations and companies forms the basis of Nordic cooperation (Rules and procedures 1988: 7; see also Nielsson 1978: 295; Wendt 1981: 40).

Participating in international cooperation may additionally highlight the similarities between the Nordic countries and facilitate their informal cooperation in international organisations and conferences. Particularly in the UN, cooperation in the form of both preparatory Nordic meetings and contacts during the sessions is well developed. It is often limited to exchange of information, but on wider UN issues, particularly economic, social and humanitarian affairs, a broader and more formalised cooperation also exists. Peace keeping and development aid have been central to Nordic cooperation within the UN. The Nordic ambassadors to the UN meet regularly throughout the year, and the traditional autumn meeting between the ministers for foreign affairs has mainly been concerned with the forthcoming meeting of the UN General Assembly. Through these meetings and the more informal daily contacts between the delegations and the ministries, the Nordic countries agree on common positions, division of work responsibilities and common voting declarations. Coordination is most developed in UNESCO and GATT;

in other organisations, such as the IMF, IBRD, OECD, ECE or the Council of Europe – particularly the Council for cultural cooperation – the Nordic countries may have a common, rotatory representative in the decision-making bodies or present joint initiatives.[14]

This kind of cooperation has often been pointed to as both consistent and effective. Nordic countries are often perceived as a bloc or a regional unit in international organisations, one of them may address the meeting on behalf of the others, and the coherence of the 'Nordic bloc' has factually been high in the analyses of voting behaviour in the UN General Assembly.[15] Without doubt, a similar coordination gives additional weight to the single Nordic countries and their policies in international fora, in addition to the tangible advantages of cost sharing and access to information. After having applied for EU membership, however, Finland and Sweden started voting more in line with the other EU members, weakening the 'Nordic front' (Værnø 1993: 174-179; Sverdrup 1996: 15).

The image of the Nordic countries as a regional unit has found a place also in the literature on security policy, despite the fact that foreign and security policy have been absent from Nordic cooperation. Quoting Deutsch, they are often referred to as a 'pluralistic security community' characterised by the peaceful settlement of disputes both among themselves and in relations with outsiders.[16] The overall security situation of the region has been called the 'Nordic balance', something that is not a mere situation but actually some kind of guarantee for the security of the Nordic countries.

According to the idea or theory of Nordic balance, the different security arrangements of the Nordic countries – Swedish neutrality, Finnish neutrality with the particular weight of Soviet relations, the Norwegian and Danish NATO membership with reservations – would actually balance each other and guarantee together the security of all the countries. As Wiberg and Wæver (1992) put it, this Nordic security community, a self-reproducing area of low tension, would hypothetically function in the following way: were the Soviet Union to put pressure on Finland, the Nordic NATO members would ease their bans on foreign bases in their territories in peacetime, a measure which would result in dissuasion (or vice versa). In their characterisation, the Nordic security community is a subregional constellation in relation to which the superpowers have come to see self-restraint as being in their own interests.

During the cold war, in fact, the idea of a Nordic balance seems actually to have functioned as a legitimate motivation for national policies and decisions. For instance, the high military expenditure in Sweden was seen to guarantee not only Sweden's own security but also, as a part of the balance constellation, overall security in the Nordic region. It also increased the legitimacy of NATO membership in Denmark and Norway. (Wiberg and Wæver 1992; Joenniemi 1992b: 64-65.) Indeed, Wiberg and Wæver see that Nordic balance has not merely been a rhetorical formula, but also something real: the Nordic countries would really have taken each other's interests into account in their security policies. In Mouritzen's view, Nordic identity has even been a significant tool in the statecraft of individual Nordic countries in foreign and security policies. The tight cooperation between the Nordic countries has been used as a tool to obtain some political concessions, as in the case of Denmark which has probably obtained somewhat more autonomy in the EC by referring to Nordic cooperation (Mouritzen 1993a: 9-10; also Jervell 1991a: 35 and 1991b: 194). In the 1990s, however, referring to a broader European framework has gradually replaced references to Nordic arrangements even in this area (see below).

Nordic institutions: deliberately in a minor role

The Nordic institutions, the Nordic Council and the Nordic Council of Ministers, together with the Helsinki Agreement, generously reflect the amplitude and variety of Nordic cooperation.[17] The agenda of the Nordic Council is in this respect particularly illustrative: in principle, no question is excluded, providing it can be said to contribute to maintain and further develop Nordic cooperation under existing agreements or be in the interests of at least two Nordic countries. In contrast to most international institutions, thus, the field of action of the Council is practically limitless. Neither the statutes of 1952 nor the Helsinki Agreement set any restrictions on the matters the Council may consider. It is therefore hardly surprising that the concerns of the Council range variously from the transplantation of bodily organs and restriction of the harmful effects of boxing to household education in the Baltic countries. An overview such as that of Wendt's gives the impression that nothing escapes the influence of Nordic Council – in fact, Wendt, a Nordist, sees that if something has not been considered by the Council, the reason may be that cooperation in that particular field already functions so well that no measures are needed (Wendt 1981: 366).

Although wide in scope, the institutions are not particularly powerful in bringing about any depth to the cooperation. The exclusion of issues of a high political nature has evidently implied that the Nordic institutions also concentrate their activities on less controversial questions, without having the formal powers to encroach on differing national choices. As a consequence, the institutions have not been able alone to sustain cooperation when sufficient will and consensus among the members have been lacking. They could be characterised, first, as being compensations for unachieved plans rather than as independent engines of cooperation, and secondly, as intentionally weak in their position and capabilities.

Almost as a rule the Nordic institutions have been established either as a substitute or compensation for more far-reaching agreements, or as a formal codification of existing practices. It has often been pointed out how setbacks, caused by some external constraints, of potential Nordic strategies and plans have led to increased motivation to develop cooperation at least in the more pragmatic form of new institutions (see, e.g., Sundelius and Wiklund 1979: 63; Sæter 1993: 8-9; Jervell 1991b: 187; Stråth 1980: 111).

The establishment of the Nordic Council in 1952 was impelled by the risk of cleavage between the Nordic countries revealed by the problems of the plans for common defence and customs union. As Andrén (1991: 291) notes, the Council was originally formed in order to balance the negative effects for Nordic cooperation of the different security loyalties emerging in 1948-1949. An institutionalisation of cooperation between the Nordic countries was thus needed to ensure that they would not increasingly drift apart. The Council was given a rather unassertive character; it was to assure the commitment to cooperation and to protect the already achieved results of that cooperation rather than to create or envisage new initiatives or more binding forms of cooperation.

In its own portrayal, the Nordic Council is an organ for joint consultation between the Nordic governments and parliaments in matters concerning cooperation between two or more Nordic countries. In addition to being an initiating and advisory body and a forum for discussion, the Council can give recommendations, proposals and statements of opinion to one or more governments or to the Nordic Council of Ministers, the implementation of which takes place under identical laws and regulations by the five states.

The Council is composed of representatives both of the parliaments and the governments of the five countries, as well as of the three self-governing regions, Åland, the Færoes and Greenland. In all 87 parliamentary representatives are elected by the national parliaments from among their members. The governments appoint an appropriate number of ministers to each Council session; there are also representatives of the executive organs of the self-governing regions.

The Plenary Assembly of the Nordic Council is required to gather at least once a year with the venue rotating each time. The Council's activities are directed by a Presidium, composed of a president and four vice-presidents with their deputies, which meets also between the Council's sessions, eight to ten times yearly (Rules and procedures 1988: 12). The Presidium follows the work of the governments and the Council of Ministers in implementing the recommendations of the Council, organises sessions and supervises the activities of the committees. It has the right to represent the Council, and in some cases, it is also authorised to approach the governments or the Council of Ministers by means of a representation without waiting for consideration of the Plenary Assembly. (Wendt 1981: 38, 56-58.) The permanent committees of the Council also meet between sessions and have their own secretaries. The committee structure of the Council was reorganised in 1996 so that the number of permanent committees was reduced from six to four. In order to avoid functional duplication and a large bureaucracy, the Council originally refrained from setting up any joint secretariat. Only in 1971 were the Secretariat of the Presidium and the Secretariat of the Nordic Council of Ministers established.[18] (Rosas 1988: 227; Wendt 1981: 47, 62.)

Similarly, the basic treaty on cooperation between the Nordic countries, the so-called Helsinki Agreement or the Nordic Cooperation Treaty signed on March 23, 1962, was motivated by external developments, in particular the decision of the United Kingdom in 1961 to apply for EEC membership. In the view of the Nordic Council, Nordic cooperation needed codification in the form of a binding international agreement which would stress its main results and outline its future development. Such an agreement would, first, make Nordic cooperation better known outside the Nordic area and help to gain recognition of the claim to maintain it in the negotiations with the EEC; secondly, it would strengthen the Nordic countries during the negotiations, as differing positions could otherwise threaten Nordic cooperation. (Wendt 1981: 39-40; Nielsson 1978: 291.) Above all, the treaty served as a guarantee of continuing cooperation; it was to define how far cooperation had progressed and to introduce certain guarantees that cooperation, once established in a particular sphere, would not be abandoned (see *Nordic Cooperation* 1972).

The Helsinki Agreement is very general in nature, a statement of intent or expression of solidarity (Solem 1977: 63), or, as Anderson (1967: 288) puts it, a joint proclamation. In addition to enumerating the main fields and forms of cooperation, it contains basic rules for the Nordic Council and the Nordic Council of Ministers. According to the agreement, the governments shall endeavour to maintain and further to develop cooperation between the countries in juridical, cultural, social and economic fields, as well as in transport and communications and protection of the environment. The agreement urges the parties to strive separately and collectively to promote Nordic interests and to consult with each other to this end in appropriate fields, including international trade. It also urges consultations on matters of common interest under debate in international organisations and conferences, the extension of diplomatic assistance abroad to citizens of other Nordic countries,[19] coordination of Nordic assistance to developing countries, coordination of statistics and joint efforts to spread knowledge abroad about the Nordic countries.[20] In all, the treaty can be seen as a mere confirmation of existing practices (cf. Turner 1982: 141).

The establishment of the Nordic Council of Ministers in 1971, in turn, was a partial compensation for the failed plans for an economic union. The Council of Ministers, a committee of senior officials and a secretariat were all envisaged in the NORDEK treaty as new permanent institutions to administer NORDEK cooperation; in the background, there was also the Nordic Council's aspiration to more effective cooperation between the governments (Wendt 1981: 77). Wendt, in fact, sees that the efforts expended upon an economic union served in carrying through reforms which implied an important expansion and strengthening of the institutions for Nordic cooperation (Wendt 1981: 45-47); Jervell (1991a: 35), on the other hand, deems the establishment of the Council of Ministers as bureaucratisation rather than a sign of new projects. In fact, the Nordic Council of Ministers did not in practice profoundly alter Nordic cooperation: cooperation between governments simply acquired an official, treaty-based form, having thus far been informal in character.[21]

The Council of Ministers is composed of one member of each member government, the composition depending on the issue; it meets in 20 different constellations (*Rapport* 1992: 42). Responsible for cooperation between the Nordic governments and for cooperation between the governments and the Nordic Council in all areas of Nordic cooperation, the Council is assisted by a secretariat, committees of senior officials and special advisory committees which prepare the decisions. (Rules and procedures 1988: 32-33.) The Council of Ministers presents an annual report to the Nordic Council on Nordic cooperation and an account of plans for continued cooperation.

Both the Nordic Council and the Nordic Council of Ministers can be characterised as deliberately weak institutions. Their powers are mainly limited to recommendations on issues of Nordic interest. Even the Helsinki

Agreement gives somewhat unstable ground for cooperation: it allows for the member countries to withdraw from the application of the treaty by giving six months notice.

The establishment of the Nordic Council illustrated well the general aim not to endanger the neutrality and sovereignty of the members – for Finland, in particular, any steps towards supranational cooperation with the Nordic countries belonging to NATO, and later to the EEC, would have been completely impossible. During its first ten years, or until the Helsinki Agreement, the Nordic Council had a peculiar constitutional foundation: instead of an international agreement, it was based on identical, parallel national legislation.[22] Thus, any country could withdraw by unilaterally repealing the legislation in question. Set up by parliaments, the Council was not an intergovernmental organisation in the strict sense (Rosas 1988: 229; Petrén 1959). For Wendt, this peculiarity was practical and natural: it assured that there was no fear that the Nordic Council would infringe on the sovereignty of national parliaments (Wendt 1981: 50); the absence of a treaty meant that no international obligations of a legal character were assumed (Robertson 1973: 280).

In practice, the powers of the Nordic Council are limited to the possibility of issuing recommendations to the member governments and the Council of Ministers. Proposals for recommendations can come from the elected members, the Council of Ministers and from the governments themselves. The recommendations are accepted either unanimously or when more than half of those present and at least 30 representatives vote in favour. Only the parliamentary representatives have the right to vote. The Council of Ministers then presents an account on the measures taken in view of the recommendations; on the recommendations addressed to particular governments, this account is presented by the governments in question. (Rules and procedures 1988: 22, 24; Wendt 1981: 69-70.)

Thus, the Nordic Council has no supranational authority: it cannot take decisions that are binding on the individual member states. The governments are not compelled to follow the Council's views, neither are they legally obliged to bring any specific issues before the Council. (Wendt 1981: 52.)[23] In reality, the Council has had problems in establishing itself as a party of its own right in the consideration of Nordic matters. The wish of the Presidium that the Council be consulted before making any crucial decisions on foreign political, economic or military alignment was only very partially fulfilled in 1971 when the Council was given the right to be heard in important questions of Nordic cooperation. However, the national governments were given a way to escape this obligation by defining the matter as urgent. (Art. 46, Wendt 1981: 52; Turner 1982: 138; Anderson 1967: 289.)

The importance of the Nordic Council is further shadowed by the fact that in many fields cooperation was habitual already before the creation of the Council, as in the case of passport union. The existence of a complete network for cooperation existing prior to the Council has, for Anderson, implied that the Council has had difficulties in making a place for itself in Nordic cooperation; in his view, the Council has instead served as a not very successful pressure group (Anderson 1967: 22-23, 117-118). It does not dispose of large financial resources, either.[24] The major source of the Nordic Council's influence on the policies of the Nordic countries has in fact been seen to be the influentialness of its members, who have traditionally been the leading and most influential members of the national parliaments. (Wendt 1981: 52.) With the generally decreasing centrality of Nordic cooperation in the national policies, then, even this source of influence is likely to diminish.

The Council of Ministers can, in principle, also take binding decisions. This possibility is, however, used rather sparingly and is subject to a series of conditions. A binding decision by the Council of Ministers only obligates those who participate in the decision, and only those concerned by it participate. Decisions, for which each minister disposes of one vote, are taken by unanimity, apart from procedural matters where decisions can be reached by simple majority. In matters where a national constitution call for parliamentary approval, neither the country concerned nor the others are bound by the decision until it has been approved by the parliament. (Art. 62-63; Wendt 1981: 77-78.)

It seems that binding decisions by the Council of Ministers in practice never occur, at least not in important matters. Instead, the area and the type of cooperation are consensual, being limited to the traditional fields of cooperation; controversial matters are not brought to the Council (cf. Turner 1982: 170; Nielsson 1978: 285). Decisions may be taken on a lower level of senior officials; more importantly, a specific issue may be considered in an informal ministerial meeting, that is, without the binding effect of the official Council decision. However, the informal and the formal meetings do not in practice differ so much: the same principle of consensus is applied in both. (Wendt 1973: 20.) Finally, the prime ministers, the ministers of foreign affairs, defence, foreign trade and development aid never meet as a Council of Ministers although they otherwise meet regularly; thus, even the possibility of making binding decisions has been excluded in their fields.

Opting for integration 209

Implications for the encounter with European integration

The examination of the achievements and institutions of Nordic cooperation reveals its remarkable breadth. At the same time, however, this scope has its downside in the risk of embarking on too many unimportant, secondary matters. As Anderson (1967: 103-104) notes, common interest being the sole limit for the subjects to be considered, the Nordic agenda becomes burdened with a variety of different day-to-day issues so that less energy is left for important ones.

Many important matters, moreover, are excluded from Nordic cooperation which concentrates on consensual, low-profile issues. As was seen above, the divergent external political and economic relations have set limits to cooperation. The few international questions on the agenda of the Nordic Council have been approached with the greatest of delicacy or with no action taken, discussing mostly whether discussion was possible (cf. Sundelius 1982: 193; Wendt 1981: 52, 343, 345-346). Instead, unanimity and solidarity are emphasised; issues where different points of view can be expected are left out of the Council's deliberations. The Council functions primarily as a vehicle for the manifestation of an already existing consensus. (Stålvant 1988: 452; Etzioni 1965: 193.)

Thus, the overall character of Nordic cooperation is vague and indefinite. There are no strong guarantees about the continuity of cooperation, notably no strong institutions or binding treaties. At the same time, there is no dynamism independent of the member states. In fact, the general appreciation of Nordic cooperation and the assurances about its importance for the countries frequently turn out to be rhetorical. Similarly, measures apparently in favour of Nordic cooperation may actually merely further national interests. For example, when Denmark has played the 'Nordic card' in the EC, it has not necessarily acted to protect Nordic cooperation, but to gain more autonomy in the EC by referring to Nordic cooperation and, conversely, in the Nordic context by playing the 'EC card' (cf. above; Mouritzen 1993a: 9-10).[25]

Finally, Nordic cooperation seems in many ways dependent on and vulnerable to external events. Even the original reason for community-building in the region has been seen as exogenous, namely the fear of great power intervention (Sundelius 1982: 179). Similarly, the 'Nordic balance' has been more a result of external forces than of any deliberate Nordic efforts. As Wiberg and Wæver note (1992, esp. 24-26), it did not emerge as a design of security experts, implemented in unison and secrecy by the Nordic countries, but gradually, by trial and error. The particular Nordic sense of community did not necessarily have an important role, either. The balance was only partly of Nordic making; as a security complex, it depended on the cold war structure, and accordingly, it has lost ground with the end of the cold war. Faced with strong outside forces, the 'naturalness' of Nordic cooperation seems actually rather volatile. As Andrén (1967: 22) puts it, the Nordic is 'fair-weather integration' with no political insurances for a rainy day; in particular, this becomes visible in relations with the EU.

The challenge of the EU: increasing incompatibility

The process of European integration has always been important for the Nordic countries. However, their participation in the process was for a long time limited by the political climate of the cold war. The end of the cold war, thus, represented an obvious catalyst for a new rapprochement. In addition, there was a further factor that considerably increased the attraction, even decisive importance, of the EC for the Nordic countries: the late 1980s' steps forward in integration, the Single European Act and, even more, the negotiations for a treaty on the European Union, made it clear that they would be increasingly influenced by the direction the process was taking and that, consequently, it was increasingly important for them not to be left outside.

In 1989, the Nordic countries, together with other EFTA members, were offered the possibility to begin negotiations for a broader participation in the process through a special agreement that would in practice extend the *acquis communautaire* to these countries; the offer was very welcome, and negotiations were initiated the same year. Already before they were concluded (1991), however, it had become clear that what the treaty on the European Economic Area would offer was not enough for the Nordic countries: it was increasingly perceived as leading to a situation in which they would be bound by the regulations of the union without any possibility of influencing them. In fact, negotiations on EU membership began in February 1993, before the EEA treaty was signed.

The Nordic membership applications revealed, once again, not only the attraction of the EU but also the relative weakness of the Nordic bond. The Swedish application for EU membership of July 1991 came as a surprise for the other Nordic countries, a particularly bitter one as it came soon after a solemn renewed commitment made by the countries to inform the others in advance about important political and economic decisions.[26] Still, the move was a mere reiteration of a similar situation in 1961 when Denmark applied for EEC membership without consulting the other Nordic governments or the

Opting for integration 211

Nordic Council. Even in 1959, the governments of Sweden, Norway and Denmark had ignored the Council when they dropped the NORDEK plan for EFTA. (Anderson 1967: 289.) These events only confirmed that the principle of Nordic consultations before important national decisions indeed has been a principle, not a practice (cf. Andrén 1984: 259).

Soon after Sweden, Finland and Norway applied for EU membership. While there had been some informal cooperation during the membership negotiations, which were conducted in parallel, once again the final decisions on membership pulled the countries apart. In fact, in the Finnish debate on EU membership in autumn 1994, the politicians stressed even the importance of making the final decision about the Finnish EU membership before the results of the Swedish referendum were known, in order to avoid any signs of dependency in relation to Sweden.

The entry of Finland and Sweden into the EU in 1995 – Norway's membership was again rejected in a referendum – has implied an escalation in what was already a situation of tacit competition between Nordic cooperation and European integration. For some time, the main interests and activities of the Nordic countries have been directed to the European level; compared to the 1950s, even the 1980s had been an idle time for Nordic cooperation (Jervell 1991a: 33 and 1991b: 189). Those aspiring to membership showed more eagerness in adapting to the EU than in cooperating with other Nordic countries. Meanwhile, Nordic activities tended increasingly to follow the European ones, being justified as making the adaptation to the EU easier. At the same time, the European arrangements functioned once again as the necessary external stimulus for progress in Nordic cooperation. For instance, the EEA was needed to achieve progress in Nordic economic cooperation (cf. Kivimäki 1992: 45).

EU membership does not leave much space for separate Nordic activities, in particular since the field of activities of the EU has constantly been widening so as to cover practically all fields of Nordic cooperation. In many ways, the EU is a serious challenge to Nordic cooperation: its size, supranationality and dynamism test both the practical possibilities, in terms of time and resources, and the motivation or interest for Nordic cooperation. Among the first basic elements of Nordic cooperation that have been actually endangered by EU membership has been the Schengen agreement with its aim of abolishing internal frontier controls, the consequent tightening of police cooperation and increased control of the outer frontiers. The Nordic passport union was immediately threatened by the fact that this outer EU frontier would run between the Nordic countries. While this problem was solved in favour of Nordic cooperation,[27] other important problems remain. First, the specific rights of the Nordic citizens are not necessarily reconcilable with the principle of equal treatment of EU nationals. Second, the informal but still important practice of cooperation in legislation and policy-making in different areas is jeopardised by commitment to EU norms, policy-making and common policies.

In this situation, to guarantee the continuation of Nordic cooperation, it would be crucial both to convince the EU about its value and to bind the Nordic countries to it. This latter task might be even more difficult than the first. Certainly, there seems to be a consensus on and a commitment to the importance of continuing Nordic cooperation.[28] On the other hand, it has also been argued that the EU membership of three of the five countries gives additional impetus for Nordic cooperation inside the EU and that, additionally, the fact that Iceland and Norway are not members makes Nordic cooperation even more important for them than before as a channel to EU decision-making. Still, these seem to be mere rhetorical moves; the indefinite character of Nordic cooperation would need specification, its contents and methods reformulation. To do this is difficult; moreover, as will be seen below, it may even be counterproductive.

Challenges to Nordic unity have thus far been answered by innovations and measures aimed at increasing the efficiency of Nordic cooperation: in the early 1950s, diverging security policy led to the creation of the Nordic Council; in the early 1960s, the EEC applications necessitated the signing of the Helsinki Agreement; in the early 1970s, the collapse of NORDEK advanced the establishment of the Council of Ministers. The early 1990s' challenge has not remained unanswered, either. This time, however, the response has not been a new institution, or a treaty, but rather a general pruning. The general aim has been to strengthen Nordic cooperation by making it more effective and more binding.

The various plans and projects presented by the Nordic institutions can be gathered under three main approaches: sharpening the profile of Nordic cooperation to assure a role for it in the future, increasing its dynamism by broadening the official scope of cooperation and widening it geographically to include, in some respects, also the Baltic states, and, finally, making the institutions and practices more efficient.

The first approach consists essentially of a new delineation of Nordic cooperation as part of the wider European context. *Norden,* it has been said, is not an alternative but a natural part of European cooperation; it is both compatible with and complementary to European integration. While Nordic cooperation can in certain fields benefit the Nordic countries in their role in European politics, participation in European integration may also be a new impulse for Nordic cooperation.[29] The Working Programme of 1990 (p. 8) notes that 'from being essentially directed towards *Norden*, Nordic cooperation has in a very few years become considered an element in European cooperation'. This new characterisation had gained ground throughout the 1980s. Stålvant (1991: 157) remarks that the 1980s economic programme of the Council of Ministers on the internal market diverged from the previous discussions in that no Nordic alternative was presented; the main aim was to assure compatibility with the EEA efforts. The report NU 1988/4, in turn, states explicitly that 'one should see integration in the Nordic countries as a part of the general integration development in Europe'.

It is generally understood that this essential compatibility with the European efforts can best be assured through concentrating Nordic cooperation on specific Nordic issues, or the 'genuine Nordic interests'. Thus, the overlapping areas, those already treated in the broader European context, should be cut as superfluous. In addition to avoiding problems of competency, this precision of Nordic cooperation would have the advantages of guaranteeing it a meaningful role and of avoiding an unnecessary waste of time and resources. Evidently, it would also help to preserve the motivation for cooperation in a situation in which the competition for the interest of both politicians and parliamentarians between Nordic and European cooperation has obviously been turning to the favour of the EU.[30] These 'genuine Nordic interests' are generally seen to be environment, culture, energy and infrastructure, and a broad citizen policy involving the rights of the Northerners, social welfare, labour market, working environment and consumer policy. Among these, culture has a been assigned a particularly prominent role, the aim being to allocate half of the budget of the Council of Ministers to culture, education and research. (*Rapport* 1992: 12; *Verksamhetsberättelse* 1993: 1-2, 8.)

The second approach to the protection of Nordic cooperation has been to give it more dynamism and impetus, perhaps also importance, through broadening and widening it in two different ways: by including issues of foreign policy and extending cooperation to the Baltic countries.

Foreign policy issues, or rather cooperation in international affairs, became a subject of committee work in the Nordic Council in the late 1980s, when a committee was established to examine how Nordic cooperation could be further developed and strengthened in international matters.[31] Including international issues on the agenda of the Nordic Council was seen as motivated by the fact that international issues were not totally detached from Nordic cooperation, but in a sense a traditional, although secondary part of it, and that the Helsinki Agreement does not explicitly hinder their examination, as it does not limit the fields of cooperation (NU 1988/4: 9; NU 1990/7). However, the mandate of the committee excluded questions pertaining to security politics; foreign policy was seen as touching the border of the mandate.

The committee work resulted in ideas on how cooperation could be made more effective in the traditional fields, e.g., in international organisations. Among the other committee proposals was the appointment of an international secretary to the Presidium, which was realised (NU 1988/4: 11-12, 20-21, 99, 144, 153-155). It was also seen as beneficial to remove all possible doubts on the status of international questions by an explicit statement in the treaty. The committee therefore proposed to complement the Helsinki Agreement by a statement on the desire of the signatories to 'improve co-operation in international questions' or 'to maintain and further develop co-operation in the field of international questions' (NU 1990/7: 89-90, 150).[32]

As shown by the guidelines for the committee work and the resulting formulation of the amendment, however, the actual significance of modifying the agreement was not to introduce something new and different, and certainly not to form a common Nordic foreign policy. Rather, the result was a simple codification of the existing practice of coordination and consultation in certain international issues. The final modification of the Helsinki Agreement (March 18, 1993) consists essentially in adding to the preamble the wish to 'renovate and develop Nordic cooperation in the light of the Nordic countries' enlarged participation in European cooperation', without mentioning international cooperation as such. In addition, article 1 now states that 'the contracting parties shall consult (*bör rådgöra*) each other in questions of common interest under examination in European and other international organisations and conferences'.

These modest formulations notwithstanding, the threshold on international questions has at least been lowered: discussion on international affairs in the Nordic context is now considered possible. Still, reaching common conclusions or demanding common action is not the aim. (See Stålvant 1988: 446.) In the Nordic Council, discussion on international affairs began actually only in the late 1980s, the 1988 session being a watershed as regards full discussion on the European dimension (NU 1989/7E: 7). A look at the discussions in the Council from 1986 onwards seems to show, however, that the debate on the suitability of discussing questions of foreign policy has continued. In addition to issues such as detente, the Nordic nuclear weapon free zone, development aid or human rights, the recommendations with a clear foreign policy character and linked to the current political situation cannot be said to be particularly prominent.[33]

On the governmental level, the representatives of the prime ministers stated in 1992 that foreign and security policy are an important part of Nordic governmental collaboration. In real terms, the agenda of the meetings of the Nordic ministers of defence (where Iceland does not participate) has, in fact, broadened: from the spring of 1993, the discussions have concerned not only the traditional UN issues, but also cooperation in Bosnia, cooperation between Sweden and Norway in the arms industry and research and collaboration in the establishment of a Baltic peace keeping force for the UN.

On the other hand, the Nordic Council itself has adopted a more active role in international relations, defining itself as an international and regional organisation the field of which naturally includes international questions.[34]

The other aspect of the attempt to broaden Nordic cooperation is that it has in the 1990s widened geographically to include a Baltic dimension in many of its activities. A dense network of bilateral relations has developed since the independence of the three Baltic states in 1990-1991, complemented by joint Nordic initiatives. They form a part of the Council of Ministers' annual programme of cooperation with the adjacent areas, prepared since 1990, and later widened to cover also Northwest Russia and the Barents region. To facilitate contacts, the Council of Ministers has established special information offices in the Baltic capitals. There is also a special pool for financing different cooperation projects with Baltic countries and Eastern Europe, for example environmental research, investment and finance, industrial and commercial cooperation and social welfare, and different sectorial initiatives.[35]

The Nordic Council also signed in 1992 a cooperation agreement with the Baltic Assembly, an interparliamentary council established in 1991. More far-reaching proposals concerning the participation of the Baltic countries in the Nordic Council have, however, not led to any firm measures. Instead, the Baltic countries have increasingly taken part in informal cooperation outside the Nordic institutions; for example, the Baltic ministers of justice participated in the meeting of their Nordic counterparts for the first time in 1993. Even Nordic coordination in international organisations has started to include Baltic countries, at least in the IMF and EBRD. (*Verksamhetsberättelse* 1993: 177, 180-181, 199.)

Finally, the third approach to protect Nordic cooperation has been to increase its efficiency. Among the most important measures envisaged are, first, increasing the participation of the executive, particularly the prime ministers, second, making cooperation more binding, and, third, reorganising the institutions and reducing their number (see, e.g., NU 1990/7: 99-102).

Accordingly, the governmental side of cooperation was reorganised in 1993. To increase the dynamism and flexibility of Nordic cooperation, the responsibility for the overall coordination of Nordic cooperation was given to the prime ministers. Meeting three to four times a year, they are assisted by the Nordic Cooperation Committee (NSK), established in 1992, which is formed by the ministers of cooperation and senior officials. The NSK takes care of daily activities and directs the secretariat for the Council of Ministers. It has full competence to make decisions in all questions where unanimity can be achieved and where the respective ministers have not reserved themselves the right of making decisions. The NSK can also receive tasks directly from the prime ministers. (*Rapport* 1992: 14; *Oppfølginsgruppen* 1992: 6.)

On the other hand, suggestions concerning the decision-making methods have been forwarded. It has been pointed out that the usual methods of Nordic cooperation are unduly time-consuming; in fact, their slowness has been seen as a reason for the failure of the large Nordic projects (e.g., Solem 1977: 75). As such, it reflects the national political 'style' of the Nordic countries: the principles of consensus and openness, or the greatest possible level of public access, imply that before a decision is taken, its feasibility and acceptability have to be ascertained, and therefore the opinions of a large number of different groups are heard. (Milas 1978: 52-53, Wendt 1981: 48-49.) In comparison with the EU, however, Nordic cooperation would need new dynamism; the lengthy procedures may hinder the necessary adaptation to the greater tempo of the European institutions.

In order to increase efficiency, more binding, even supranational methods have been proposed, something that could seem to change the style of Nordic cooperation quite dramatically. The report NU 1990/7 (pp. 83-84) envisages that the Council of Ministers could make a decision even with one country disagreeing, a method called the '4/5 consensus'. By this method a country which is not ready to take part in a decision can be left out but still have the possibility to enter the decision later. Even if adopted, however, this would not introduce supranationality to Nordic cooperation, but at most add to its 'multi-speed' nature (since the decision does not bind the disagreeing country, it cannot be said to be a majority decision; it is still unanimous in terms of those who are bound by it).[36] The report uses the term 'supranational' rather ambiguously. On the whole, it is underlined that there is no need for new organs. The committee also stressed the differences between the European Community and Nordic cooperation, outlining the latter as cooperation which does not limit the national decision-making competence, as 'co-existence and understanding to benefit all Nordic citizens', not integration. (NU 1990/7: 82-83, 113-115.)

Until now, effectiveness has been furthered through institutional simplification; the *Rapport* 1992 (pp. 42-43) points out that there is less need for the machinery of civil officials and that the institutions and projects (some 800) that partly or wholly depend on the Nordic budget should be revised and their number perhaps reduced. After some debate, reductions have been made. The number of minor Nordic institutions has been cut, the secretariats of the two Councils have been relocated. The reorganisation of the permanent committees, mentioned above, can also be seen as a move in this direction.

As a whole, however, the measures aimed at protecting Nordic cooperation raise two questions: are they really sufficient, and do they really have the desired consequences? They do not seem to alter the character of Nordic cooperation to the extent necessary to face the challenge of the EU. It still lacks the EU's central assets: the calculability provided by binding decisions, directly applicable legislation and a court of justice; the weight of size and the agenda with crucial issues of economy and politics; and a logic and dynamism independent of its member states, assured by the strong institutions and the long-term political goals. There is not even a hegemonic power in the Nordic context capable of being the driving force for cooperation (cf. Jervell 1991a: 37). In the past, these differences have explained the scarcity of tangible results in Nordic cooperation; now, they can hardly be supposed to contribute to its resistance.[37]

A basic problem is that the original motives for Nordic cooperation seem now to work against it. In contrast to the EC/EU, which proceeds by the force of political commitment to ambitious long-term goals of economic and political union, Nordic cooperation has progressed in more modest and uncontroversial steps. It has concentrated on fields where the concrete goals of the different countries actually converge, where it is seen as tangibly beneficial by all participants. NU 1989/7E (p. 61) specifically states that the motive of Nordic cooperation is to save money for the individual Nordic countries, while the *Rapport* of 1992 (p. 20) declares that basic idea of Nordic cooperation is to be led by demand (cf. Stålvant 1988: 452). Quite understandably, then, when measured against a more advantageous alternative, the superior benefits of a wider and more effective integrative framework, Nordic cooperation risks losing its impetus. In an interview at the Presidium secretariat in May 1994, this was expressed very straightforwardly: Nordic cooperation can be dispensed with if it is not necessary – something one could hardly hear about the EU.[38]

Moreover, all the supporting measures envisaged involve features which may actually turn them against Nordic cooperation. For the first, widening into foreign policy is perhaps more a reflection of external developments than a measure which increases the weight of Nordic cooperation or its practical importance for parliamentarians and members of government involved in the new EU issues. With the disappearance of the bloc division, the reasons for not discussing international issues also disappeared – as was well shown by the commitment of the aspirant EU members to the development of the common foreign and security policy of the EU. Moreover, the widening did not bring anything new to Nordic cooperation; it only codified the traditional, pragmatic Nordic consultations and background discussions. One could even see that the fact of explicitly stating the competence *limits* the possibilities of cooperation, if the agreement is understood literally as comprising only consultations in the context of organisations and conferences. Since this has traditionally been the case, the explicit statement tends to exclude new forms of cooperation in international matters, such as binding Nordic commitments or joint actions. After all, increasing Nordic foreign policy coordination would only increase the possible collisions with a similar European coordination.[39]

Similarly, then, the new Baltic – and more generally regional – dimension of Nordic cooperation can also increase internal divisions instead of being a source of dynamism, evidence of its attraction as a model of regional cooperation or a springboard to wider European relations (cf. Jervell 1991b: 192). The interests of the Nordic countries do not necessarily coincide in relation to the Baltic states,[40] and the same is true for regional cooperation, for example, in the Arctic region. These projects might, thus, also result in conflicts with the internal regionalisation in *Norden*, when, for instance, the 'Västnorden' – the Færoes, Greenland and Iceland – feel that they get too little attention compared to the Baltic countries (*Rapport* 1992: 50).

Concentrating Nordic cooperation on genuine Nordic interests, then, is also a problematic strategy. It has always been pointed out that the Nordic countries do not really have many truly common interests. In vital economic issues such as agriculture, fisheries or industry, the interests of the Nordic countries are, in fact, very different (cf. Wæver 1992a: 94; Wiberg 1992: 246; Stålvant 1991: 176-177). It has also been stressed that increasing convergence in the economic and political directions does not necessarily mean more reasons for collaboration, either, but rather increasing competition (Hettne et al. 1991: 27-28).

Moreover, several Nordic scholars see that even the basic sense of community and Nordic identity is now seriously threatened. If in the past, Nordic identity essentially consisted of a 'difference' based on remaining outside the military divisions and of a moral and abiding 'superiority' in relation to the 'European', this now appears increasingly hollow as the bloc division has disappeared and, perhaps more importantly, as the 'European' model now has taken the lead.[41] Previously, it was often remarked that Nordic cooperation had in many fields proceeded further than European integration (see, e.g., Goldschmidt 1990: 92, 97); now, however, as equally high or even higher results of cooperation has been achieved in the European context, the 'Nordic' has lost its role as a model and even become peripheral. The progressive, integrated and market-based European setting offers an attractive, alternative object of identification (cf. Wæver 1992a: 86-87 and 1992b; Joenniemi 1992b). In actual terms, the process of European economic integration has not only been a model for or influenced the development of Nordic cooperation, as when the establishment of the EEC influenced the plans for a Nordic customs union or the developments in the 1960s those for NORDEK (cf. NU 1988/4: 56). Increasingly, specific Nordic measures are justified as adjustment to European cooperation.[42]

Consequently, if this Nordic identity previously could be used instrumentally as a tool in international relations, it has now lost its credibility, and in fact now seems forsaken. Mouritzen notes that for the Swedish bourgeois government (from 1991), the Nordic model was no longer consistent with perceived Swedish national interests; instead, reference was made to European identity (Mouritzen 1993a: 1, 12-13, 21-22). He interprets this as a paradigm example of adaptive acquiescence: the membership application made it necessary to appear as good Europeans, while stressing the Nordic, or even Swedish, identity was seen as counterproductive and might sustain fears among the southern EU members (*idem:* 15-18). Similarly, Wæver (1992a: 78) sees that in 1989 to 1990, there was particularly in Sweden an almost complete acquiescence to the perceived necessity of joining the European Community. This showed the volatility of the 'Nordic' also by casting one of the basic pillars of Nordic cooperation – reluctance to supranationalism – in a rather odd light.

A second problem in the concentration on 'genuine Nordic interests' is that the diminishing share left for Nordic cooperation and the nature of this remainder are not necessarily conducive to upholding interest in Nordic cooperation and the motivation of politicians to support it. In the 1960s, when the Nordic countries faced the same problem because of the unclear effect of Denmark's and Norway's potential EEC membership for Nordic cooperation, it could still be argued that Nordic cooperation was not thwarted, since many of the areas it covered – cultural activities, transport, environment, social welfare, regional cooperation, major traffic projects – were outside the Treaty of Rome or unaffected by EEC-cooperation (Wendt 1981: 141-144). Now, the situation is obviously different. In particular, the increasing centrality of cultural cooperation lowers the profile of Nordic cooperation, making it less important and less interesting (cf. Jan P. Syse, Council President, in *Helsingin Sanomat,* January 30, 1994) while it also cuts resources from other fields of cooperation. The necessary compatibility of Nordic cooperation and European integration may marginalise the former, making it a function or echo of the wider process.

Similarly, the increasing role of the executive and the prime ministers could be interpreted as a way of assuring the compatibility between the Nordic and the European rather than as a measure furthering Nordic unity. In practice, prime ministers now have a leading position in both contexts. Their cooperation in the Nordic context is informal and unbinding; it takes place outside the institutions. Moreover, a generally more informal role has been envisaged for Nordic cooperation following Finland and Sweden's EU membership. It has been seen that formal cooperation could take place in the EU, while Nordic cooperation would appear in different informal frameworks and forms (cf. Kivimäki 1992: 24, 26-27; *Rapport* 1992: 10). This reduces the position of the Nordic institutions, especially the traditional role of parliamentary cooperation in the Nordic Council.

Finally, efforts towards more binding Nordic cooperation do not seem very promising either. On the one hand, they would seem feasible only in the most uncontroversial issues. On the other, they would go against the conditions of EU membership. The possibilities of the Nordic countries cooperating tightly inside the EU as some sort of a Nordic bloc are reduced both by the scarcity of common interests and the practical impossibility of combining two binding commitments without either making them coincide or halting the progress in the European context. Symptomatically, the idea of a common information office in Brussels is opposed to because of the different points of view between the countries (report NU 1988/4: 144, 153-155). It has also been pointed out that the growing aspirations and independent actorship of the Nordic Council are problematic in that they seem to surpass the limits of political will and the outlines of the governments, questioning the legitimacy of the Council. Thus, they might decrease, rather than increase, the influence of the Council. (Værnø 1993: 240, 249, 270-275, 293.)

There has been some optimism about the possibilities of forming a grouping inside the EU, even emphasising the Nordic framework as one level of decision-making by applying the principle of subsidiarity. However, Nordic politicians have been wary of provoking the EU with speculations about bloc-like behaviour within the Union. As the *Rapport* (1992) cautiously observes, while it is common in the EC that the members cooperate with like-minded countries in forwarding their national priorities, permanent groupings are not common.[43] Therefore, Nordic cooperation in the EC would consist in mere informal consultation which would let the Nordic countries know each others' points of view and coordinate where possible. At the same time, the Council of Ministers stresses the importance to avoid duplicating work in the form of separate Nordic and European levels, and thus, of avoiding a parallel Nordic decision-making level. (*Rapport* 1992: 13, 37; Kivimäki 1992: 25-26, 31, 45; *Planer* 1993: 6.)

In all, it is accepted that the credibility of the EU would not allow for a form of Nordic cooperation based on systematic, binding commitments. Instead, it is seen that Nordic cooperation could perhaps find a *raison d'être* in informal consultations and in the contribution the Nordic members would give to the EU on the basis of their tradition of collaboration, for instance the practice of subregional cooperation (Stålvant 1991: 163-168, 171-173), compensation for the democratic deficit (Jervell 1991b: 206-207, 210) or concrete achievements in environment, labour market, social policy, cultural and educational cooperation (Working programme 1990: 81). Equally, areas such as transparency and openness or the development of relations with countries and areas outside the EU could be among the Nordic contributions.

The possibility of making real contributions seems, however, to require rather tight knit Nordic cooperation. In all, therefore, the Nordic countries are caught up in a dilemma. To preserve at least some of the distinctive achievements of their cooperation, they would have to sharpen their profile and fix their joint efforts. A sharpening of this kind, however, could, by increasing the credibility of Nordic cooperation, go against that of the EU. In the end, therefore, there does not seem to be much room for systematic Nordic cooperation unless it is definitively redefined as something not distinctive, but conforming to the goals and methods of European integration. As part of the larger process, it could perhaps have an autonomy comparable to that of Benelux cooperation, to the extent it brings forward the general process of integration (e.g., Jervell 1991b: 208). Another question is, then, how the necessary political will for and unanimity on a similar redefinition could be found in the Nordic countries.

Notes

1. Sometimes also the term 'Scandinavian' is used. While 'Nordic' includes all the five countries, 'Scandinavian' actually denotes Denmark, Norway and Sweden, at times also Iceland.
2. Both Norway and Denmark, however, made reservations when joining NATO, prohibiting foreign bases and the storage of nuclear weapons on their territory (see Miljan 1977: 80-81, Turner 1982: 116-117).
3. Helge Pharo, seminar at the EUI, November 8, 1993.
4. Helge Pharo, seminar at the EUI, November 8, 1993.
5. Founded in 1948 at the behest of the United States to ensure the fair and effective distribution of Marshall aid and to try to prevent a recurrence of protectionism, working towards the removal of import quotas (Turner 1982: 112).
6. At that time, Sweden supported the wider free trade arrangement, while Denmark was for closer links with the EEC. On the other hand, the support for a Nordic common market was more widespread in Sweden than in the other countries.
7. The undeniable interest in European cooperation was balanced by declarations aiming to reassure the people that even the Nordic framework still mattered; Denmark, Norway and Sweden all stressed their interest in preserving Nordic relations or Nordic unity. To minimise any division which might be caused by Denmark and Norway joining the EEC, the Nordic Council urged the governments to enter into a formal agreement on cooperation. As a result, the Helsinki Agreement was signed in 1962 (see below). The EEC negotiators, in turn, pointed out that for Denmark a proclamation on Nordic cooperation would not prejudice the Danish application, provided it was of a non-binding nature (Anderson 1967: 290; Wendt 1981: 116-117).
8. 'Nordek' is an abbreviation of 'Nordic economic', symptomatic in that the noun was omitted – Turner, among others, notes that the word 'union' had unfavourable connotations for Finns and Norwegians (Turner 1982: 145; cf. Solem 1977: 79).
9. Among the minor 'privileges', one could mention the principle of the Nordic Postal Association that Nordic mail can be posted on domestic rates, a good example of how this kind of 'positive discrimination' gradually erodes due to both diverging European norms and privatisation.

10. Nordens folk om Nordiskt samarbete. En attitydundersökning i Sverige, Norge, Danmark, Finland och Island våren 1993. TEMO AB för Nordiska Rådet och Nordiska Ministerrådet.
11. In fact, Wæver (1992a: 94) notes that in the debate on EU membership, furthering Nordic cooperation was an argument which both the opponents and the supporters could use to strengthen their positions. Relying on the popular support for Nordic cooperation, the opponents of EU membership depicted Nordic cooperation as a (better) alternative to European integration, while European integration was, in the supporters' view, a very good base for the development of Nordic cooperation.
12. Indeed, one should not forget that a strong legal unity developed within the two kingdoms of the region after 1523. On the one hand, Danish law was increasingly applied in Norway and influenced Norway's national law. On the other, Sweden-Finland had a joint legal foundation in a common statute-book from about 1350. The code from 1734 was particularly important for the Nordic community of law, as it retained its validity after Finland's separation from Sweden and preserved thus its juridical affiliation with Scandinavia even as a Russian grand-duchy. Furthermore, the union between Sweden and Norway in the 19th century undoubtedly had similar unifying consequences. (Wendt 1981: 257.)
13. See, e.g., Karvonen's (1981) study on policy diffusion from Sweden to Finland in the form of the conscious introduction of Swedish models into the Finnish system, sometimes through Nordic cooperative contacts. Cf. also Solem's (1977) efforts to discern the consequences of Nordic cooperation for national policies and decision-making, realised in a form of a survey of the opinions of civil servants, parliamentarians and ministers. No clear consequences emerge; Solem notes the difficulties in assessing the degree to which unity has come about specifically because of the Nordic Council – which itself is also a consequence of this unity.
14. See NU 1988/4: 38-39, 50, 64-65, 67-71; Wendt 1981: 367-373, 381-387; see also Landqvist 1968, *Verksamhetsberättelse* 1993: 196 and 1992.
15. See, e.g., *Cooperation and Conflict*, volume II, 1967.
16. Compared with the extension to which it has been quoted in the Nordic literature, Deutsch *et al.* (1957) is actually quite brief about the Scandinavian security community. On the basis of an historical case study on the relations between Sweden and Norway, it notes that the Scandinavian security community is characterised by limited functional amalgamation. The most important functions, however, have not been amalgamated: the common laws must be adopted by national legislatures, the common parliamentary body can only make recommendations, and it has no common defence forces, police, or control over the political and economic systems of its members (Deutsch 1957: 22-23).

224   The Plurality of Truth

17. As a thorough introduction to Nordic cooperation, Wendt's book of 1981 is indispensable; however, no similar general accounts have since been published. Therefore, the reports on activities and plans by the Council of Ministers is perhaps the best way to get an overview of Nordic cooperation. Another way is to have a look at the 2000-page 'blue books' about the Nordic Council sessions. In the past, the Council published overviews on its activities over some years, but the latest of this kind only covers the period until 1986. Yet another way of getting acquainted with the various fields of activities is the list of publications by the Councils and other Nordic institutions, e.g., *Trykt og Udgivet 1994* (Nordisk Ministerråd, København 1994). A recent analytical overview is presented in the special volume of *Den Jyske Historiker,* 'De Nordiske Fællesskaber', vol. 69-70, 1994.

18. Both are now placed in Copenhagen. Originally, the secretariat of the Council of Ministers was placed in Oslo and that of the Presidium in Stockholm. In 1986, the former moved to Copenhagen as a result of the merger with the secretariat for Nordic cultural cooperation, joined by the presidium secretariat in 1996. The secretariats, which consist of Nordic civil servants on fixed-term contracts, have never been massive. Before the latest relocation, there were some 30 persons at the secretariat of the Presidium, 80 in the secretariat of the Council of Ministers and 40 in all the national secretariats together (cf. Wendt 1981: 63-65).

19. There has been much informal cooperation between Nordic consular representatives abroad, encouraged also by Nordic Council recommendations by the Nordic Council (see NU 1988/4: 29), but it has been seen by the governments as unsuitable for general agreements (Wendt 1981: 363-365).

20. In addition, separate Nordic cooperation treaties have been made in different fields, e.g., the Convention on Nordic labour market (1982, replacing one from 1954), the Nordic Treaty on work environment (1989), on cultural cooperation (1971), on environmental protection (1974), on social security (for the first time in 1955), and on transport and communications (1973). (See *Nordiska samarbetsavtal,* Nordiska rådets presidiesekretariat/Nordiska ministerrådets sekretariat, Stockholm 1993.)

21. Ministerial meetings had begun in almost all areas by the end of the 1960s. In the 1960s, two ministerial committees were formed, one for economic cooperation and the other for the coordination of aid to the developing countries. In other respects as well, the executive has been linked to Nordic cooperation long before the actual establishment of the Council of Ministers. Ministers participate in the work of the Nordic Council; in each ministry, a special liaison official works as a link between the ministry and the national delegation to the Nordic Council. Finally, one minister from every government is appointed as minister for Nordic cooperation with the tasks

Opting for integration 225

of coordination, supervision and encouragement. These ministers have as their deputies specially appointed civil servants, who form the Committee of Co-operation Ministers' Deputies (*ställförträdarkommittee*). (Wendt 1981: 75-76, 78, 81; Rules and procedures 1988: 32.)

22. See Anderson (1967: 24, 26); Lange (1954: 288); Wallmén (1966: 16); cf. also Wendt (1981: 34-36) and Solem (1977: 45-46).

23. Wendt and Anderson argue that the authority of the decisions by the Nordic Council has also been diminished by the fact that the government members have no right to vote in the Council. This had been planned for in the draft statutes, but the ministers for foreign affairs changed the draft in 1952 so that the members of government were only given the right to speak. (Wendt 1981: 35.) The representatives of the governments actually deleted all the binding provisions and weakened other sections of the draft (Anderson 1967: 281).

24. For instance, in 1993 the budget for the Council of Ministers was 650 million Danish crowns. Additional resources for Nordic cooperation come from the national budgets of the member states. (Wendt 1981: 82-83, 88; Rules and procedures 1988: 28; *Verksamhetsberättelse* 1993: 3.)

25. Similarly, while the NORDEK plan was Denmark only a bridge to the EEC, Stråth (1980: 110-111) argues that even the 'much-publicized close cooperation' in the GATT negotiations of 1964 was hardly more than tactical cooperation in order to achieve non-Nordic goals.

26. Interview at the Presidium secretariat, Stockholm, May 30, 1994.

27. The result of the Schengen negotiations was that the Nordic passport union could continue, despite the fact that Norway and Iceland are not EU members: they were given observer status, while Finland and Sweden signed the treaty together with Denmark in December 1996 (*Helsingin Sanomat*, December 17, 1996).

28. Such solemn endorsements of Nordic cooperation are easy to find; one might cite the EEA clause on the possibility of continuing regional cooperation arrangements, among which Nordic cooperation, or the joint declaration by Finland, Norway, Sweden and the EU in early 1994 confirming that Nordic cooperation will continue independently of the EU membership of these countries (Per Stenbäck in *Nordisk Kontakt*, 2/94). These statements find an echo in the equally habitual declarations by the governments on the value of Nordic cooperation, e.g., that '[T]he Nordic countries find it very important to continue and strengthen the existing Nordic cooperation which is of great value in itself' (Working Programme of the Council of Ministers 1990: 7), that Nordic cooperation and its widening is both natural and self-evident (Swedish ministry for foreign affairs on Nordic cooperation in 1979), or that a further development of Nordic cooperation is for cultural, political and economic reasons a privileged goal in Swedish government policy (similar

report of 1986).
29. In the view of the personal advisors to the prime ministers, Nordic cooperation is needed to strengthen the genuinely Nordic interests and to help participation in the EEA and the EC. Its tasks are, therefore, to secure *Norden* as a home market, to strengthen the aspects of a value community (identity and mutual understanding), to increase the competitiveness of Nordic industry, and, finally, to have a role in securing national interests (*Rapport* 1992: 9).
30. The motivational problems are not new; Sundelius and Wiklund (1979: 74) and Solem (1977: 138) remark that the general approval of Nordic cooperation by, e.g., all political parties may be a facade for inertia instead of proof of a will to continue while no one feels obliged really to push for the implementation of concrete Nordic measures. The problems might be further exacerbated if the European Parliament was to acquire a more prominent role in the future (cf. Per Stenbäck in *Nordisk Kontakt* 2/94).
31. Recommendation 22/1986 to the Council of Ministers. The committee, called the Nordic Council's committee on international cooperation, issued two reports, the so-called Söder I (NU 1988/4) and Söder II (NU 1989/7), quoted in the following by their serial numbers. A third important report in this respect is that of the organisation committee (NU 1990/7).
32. What 'cooperation in international questions' actually means is not necessarily clear. Moreover, the proposal differs according to the language used both as to whether the question is about introducing or further developing cooperation in the field and to whether the proposed cooperation concerns foreign policy (as in the Finnish version) or international questions (Swedish and English). Similarly, the nature of cooperation varies, the Swedish *'samråda'* (consult, confer) being the least ambitious of the three, without doubt less than 'cooperation'.
33. In 1993, for instance, the only recommendation of this kind urged the governments to strengthen their demand about the withdrawal of the Russian troops from the Baltic countries (rec. n. 18/93/P; *Verksamhetsberättelse* 1993: 218, 227). - In the absence of recent overviews on the activities of the Council, the sources used here are various unpublished compilations by the presidium secretariat of citations and ideas expressed in the Plenary Assembly and summaries of recommendations and activities in international issues, prepared for various purposes of internal information.
34. The Council considered developing contacts with the parliamentary organisations of the CSCE, WEU and NACC, as well as widening its traditional contacts with the interparliamentary assemblies of the CIS, EFTA and EEA into the field of security policy. See *Nordiska Rådets internationella verksamhetsplan för 1995-96* (Presidiesekretariatet, Stockholm, May 30, 1994) and *Nordiska Rådets relationer till rådets*

internationella samarbetsparter (Presidiesekretariat, Stockholm, December 24, 1993, including pro memoria of the international cooperation of the permanent committees).

35. See *Rapport* 1992: 56-59 and *'Nordisk ministerråds arbejdsprogram for Baltikum og Østeuropa'* (October 9, 1990; revised October 8, 1992); 'Nordic Working Programme for the Baltic Region and Other Adjacent Areas 1993' and 'Nordic Working Programme 1994 for Areas Adjacent to the Nordic Region'.

36. In fact, Nordic cooperation shows a remarkable 'variable geometry' in that often an agreement involves only some of the countries; there is also a tendency towards further bilateralisation (e.g., an agreement on industry and energy between Sweden and Norway in 1981; interview at the Presidium secretariat, Stockholm, May 30, 1994, and Wiklund 1984: 218). One might ask whether, formally speaking, bi- or trilateral cooperation can be seen as a part of Nordic cooperation; if not, the contents of Nordic cooperation are considerably reduced (cf. Joenniemi 1992b: 37-40).

37. Cf. Jervell 1991a: 36-37; Stålvant 1991: 174; Etzioni 1965: 223-226; Andrén 1967: 10; Milas 1978: 18.

38. An example of the difficulties to motivate the efforts towards more efficiency could be when the practice of one annual Council session was changed from 1992 to two annual sessions, it did not take long to see that the second meeting was not really needed, and the Council returned to the former practice.

39. Similarly, the definition of security policy has become broader. In fact, when the prime ministers mentioned in their Bornholm declaration security policy as a field where the Nordic countries have common interests in participating in the European cooperation and where Nordic governmental cooperation should be developed, they also state that the concept of security has a new dimension, including also non-military matters (*Rapport* 1992: 11). The new forms of cooperation concentrates on these more technical issues, being economically advantageous; the political side still remains outside.

40. Hettne *et al.* (1991: 39) note that attempts at finding a common Nordic line on the issue have been insufficient in relation to the temptations for individual politicians to engage in grandstanding. The Nordic countries have taken different stands – the closer to the Baltic states, the more eager the state has been in practical cooperation but the more cautious in political issues. Thus, for instance in a meeting of the Nordic foreign ministers in November 1990, the Danish and Norwegian ministers urged regular meetings with those of the Baltic countries, while their Swedish and Finnish counterparts were less enthusiastic, emphasising a more encompassing cooperation including the Soviet Union and Poland (Wæver 1992b: 164).

228 The Plurality of Truth

41. For examples on how the Nordic countries are sometimes lavishly depicted as particularly virtuous and profoundly well-meaning, even altruistic, e.g., Miljan (1977: 97); Turner (1982: 2); on the specifically virtuous nature of Nordic cooperation, e.g., Nielsson (1978: 278-279, 281); Sundelius (1978: 61-62); Sundelius and Wiklund (1979: 71). There has been a tendency to characterise the Nordic countries by low military tension, anti-militarism, high social stability and standard of living and a small state philosophy of being morally superior to the larger states (see Jervell 1991a: 15-16) and to see Nordic cooperation as better than the EC because of the prevalence of societal actors, voluntary, informal and consensual nature – the absence of formal agreements equalling moral superiority (Neumann 1992: 17). On the other hand, Wiberg (1992: 247-248) argues that there have always been competing identities and differing links to outside countries, and that these, in fact, have caused the failures of the grand Nordic cooperation schemes.

42. A first gauging of the degree to which Nordic cooperation is influenced by the development of the EC's home market is presented in the report of the Nordic Council of Ministers on Nordic cooperation 1987 (C1/1988), final report *Norden i Europa* 1988 and a complementary report. Economic integration seems, in fact, to proceed *pari passu* with the EU, or imitating it (cf. the working programme of the Council of Ministers 1990: 10-11).

43. In fact, the Nordics were reminded of the priority of European integration already when the question of broadened Nordic cooperation was taken up by Denmark in its membership negotiations, the EC answering with a counter-declaration to this effect (Stålvant 1991, referring to *Agence Europe*, November 10, 1971).

5 Nordic integration: elements of a model

The 1990s: new dynamism for Nordic cooperation

For many observers, politicians and scholars alike, the 1990s have profoundly changed the conditions for Nordic cooperation. Several factors – decrease of the particularity of the 'Nordic model' in social policy, increasing participation in European integration by the Nordic countries, the end of bipolarity in international relations – converge, in their view, in gradually eroding the very foundations of Nordic cooperation. It now faces serious competition from the EU for resources, time and motivation. The binding nature of EU integration makes parallel Nordic efforts incompatible and illegitimate, while Finland and Sweden's EU membership may even induce new conflicts of interest between the members and the non-members.

The various changes, summed up by Sverdrup (1996) as 'Europeanisation', are seen to lead to increasing informality, a lessening of Nordic cooperation in international organisations, and decreasing resources and interest. Nordic cooperation seems in retreat, judging from the cutting of institutions and the concentration on fewer issues, selected by applying the criteria of utility and 'genuine Nordic interests'. Furthermore, it has lost credibility as a tool in the policies of the Nordic countries (Mouritzen 1993a); Nordic identity is endangered by the loss of its particularity and leading role due to the end of bipolarism and the superior dynamism of European integration. Wæver even argues that, despite a temporary revival of 'Nordism' in the current phase of adaptation and transformation, Nordic cooperation will be 'dead by the late 1990s', except for culture and education (Wæver 1992a: 95 and 1992b: 149; cf. Joenniemi 1992b). Others claim that it is not that the 'Nordic option' has now lost ground; it might never even have existed as a real option or an alternative to the EU. As Andrén (1984: 261), for example, has maintained, real Nordic integration would require a total insufficiency of the national systems and unacceptability or unavailability of European solutions.

These pessimistic views stem, however, from the manner in which Nordic cooperation is compared to EU integration. Assuming that the two are essentially similar in terms of their tasks and goals, they are either seen as incompatible or merely overlapping. In both cases, Nordic cooperation is the weaker, the less binding, less successful, dynamic or effective, and therefore it seems clear that the choice between the two falls with EU integration. For both Nordic politicians and scholars, the EU seems more rewarding and interesting and thus for the time being it absorbs a major part of their energy.[1]

Nordic cooperation, like European integration itself, has every now and then experienced periods of diminished interest. Contrary to the European process, however, the reason for this decline has not been deceleration or problems in reaching its goals, but the very success and stability of Nordic integration. Its largely self-evident nature has not been inspiring, but has turned the attention to more demanding fields. For this reason, new challenges imply new incentives for Nordic cooperation. In particular, the end of the cold war and Finnish and Swedish EU membership can provide Nordic cooperation with the necessary new dynamism. As three of the five Nordic countries now are EU members, the two forms of integration, Nordic and European, are much closer connected than before. This implies an increasing need and possibility for collaboration between the Nordic countries in the European context, while the achievements in the latter may also inspire similar measures within Nordic cooperation.

Even more importantly, however, the ensuing need for comparison and adjustments creates a new consciousness about Nordic cooperation, its nature and achievements. New plans in EU integration tend to highlight that not only has a similar plan already been realised in the Nordic context, but also that it functions smoothly and appears self-evident – as is shown by the measures linked to the free movement of people. This kind of comparison also furthers 'Nordic identity'. Indeed, one can hardly see that Nordic identity could be threatened because of contacts with the 'European'; actually, it is through these contacts that a special Nordic identity can develop, based on perceived common attitudes and principles which are seen to differ from European ones.

At the same time, one can also achieve an improved picture of the EU through the differences and similarities between the Nordic and the European processes. A similar comparison shows the extent to which Nordic integration is still a distant model for the European process due to, for instance, its considerable advantage in duration. It also indicates fields in which Nordic cooperation could serve as a model for the larger process, as well as fields in which Nordic cooperation could benefit from that process.

The peculiar extent and methods of Nordic integration

The apparent clarity of the term 'Nordic cooperation' easily misleads scholars to concentrate on the area literally characterised as being 'Nordic' and 'cooperative'. This is a small, although significant, field of agreements and arrangements common to all the Nordic countries and involving measures which can be seen as cooperative – nothing more and nothing less. In reality, there is not much 'Nordic' cooperation in the sense of it being common to all the Nordic countries, even less exclusively to them. There are treaties and practices which concern only some of the countries, and few interests link them in questions such as relations to adjacent areas. Rather than being a separate field of its own, the 'Nordic' component is an aspect or the overlapping part of the different national realms. Moreover, 'cooperation' takes many different forms, some of which could just as well be characterised as harmonisation, unification or joint action. Thus, the literal interpretation of 'Nordic cooperation' reduces both the extension and the depth of the phenomenon, depicting it as unduly low-profile and modest in its aspirations.[2]

On the other hand, hasty conclusions from the failed large-scale plans for union and from the formal aspects of Nordic institutions and agreements[3] may mean that two particularities of Nordic cooperation pass unnoticed. First, there exists a large informal cooperation which might not be easy to approach but which in practice hardly differs from the formal as to its real importance. Second, the low-profile nature of Nordic cooperation has often been emphasised by the involved actors themselves as a kind of self-definition, even camouflage, in order not to give cause for opposition to Nordic cooperation, be it from domestic opinion or the external environment.

Actors and fora

The basic treaty on Nordic cooperation, the Helsinki Agreement of 1962, alludes to its variety of issues, actors and forms. This agreement seeks to sustain and to develop Nordic cooperation in the fields of legislation, culture, social policy and economy as well as in those of transport and communications and environmental protection, the general aim being the widest possible similarity as regards different national norms and an appropriate division of labour between them wherever suitable preconditions are to be found (preamble; art.1). Thus, rather than creating or urging cooperation, the agreement gives an overview of existing cooperation, stating the signatories' commitment to it. On the other hand, it does not limit cooperation to the fields explicitly mentioned. Nordic cooperation is above all characterised by two features: the limitless range of issues and the variety and variability of the actors concerned as well as of the fora in which it takes place.

The matters pertaining to the competence of the Nordic Council are practically unbounded.[4] The only criteria by which the Helsinki Agreement (art. 44) delimits them is interest to more than one Nordic country: the Council may take initiatives and give advice on all matters concerning collaboration between all or some Nordic countries. Similarly, the decision-making competence of the Council of Ministers comprises the entire field of Nordic cooperation (art. 60). In practice, only one area has been kept out of formal cooperation, namely, that of foreign and security policy. The Nordic countries have not been willing to give the impression that binding common stands could be taken in this field. At the same time, it was assured that these matters were not formally excluded, either. As foreign policy issues tended to come up in the discussions, it was frequently debated whether or not the Council actually was authorised to discuss them. In 1964, the Presidium therefore stated that the Council indeed had the formal competence to discuss foreign policy and defence, warning against any decision of principle or alteration of the statutes which would formally exclude such matters. This was motivated by the possibility that in the future, situations could arise in which it would be natural for the Council to examine such matters. (Wendt 1981: 249-250.) In the 1990s, this has clearly become the case.

According to the Helsinki Agreement, cooperation takes place – in addition to the Nordic Council and the Nordic Council of Ministers – in the meetings between prime ministers, ministers for foreign affairs and other ministers, in special organs for cooperation and between the public authorities of the countries (art. 40). The diversity of issues implies also a variety of participants. In fact, it is taken for granted that not only Nordic public bodies but also organisations and companies should be able to cooperate with the minimum of formality. Thus, different interest organisations, including trade unions and political parties, traditionally cooperate with their Nordic counterparts (Rules and procedures 1988: 7, 16).[5] The sphere of private Nordic cooperation comprises, for example, regular Nordic meetings of different professionals, going back to the 19th century, and the *Norden* associations, established by civil servants, politicians and business leaders, the general aim of which is to promote Nordic cooperation through inspiring different Nordic initiatives and spreading knowledge of other Nordic languages and cultures.[6] (Wendt 1981: 18-22; Kivimäki 1992: 14.)

Nordic integration: elements of a model 233

As regards the fora and levels where Nordic public authorities cooperate, five different types can be distinguished: subnational, national, Nordic, regional and international. The subnational level consists of cooperation between municipal and regional authorities. The practice of direct transborder correspondence between municipalities was codified in the Helsinki Agreement (art. 42); the Nordic Council has particularly encouraged cooperation in border regions. Furthermore, a convention between Denmark, Finland, Norway and Sweden on municipal cooperation across the Nordic state frontiers was signed in 1977 to ease collaboration in the field of municipal competence, which in the Nordic countries is extensive and comprises, e.g., health care, transport, culture and the environment. Assisted by regional loans from the Nordic Investment Bank, municipalities in different countries share, for instance, schooling and health care services. (Kivimäki 1992: 14; Wendt 1981: 243-246.) Transborder cooperation can also take place between larger units than municipalities. There are, in fact, several large Nordic subgroups which reflect regional or local identities and interests, and together they form an informal cooperation council (*Rapport* 1992: 50-51).[7]

The national level comprises cooperation between various Nordic state authorities taking place beyond the Nordic institutions. A concise way of describing it would be to say that practically all state authorities cooperate with their Nordic counterparts, something that has given rise to the metaphor of a 'cobweb model' of integration; this is part of the informal or unofficial Nordic cooperation which parallels and completes the cooperation taking place within the institutions. On the one hand, there are Nordic meetings between the heads of governmental bodies such as state archives, post and railways, the supreme courts and central banks (Wendt 1973: 17-18). On the other, there is extensive cooperation on different levels between the ministries.

Practically all ministers have regular Nordic meetings, irrespective of whether they also meet as the Council of Ministers. This practice began already in the years of 1929-39; for instance, the ministers for foreign affairs have met regularly at least twice a year since 1932, and those for development affairs and defence have also met twice a year (Wendt 1981: 24; NU 1988/4: 118-124). The prime ministers have since 1993 had a particular responsibility for the overall coordination of Nordic cooperation; they meet three to four times a year. One minister from every government is appointed as the minister for Nordic cooperation with the task of coordinating, supervising and encouraging it. They assist the prime ministers together with a special cooperation committee composed of senior officials (NSK, *Nordisk samarbetskommitté*) which was established in 1992. The NSK heads the secretary for the Council of Ministers and takes care of day-to-day activities. It also has full competence to make decisions on all questions where unanimity can be achieved and where the respective ministers have not reserved themselves the right of making decisions.[8]

In addition to ministers, cooperation across ministries takes place at lower levels. While the foreign relations of particular ministries have traditionally passed through the ministry for foreign affairs, this has never been the case for Nordic contacts. Indeed, Sundelius (1978: 57-60) has argued that the foreign ministries have had very limited opportunities to coordinate Nordic policies because of the well-established practice of direct communications and informal contacts. In each ministry, a liaison official is appointed as a link between the particular ministry and the national delegation to the Nordic Council. Wendt (1973: 17-18) also mentions that the chiefs for administration, trade and press of the ministries for foreign affairs regularly meet their Nordic counterparts.

The formal Nordic level of cooperation comprises the two main institutions, the Nordic Council and the Nordic Council of Ministers, established respectively in 1952 and 1971. The Nordic members of parliament had met regularly since 1907 in the semi-private Nordic Interparliamentary Union, NIPU, a regional organisation within the worldwide IPU. Its ambit was exchanges of opinions, and occasionally, it inspired legislative initiatives, although it had no institutional authority.[9] (Wendt 1981: 33.)

The idea of a Nordic parliamentary council was expressed as early as 1938. Once established, however, the Nordic Council came to be more than a mere parliamentary assembly: it became an organ for joint consultation between the Nordic governments and parliaments. It is composed of 87 parliamentary representatives and a variable number of representatives of the five governments and the three self-governing regions. In practice, a large majority of the executive has usually participated in the plenary sessions.[10] The Council can give recommendations, proposals and statements of opinion to one or more governments and to the Nordic Council of Ministers. It also has the right to be heard in the most important questions of Nordic cooperation, when this is not made impossible through lack of time. The Council can also pose questions to the members of governments on all matters pertaining to Nordic cooperation. (Rules and procedures 1988: 22, 24; Wendt 1981: 52, 69-70.) Although the governments are not formally compelled to follow the Council's recommendations or to bring any specific issues to it, it is often pointed out that the recommendations approved by a broad majority of the Nordic Council have considerable weight in the national parliaments and governments and are to a large extent implemented. Wendt sees the reason for this in that the political parties generally elect their leading and most influential members to the Council. Thus, in a way, the Nordic parliamentarians may exercise power over the governments; in the Council, the latter can present proposals, but they do not have the right to vote. In addition, the members of the organs of the Council, the permanent committees and the Presidium, are elected among the parliamentarians; the government representatives have access to the committees, but without the right to vote.

The Presidium of the Nordic Council, which takes care of cooperation between the annual sessions, has considerable autonomy in that it can address a 'statement' directly to the governments or the Council of Ministers without awaiting consideration of the plenary assembly. In addition, the Presidium has the right to represent the Council. (Wendt 1981: 38, 56-58.) The Presidium coordinates and is responsible for the international activities of the Nordic Council. Both the Nordic Council and its four permanent committees have contacts with similar international organisations or institutions; for example, the Nordic Council signed in 1990 a cooperation protocol with the Council of Europe about mutual observer status, it has been an observer in the IPU since 1992, and has contacts with the parliamentary organs of Benelux, CIS, EFTA and EEA. The Nordic Council is also member of one of the 24 interparliamentary delegations to the European Parliament, together with Finland, Iceland and Sweden (NU 1988/4: 68). The international activities of the Council have expanded in recent years, and it defines itself increasingly in terms of an actor in its own right with contacts even to organisations of which the Nordic countries are not members. There have been discussions on the possibility of establishing contacts with security organisations such as the OSCE, NACC and WEU. In its relations to the EU, the Nordic Council has established contacts with the Committee of regions and is willing to take an active role as a regional policy actor in Europe.[11]

The establishment of the Nordic Council of Ministers implied a strengthening of governmental cooperation. It is composed of one or more members of each government, with the participation of the representatives of the self-governing territories. Convening as a Council of Ministers, the members of governments have the power of taking decisions by unanimity that are binding for the individual countries. Usually, however, the Council of Ministers proceeds on the basis of consensus. Thus, it does not much differ from the equally consensus-based informal meetings between ministers which are in addition to their meetings as the Council of Ministers. Some ministers never meet as a Council of Ministers; the difference between the two types of meetings is not very clear, however, and a meeting can even begin as one and end as the other (Wendt 1973: 20).[12] The Helsinki Agreement (art. 67, 40) also equates the two, stating that consultation between governments can take place, in addition to the Council of Ministers, also in Nordic ministerial meetings. Responsible for cooperation between governments and between the governments and the Nordic Council, the Council of Ministers submits an annual account to the Nordic Council detailing Nordic cooperation and future plans, as well as a budget proposal; in addition, it presents a report on the measures taken in light of the recommendations of the Council. Furthermore, the prime ministers and the ministers for foreign affairs give an annual report on their activities. (Rules and procedures 1988: 32-33; *Planer* 1993: 5.)

In evaluating the Nordic institutions, it is important to note that they differ in two central ways from many other international institutions. For the first, their main function is not that of a locomotive of cooperation; they should not be evaluated in terms of what they have devised or achieved, since this is not necessarily their role. Instead, they coordinate and strengthen existing activities. While the establishment of the Nordic Council was more a way of assuring the Nordic countries' commitment to cooperation than an effort at creating new forms of cooperation, the objective of the Helsinki Agreement was to define how far cooperation had progressed and introduce certain guarantees that cooperation, once established, would not be abandoned. (Cf. Sundelius and Wiklund 1979: 69; Nielsson 1978: 282-283, 295.)

The second main difference is that the Nordic institutions are not intended to be above, or even completely separate from, the national administrations. Again, evaluating them on the basis of formal authority *vis-à-vis* the member states, their own resources and independent goals would be mistaken as they would appear unduly weak (e.g., Ørvik 1974). Relatively few people work on a full-time basis for Nordic cooperation; the secretariats of the Nordic Council and the Nordic Council of Ministers are quite small – some 150 persons in all, including the national secretariats – and are getting smaller rather than growing through the recent relocation of the secretariats under the same roof in Copenhagen. However, the number of staff does not say much about the productivity of cooperation. In a particularly important phase of Nordic cooperation such as the 1950s, when a large part of the *acquis nordique* (see below) was created, one could hardly speak about personnel at all: Petrén (1959: 119) remarked that the only official working on a somewhat more permanent basis in the Council was the person who took care of the transcriptions of the Council discussions (cf. also Anderson 1967: 55).

The basic idea, in fact, is not that a single, separate secretariat should alone take care of Nordic interests and activities, but that all civil servants in the Nordic countries have the possibility of working for a fixed time period (four to six years) in the Nordic secretariats. Thus, there is no independent Nordic administrative career. The 'Nordic' is rather an aspect of the work in the national administration, which contributes to a bureaucratic interpenetration of Nordic cooperation in the national administrations (cf. Sundelius 1978: 105-106).[13] Similarly, the 'Nordic' is an aspect of the national in terms of its resources. The Nordic budgets are not large, but they do not account for all the money spent on Nordic cooperation as some expenses of the Councils are financed entirely via the national budgets of the member states. Each national delegation also has a budget of its own in the framework of its own parliament. It is difficult to assess the total amount of money spent on Nordic causes because it is hard to distinguish between expenditure for national and for Nordic purposes. (Wendt 1981: 63-65, 82-83, 88; Rules and procedures 1988: 28.)

Regional level cooperation between the Nordic countries and the adjacent areas is of increasing importance for Nordic cooperation, reflected also in the reform of the permanent committees of the Nordic Council: there is now a Nordic committee, an EU committee and a committee for neighbouring areas, in addition to a fourth, controlling committee. At the government level, several initiatives have been taken especially in relations with the Baltic countries; cultural cooperation is also developing within the Arctic region which includes the United States, Canada and Russia. Since 1990 the Council of Ministers has prepared a special yearly working programme for cooperation with adjacent areas; since 1992, these have covered not only the Baltic countries but also Northwest Russia and the Barents region. There is also a special pool of funding of different cooperation projects with Baltic countries and Eastern Europe and sectorial initiatives such as the Baltic Investment Programme (BIP), while the Nordic Investment Bank (NIB) has for a long time been active in Eastern Europe, especially in the Soviet Union. Cooperation with adjacent areas also involves collaboration with different newly established regional bodies both in the level of governments and through the Nordic Council. Among these are the Baltic Assembly, the

Council of Baltic Sea States (est. 1992), the Barents Council (est. 1993) and the Arctic Council (est. 1996).[14]

In recent years, Nordic cooperation has been widening to include a Baltic dimension. In addition to practical assistance in the framework of the working programme for neighbouring regions, cooperation takes place also at the governmental level. For instance, the Baltic ministers of justice participated in their Nordic counterparts' meeting for the first time in 1993, and similarly, the Baltic prime ministers have met the Nordic ones in connection with Nordic Council sessions. The Nordic countries have also aided in the establishment of a Baltic peace-keeping force for the UN. Recently, Nordic cooperation in IMF and EBRD has also started including Baltic countries. (*Verksamhetsberättelse* 1993: 177, 180.) In April 1996, the first meeting between Nordic Council and the Baltic Council took place in Vilnius, together with a meeting between the Nordic ministers for cooperation and the newly formed Baltic Council of Ministers (*Helsingin Sanomat*, April 15-17, 1996).

Cooperation in international organisations, the fifth level or fora of Nordic cooperation, is actually one of the first forms of Nordic cooperation. By the 1920s, Denmark, Norway and Sweden were cooperating in the League of Nations, holding, for instance, a rotating Nordic seat. Subsequently, they were in close contact with Finland (Landqvist 1968: 85). They also cooperated in other early international bodies like the ILO or the UPU, where the Nordic Postal Union from 1935 and its successor, the Nordic Postal Association has been the foundation for joint action (Wendt 1981: 23, 193-194). Subsequently, cooperation in the United Nations has been central in the foreign policies of the Nordic countries. Cooperation takes various forms, such as preparatory meetings before the sessions between government members and continuous consultation and exchange of information during the sessions. The Nordic ambassadors to the UN meet regularly throughout the year, and the ministers for foreign affairs and defence have traditionally considered the upcoming General Assembly issues in a meeting before the session; peace-keeping and development aid have been among the central areas of cooperation.[15] Through these meetings and the more informal daily contacts between the delegations and the ministries, the Nordic countries agree on common statements, division of work responsibilities and common voting declarations. In fields other than economic, social or humanitarian, cooperation is generally limited to exchanges of information. Formally, however, the countries' stands are based on national decisions, even if the preparatory work is done jointly. Among the special agencies, coordination has been particularly developed in UNESCO and GATT, comprising a far-reaching and formalised division of labour. In GATT, well-organised cooperation has occurred between Finland, Norway and Sweden with the participation of Iceland when possible. There has been some coordination also between all the five Nordic countries despite the fact that Denmark has participated in the EC delegation. (NU 1988/4: 38-39, 48, 50.) In IBRD, IDA, AFDB and IMF the Nordic countries have a joint rotating seat. (Wendt 1981: 381-387.)

Similarly, cooperation has been regular in the OECD, where the first common Nordic action was taken in 1983. In the Council of Europe, cooperation is based on the similar directions the countries' delegations receive from their ministries for foreign affairs. The Nordic ambassadors in Strasbourg meet regularly. When Denmark was still the only Nordic EC member, it acted as a bridge between the EC and the other Nordic countries: Nordic ambassadors in Copenhagen were continuously informed about EC issues. Moreover, the Danish parliament has contacts with other Nordic parliaments which can be used as information channels in EU issues. (NU 1988/4: 64-65, 67, 69; see also Turner 1982: 140; Wendt 1981: 146, 367, 373.)

In practice, the Nordic countries have coordinated their policies in international organisations to the extent that they are often seen as a fixed regional grouping with a virtual claim to be represented as such, usually through one rotating representative in the highest organs of decision-making (see Wendt 1981: 373). In fact, in the analyses of voting behaviour in the General Assembly, the coherence of the 'Nordic bloc' has been remarkably high compared to other groupings. The Nordic NATO members sometimes vote differently from the other Nordic countries; the introduction of consultations on foreign policy matters among the EEC members, in turn, did not deter Denmark from voting with the other Nordic countries rather than with the EEC group. (Wendt 1981: 368-369.)[16] The practice of cooperation in international organisations in the form of consultations on questions of common interest or joint appearance and measures has also been codified in the Helsinki Agreement (art. 1), the Nordic treaty on cooperation in the fields of transport and communications (art. 3) and in the treaty on cultural cooperation (art. 2).

240   *The Plurality of Truth*

Aims and method

It is often underlined that the aims and motives of Nordic cooperation are very practical in nature: the purpose of cooperation is to decrease formalities, share costs and increase the single Nordic countries' possibilities to resolve different problems. In addition, motives for cooperation have been seen in concrete gains in defending the region from outside forces, strengthening the international influence of the Nordic countries, achieving certain domestic objectives and securing collective prosperity (Sundelius 1982: 182, 190-193; Sundelius and Wiklund 1979: 71).

The various Nordic cooperation treaties seldom go beyond stating the simple aim of increased cooperation in a given field. The preamble of 1962 of the Helsinki Agreement, however, also refers to the purposes of encouraging close community between the countries, cooperation, uniform rules and, where possible, an appropriate division of labour. According to the Helsinki Agreement, cooperation takes the form of continuous consultation and, when needed, coordinated measures. The practices of cooperation in the international fora were presented above; coordination of national policies and rule-making will be closer examined below.

Both the aims and methods of Nordic cooperation could be characterised as gradual, functional and cautious. It advances step by step, and each step is carefully planned, involving broad consultations and a general openness to the public to ascertain its feasibility and acceptability. Following the principle of transparency common to the Nordic public administrations, Nordic cooperation aims at widest possible openness to the public (Helsinki Agreement, art. 43). Thus, its tempo is rather slow, and controversial steps are avoided. These are often pointed out as basic problems in Nordic cooperation. In Etzioni's view, the fact of being highly egalitarian and concerned with unanimity may be helpful in maintaining commitment, but it is not conducive to action, and the lack of action can have an alienating effect (Etzioni 1965: 195-196). The Nordic institutions have also themselves pondered the necessity to respond to the faster rhythm of work of the EC by making Nordic cooperation more effective, arguing that 'it should also be possible in many cases to formulate political goals without waiting for the results of studies of various kinds' (NU 1989/7E: 15, 19-22).

However, these features are also advantageous. The fairly decentralised, practical-functional (cf. Lange 1954: 286) style has helped Nordic cooperation to expand, inconspicuously but steadily (Anderson 1967: 147, 149). Almdal even sees it as a serviceable approach to integration which focuses on the process rather than the end (Almdal 1986: 5-8, 16). The treaties do not set any limits to cooperation, and it actually has widened both functionally and geographically. As Wendt (1981: 51-52) points out, it is easy for the Nordic Council to assume new duties: according to the Helsinki Agreement, the Council 'in general has those tasks which are apparent from this and other agreements'. Often, this widening has followed the 'spill-over' model: the consequences of cooperation in a certain field have made it necessary to cooperate in related fields as well. For instance, the functioning of the common labour market led the ministers for education to call for a common Nordic school system, the result being a recommendation towards continued unification of school systems (Siikala in NU 1969/21: 59-60). Sundelius and Wiklund (1979: 64-65) have also observed 'spill-around' taking place in the form of spill-over from failure in one field to success in another: notably the treaties and institutions have been seen as achievements that compensate for setbacks in other areas. For instance, the plan for defence alliance led to the establishment of the Nordic Council, the applications for EEC membership to the Helsinki Agreement, and the NORDEK plan to the Council of Ministers.

The cautious aims and methods of Nordic cooperation may also serve an important purpose in making agreement easier to achieve, and general acceptability, both domestically and internationally, has been sought by deliberately underlining its non-binding and pragmatic character. In particular, this kind of *sordino* was needed during the cold war to enable Finnish participation in Nordic cooperation, which for the Soviet Union seemed to be linked to Western European organisations. In practice, Nordic cooperation had to be defined in terms which did not impinge on the neutrality and non-alignment of its members. On the other hand, in relations with the EC/EU, it has been important to stress that Nordic cooperation is compatible with the broader integration process.

One could discern a practice of self-definition by the Nordic institutions, and by many scholars alike, which by so convincingly stressing the modest and thus 'harmless' nature of cooperation, actually covers much more advanced forms of coordination and harmonisation. In a way, the Nordic institutions have had a certain monopoly over their own definition, being able to decide about the nature of the information offered. It could be argued that this has allowed the individual Nordic countries to benefit from Nordic cooperation in different ways, and perhaps protected the very existence of Nordic cooperation in relation to European integration.

A need for particular information activities arose in the early EEC negotiations, as it was important to provide the EEC with an understanding of the objectives and results of Nordic cooperation. As Wendt put it,

> [S]ince the governments intended to insist upon the continuation of Nordic cooperation both within the framework of the EEC and with the Nordic countries outside it, the EEC authorities naturally might desire to know exactly what this Nordic cooperation involved. It would not be easy for the Nordic representatives to explain. Nordic cooperation had always been free and informal in style; the individual countries generally approved uniform legislation, or each one of them introduced measures upon which all could agree. The results of cooperation were only to a limited extent expressed in conventions. (Wendt 1981: 39-40, 376-379.)

The principal means of informing about Nordic cooperation, then, was the drawing up of the Helsinki Agreement in 1962. The agreement is, however, rather general in nature; in fact, the formal documents hardly give a clear or complete picture of the subject.[17]

One of the first statements which had the effect of depicting Nordic cooperation as singularly informal and 'low political' in nature was the declaration by the Finnish government when Finland joined the Nordic Council in 1955. The government stated that the Nordic Council's activities were restricted to issues concerning the Nordic countries and mainly to administrative, social and economic affairs. Moreover, it was emphasised that the representatives of Finland should not participate in the Council discussion if the Council, against accepted practice, were to discuss military questions or conflicts of interest between the great powers. (Wendt 1981: 35-37, 343-344.) Through these statements, Finland was, in part, defining the defined: there was already a general consensus that Nordic cooperation was not aimed at influencing the countries' foreign and security policies.[18] This was also confirmed by the NORDEK draft treaty of 1969 which stated that cooperation should not influence the foreign or security policies of the Nordic countries (*idem:* 346-347, 351).

The low profile is particularly emphasised in the publication 'Nordic Council: Rules and Procedures', where the presentation of Nordic cooperation begins by stating – rather surprisingly – that the [Nordic] region 'is not a federal state' (p. 7). Further, it is observed that 'decisions on foreign and security policies cannot be taken by joint Nordic bodies' (p. 8) and that 'as unanimity is required, the Council of Ministers is not vested with supranational powers of any kind' (p. 31). Nordic cooperation is presented as something informal, not impinging on national decision-making capacity. It is also presented as a model for other regions showing that sovereign states are able to cooperate in joint projects without having to base their cooperation upon common defence and foreign policy (e.g., Council of Ministers' working programme for adjacent areas; also Wendt 1981: 380-381). In fact, the practice that the ministers for foreign affairs and defence do not meet as a Council of Ministers and cannot, thus, make binding decisions, underlines the exclusion of their fields from the formal Nordic cooperation. This does not mean, however, a total absence of foreign and defence policy from the field of cooperation: rather, they have been treated in other, more informal ways.

It is difficult to say whether this practice of self-definition reflects a strategy. Several authors seem to be inclined to think that it does, pointing to the benefits it yields. Anderson argues that the Nordic type of low-key international cooperation is often less threatening to outside forces than a comprehensive, supranational strategy in which defence and foreign policy dimensions can easily come to dominate the picture: it antagonises neither domestic groups nor neighbouring countries (Anderson 1967: 147, 149). Sundelius and Wiklund (1979: 72-74) note that the practice of handling politically sensitive issues outside the Council of Ministers has been useful in maintaining flexibility and discretion. Also Joenniemi (1992: 48-49) maintains that the choice of profile is intended. For him, the Nordic countries seem to be well aware that they must not challenge the conventional understandings of international relations too openly. In Joenniemi's words, they must define themselves as a normal case of international relations, drawing attention away from the fact that their relations actually are not 'international' in character – something which we will return to.

Whether or not the 'image' of Nordic cooperation has been a result of conscious strategy, it seems to have directed research to emphasise the low profile, even though rather interesting scholarly manoeuvres have sometimes been needed in order to confirm that Nordic cooperation in fact is what it has been defined to be. An illustration can be found in Sundelius (1978). His starting point is that there is a clear difference between the EEC, characterised by formal commitment to supranationalism and eventual political union, and Nordic cooperation, which is mere joint 'management of transnationalism' motivated by the countries' small size and vulnerability. He underlines that the Nordic institutions are in no sense supranational decision-making centres independent of the governments, and that even though Nordic relations are more like an extension of domestic policy formulation than traditional foreign policy making, this does not concern issues of vital national political importance. (Sundelius 1978: 5-10, 105-106.)

In analysing Nordic cooperation, then, Sundelius applies a list of policy areas intended to analyse the scope of the EC. The application shows the extremely broad scope of Nordic cooperation which, in fact, includes all the issue areas listed.[19] What does not appear, however, is the difference between the spheres of high and low politics assumed by the theories Sundelius refers to. He quotes Lindberg and Scheingold who expect integration to start in the sphere of low politics, proceeding in a particularly advanced stage eventually to that of high politics, and Hoffmann who doubts whether even successful regional integration ever reaches beyond low politics. Interestingly, when Sundelius examines Nordic cooperation in the light of Lindberg and Scheingold's typology of high and low politics, no significant differences emerge in the scope or intensity of joint policy between the two types of issues.[20] This result could lead to the conclusion that the Nordic case presents characteristics of particularly advanced integration. Sundelius, however, constructs a new order of salience of issues[21] which permits a result coherent with both the assumption about the progress of integration from low to high politics and about the low profile nature of Nordic cooperation, concluding that joint management in Nordic cooperation is most successful in less salient issues. (Sundelius 1978: 99-100.)

Recently, this cautious self-portrayal has appeared in particular in the relations with the EU. As early as in 1961-1962, when Denmark, Norway and Sweden applied for EEC membership or association, Denmark stressed in the motivations for the application its interest in preserving Nordic relations and the need to continue the Nordic labour market. Similarly, Norway and Sweden took a strong stand for Nordic unity. (Wendt 1981: 116-117.) While the Nordic countries have repeatedly stated their commitment to continuing Nordic cooperation despite the EU membership of some Nordic countries, they have asserted, at the same time, that this commitment does not imply anything incompatible with EU membership. For the EEC negotiators, the low profile of Nordic cooperation was clearly a prerequisite for its acceptability: they stressed that a joint proclamation on Nordic cooperation would not prejudice the applications as long as it was non-binding (cf. Anderson 1967: 290).

In a similar vein, the compatibility of Nordic cooperation with European integration was stressed in the EEA agreement which states that

Nordic integration: elements of a model 245

The provisions of this Agreement shall not preclude cooperation: (a) within the framework of the Nordic cooperation to the extent that such cooperation does not impair the good functioning of this Agreement; [...] (Art. 121, part IX).

Finally, when signing their membership treaties, Finland, Norway and Sweden gave a joint declaration together with the EU stating that

The Contracting Parties record that Sweden, Finland and Norway, as members of the European Union, intend to continue, in full compliance with Community law and the other provisions of the Treaty on European Union, Nordic Cooperation amongst themselves as well as with other countries and territories (Corfu Protocol; August 17, 1994; Part E, joint declarations, n. 28).

These statements actually assure the compatibility of Nordic cooperation and European integration in a manner largely favourable to the Nordic countries in that the declarations remain silent about what Nordic cooperation means. In fact, at the level of formal agreements, Nordic cooperation and EU membership could hardly be found to be incompatible due to the 'low profile' definition of the former. Therefore, these defining statements can be seen as 'protecting moves' which, although weak in appearance, actually serve particularly well the purpose of consenting the further continuation of Nordic cooperation. On a closer look, some of them even leave the low profile behind. In the last example cited above, the geographically extensive definition of Nordic cooperation is remarkable, permitting, for example, the possible development of it with the Baltic countries. Even more remarkable in this sense is the Danish statement accepted to the protocol in the SEA negotiations where

...the Danish government takes note that the adoption of section three (in the Act) on European political cooperation does in no way affect Danish participation in the Nordic foreign policy cooperation *(Dansk Udenrigspolitisk Årbog* 1986, Copenhagen 1987, p. 310, quoted in Pedersen 1990: 104).

This is a rather puzzling statement in light of the fact that 'Nordic foreign policy cooperation' did not exist at all according to the usual definition of the contents of Nordic cooperation.[22] Yet, it cannot be taken as a mere solemn declaration without definite consequences. This is demonstrated in particular by the effectiveness of the Nordic stand in the negotiations on the Schengen agreement. Denmark's declaration that it will not accept any EU norm implying an encroachment of the Nordic passport freedom (NU 1988/4: 96-97) was, in fact, not rhetorical. Associating non-EU members to the Schengen agreement, the Nordic passport union came to form a singular exception to an agreement which is one of the most advanced and important steps towards political union between the EU members, permitting the free movement of people between the member countries while closing to a larger degree the outer borders. Finland, Iceland, Norway and Sweden all became observers in May 1996, and the EU members signed the treaty in December 1996. Iceland and Norway, in turn, are associated with Schengen through a cooperation treaty which gives them the right to participate in working groups and ministerial meetings. (*Helsingin Sanomat*, February 22, April 19, December 17, 1996.)

The *acquis nordique*

The core of the wide array of treaties, common laws and practices of collaboration which Nordic cooperation involves and which so easily eludes precise definition can best be summarised by Hveem's (1992) telling term *acquis nordique*. It contains the common labour market, passport union and harmonised public administrative systems and social welfare together with permanent cooperation and wide common representation in international organisations. While pointing out the comparability with the *acquis communautaire*, the word *acquis* is particularly fitting in that it gives the idea of something acquired, helping to explain the concurrent invisible and solid nature of Nordic cooperation.

The main achievement of Nordic cooperation is without doubt the existence of a virtual Nordic citizenship based on the free movement of people, achieved already in the 1950s. In 1954, an agreement on the Nordic labour market was signed, including the free movement of labour without the need for work permits. The final step in establishing a passport union was taken in 1957 when passport control for foreigners was abolished at the inter-Nordic borders. Initially, the labour market convention did not include professions demanding authorisation or specific certificates; subsequently, however, measures have been taken to establish, for instance, a medical labour market. (Wendt 1981: 188-189, 223.)

The Nordic labour market measures were accompanied by a Nordic social security convention which replaced different bilateral agreements in

1955 and which has subsequently been revised and extended on various occasions. The aim of this convention is to guarantee in principle equal welfare for each country's citizens and for other Nordic nationals, e.g., in case of sickness or unemployment and for old age pensions. (Wendt 1981: 213-218.) In contrast to the EU, Nordic social security has not been linked to economy and working dimensions: the freedom of movement and equality with the citizens of the host country does not require employment (*Eurooppa*, October 27, 1992: 11; cf. Working programme 1990: 52). Nordic citizenship implies the possibility of living and being active in another Nordic country partly under the conditions applying to citizens of that country, partly under conditions which are similar to those of the home country. The different 'infrastructural' arrangements which facilitate Nordic citizenship in practical terms would be impossible to enumerate. Examples of the many details which make freedom of movement easier to realise are the validity of medical prescriptions and driving licences in all the Nordic countries.

Further, the rights of the 'Northerners' include the right to vote and be elected to local government as well as the acquisition of citizenship quicker and with less formalities than citizens of other countries.[23] The so-called 'citizen policy', aimed at safeguarding and developing these rights, is one of the primary areas of Nordic cooperation. According to the Helsinki Agreement, the parties shall continue to work to attain the highest possible degree of juridical equality between resident nationals of other Nordic countries and their own citizens.

Nordic citizenship, and the *acquis nordique* more generally, are based on a long history of legal harmonisation and general encouragement of cooperation in different fields. They have resulted in a degree of community of law in the Nordic countries which has been estimated to be greater than in many federal states. The aim of continuing legislative cooperation in order to attain the greatest possible uniformity in private law, strive to create uniform provisions regarding crime and consequences of crime and work for mutual imposition of sentences are also codified in the Helsinki Agreement. The work in the Nordic Council is based on the principles of continuous collaboration as well as harmonisation or, where possible, the uniform formulation of legislation or joint legislative measures, and the Council of Ministers gives a yearly report on long-range Nordic legislative cooperation. (Wendt 1981: 264-265.)

This Nordic legislative cooperation began already in the 19th century. From 1872, regular Nordic meetings of jurists were organised, designed to encourage the widest expert agreement on issues concerning legislation and the administration of justice in questions which were important for the Nordic countries. The first joint Nordic law was issued in 1880 on bills of exchange: the same draft was approved by all parliaments, prepared by national commissions individually and collectively. In the 1880s and 1890s, Denmark, Finland, Norway and Sweden prepared common laws on such things as trade marks and maritime regulation. In 1901, the Nordic civil law commission was established. The area of legislative cooperation was subsequently widened and extended to criminal law in the 1940s, when a Nordic committee for legislative cooperation composed of all the five countries was set up. Subsequently, the legal committee of the Nordic Council urged synchronised cooperation already in the phase of investigations and between departments. (Wendt 1981: 258-261; 266-286.)

Legislative cooperation is, however, not the only field of Nordic cooperation with origins in the 19th century. The Nordic 19th century was a mixture of increasing national awareness and emphasis on elements of a common identity, in particular in the form of 'Scandinavianism', a movement among young academics especially in the 1840s and 1850s. It inspired research on common history and culture as well as more general collaboration, including the aim of legislative uniformity. At that time, cooperative relations were quite new in the Nordic relations, and without doubt not self-evident for all.[24]

Cooperative efforts were also inspired by developments abroad, for example the German *Zollverein* or the Latin Monetary Union, constructed around France in 1865, and the German unified monetary system. The 19th century plans for Nordic cooperation were extremely wide, ranging from expanded instruction in other Nordic languages and mutual recognition of university degrees to standard weights and measures, tariff union, common currency and a joint monarchy. A postal union was being prepared, and professional Nordic meetings began; for example, the first Scandinavian meeting of national scientists was held in 1839. Also labour movements established Nordic contacts. (Wendt 1981: 18-21.) The Scandinavian monetary union was established between Denmark, Norway and Sweden in 1875. Its last fragments lapsed only in 1924, the year of Iceland's entry to the convention. Cooperation between central banks, initiated with the union, still continues (*idem:* 100). Not all the plans materialised, however; notably, those for a dynastic union, military alliance and customs union failed. The Danish proposal for a defence alliance against the German threat was deluded by the other Nordic countries which adopted a neutral position when Denmark was attacked in 1864, and the hopes for customs union suffered a setback in the 1880s. (*Idem:* 92-99.)

The weight of such a long history seems sometimes to distort the interpretation of Nordic cooperation. A perspective of more than a hundred years is difficult to take into account in research, and the causes and consequences of Nordic cooperation tend to get inverted: a factor such as similarity of administrative structures and legislation comes to be seen as a mere fortunate prerequisite or cause for Nordic cooperation, while, in reality, it results from long-lasting, at times difficult cooperative efforts. Thus, the *acquis nordique* is often taken to be a condition and point of departure rather than an achievement. In addition to its long history, the unfocused and undramatic manner in which cooperation is achieved contributes to this misunderstanding. Often, in fact, the accomplishments lack direct links to Nordic institutions, as they may originate in the national or international contexts or be, for instance, initiatives of the Nordic interest and parliamentary groups.

Similarly, cooperation in different fields is often seen as self-evident. However, the *acquis nordique* also comprises practices of regular cooperation in three fields where cooperation is actually far from self-evident, due to the differences between the Nordic countries, namely, culture, economy, and foreign and security policy (cf. Hveem 1992).

Nordic cultural cooperation is seen as a cornerstone of joint efforts. It tends, however, to evade exhaustive definition because of its remote origins and the variety of actors and initiatives involved.[25] At the ministerial level, a Nordic cultural commission was set up by the ministers of education in 1946 to assist the governments in cultural affairs. In 1966, the Nordic cultural fund was created to promote cultural activities and cooperation in research and education. In 1971, the Nordic countries signed a treaty on cultural cooperation which expressly mentions cooperation at different levels of education, research, arts and the media. It also aims at a coordination of the Nordic countries' participation in international cultural cooperation.[26]

Among the various achievements chalked up are the various Nordic research institutes and programmes, the private Nordic Summer University, which started in 1950, literary and music prizes and a film and television fund, established in 1990 (Wendt 1981: 305-310; *Verksamhetsberättelse* 1993). The depth of Nordic cultural cooperation is, however, best shown by the two dimensions which concern the basic features of the national societies: cooperation regarding the structure, goals and contents of the educational systems and the position of languages. Particularly interesting early efforts in these fields were the Nordic orthography meeting in 1869 which succeeded in harmonising some features of the Scandinavian languages (see Wendt 1981: 326) and the revision of history and geography textbooks in the 1930s which consisted of recommendations to the publishers for measures intended to increase mutual understanding in *Norden* (Andersen in NU 1969/21: 55; Wendt 1981: 91).

The efforts concerning the mutual understanding of languages and cultures more generally were first concentrated on the different Scandinavian languages, while the position of Finnish and the minor languages in the Nordic countries was relatively weaker. In fact, eight different languages are spoken in the region, three of which, Finnish, Greenlandic and Sámi, are not even Scandinavian. Subsequently, all languages have been involved; the idea is both to promote mutual understanding and to help preserve the cultures and languages. For this purpose, a Nordic language secretariat and a council for the protection of each language have been established. (Wendt 1981: 324-328.) Particularly important from the point of view of the principles of the Nordic community is the Nordic language treaty, signed in 1981. Covering the five principal languages of the region, it gives the right to use one's own language in communications with the public authorities of other Nordic countries, for example the police, public health service and school administration.

It is perhaps emblematic that the language treaty entered into force only in 1987, while Nordic treaties as a rule enter into force soon after they have been signed. Cultural cooperation is, in fact, not necessarily a matter of course between the Nordic countries, as it has often been depicted. Instead of being facilitated by their 'cultural similarity', it has often actually highlighted mutual cultural differences and a certain antagonism. After all, Nordic national identities have, to some degree, been created against each other; the memories of the relatively recent 'intra-Nordic colonisation', as Hveem (1992) puts it, of Iceland, Finland and Norway, and a strong nationality identification persist (cf. Nielsson 1978: 308). This has been particularly clear in issues of education and research, where the Nordic plans have not always succeeded. The differences in national education systems, which from the perspective of an outsider could appear rather small, have not been easy to overcome. Wendt (1981: 303) points out the 'disappointingly slight practical results' in the mutual recognition of examinations,[27] while Solem notes that a recommendation by the Nordic Council in 1961 aiming at a systematic division of labour in Scandinavia within research and scientific education was unacceptable to the governments (Solem 1977: 111, 118-119). Similarly, the discussions on a joint Nordic television satellite highlight the closeness of questions of cultural cooperation to those of national identity and sovereignty. In fact, while for some, the satellite would favour the Nordic objectives of mutual understanding and knowledge, easing the differences of living in another Nordic country, others thought it would undermine national culture (Wendt 1981: 321-322; see also *Verksamhetsberättelse* 1993: 19).

In fact, it would be mistaken to see culture as a neutral field of 'low politics'. This is also shown by the slow progress in this field in the EU. Cultural cooperation – developing a European cultural area, safeguarding cultural heritage, developing cooperation in the audiovisual field and in education – entered the EC only in 1987 via the Single European Act and a framework programme for cultural cooperation (NU 1988/4: 87-88). Moreover, in the Maastricht Treaty, the harmonisation of laws is explicitly excluded in education and culture (cf. Burley and Mattli 1993: 73-74). That Nordic cultural cooperation nowadays appears as self-evident as it does proves the importance of the steps taken.

Many analysts have also pointed out the importance of cultural cooperation as a prerequisite for solidarity and successful cooperation in other fields or necessary for the progress of economic collaboration (Andersen in NU 1969/21: 47). Solem (1977: 14, 118) further remarks that the social and cultural fields might well become increasingly central in integration, as the economic dimension becomes gradually depoliticised through becoming subject to technological and scientific planning and management.

The second field in which Nordic cooperation exists despite the rather unfavourable preconditions is economy. Indeed, the efforts at Nordic cooperation have been hampered both by clearly diverging economic interests and by the competition caused by economic similarity. In particular, the conditions for agriculture vary considerably, the countries have different trading partners and even compete with each other directly in certain sectors, such as pulp and paper. Yet, although the plans for a Nordic economic union never materialised and despite the division of the Nordic countries in their economic affiliations between, first, the EFTA and the EEC, and, later, the EU and the EEA, economic cooperation has been a constant factor of Nordic cooperation.[28] It is also one of the main areas of cooperation mentioned in the Helsinki Agreement (art. 18-25) according to which the Nordic countries shall promote cooperation in the fields of production and investment, including an appropriate division of labour, and work towards facilitating direct cooperation between Nordic firms and economic cooperation in the border regions. In addition, they shall aim for free capital movement and the abolition of trade barriers. In questions of international trade policy, the countries shall, individually and collectively, promote the Nordic interests. The different attitudes towards the EEC did not, in fact, impede practical Nordic economic cooperation in such forms as a joint negotiating front in GATT. Already in the GATT conference of 1956, Norway, Sweden and Finland had a joint negotiator (Turner 1982: 139) and in the Kennedy Round (1966-1967), Nordic cooperation was particularly successful. It was based on a special agreement between Denmark, Finland, Norway and Sweden giving the common negotiator the exclusive right of making binding proposals and decisions in the negotiations (Gustafsson 1968: 170).

In addition to cooperation in the Bretton Woods institutions and between central banks, Nordic economic cooperation has also developed in special Nordic institutions such as *Nordforsk*, the Scandinavian council for applied research, founded in 1947, *Nordtest*, an institution for standardisation and material testing (1972), the Nordic fund for technology and industrial development (1973) and the Nordic Investment Bank (1975), which gives loans and guarantees for the realisation of Nordic projects and finances exports of Nordic interest. The NOPEF *(Projektexportfonden)*, functioning from 1982, became a permanent cooperation organ in 1988 with the idea of strengthening international competitiveness through exports to developing and state-trading countries. (NU 1988/4: 62; NU 1989/7E: 40; Wendt 1981: 148-153, 165-166, 167-181.)

Both the EFTA and the EEA agreement have considerably increased Nordic economic cooperation. In the 1960s, EFTA led in practice to the removal of tariff barriers in Scandinavia:[29] by the end of 1969, all duties and restrictions on industrial goods were removed. Trade between the Nordic countries increased considerably. (Wendt 1981: 111-115.) The EEA agreement, which entered into force on January 1, 1994 comprising all the Nordic countries together with the EU countries, Austria and Liechtenstein, further widened and deepened economic cooperation between the Nordic countries. In its field, it has been seen as one of the most important treaties which regulate relations between Nordic states. It has also led to increased legislative harmonisation in fields new to Nordic cooperation (Kivimäki 1992: 45; *Verksamhetsberättelse* 1993: 198).

While Nordic legislative cooperation has for a long time followed the developments in similar efforts between the EC countries, encouraged by the Nordic Council (Wallmén 1966: 38), also the EC plans for economic cooperation have inspired similar Nordic initiatives. For example, in 1985, a plan for economic development and full employment was given, containing the establishment of a Nordic home market and measures to promote exports, industrial policies, research and development. In 1987, a programme for abolishment of barriers to trade was presented. A certain liberalisation concerning free capital movement and establishment rights has taken place (see NU 1988/4: 61) – a decision was made to remove the remaining barriers to capital movements across frontiers on July 1, 1990. (Working programme of the Council of Ministers 1990: 10-11; NU 1988/4.)

The third and last area of Nordic cooperation where one would least expect it is foreign and security policy. In principle, the Nordic countries' foreign and security policies have been truly different because of their varying affiliations: Denmark, Norway and Iceland are NATO members, while Sweden and Finland are neutral, the latter having also been bound for a long time by a cooperation on friendship, cooperation and mutual assistance with the Soviet Union. Still, cooperation has extended even to these fields, although it has become more prominent only in recent years.

During the cold war, there was a general consensus that questions of foreign and security policy did not belong to the field of formal Nordic cooperation (Wendt 1981: 343-344; Lange 1954: 289-291; cf. above, p. 13). Although these issues were in principle not discussed in the Nordic Council, they came to the agenda every now and then.[30] The Finnish communists were particularly active in introducing elements of foreign policy to the Council.[31] In addition to purely Nordic issues, matters linked to UN resolutions and international relations more generally were discussed, such as the Russian intervention in Afghanistan (Wendt 1981: 249, 352, 358-359). The Council also acted in an international dispute – although not as an institution – when relations between Iceland and the United Kingdom were severed by a dispute over Iceland's fishing limits, leading to the three so-called 'cod wars' (1958-1961, 1972-1973 and 1975-1976). Cautiously, Iceland was assisted by the Presidium of the Nordic Council and the Nordic foreign ministers, as well as by NATO. (See extensively in Wendt 1981: 388-394.)

On the informal side, however, consultation on foreign policy and defence has been regular at different levels, including the meetings of ministers for foreign affairs and defence (see above). Moreover, the Helsinki Agreement furnishes the Nordic Council with a range of practical issues having to do with foreign policy or international relations. The section 'Other cooperation' (art. 33-36) encourages cooperation in foreign service, development aid and information activities on Nordic cooperation abroad. According to the treaty, Nordic foreign service officials on assignment outside the Nordic countries, shall, to the extent compatible with official duties and in accordance with the host country, assist nationals of another Nordic country, if that country has no representation in the locality concerned. In practice, also joint representations and some sharing of functions have taken place in the consular field; there has been much informal cooperation between Nordic representatives abroad and exchange of information between the Nordic countries on, for instance, new opening plans for embassies has been encouraged. (Wendt 1981: 363-365; for the Nordic Council recommendations on these issues, see NU 1988/4: 29.)

In the late 1980s, international questions became increasingly dominant in the Nordic Council. In 1985, a member proposal was made on a committee to examine how Nordic cooperation could be further developed and strengthened in international matters. The ensuing committee work was based on the perceived need for further cooperation in this field; it was observed that while the Council had always examined questions of international character, they had not played a central role. The mandate of the committee for international co-operation was limited to 'various international issues', explicitly excluding only questions pertaining to security politics. From 1988, the discussion on European integration started fully in the Nordic Council, while recommendations were also given on detente, the superpowers' arms race, the conflict in the Middle East, refugee policy, South Africa and the Baltic countries. (Cf. NU 1989/7E: 7 and NU 1990/7: 91.)

The proposals of the reports about the strengthening of the international dimension led to the establishment of an international secretary to the Council and to a revision of the Helsinki Agreement which was to remove the doubts concerning the competence of the Council in the field of international issues by stating them explicitly (NU 1988/4: 11-12; 20-21; NU 1990/7: 89-90, 150). On the basis of a proposal by the personal advisors to the prime ministers, the Helsinki Agreement was modified in 1993: it is now less conditional and contains clearer indications on cooperation in international questions.[32]

The ease with which these modifications were made shows that the question was not about introducing something new to Nordic cooperation, but rather about consolidating traditional practices. Interestingly, in the eyes of the general public, Nordic cooperation in foreign and security policy seems not only acceptable but even central; in a large Nordic opinion poll in 1993, foreign and security policy were seen as a very important field of Nordic cooperation, second only to environmental protection, free possibility of study in other Nordic countries, recognition of exams and the possibility of free trade across frontiers. Yet, the significance of this cooperation was again undermined in the official interpretation: the incentives for the recommendation to the Council of Ministers about strengthening cooperation in the international context (22/1986) stressed that the aim was not to form a common Nordic foreign policy, only to coordinate the nationally decided policies. In the Nordic context, however, as cooperation primarily takes place at the level of policy formulation and preparation, the difference between a Nordic policy and a coordination of national policies is not necessarily evident.

Recently, questions of security and defence have become increasingly important. The personal representatives of the prime ministers stated in 1992 that foreign and security policy were an important part of Nordic collaboration at the level of governments, pointing to the wide existing practice of cooperation. They also defined it in ambitious terms, noting that cooperation in these fields appears chiefly as an active initiatory cooperation in order to influence current issues of substance (*Rapport* 1992: 29-30). The novelty of the 1990s is the gradual emergence of security policy in institutional cooperation: for instance, the plan for international activities of the Nordic Council for 1995-96 states that in accordance with the active role of *Norden* in the fields of foreign and security politics, questions of security policy should be treated when they have common Nordic importance.

Traditionally, the Nordic ministers for defence have met regularly; the issues dealt with, however, have been carefully distributed between the different fora. Thus, the ministers for defence have not met as the Council of Ministers; in the ministerial meetings, mainly UN issues have been discussed, while other issues have been treated in informal breakfast meetings. Besides, the ministers usually consult each other by phone several times a week.[33] Again, the practice of informal consultation seems to have been more important than the official diverging security policy affiliations of the Nordic countries for the general perception of the region. Similarities seem to outweigh differences: scholars refer to a Nordic security community, Nordic balance (cf. Joenniemi 1992b, Wiberg and Wæver 1992) and negative policy coordination (Sundelius 1978: 80-81) implying that the Nordic security policies are not only mutually supportive – e.g., Denmark's and Norway's NATO policies[34] lessening the pressure on Finland and Sweden – but also fairly similar. The different alliances have not prevented the Nordic UN votes from being remarkably uniform; the mere possibility of writing a book such as *Foreign policies of Northern Europe* (1982) where the foreign policies of the Nordic countries are seen as sufficiently similar and yet various for comparative study is illustrative of the transformation of the difference between neutrals and NATO members into a 'Nordic foreign policy'.

In 1992, a working group was set up by the ministers for foreign affairs to examine issues linked to security in Northern Europe.[35] Since 1993, the meetings of the ministers of defence have been characterised by an enlarged agenda, comprising the joint Nordic troops in Bosnia and cooperation between Sweden and Norway in the arms industry and research. In November 1994, an agreement on joint procurement and cooperation in the weapons industry was signed between Sweden, Denmark, Norway, Denmark and Finland (see also Værnø 1993: 120). The military commanders-in-chief also expressed favourable opinions on cooperation in defence. In fact, Neumann (1995) sees that cooperation in the field of security may become an increasingly important part of Nordic cooperation as the end of the cold war has made Nordic security concerns increasingly similar. Security might also become relatively more central as other fields of cooperation have partly been transferred to the EU/EEA level (cf. Stålvant 1991: 184).

Meeting of two methods of integration

The Finnish and Swedish EU membership has once again made a comparative evaluation of European integration and Nordic cooperation expedient, showing both their partly similar, even overlapping content and the differences in their methods of integration. The comparison highlights the particular characteristics of Nordic cooperation, its rather vague appearance, commitment based on a sense of community rather than obligations, and its nature as informal integration or domestic politics rather than inter-state interaction.

Consciousness of the contents of Nordic cooperation and the meaning of the 'Nordic' is increased specifically through discussions on the consequences of EU membership. For example, the Nordic citizenship, and even the passport union, were probably not well known to the public until they were raised by the discussions of and plans for a European passport union. The emerging differences in the methods and achievements of the two processes in matters such as openness or consumer protection not only increase awareness of the 'Nordic' but may also be turned into an activation of a Nordic identity. The new situation shows the importance of international participation for forming a collective identity. In the cold war era, traditional Nordic cooperation in international organisations was almost the only way which induced other states to perceive the Nordic countries as similar to each other or as a unit (cf. Værnø 1993: 196), thereby contributing somewhat to a 'Nordic identity'. Now, after this interlude which limited both the fields of Nordic cooperation and their participation in European integration, this effect is strengthened.[36]

The comparison of Nordic and European integration shows the strengths of Nordic integration, notably its flexibility, pragmatism and legitimacy, which result in part from its long traditions. At the same time, it helps to identify ways to develop both processes.

A first strength of Nordic cooperation lies in its flexibility. Nordic cooperation is, in fact, a paramount example of 'variable geometry'. The number of the Nordic countries actually participating varies from case to case: often, some of the countries are not included at all or have joined the arrangement later. Thus, to mention a few examples, Iceland joined the agreement on the Nordic labour market and passport union some ten years after its launch (Wendt 1981: 188-189), and has not participated at all in the meetings of the ministers for defence. Finland, in turn, joined the Nordic Council only in 1955; in the 1930s and 1940s, it temporarily suspended participation in the meetings of the ministers for foreign affairs (Wendt 1959: 24, 39). Subsequently, even Baltic countries have been included in many undertakings. It is important to note that even cooperation between only two Nordic countries is comprised in official Nordic cooperation, rather than being understood as bilateral cooperation. Bilateral matters share the general methods of Nordic cooperation – direct links between authorities, etc. – and can also be brought to the Nordic Council. According to the Helsinki Agreement (art. 44), the Council can take initiatives and give recommendations in matters concerning cooperation between all or some of the Nordic countries and self-governing territories.

In addition to the variability of participants, the issues considered are in practice unlimited. The consensual and functional base of participation ensures high legitimacy: while there are different motivations and reasons behind different Nordic projects, there are, on the other hand, no grounds to oppose Nordic cooperation. Broad participation also implies that the continuation of Nordic cooperation is not dependent on the level of states; the 'motors' of Nordic cooperation can be found also at a subnational or regional level. Proceeding in an open and gradual way on the basis of concrete common interests, Nordic cooperation cannot be said to have negative side-effects (cf. Almdal 1986: 95, 101); the characteristic 'piece-meal microintegration' has also be seen as important for finding the 'point of diminishing returns' (Solem 1977: 113, 165-166). This pragmatism together with the consolidation and habitual nature of Nordic cooperation contribute to its general popularity.[37]

While a certain vagueness may help the Nordic countries in their using Nordic cooperation as a tool for different national purposes, the credibility of Nordic cooperation as such a tool in different contexts (see Mouritzen 1993a: 9-10; Jervell 1991a: 24, 35) demonstrates the existence of substantial commitment. Compared with commitment to the EU, that of Nordic cooperation is more informal: it is not based on binding commitments or supranational decision-making capacity, but rather on a general sense of community, perhaps the 'unique Nordic transnational community' (Sundelius 1978). It manifests itself in the usual acceptance of seeing something in terms of 'Nordic' or likening Northerners to each other,[38] and is a result of a lengthy period of cooperative efforts and intentional creation of community and common identity through the involvement in the cooperation of various parts of the population.

Nordic cooperation has had success in region-building (cf. Wæver 1992a: 99 and 1992b: 159). It has transformed differences into similarities while being able to overcome the negative effects of excessive similarity and proximity. The achievements of Nordic cooperation are often seen as rather self-evident in that the countries are so similar. In reality, however, the self-evident character of the cooperation is itself an achievement. It is important to examine why the countries actually are similar and to see the degree to which this similarity results from cooperation, e.g., the deliberate efforts at legislative harmonisation. Moreover, mere similarity[39] as such does not determine the success of cooperation; it may even be counterproductive. As Etzioni points out, similarities do not make a union in themselves: the effect depends on what is made of them (Etzioni 1965: 220; cf. Neumann 1992: 32). Similarity and geographical proximity together with joint experiences or history may have dysfunctional effects on integration when creating impediments and resentment (Solem 1977: 39-40). The hypersensitivity towards the notion of Nordic union or the Finnish politicians' obsession to decide on the EU membership before Sweden are evidence of these problems.

Nordic cooperation has also transformed inter-state relations into something closer to domestic politics. The Nordic relations are more like an extension of domestic policy formulation without central governmental control or coordination than traditional foreign policy (Sundelius 1978: 6-10; cf. Stålvant 1991: 183). Referring to Deutsch, who placed the Nordic region within the domain of the domestic, Joenniemi (1992b: 53-56) points out that the Nordic relations are characterised by a communality which is usually located in the 'inside' of a community; thus, *Norden* falls in between international relations and domestic-societal properties.[40]

While not supranational in the sense of transferring national competencies to a level above the states or involving binding majority voting, Nordic cooperation has nonetheless been effective in influencing the Nordic states and societies. As Solem notes, the frequently advanced statements that recommendations dealing with noncontroversial issues have little effect on political integration, that non-binding decisions and informal procedures mean that the impact of Nordic cooperation on political integration is minimal, and that the Nordic Council does not play an active or important role in the integrative process of Scandinavia because it has no supranational powers, are at best misleading, at worst incorrect (Solem 1977: 13). Where others would see a need for strong common institutions, the Nordics do not, because the national ones act as if such institutions did exist, as Etzioni (1965: 226-227) points out. In fact, through the practice of collaboration in legislation and the domesticisation of Nordic institutions, Nordic cooperation may actually have a more profound impact on the states and societies than it would have through the formal possibility of making binding decisions by majority vote. The Nordic method, called 'the parallel national action process' by Nielsson, may in practice mean political integration as cooperation becomes a constant factor in national decision-making, leading to identical decisions (Nielsson 1978: 270).

Yet, Nordic cooperation cannot be characterised as intergovernmental, either. The governments are but one participant in the process; the executive, legislative and jurisdictional branches are all involved and the role of parliaments is particularly central (cf. NU 1989/7E: 54). Accordingly, Nordic cooperation has been characterised as transgovernmental or transnational, as a process which reaches across the national administrations, parliaments and ministries instead of functioning above the national level (Sundelius 1978: 77). Equally, it could be seen as informal integration. The actual basis of the influence of the Nordic institutions might well reside, as Sundelius claims, in the merging of the Nordic with the national, or their involvement in effective governmental policy-making, rather than in their independence of the states.

Similar comparisons between the two processes have already lead to measures taken to secure a role for Nordic cooperation and develop it further. To render it more effective, the Nordic governments and institutions seem ready for a fresh dynamism of Nordic cooperation and for new steps inspired by European methods. It is felt that closer contact with the EU gives a new impetus to Nordic cooperation and thereby increases its attractiveness. The dynamism of the continuation and deepening of cooperation is important for political support.[41] The EU membership of three of the Nordic countries gives a new fora for Nordic cooperation; moreover, the EU could also give the possibility of emphasising the Nordic regional framework as one level of decision-making through the principle of subsidiarity (cf. *Rapport* 1992: 13, 37; Kivimäki 1992: 31).

Interestingly, the European process seems now even to contribute to making supranationalism acceptable in *Norden*. There have been several suggestions by the Nordic institutions into this direction. The need for resorting more frequently to binding decisions has been mentioned. Report NU 1988/4 (pp. 28, 31) regrets that Nordic cooperation has in recent years less than before been directed towards binding conventions. While this is considered appropriate in the Nordic context, it is also seen as a potential hindrance in the wider context of European cooperation; particularly measures such as those concerning the Nordic home market would need obligations in order to function well. The need of catching up with EU integration in those fields where it has advanced further has been evident. Report NU 1989/7E asserts that the Nordic Council needs more ambitious and precisely defined goals, a greater sense of direction and effectiveness: Nordic ambitions should not be below those of the EC, but at least on a par with them.[42]

In particular, report NU 1990/7 reflects on supranationalism. Observing that the Helsinki Agreement does not set limits as to how deep cooperation can be, it states that 'in certain cases it may be necessary to resort to majority decision', and considers the possibility of making decisions in the Council of Ministers with a '4/5 consensus' which would allow the Council to decide even in the case of one member country disagreeing. Although the report is unclear as to what this decision-making method would imply, it seems to take supranational methods seriously in that it is concerned about the fact that Denmark cannot automatically comply with the supranational decisions of two organisations. (NU 1990/7: 82-84.) The report also evaluates a member proposal on the establishment of a Nordic commission as an initiatory, preparatory and executive organ, following the example of the EU, noting that '[I]f, at a later stage, some supranational elements are taken into the cooperation, consideration can be given to the establishment of a commission' (*idem:* 113-115).

Efforts have also been put into defining the area of the 'genuine Nordic interests' where Nordic cooperation would concentrate in the future. This 'profilation' has been seen to help to avoid problems of overlapping competence with the EU and a waste of resources. In particular, Nordic cooperation should secure *Norden* as a home market, strengthen identity and mutual understanding or the value community and increase the competitiveness of trade and industry, while having a role in securing national interests (*Rapport* 1992). In practice, however, the agenda of Nordic cooperation does not seem in any way reduced by this profilation; rather, a clearer upgrading of certain interests to the common Nordic level has taken place.[43]

Finally, a comparison of the two methods of integration also increases the understanding of the European integration process and points to areas where its Nordic counterpart could, in turn, give new inspiration. In particular, it opens up discussion on whether the rhetorics of continuous process and the abstract, ambitious goals typical of European integration are really necessary for integration. The ambitious goals risk, in fact, compromising the smaller-scale achievements in that they easily provoke general opposition. Similarly, it is not clear that independent institutions would serve integration better than coordinated national bureaucracies, as these institutions might not only advance integration but also develop their vested interests, being difficult to control, in particular if they lack transparency. Finally, the democratic deficit of the European institutions, in clear contrast with the parliamentary nature of the Nordic Council, points out the importance of broad participation.

Compared to Nordic cooperation, the EU seems to remain in the discourse of traditional international relations. It is characterised by the 'hard' methods of majority voting and directly applicable common regulations, which are seen to be needed to make the member states comply with the common plans, and by risk-taking in the form of denying the viability of a 'stable', seemingly non-progressive union and warning against occasional steps backwards. The comparison with Nordic cooperation may, in fact, lead to observations that there is both the room and need for a Nordicisation of Europe (cf. Joenniemi 1994b: 37) through strengthening the informal and transnational methods of the Nordic type. As the Working programme (1990: 81) puts it, Nordic cooperation is not only well suited by its organisation and nature for being developed parallel to such organisations as EFTA and the EC and for learning from them, but is also capable of holding its own in relation to European integration process, even inspiring it. In essence, the assets of Nordic cooperation are flexibility and adaptability which, combined with pragmatic aims, make it developing and open-ended, but also so well 'tolerated'. As Joenniemi (1994b: 33-34) notes, Nordic cooperation is often seen incompatible with the apparently more established and coherent EU, and it is thus argued that the 'Nordic' can be preserved only if made as similar as possible to the EU. It might well be, however, that the EU with its somewhat mechanical and possibly counterproductive methods could do well to take account of the Nordic experience.

Notes

1. Etzioni seems to have been a trend-setter in diffusing an 'academic image' of Nordic cooperation as completely colourless: in his comparison of different unions, he claims that '[...] the Nordic Union is just a noninspiring, indecisive, high consensus-commanding, egalitarian endeavour' and that '[T]he sessions of the Nordic Council are sporadic, short and dull' (Etzioni 1965: 195-196, 226).
2. The trend described above of underlining the comparative disadvantages of Nordic cooperation and the unique nature of European integration seems prohibitive concerning further research interest in Nordic cooperation. In earlier literature, however, the trend was different. The terms 'union' and 'integration' were frequently applied in the Nordic context. Franzén ('Will There Be a United States of Scandinavia?', 1944) discusses the then actual debate on the creation of a Scandinavian confederation and notes the proliferation of publications on the subject. Etzioni (1965) compares different unions or plans for a union, among which the 'stable union: the Nordic associational web' – although he has subsequently been quoted more for 'associational web' than for 'stable union'. Finally, Turner (1982) entitles his comparison with the EEC 'the Other European Community. Integration and Co-operation in Nordic Europe'.
3. The studies of Nordic cooperation tend to give particular importance to institutions as the motor of integration (e.g., Etzioni 1965, Jervell 1991a: 37), partly due to the simple reason of feasibility. Institutions are accessible and tangible as objects of study (cf. Ørvik 1974: 68). Thus, although for many authors the institutions of Nordic cooperation matter relatively less, while the informal side is particularly relevant, they rarely consider the latter more thoroughly. For example, Jervell (1991b: 187) notes that informal cooperation is a unique feature in Nordic cooperation; however, he relieves himself from further consideration by stating that it is difficult to analyse, and analyses instead institutionalised cooperation.
4. For an idea of the broad scope of activities, see, e.g., the proposal for organisation of committee work in the Nordic Council by the organisation committee, NU 1990/7: 203.
5. Ideas for a Nordic trade union had been presented already in the late 19th century (Wiklund 1968: 147), but they materialised first in 1972 in the form of the NFS, *Nordens fackliga samorganisation*. In 1982, the industrial

associations formed a joint secretariat. Cooperation between employers has been more informal. (Wiklund 1984: 216.) The social democratic parties have a long tradition of close cooperation; other political parties institutionalised their cooperation in the mid-1970s (Karvonen 1981: 101).
6. Every country has its national association. In Denmark, Norway and Sweden, the association was founded in 1919, in Iceland in 1922 and in Finland in 1924. Subsequently, *Norden* associations have been established in the Færoe Islands (1952) and Åland (1970); the latest newcomers are the *Norden* associations in the Baltic countries.
7. Among the subgroups, one might point out Nordkalott (the northern parts of Finland, Norway and Sweden), Västnorden (Greenland, Iceland and the Færoes), the archipelago (Stockholm, Åland, Åbo), and the Sound. For the Sámi population living in the northern parts of Finland, Norway and Sweden, transborder cooperation is natural and the openness of national borders important because of the special characteristics of the reindeer culture. The Nordic Sámi Council was established in 1956; subsequently, it established contacts with the Sámi people in Russia and became the Sámi Council (*Verksamhetsberättelse* 1993: 25; see also Wendt 1981: 248-254).
8. Wendt (1981: 75-76, 78, 81); Rules and procedures (1988: 32); *Rapport* (1992: 14); *Oppfølginsgruppen* (1992: 6).
9. Finland and Iceland joined the NIPU in the 1920s (Anderson 1963: 30 and 1967: 16).
10. The Rules and procedures of 1988 give the number of some 80 government representatives, which is remarkable taken into account that only five countries participate.
11. See *Nordiska Rådets internationella verksamhetsplan för 1995-96* (Presidiesekretariatet, Stockholm 30.5.1994); *Nordiska Rådets relationer till rådets internationella samarbetsparter* (Presidiesekretariat, Stockholm 24.12.1993, including pro memoria of the international cooperation of the permanent committees); NU 1988/4: 69-70.
12. Pragmatism seems to prevail over formalities, even to the extent that different sources give different views on which ministers do not meet as the Council of Ministers: NU 1990/7 and Wendt (1981: 366-367) list those of development affairs, foreign trade and foreign affairs, while the Rules and procedures (1988: 30) mention prime ministers and the ministers for foreign affairs and defence. A somewhat similar pragmatic curiosity was found by Anderson (1967: 40) in former Rules of procedure for the Nordic Council according to which the Presidium could reach unanimous decisions without actually meeting, while in more routine activities, particularly those regarding their own national secretariats, the members of the Presidium could act individually, without mutual consultation.

13. Still, the secretariat of the Presidium is also an actor of its own. On the one hand, both secretariats have power in initiating, vetoing and broking decisions to the extent that they may even reduce the influence of the parliamentary members of the Council (Sundelius 1978: 68-69). On the other, with the establishment of an international secretary to the Presidium, the international contacts of the Council have considerably developed. For example, in 1992 it signed an agreement on parliamentary cooperation with the newly established Baltic Assembly.
14. See *Rapport* (1992: 56-59) and the following documents by the Council of Ministers: *Nordisk ministerråds arbejdsprogram for Baltikum og Østeuropa* (October 9, 1990; revised October 8, 1992); *Nordic Working Programme for the Baltic Region and Other Adjacent Areas 1993* and *Nordic Working Programme 1994 for Areas Adjacent to the Nordic Region*; Værnø (1993: 165-166); *Helsingin Sanomat*, September 22, 1996.
15. See Nielsson (1978: 306); Wendt (1981: 369-371). – In 1989, a Nordic Development Fund was established (*Verksamhetsberättelse* 1993: 196; more in the same of 1992).
16. The importance attached to the uniform voting behaviour is shown by the consequences which an exception to this rule comported. In 1965, the usual cooperation suddenly failed as Denmark changed its opinion about sanctions against South Africa without informing the other Nordic countries. This created bewilderment, and the matter was brought to the Nordic Council session in 1966. Some members of the Council demanded a revision of the Helsinki Agreement in order to change the expression 'should consult' to 'must consult'. Although no action was taken in the matter, the importance of consultations was emphasised. (Wendt 1981: 371-372.)
17. A coordinated long-range information plan on the Nordic Council and Nordic cooperation came into effect in 1976; for instance, the Council has organised conferences for other international organisations in Europe (see the report NU 1969/21 which is a collection of papers presented in such an information conference).
18. By further emphasising the low profile, the Finnish 'definition' actually shed a doubt on whether the profile in reality was that low. The definition was also permissive in that the issues considered were said to be 'mainly' restricted to social and economic questions, and as the possibility of discussion on foreign policy in the Council was, even if exceptionally, recognised.
19. In fact, Nordic cooperation is noted to comprise, for example, negative political coordination (compatible policy outputs) in security policy ('Nordic balance'), coordination in foreign policy, joint measures in trade policy, intensive policy coordination in public health and safety and in the maintenance of order, creation of uniform Nordic law in practically all areas,

substantial results in economic development and planning and, finally, free movement of goods, services and labour. (Sundelius 1978: 80-96.)

20. For them, high politics includes military security, diplomatic influence, political participation, public safety and order, economic and military aid and legal-normative system. Low politics consists of community relations, economic development, business regulation, labour and agriculture, control of economic system and of monetary and fiscal policy, culture, social welfare, education and research.

21. The new rank-ordering is, thus, 1. security policy, 2. economic issues, 3. political participation, public order and health, 4. welfare and education, 5. culture and recreation.

22. Moreover, Denmark proposed a new article to the Treaty of Rome on third country participation in EC cooperation. In principle, the proposal, if adopted, would have made Nordic participation possible in all EC activities. Denmark also tried to obtain a privileged status for Norway within the European Political Cooperation; what it obtained was that a statement was added to the act spelling out the EC's openness towards other democratic countries in Europe. (Pedersen 1990: 104.) See also Værnø (1993: 115-119) on the Danish reservations on the Maastricht treaty, possibly aimed at serving also the other Nordic countries.

23. In fact, after a period of residence, a Nordic citizen has the right unilaterally to declare the assumption of a new citizenship, without applying for it.

24. Until the 19th century, in fact, conflicts outweighed cooperation; the short period of the Kalmar Union (1397 to 1448), which gathered Denmark, Norway and Sweden under a common king with common foreign policy and defence, was rather exceptional and motivated by the common threat constituted by the North German Hanseatic states which sought to dominate the area (Wendt 1981: 13). More usually, there were three competing states in the region, Denmark, Norway and Sweden; after the Kalmar period, the two main states, Denmark-Norway and Sweden-Finland, were at war with each other on several occasions, as the Scanian War (1675-1679) and the Great Nordic War (ending in 1721). The Nordic states also took different stands in the Napoleonic wars. In the 19th century, Norway and Sweden formed a personal union, while Finland was an autonomous grand-duchy under the Russian czar.

25. As the former Danish minister of education K.B. Andersen eloquently expressed in his speech 'The Nordic countries as a cultural community' (NU 1969/21: 47), 'Attempts to describe something requires first of all an isolation of the subject from its environment, and then a delimitation as well as a comprehensive view. It is, however, not so easy to apply these requirements to the theme of this paper: "Cultural Cooperation in the Nordic Countries, and its Popular Background". Nowadays the Nordic community

of culture is both in practice and in principle a matter of course to such a degree that it defies any really exhaustive and satisfactory description. It is like the incidental music to a film: it forms an integral part of the whole, and is, therefore, not easily experienced as a separate element; indeed, we may not notice it at all – though we do know it is indispensable to the overall impression.'

26. Cultural cooperation was first financed through a special common budget, which was also the first joint Nordic budget; now, it is financed through the budget of the Council of Ministers. In the beginning, there was also a special secretariat for cultural cooperation (Wendt 1981: 289-299).

27. In May 1994, however, the ministers for education signed an agreement on the free movement of students (*Helsingin Sanomat*, May 31, 1994).

28. For instance, cooperation in the framework of the Oslo convention of 1932 which also comprised the Benelux countries, Finland joining in 1933 (Wallensteen *et al.* 1973: 50, 53) and UNISCAN, a British-Scandinavian economic committee, established in 1949. Meetings between the heads of the trade departments of the Nordic foreign ministries started in the early 1950s (Turner 1982: 140) and a Nordic permanent committee of ministers for economy was formed in 1960 (Wendt 1981: 111-115; see also 100-101). – On the first 100 years of Nordic economic cooperation, see K. Møller, *Nordisk økonomisk samarbejde gennem 100 aar*, Nordens serie 11, Stockholm 1945.

29. Finland became an associate member in 1961 and a full member in 1986; Iceland joined EFTA in 1970.

30. Attempting at exemplifying this restriction in practice, Wendt gives an account of discussions on international issues as something exceptional and provocative. However, rather than showing how rare exceptions confirmed the rule of non-discussion, he unintentionally shows that foreign policy issues have been constantly present in the Council. He also directly alludes to this when noting that 'in recent years, there has been a growing tendency to vote on party lines, *particularly concerning foreign policy matters,* multinational companies and economic problems [...]' (Wendt 1981: 55, italics added).

31. They proposed, e.g., to add peace and disarmament to the aims of the Council; they were also interpreted in 1976 to wish to give the Soviet Union a place in Nordic cooperation (Wendt 1981: 351, 355; cf. Ørvik 1974: 87).

32. The preamble now notes the countries' wish 'to renovate and develop Nordic cooperation in the light of the Nordic countries' enlarged participation in European cooperation'. According to art. 1, the contracting parties shall consult *(bör rådgöra)* each other in questions of common interest under examination in European and other international organisations and conferences. Thus, the previous conditionality was removed: the article had

stated that the parties shall consult each other *when possible and appropriate*. Art. 33 adds that while participation in European and other international cooperation provides good grounds for cooperation to the benefit of Nordic citizens and firms, the governments have in this respect a special responsibility in safeguarding common interests and values. Finally, the meetings of prime ministers and the ministers for foreign affairs are explicitly mentioned as fora of Nordic cooperation (art. 40). (Cf. *Rapport 1992.*)

33. Interview at the Swedish ministry for defence, Stockholm, May 31, 1994.
34. See, e.g., Turner (1982: 116-117) and Miljan (1977: 80-81).
35. See *Norden og nordisk samarbeid*, Oslo 1992.
36. Many authors claim, on the contrary, that Nordic cooperation faces serious problems with the end of the cold war in that the need for cooperation and the Nordic identity itself were based on the conditions of the cold war, that adaptation to the EU implies a need to abandon the Nordic identity as potentially counter-productive (Mouritzen 1993a) or vanishing attraction of the Nordic and disappearing identity (Wæver 1992a and 1992b; Joenniemi 1992b). This argumentation, however, rather strangely implies that Nordic cooperation was born, in practice, only with the cold war; it also seems to take identity as given, rather than constructed, something which is quite clear as to the European identity currently under construction.
37. Typically, a large Nordic opinion poll conducted in 1993 revealed a very positive attitude to and a rather scarce knowledge of the actual contents of Nordic cooperation in the sense that the field in which it was seen legitimate and consolidated, even self-evident, was larger than the official contents. 74% of the almost 5000 respondents also welcomed increased cooperation.
38. E.g., the possibility of referring to 'genuine Nordic interests' in the EU context or the principle of equating the interests of the other Nordic countries and their citizens with the own in the Nordic environmental cooperation (NU 1988/4: 103-116).
39. The Nordic countries *are* in many respects similar in, e.g., being small and homogeneous societies, welfare states with large municipal autonomy etc. (see Turner 1982: 243-246; Kivimäki 1992: 9, 11-12; Mouritzen 1993a: 5-7). However, there are no similarities without exceptions. It might be difficult really to say what 'Nordic' is in terms of characteristics shared by all the Nordic countries. In answering the intriguing question of whether Finland is a Nordic country, Engman arrives, in fact, at the conclusion that no Nordic country is 'more Nordic' than Finland, or that Finland appears, despite the obvious differences such as language, as Nordic as the others. He points out that *Norden* comprises many different historical and geographical realities – the Atlantic region, the Baltic world, the Northern Kalott region, island and non-island societies, new and old states – and none of the

268   *The Plurality of Truth*

countries belongs to all of them. (Engman 1994, esp. 76-77.)

40. In fact, Karvonen (1981: 103) suggests that Nordic relations should be studied more as domestic than international politics; on the other hand, he adds that it is also commendable to study the Nordic case from the point of view of international politics as 'the Nordic experience has been one of the important empirical inspirations for students of international politics striving to break the boundaries of the high politics dominated traditions of their discipline.'

41. Cf. Per Stenbäck, secretary general of the Council of Ministers, in *Nordisk Kontakt* 2/1994.

42. As an immediate reform, the report proposes the establishment of a Nordic *ombudsman* who would also have the task of receiving complaints from private persons who consider that their rights as Nordic citizens have been infringed and of making the implementation of resolutions more effective – in short, performing some functions of a common court of justice. Thus far, similar complaints – the very existence of which actually shows that the 'Nordic citizenship' is not an empty term for the public – have been addressed to the Presidium. (NU 1989/7E: 15, 19-22, 34-37.)

43. In fact, the lists of the 'genuine Nordic interests' which have been presented are both comprehensive and divergent. Put together, they resemble the traditional, unlimited view of Nordic activities. The prime ministers' Bornholm declaration (1992) includes in these interests environment, citizen policy, energy and infrastructure; the report to the prime ministers lists culture, citizen policy, environmental protection and economic policy (*Rapport* 1992: 12), and the report on the activities of the Council of Ministers (*Verksamhetsberättelse* 1993: 1-2) lists as politically preferential areas of cooperation culture, education, research, environment, fisheries, social questions, health, labour market and work environment, consumer policy, energy, commerce and industry, regional policy, agriculture and forestry, legislation and equality. To these, *Planer* (1993, p. 6) further adds general economic-political cooperation.

6 Finnish EU membership: an integration policy turned on its head

The customary principles of neutrality and sovereignty in Finnish integration policy

Surprisingly, Finland's joining the European Union – a decision whose significance was compared to the declaration of independence in 1917 – was promptly announced to be a logical continuation of traditional Finnish integration policy. As we will see, this kind of continuity is purely rhetorical, constructed as an explanation and justification of the membership decision through a redefinition of central concepts and a certain interpretation both of the nature of the policy and of the process of integration. In reality, membership of today's EU does not allow for the continuation of the sort of policy Finland has had. It implies a disruption of traditional Finnish policy towards Western European integration, as well as, in a long run, major political changes in Finnish domestic and foreign policy, political culture and identity.

Until the early 1990s, Finnish integration policy was based on a confluence of two types of objectives, or two imperatives, as Törnudd has called them, the one economic, the other political. An obvious aim has been to further Finnish economic interests, competitiveness, growth and stability. In particular, the economic imperative stated that Finland must not remain outside any preferential trade arrangement that includes Norway or Sweden together with any principal trading partner. At the same time, Finland's participation in economic cooperation was not to compromise its political autonomy. As a part of foreign policy and closely linked to security political considerations, Finnish integration policy has aimed at safeguarding neutrality and sovereignty, or a certain room for manoeuvre and autonomous decision-making capacity. By resorting to carefully tailored arrangements and avoiding supranational institutions and political obligations, Finland has been able to participate in Western economic cooperation without compromising its relations with third countries, mainly the Soviet Union. At the same time, it has defended itself against being overruled by other Western states within the supranational institutions. (Cf. Törnudd 1969: 64-65; Möttölä 1993: 64; Himanen 1993: 26.)

Basing the policy of integration on neutrality has been motivated by *Realpolitik* and respect for status quo, notably bloc realities. It has implied placing the political before the economic, something that for Finland has been a deliberate choice and an aim in itself, accepted also by the economic interest groups. As a neutral country between the blocs, Finland has been able to play the role of a bridge-builder. (Antola 1991a: 146-147.)

This political imperative has been manifest, first, in various special arrangements and reservations through which Finland has aimed at separating the political from the economic: while participation in economic cooperation has been possible, political cooperation has been more restricted, especially in matters involving a confrontation between the great powers and institutions based on the bloc division. Secondly, Finland has aimed at ensuring 'parallelism' by building symmetric relations with the two blocs through similar economic arrangements. Thirdly, it has emphasised autonomy, accepting an intensification of cooperation only when an independent decision-making capacity could be preserved. Thus, the policy rested on a clear organisational differentiation, aiming at keeping EFTA, an organisation which allows for neutrality, separate from the supranational EEC/EC. While membership of the EEC/EC was categorically excluded, Finland was rather cautious also as regards other organisations, perhaps even overpoliticising the Nordic Council, the OECD and the Council of Europe. (Antola and Tuusvuori 1983: 246-250; Antola 1990b: 166, 1991a: 148 and 1991b: 17-18.)

These elements are clear in the main settlements between Finland and the various West European integrative institutions from the late 1940s onwards. A first instance of Finland's policy can be seen in its reaction to the Marshall Plan. The Soviet Union followed by the Eastern European countries rejected the plan and, thus, it came to be seen in Finland as linked to the bloc division of Europe and disputes between the great powers. Moreover, the coordination of national policies proposed in the plan also involved some supranational features. Finland therefore turned down the invitation to participate in it.[1] Instead, some purely economic arrangements were made to secure foreign capital for the relaunch of production and exports. For this purpose, Finland received loans from the United States and Sweden. More credit was subsequently received through membership of the Bretton Woods organisations IMF (1948) and IBRD (1949), which had been created to further exchange stability and expansion of trade and to facilitate investment in production, reconstruction and development. (Antola and Tuusvuori 1983: 122-124; Antola 1991a: 146; Hjerppe 1993: 67, 69.)

GATT and Nordic cooperation were subsequently found as suitable means for Finland to participate in Western economic cooperation and support Finnish export industries. The GATT was established in 1947 to further negotiations between the signatories towards nondiscriminatory tariff concessions and trade liberalisation; originally, the socialist countries did not join it, as they did not join IMF and IBRD, either. The Finnish accession treaty of 1949 came into force in 1950. For Finland, GATT secured wide and multilateral markets; an important prerequisite for joining was that it gave the possibility of applying the most favoured nation (MFN) principle to countries outside the agreement. Thus, it did not contradict the bilateral trade treaty between Finland and the Soviet Union in force since 1947. (Antola and Tuusvuori 1983: 124-125; Hjerppe 1993: 69.)

Nordic cooperation was advantageous for Finnish integration policy in that it implied possibilities for both economic and political cooperation without formally limiting its members' political room for manoeuvre. Safeguarding national sovereignty was also important for other Nordic countries: the Nordic Council was not given any decision-making power, and it was agreed that it would not discuss matters of foreign and security politics. (Wendt 1981: 343-344.)

For the Soviet Union, however, Nordic cooperation was too closely connected with the Western bloc – after all, the majority of the Nordic countries were NATO members. Finland's approach was therefore initially rather cautious. It had not participated in the Nordic plans for a customs union in the 1940s, although it was involved in different cooperative arrangements with Nordic countries. It also participated in the preparatory work for the creation of the Nordic Council but did not join it when it was established in 1952. Instead, it suspended its membership until 1955 when the critical Soviet attitude changed in the more general relaxation of international relations. Furthermore, on joining it emphasised the low profile nature of the Council: membership would not lead Finland to abandon its neutrality. Finland also made the reservation that its representatives would not participate in the Council's deliberations, if against accepted practice, they were to cover military questions or matters that would lead to taking a position on conflicts of interest between the great powers. (Wendt 1981: 35-37, 343-344; also, e.g., Forsberg and Vaahtoranta 1993: 238.)

Nordic cooperation soon gained an important role in the Finnish economy. In 1956, Finland joined the Nordic economic cooperation committee, which planned tariff reductions; the same year, a Finnish national committee for Nordic cooperation was established. Separate and independent Nordic integration together with measures aimed at developing economic relations between Finland and the Soviet Union came to characterise the Finnish response to Western European integration. (Antola and Tuusvuori 1983: 126-127.)

Gradually, Finland also came to accept the plans for deepening Nordic cooperation towards a Nordic common market. The plan, however, did not materialise. At the time Finland was ready for this new step, the other Nordic countries were no longer aiming at a purely Nordic arrangement. As a follow-up to negotiations between some OEEC members on the possibilities for a wider free trade agreement, they had been negotiating for a European Free Trade Association, and the Stockholm Convention establishing EFTA was signed in 1959 by Austria, United Kingdom, Portugal, Switzerland, Norway, Denmark and Sweden.

Preferring bilateral agreements, on the one hand, and broad economic organisations on the other, Finland stayed outside the Council of Europe, the OEEC, and obviously, the EEC's common market integration. The Council of Europe was too clearly linked to cold war divisions and therefore incompatible with neutrality (Antola 1990b: 164). Moreover, at the time of its formation, the organisation showed clear supranational ambitions. Finland became a member of the Council only in 1989. A practical reason for Finland's position towards the Council was the Finnish rejection of the Marshall Plan, which determined its relations with both the Council of Europe and the OEEC. While the OEEC was established as the European coordinating organisation demanded by the Marshall Plan, the OEEC members were invited to become members of the Council of Europe; all accepted the invitation except for Switzerland. Finland was therefore not even invited to become a member (Antola and Tuusvuori 1983: 229-231).

Finland had not participated in the negotiations between the Seven, or, understandably, in those between the Six for the establishment of the EEC. The question of EFTA membership was, from a political point of view, more complicated for Finland than a Nordic solution would have been. Soviet suspicions concerning Finnish domestic politics and growing interest towards Western integration had culminated in the so-called 'night frost crisis' in Finnish-Soviet relations in 1958. However, Finnish EFTA membership was not excluded in principle, provided it did not include supranational organs or political obligations in contrast with Finnish foreign policy.[2] In fact, EFTA was a pragmatic, purely economic organisation. Following the article XXIV of the GATT treaty which allows for two exceptions to the MFN principle, customs union and free trade agreements, it aimed at realising free trade, establishing rules on competition, economic growth and better living standards, together with the harmonious development, expansion and liberalisation of world trade. According to the Convention, although the EFTA Council can make binding decisions, it does so mainly by unanimity. The convention also includes security clauses and exceptions. Moreover, agriculture – a central concern for Finland – was left almost wholly outside the convention. (Antola and Tuusvuori 1983: 93-96.)

Despite the fact that the organisation was clearly of a non-political nature with no elements of supranationality, and that it included the Nordic framework as well as the other neutral countries of Austria, Sweden and Switzerland, some problems remained. Finnish membership was hampered not only by a negative Soviet attitude; the United Kingdom also opposed it (Antola and Tuusvuori 1983: 131; af Malmborg 1994: 381-383; cf. Hakovirta 1976: 200-202). Two additional measures were therefore seen as necessary to make Finnish participation possible. First, Finland prepared parallel agreements with the Eastern countries. Before the FINEFTA treaty could come into force, the question of Eastern trade had to be settled by signing, concurrently, a Finnish-Soviet agreement about tariff reductions to give the Soviet Union the same position as the EFTA countries in the Finnish market. (Antola and Tuusvuori 1983: 131-136; Antola 1991a: 148.)

Secondly, Finland did not actually become an EFTA member, but opted for a particular form of association. In March 1961 it signed a special association treaty called FINEFTA. In practice, the status as associate member gave Finland the rights of a full member but guaranteed its special interests, notably in bypassing supranational ard political commitments. The FINEFTA treaty included all the stipulations concerning trade and economy of the Stockholm Convention with the exception of a slower reduction of duties to protect the weak Finnish home market industry.[3] Furthermore, bilateral trade with the Soviet Union was able to continue undisturbed due to the proviso that the removal of quantitative import restrictions did not apply to Finland for, e.g., liquid and solid fuels and fertilisers, which were central to Finnish-Soviet trade. (Antola and Tuusvuori 1983: 134-135.)

The association treaty also differed in an important way from the Stockholm Convention as regards its allusions to economic arrangements between the Western European countries. According to the convention, EFTA aims at closer contacts with other states, associations of states and organisations; its introduction explicitly mentions closer economic cooperation between OEEC members, including the members of the EEC. These allusions were seen as potentially involving political commitments not consistent with the Finnish policy. Therefore, they were omitted from the FINEFTA treaty. (Cf. EFTA Convention, art. 32 and 36.)

Somewhat similarly, Finland also found a particular way to join the OEEC which was seen to represent rather developed coordinating integration (Antola and Tuusvuori 1983: 125-126). In 1957 Finland signed its own agreement, the Helsinki Protocol, with the members of the OEEC, a move which was of special importance for the liberalisation of trade with Western European countries. The political reasons for remaining outside the OEEC were, however, gradually removed: with the establishment of EEC and EFTA, the OECD – the successor to the OEEC from 1961 with the entrance of Canada and the United States – lost its political significance and became more clearly concentrated on purely economic matters (Muoser 1986: 155). Membership of such an organisation was seen to improve Finland's chances to influence trade and economic policies, as well as to enhance both its international status and access to information (Antola and Tuusvuori 1983: 142-143). Finland therefore joined the OECD in 1968. However, analogously to the case of the Nordic Council, Finland made it explicit that membership would not affect its sovereignty and neutrality. The declaration of the Finnish representative stated that

> [I]n acceding to the Convention of the OECD the government of Finland does not commit itself to anything that conflicts with the foreign policy pursued by Finland and with her recognised neutrality. [...] The government of Finland notes furthermore that the rules and aims of the OECD do not limit Finland's possibilities to develop her trade relations with countries outside the Organisation. (Protocol of the Paris meeting in which Finland joined the organisation, quoted in Muoser 1986: 155.)

The question of Finland's relations to the EEC was brought up by the fact that several EFTA members applied for EEC membership soon after EFTA had been established.[4] The applications were, however, unsuccessful. This gave new impetus to plans for a Nordic customs union and negotiations on NORDEK began in 1969. For Finland, a Nordic common market would have been beneficial in that it would have strengthened the position of the country without jeopardising its vital interests. Again, however, considerations of

EEC membership intertwined with the Nordic plans: for Denmark especially, NORDEK was to become a bridge to the EEC, something that made the Finnish attitude to the plan more critical. In the end, when the NORDEK treaty was in practice ready to be signed, the Finnish government declared it could not sign the treaty as in light of the beginning of negotiations between Denmark, Norway and the EEC, it did not fulfil Finland's demands for stability and permanence. (Antola and Tuusvuori 1983: 144-146.)

Finland aimed to find a way to organise its relations with the EEC which would secure neutrality and the privileges it had already acquired, while permitting, at the same time, an all-European development without the need for EEC enlargement (Antola and Tuusvuori 1983: 137-142). To this effect, negotiations on a free trade agreement between Finland and the EEC were launched at Finland's initiative in spring 1970 – a measure which occasioned a unique debate in the country, prompting a large pamphlet literature.[5] Finland had to reconcile its traditional policy of maintaining neutrality, trade with the Soviet Union, free trade with EFTA, Nordic cooperation and previous international agreements, especially GATT, with the need to avoid possible discrimination and isolation. An agreement was necessary to avoid the reintroduction of tariffs in trade between Finland and the United Kingdom and Denmark, both of which left EFTA and joined the EEC in 1973 (cf. Laine 1973: 21).

In contrast to Sweden, which was also negotiating a free trade agreement, Finland was not ready to discuss all possible areas of cooperation. It wanted to stay apart from EEC economic policy, agreeing only on the removal of duties for industrial products (Antola and Tuusvuori 1983: 148-150). The Finnish free trade agreement of July 1972[6] thus differed in some respects from the free trade agreements signed by the other neutral EFTA members. As in the case of FINEFTA, these differences were both economic and political. The economic exceptions agreed in FINEFTA were maintained and the treaty included the protection of weak industries for both parties – for the EEC, they were the paper and wood industries. On the political side, it was made easier for Finland to annul the treaty, the term of notice being only three months instead of the twelve of the other treaties.

Even more importantly, the treaty committed Finland only as far as the actual text of the free trade treaty was concerned, and not with a view to possible future developments. By contrast, the other free trade agreements contained an evolution or development clause stating that the parties could propose the extension of their relations to areas not covered by the agreement when this was seen to be beneficial to both sides. This was seen as a commitment which might endanger Finland's freedom of action, and so was omitted from the Finnish treaty. (Antola and Tuusvuori 1983: 157-158, 165-166; cf. the introduction of the treaty and art. 32.)

Finally, as in the case of the FINEFTA treaty, a comprehensive arrangement was developed according to the principle of parallelism, which granted the same customs privileges for trade with both East and West. The free trade agreement with the EEC was accompanied by a cooperation agreement with the Council for Mutual Economic Assistance (COMECON or CMEA)[7] and the so-called KEVSOS system of bilateral treaties for the reciprocal removal of trade barriers with the socialist countries other than the Soviet Union.[8] In addition, the Soviet Union was provided with advantages in trade equal to those of the Finnish trade in Western Europe through a bilateral trade agreement. The Finnish policy was to support the development of economic cooperation in Europe between all three organisations, EFTA, the EEC and the CMEA. (Antola 1989: 56-57; Antola and Tuusvuori 1983: 156-157.)

The EEA: a step into a whirlpool

Until the late 1980s Finnish integration policy was, thus, characterised by caution. The freedom of action and autonomous decision-making capacity, required to guarantee Finland's neutrality and sovereignty, were not endangered by hasty steps towards new agreements or organisations. Rather, Finnish policy was based on weighing the necessity, advantages and disadvantages of the different forms of cooperation, and on striving for particular arrangements that would reconcile the economic needs for cooperation with the maintenance of autonomy. Understandably, this has often been time-consuming. In all, it has not been common to accept international arrangements without accommodating the Finnish concern for room for manoeuvre and freedom from political commitments. Suitable conditions for participating and a clarification of the situation in European integration have been awaited before action has been taken, something that Hakovirta (1976) has labelled as a 'wait-and-see' policy.

At the same time, the Finnish attitude to integration has been pragmatic. Instead of viewing it idealistically as something overwhelmingly positive – or negative – integration has been approached as a phenomenon whose consequences are not self-evident. Prompted originally by political considerations about the possible threats and disadvantages of integration, notably the economic threat of exclusion and the political challenge to the prevailing order with ensuing insecurity (cf. Antola 1990b: 163), this attitude has without doubt been fruitful. It has contributed to the development of a balanced view on the process; moreover, the stance of being a relative outsider has not only permitted wide relations across various organisational boundaries, but has also functioned as a counterweight to excessively closed economic groupings.

The agreement on the European Economic Area, EEA (at first also called the European Economic Space, EES) originally seemed to suit this picture. As an alternative to EC membership which would guarantee the Finnish special interests, it was seen as a further step for and continuation of Finnish integration policy. Moreover, it seemed to evolve quite naturally from EFTA cooperation.

However, the road from EFTA membership to the EEA was not as straightforward and logical as might be depicted, and, moreover, it went further than expected. Finland's free trade agreement with the EEC was actually the top achievement of the country's neutrality policy: it could organise relations with the EEC purely on the basis of free trade, notwithstanding the common market character of EEC integration (Maude 1976: 122-123). Little more could be achieved without renouncing neutrality. On the way to the EEA, however, a qualitative leap took place, implying an acceptance of supranationalism and rejection of neutrality which reversed the traditional policy. To paraphrase Antola (1989: 55), Finland was pushed into taking these decisions by events in its closest and the most important market area, Western Europe.

In essence, the EEA was aimed at coordinating the EC and EFTA into a common market. The two organisations had been gradually approaching each other since the 1970s. The Finnish stand on this development was originally cautious, as was shown by the omission of the allusion to relations with the EC from the FINEFTA treaty.[9] The *rapprochement* acquired more impetus in the 1984 Luxembourg meeting between EFTA and the EC, where the aim of creating a dynamic European economic area and the idea of widening the internal market to EFTA were presented. As a result, EC-EFTA relations were put on a more systematic, albeit still informal, basis, and cooperation between the two was enlarged and intensified. (Hurni 1989; Rehn 1993: 194.)

This development first made Finland anchor its policies more clearly to EFTA. As Antola put it, a new Finnish 'EFTA-card policy', or cooperative integration strategy, began: Finland now saw EFTA as the main tool in the integration policy of its members. More emphasis was put on the importance of cost-sharing with other EFTA countries. As all EFTA members were faced with the threat of marginalisation in the integration process, increased unity between them was seen to be in the interests of all. For Finland in particular, a steady and unified EFTA could insure that Finland would not be left alone to cope with the relations to the EC. So, it was seen to be in Finland's interests to strengthen EFTA, not as an end in itself but because of the common interests of its members. In other words, Finnish integration policy was gradually shifting from separately tailored unilateral agreements to an EFTA-based, multilateral approach. (Antola 1989: 61-62; 1991a: 150.) Accordingly, Finland also decided to become a full member of EFTA. The agreement of September 1985 entered into force at the beginning of 1986. By that time the character and membership of EFTA had become more 'neutral', making it easier for Finland to be a full member: EFTA had been joined by Iceland and Liechtenstein, while the NATO members Denmark and United Kingdom left EFTA in 1973 and Portugal in 1986. (Cf. Muoser 1986: 182-183.)

That Finland's integration policy had begun to change became manifest when in November 1988 the government addressed a report or white paper to the parliament on the country's stand on economic integration in Western Europe. It could be argued that the very need for such a paper and its emphasis on the elements of continuity in Finnish policies revealed that the line was starting to change. Indeed, the paper was but the first in a series of four white papers on Finland and integration in little more than four years. These reports show tangibly the rapid turn in Finnish integration policy, while reflecting, at the same time, the government's concern for stressing continuity and justifying change.

This first government report endorsed the traditional elements of Finnish neutrality-based integration policy. As neutrality required a national decision-making capacity, including its own rulings on economic policy, it could not be combined with membership in a EC aiming for a European Union, common foreign policy, supranationality and majority decision-making. Membership being excluded, the Finnish aim was the closest possible cooperation with the EC in order to safeguard Finnish interests in Western European integration. In general, the report saw Finland as an active supporter of European economic cooperation: it was seen that pooling economic capacities offered new possibilities for Finland. The importance of economic relations with the Soviet Union and other Eastern European countries was also mentioned. (Government report 1988: 5-7.) According to the report, EFTA was the primary channel for securing Finnish interests. EFTA countries had similar interests in many issues; together, they formed the most important trading partner of the EC. They could also best avoid discrimination through joint negotiations and by aiming at common views on as many issues as possible. Therefore, it was felt that EFTA should be reinforced – without, however, changing its nature to resemble that of the Community. (*Idem:* 16-17 *et passim;* see also Antola 1991a: 152.)

It was here that the report actually pointed to a central dilemma. The deepening of EC integration from the mid-1980s had twofold consequences: it made EFTA countries increasingly dependent on good relations with the EC, but it also increased the differences between the two organisations. EFTA countries had to find a way to avoid being left out of the process of integration. At the same time, the increasingly supranational character of the Community made membership of it even less compatible with the requirements of neutrality. As Hakovirta (1987: 266-268) notes, the improving competitiveness of the EC, the prospective of an arrangement which could ensure participation without immediate risks for neutrality and the possibility that EFTA would lose importance if more members were to leave it pressed Finland and Sweden towards integration with the EC.

On the other side, however, the EC had set clear conditions to closer cooperation with EFTA countries; the neutral countries were not to be allowed to select economic benefits without bearing the same economic burdens and responsibilities as the ordinary members, and without taking on the Community's political purposes. These principles, laid down in the Luxembourg meeting of 1984, were repeated in the EFTA-EC ministerial meeting in Interlaken in May 1987: the EC gave priority to internal integration over any agreements with third countries, emphasising the balance of benefits and obligations in agreements between the EC and third countries. Furthermore, it was stressed that the autonomy of EC decision-making was not to be undermined or made over-complicated through third country participation. In all, the EC was limiting the possibilities of the influence of third states. (Antola 1989: 61; cf. Pedersen 1991: 137-138, Cremona 1994: 510-511.)

In this situation, the proposal made by the president of the Commission, Jacques Delors, in January 1989 to extend the common market to EFTA countries through the EEA as a third way between membership and the risk of marginalisation met the wishes of the EFTA countries halfway. It gave them the chance to increase their participation in the integration process without having to compromise their national policies. For Penttilä (1994: 21), it was like a proposal invented by the Finns themselves: participating in the common market without getting politically involved was well suited to Finnish integration policy. In fact, Finland soon became strongly devoted to the EEA plans as a suitable alternative to EC membership (Antola 1991a: 150-151). At the same time, the EEA let the EC profit from the widening markets and thereby strengthen its competitiveness without risking interference with or retarding the deepening of Community integration and without undermining the position of Community institutions. (Rehn 1993: 194; Cremona 1994: 508.)

Finland also remained firmly in favour of the EEA even though almost immediately, the EEA came to be seen by other EFTA countries as a temporary stop on the way to EC membership rather than as an autonomous long-term solution. In fact, Austria applied for EC membership as early as July 1989, before the start of the formal EEA negotiations in 1990. (Cf. Rehn 1993: 194-195; Cremona 1994: 508.)

This new EEA policy was reflected in the second government communication on Finland's position towards Western European integration (no longer 'economic' integration) of November 1989. Recapitulating the stand taken in the report of 1988 about the importance of cooperation with EFTA countries, the key role of national measures and competitiveness and the interest for a wider pan-European collaboration including Eastern European countries, the government considered that active participation in negotiations on a wider, general agreement between EFTA and the EC was needed to safeguard Finnish interests. Participation, however, was to be based on the country's own premises. Moreover, it was noted that the EEA would apply also to the relations between EFTA countries and between the Nordic countries, thus guaranteeing that Finland could maintain its relations with these important reference groups (government communication 1989: 32).

The government saw several positive features in the EEA agreement: it would guarantee equal rights and mutuality with an independent right of initiative for the EFTA pillar, participation in the preparatory work as well as homogeneous and efficient application and control of the EEA norms in the whole area. The agreement would essentially be a free trade agreement, not a customs union. It would not include foreign and security policy, or common policies in economy or industry, even less so in agriculture: there would be no free trade in agricultural products comparable to free trade in industrial goods. Although it was acknowledged that joint decisions would decrease the freedom of action of the country, it was also underlined that decision-making in the EEA would be consensual, not supranational. (Government communication 1989: 11-14, 27-28; see also Antola 1991a: 152-153.)

There was, however, a growing discrepancy between the views held on the EEA by the EC and EFTA countries. In the EFTA view, the EEA was to be an organisation based on two equal pillars, EFTA and the EC. Real mutuality was also one of the conditions for negotiations set by the EC, but rather in the sense of ascertaining that EFTA countries could not circumvent the common norms. In fact, the EC's emphasis on protecting its decision-making autonomy implied that the two pillars were in a quite unequal position: the factual capacity of deciding on EEA norms as norms of the Community would pertain to the EC only.

The third government report on integration of March 1990 considered these problems while giving a highly positive picture of the economic consequences of integration.[10] The EEA was to guarantee equal competition and safeguard the Finnish interests in the integration process, particularly since Finland's goals in economic policy were very similar to those of the EC. Competitiveness was needed to benefit from the new possibilities offered by integration. As such, increased competition could cause problems of adaptation; however, these problems would arise even outside the EEA. At the same time, remaining apart from deepening integration would decrease competitiveness. (Government report 1990: 9.) Somewhat confusingly, competitiveness was thus seen simultaneously as a consequence of integration and a means, or prerequisite, for benefiting from it.

The report noted that the EC had expressed concern about the application of EEA norms in EFTA countries arguing that there was a risk of selective application, and that it would be possible for EFTA countries to re-write these norms as national ones, thereby being able to change them. Furthermore, the EC was concerned over the unequal position of individuals and firms of the EC countries in that they would not have the same rights to appeal to courts and administration in EFTA countries as the individuals and firms from EFTA countries have in the EC. (Government report 1990: 120.)

It was clear by now that EFTA countries had to accept in some way or another the direct applicability of EEA norms. The Finnish government, however, did not intend to give the agreement a supranational character. In fact, according to the report, the Finnish intention was that the EEA would enter into force through a national measure, resembling an international agreement (*idem:* 121). It was also made appear less demanding by comparing it to the Council of Europe. The government did not see any hindrances in accepting an EEA court which could judge whether Finland had fulfilled its obligations stemming from the treaty as Finland actually already had accepted a similar competence of an international court as to whether Finnish legislation is compatible with an international agreement when it became a member of the Council of Europe. (*Idem:* 123.)

Thus, in Finland it was still thought that the EEA could be a way of combining political neutrality and full participation in economic integration, that is, a solution to secure economic interests without political participation. In 1990, prime minister Holkeri compared the task of combining neutrality and EC membership to the task of squaring a circle. At the same time, the importance of the EEA was in both political and economic terms greater for Finland than for other EFTA countries. (Cf. Rehn 1993: 195.)

However, as Antola notes, the government was pursuing rather disparate objectives as it aimed at access to real influence with the possibility of some 'opting-out' and the retention of a meaningful role by the national institutions, notably parliament and the president. Real influence in the rule-making, however, was possible only through participation. Although EC membership was still excluded in the second and third government reports, rejection became less categorical so that membership came finally to be seen as the second option if the EEA did not materialise. Public opinion was also becoming favourable: in opinion polls conducted in May 1990, 60% were for and 13% against. On the other hand, 22% believed that Finland already was a member. (The EC Bulletin May 31, 1990; Antola 1991a: 153-156.)

In all, the political imperative of Finnish integration policy was gradually turned on its head by a largely rhetorical manoeuvre. Whereas political commitments had previously been avoided in order to safeguard the political freedom of action and sovereignty, they were now seen as the means for securing greater political influence. The 'political' was no longer separable at will; involvement without political commitment implied a factual loss of influence. In fact, in the course of the negotiations the expectations changed and the EEA came to be seen deprived of decision-making capacity for the EFTA countries.

After considerable delay both before signing and before ratification, the EEA treaty finally came into force on January 1, 1994.[11] The agreement involves the EU countries and the EFTA countries excluding Switzerland; in addition to the individual countries, the EU and the ECSC are also parties to the agreement. In short, the EEA implies that the five EFTA countries are an integrated part of, and participate on an equal basis with, the EU countries in the internal market as far as the free movement of people, services, goods and capital are concerned, and cooperate with the EU in other areas, such as research and development, environment and education. The intention is to maintain a homogeneous and dynamic economic area which implies that new, related EU norms have to be incorporated in the EEA. EFTA countries are informed and consulted in the process of shaping new EU legislation relevant to the EEA, and they can participate in preparatory committees. New EEA rules must also be formally approved by EFTA parliaments within a six month period of the EEA decision. All decisions in the Joint Committee must be taken by unanimity between the two 'pillars', the EU and the EFTA states, in new, joint institutions.[12] (EFTA Bulletin 1/94, esp. 6-7; EFTA News 1/1994.)

The agreement was in many ways advantageous for Finland and the other EFTA members. It does not involve any doctrine of primacy or direct effect of common law, nor transfer of sovereign rights to its intergovernmental institutions. The agreement states that it does not restrict the decision-making autonomy or the treaty-making power of the parties and that it is based on equality and reciprocity and an overall balance of benefits, rights and obligations for the parties. Automatic application of the EEA norms is not envisaged: they have to be made part of the internal legal order. Their primacy, therefore, will not derive from their character as EEA norms, but from national law, confirming the approach of the Nordic EFTA states. Furthermore, Cremona sees that an EFTA state effectively can 'opt out' of a particular legislative act. Finally, the EEA is concerned solely with the promotion of trade and economic relations between the parties; it does not contain common tariffs, trade policy or references to economic and monetary union, nor is it intended to be an area without internal frontiers. (Cremona 1994: 519-522, 524; cf. Protocol 35.)

In fact, the agreement met practically no political resistance in Finland, though it was controversial in both Norway and Switzerland.[13] It was understood that the support for the EEA stemmed from the very fact that it did not include the two areas most sensitive for Finland – agriculture and foreign policy – while it met the needs for equal access to the EC's internal market for Finnish business (Väyrynen 1993: 39).

Yet, the EU also secured its own position with the agreement. Being a contracting party on an equal footing with the states, its decision-making and legislative autonomy is equally safeguarded by the treaty. The EU opposed a one-pillar solution which would have implied surrendering power to EFTA members in an extended Council of Ministers for the EEA law-making. (Cremona 1994: 510-511, 520.) As regards EU norms, EFTA countries are in a less favourable position. The EU retains its legislative power. The EEA joint committee cannot make binding decisions, and the EU Commission has the monopoly of initiative; EFTA countries can only participate in the preparatory work, possibly consulting together with the EU member countries and through experts and committee members. (*Eurooppa* 27.10.1992, p. 18.)

This consultation has not been made a formal part in the process of adaptation of Community legislation; the EEA was drafted in such a way as not to require amendment of the EC treaty (Cremona 1994: 512).

The Finnish government came to see these negative features as a decisive burden. It had aimed at a result that would not allow for decisions binding Finland against its will and would secure the position of the national organs of government, but the result of the negotiations was seen not to conform to these aims. The government saw that the EU did not accept the real joint decision-making proposed by the EFTA countries who had no real possibility of opting out. (*Eurooppa* 27.10.1992, pp. 4, 19, 29.) Before even having entered into force, the EEA was overtaken by the goal of EC membership. The sense of necessity to join was increased, as the EEA produced a gap between rights and obligations which previously did not exist, and could be remedied only by choosing between membership and the abrogation of the treaty.

Finland had stepped into a whirlpool by consenting to quite a number of conditions. In practice, with the EEA Finland accepted a large part of the Community legislation, excluding only the common policies in trade, agriculture and foreign policy, as well as the contents of the Maastricht Treaty regarding the aim of economic and monetary union and cooperation in internal affairs. Nor was foreign policy completely absent from the EEA: what was stated was that *security and defence* were outside the treaty.[14] The EFTA countries were required to accept the *acquis communautaire* with at most temporary exceptions and emergency clauses, to establish an organ of control for competition policy and to contribute to the economic and social cohesion fund for Southern Europe. In addition, concessions were required in fisheries and agriculture (access to Norwegian and Icelandic fishing waters in exchange of access by their fishery products to the EC market). (Pedersen 1991: 137-138.) Indeed, even the Court of Justice was accorded in the EEA a *de facto* pre-eminence in the judicial structure (Cremona 1994: 517).

The rhetoric of application and the implications of membership

It is obviously difficult to say whether the EEA agreement would in reality have led to an intolerable loss of influence by the EFTA countries or whether it could have been a good solution in line with their previous policies, as it was immediately overruled by the membership applications. In the short interval between the treaty and the EC membership, hardly any serious efforts could be made towards applying the agreement, even less towards developing it further. For Finland, the decision to join the EC was in practice implicit already in the fourth government report on integration of January 1992. This time, the report concerned the impact of EC membership for Finland. The government acknowledged the importance of the EEA in safeguarding the central economic interests of the country, but noted that it might only be temporary. Therefore, the best way fully to secure the Finnish interests seemed to be EC membership, that is, by participating in the decision-making. The report formed the basis for a government communication to parliament on March 16 in which the membership application was proposed. The communication was approved,[15] and on March 18, Finland applied for EC membership.

This turn in Finnish integration policy was expressed and explained in terms which made it seem understandable, even a continuation of the traditional policy. On the one hand, the government made the decision comprehensible through referring to the changes in the environment which seemed to require reactions. Thus, the government report mentions the disappearance of the bloc division in Europe, the Maastricht summit of December 1991 together with the EU's statement that negotiations on membership with the applicants could begin in 1992, the fact that the EU was becoming a new type of actor in international relations, and, finally, that Sweden had applied for membership in July 1991. Sweden's applying for membership was the most immediate reason for Finland to follow suit: it was thought that the Swedish membership would imply a comparative advantage for the industry of Finland's closest competitor. (Government report 1992: 5-7.) On the other hand, the turn in Finnish integration policy was underplayed through the way in which the government presented the EEA and the consequences of an eventual EC membership. The evaluation of the consequences was further coloured by considerations of the domestic situation, notably the economic crisis, and the uncertain situation in Russia.

The EEA was essentially a springboard for full EU membership in that it already implied the adoption of a large part of the *acquis communautaire* and, thus, lessened the amount of additional changes required while, at the same time, increasing the momentum towards membership. The government saw that the EEA would allow only minor leeway for influencing EC norms in contrast to full membership:[16] in the EEA, Finland could influence the contents of EC law only indirectly and with support from other EFTA countries. Although the government admitted that in the EEA, Finland could impede the adaption of new norms or hinder unacceptable decisions – which would be possible in the EC only when the decision is taken by unanimity –

it pointed out that this could lead not only to pressure from the other members but even to a partial annullation of the treaty. (Appendix 1992: 103-104.)

The assessment that national interests were best achieved or secured through EC membership was motivated by both political and economic considerations, and subsequently also in terms of security. Political motives centred around the possibility of participating in decision-making which in any case would have a bearing on Finland. Economically, membership was seen to be the best solution, although it was noted that the economic consequences of membership were difficult to estimate more than hypothetically and that, indeed, rather dissimilar results had been reached in the various evaluations carried out. The deep economic crisis in Finland with a sudden leap in unemployment to almost 20% was one of the background factors that worsened the economic forecast for staying outside the EU.[17] Later, security considerations entered the calculations of the consequences of membership, becoming gradually central in justifying the membership. Instability in Eastern Europe and Russia increased the attraction of integration as a possible security mechanism; as Arter (1995: 372) argues, a covert recognition of a potentially considerable 'security bonus' to be gained through EU membership made the EEA alternative disappear. (Cf. Salovaara 1994: 11, 13, 37; Penttilä 1994: 24-25.)

Finally, what was important for justifying the reassuring view that membership would actually not imply dramatic changes for Finland was obviously that the government depicted EU integration in rather generic and loose terms as an all-European process in which Finland was seen to be able *grosso modo* to continue with its own policies. According to the government, membership would not change the basis and essential aims of Finnish foreign and security policy; the core of neutrality would remain unchanged, and continuity would also characterise Finland's relations to the Nordic and Eastern countries. The responsibility for defence would remain national, and a decision on relations with the WEU would be made later. In the government's interpretation, in fact, the common foreign and security policy of the EU is characterised by its general aims of peace, security and promotion of human rights rather than, for example, the aim of formulating common positions and eventually a common defence. Moreover, the government emphasised the importance of unanimity or/and essential common interests in the common foreign policy. Similarly, the envisaged common defence policy would be based on the respect for the basic security and defence arrangements of the member states. In addition, the government saw that the Maastricht Treaty allows for special bilateral or multilateral treaties between the members, being compatible with the obligations stemming from NATO membership as well as with neutrality. Moreover, both Austria and Sweden had stated that military non-alignment is compatible with the Maastricht Treaty. (Government report 1992: 8-10, 25; Appendix 1992: 35-37.)

Just as Finland's foreign policy could continue, its trade policy would not be dramatically altered either, since the basic aims of EC trade policy do not differ from Finnish ones: national trade policy is simply carried out in the framework of EC membership. Indeed, the government points out that as a great power in trade policy, the EC can effectively defend the interests of its members. (Government report 1992: 12.) Membership would increase Finland's possibilities to influence international issues; the EC would be a stronger means of enforcement and would increase the importance of Finland for other EC countries (Appendix 1992: 35-37).

In reality, however, the membership decision indicated that a twofold change had taken place in the orientation of the government. Firstly, membership was no longer a secondary option, perhaps it was not even an option at all; secondly, the decision had to be made promptly: a 'wait-and-see' stand was no longer possible. The speed of the process was considerable: the decision was quite suddenly made after only two years of public debate on the possibility of membership. The government had several reasons for not wanting to dwell on the question for too long. Sweden's membership application was one accelerating factor; the government hoped that Finland's eventual membership application would be examined together with those of Austria and Sweden, and this meant that the application had to be submitted in early 1992. (Government report 1992: 5-7.) Reference was also made to the importance of joining in time to participate in the intergovernmental conference of 1996 where the contents of the common foreign and security policy were to be specified (see Himanen 1993).[18]

Without doubt, the membership decision was linked to a broader change in Finnish foreign policy, a change which essentially consisted of discarding the policy of neutrality. In fact, neutrality had anyway been gradually eroding, or it had been come to be increasingly restricted in terms of its application during the 1980s. First, the neutrality doctrine in broad humanitarian issues had been renounced to apply only in cases where the interests of the great powers were in direct conflict. Secondly, economic integration had been detached from the field where neutrality policy was applied, and in autumn 1987, it was made clear by the prime minister and the minister for foreign affairs that participation in Western European integration was no longer a component of the Finnish policy of neutrality. The chief purpose of this redefinition was to avoid the comprehensive economic-political packages by which Finnish political commitments to the East and economic ties with the West were previously balanced. In fact, the EEA treaty no longer involved the principle of parallelism. Thus, neutrality came to be reduced to the military field and narrowly defined matters of security policy. (Väyrynen 1993: 36; Möttölä 1993: 90-95.)[19] In fact, in the Government report of 1992, what is left is the 'core of neutrality', that is, staying outside military alliances in order to enable neutrality in war, supported by a credible national defence.

As Möttölä (1993: 90-95) notes, Finnish neutrality began to lose significance at the very time when it was recognised officially by the Soviet Union; Arter (1995: 372) sees even an irony in that Finland sought to abandon its neutrality when there was finally the possibility of giving it real substance and credibility.[20] In fact, two important changes had taken place. The traditional subordination of foreign policy to security policy was if not reversed, at least abandoned, and the importance of participation outweighed the need for retaining a certain freedom of action.

A new Finnish foreign policy doctrine started to emerge in the early 1990s. The rapidly revised interpretations of the Paris peace treaty and the FCMA in September 1990 were signs of major change; as Majander (1991: 37-38) put it, the FCMA treaty had been 'brought down from the inviolable realm of holy liturgy to the sphere of mortal elements of foreign policy'. The new doctrine comprised a decreasing centrality of security and defence, and an active integration strategy based on the possibility of EC membership and harmony between the interests of the EC and Finland (Patomäki 1991: 81-82).

This change has been interpreted as the beginning of an altogether new epoch in Finnish foreign and security policy. Finland was gradually seen as less particular and more like any other country as to its characteristics and policies. More weight was put on participation than on the need to keep distance and maintain autonomy. Finland was becoming, in all, increasingly comparable and similar to other countries. (Joenniemi 1995: 106-108, 113; cf. Joenniemi 1992a.) At the same time, even the traditional consensus (cf. Antola 1991a: 152) on foreign policy disappeared.

One could even see that the aim of membership forced this radical change in the Finnish attitude to its foreign policy. As Tiilikainen explains, there could be no doctrine more distant from the basic ideal and aims of the European Union than the traditional Finnish one. She argues that the Finnish doctrine rather boldly subscribes to the idea that the state is authorised to act egoistically to secure its existence and interests. The Union, on the contrary,

An integration policy turned on its head 289

is based on the view of the inadequacy of the traditional state and the harmfulness of the national identities they have established. The state's task of furthering its own interests is increasingly replaced by tasks subordinated to the European goals of harmonisation and mediation. Thus, the Union questions not only the Finnish type of political realism, but also neutrality, autonomy and the division between foreign and domestic politics. (Tiilikainen 1992: 15-16, 18-19.)

What makes the Finnish policy change particularly interesting, and also problematic, is its magnitude. On the one hand, it seems that there has been an authentic willingness to change direction; on the other, the willingness to do so has perhaps led to an unintentionally dramatic reversal of policy, the consequences of which are more profound than expected. Above all, the rhetoric of continuity, the way of depicting the Finnish membership decision as a logical step in the customary direction, is bound to ring increasingly hollow.

In fact, Finnish integration policy has been turned on its head: the traditional avoidance of political commitments and supranationality has been replaced by what could even be seen as an eagerness to welcome both, and the search for specially tailored arrangements has turned into a promotion of common policies. Yet, the elements of continuity were emphasised in the discussion both by the government and by several researchers. Integration was seen as a complement to national policies rather than an alternative to them (e.g., Himanen 1993: 29-30) and as an additional means for furthering national interests; it was argued that Finnish integration policy had not changed, but that the environment had (Rehn 1993: 217).[21]

It is clear that these claims would only be true if the European Union were still a mere intergovernmental community to be used for furthering particular interests. This was actually what was maintained. As Lempiäinen (1994: 130) put it, the European Union, instead of being federalistic in nature, is characterised by closer cooperation between nation-states and serves the national interests. Understandably, this is how it was also depicted by the government before the membership. It noted expressly[22] that Finland, considering that membership was seen as the best way of securing its national interests and international goals, would further these with the help of the Union; it would also in the future independently define its own interests. In full equality with other member states, Finland would be loyal to them, while expecting solidarity in turn. As the common foreign and security policy has developed on the basis of unanimity and as an independent defence conforms with the Maastricht Treaty, the bases of Finnish foreign and defence policy may remain.

Further, the government let it be understood that 'the EU involves independent and sovereign states having freely decided to exercise in common some of their competencies', and that it would be only normal to pursue the own interests in the negotiations, where 'we will defend our own views and pursue our interests just as others do'. Finland would be an active participant, but on 'the basis of our own views', as, indeed, 'it is in the interests of the Community as well to ensure that the interests of a new member are duly safeguarded'.[23] It was, thus, only natural that the Finnish government refer to the decision of the German constitutional court of October 1993 which states that the Maastricht Treaty is not in contradiction with the German constitution, that the treaty does not imply the establishment of a federal state, that there is no automaticity in the treaty and that Germany will remain a sovereign state, retaining also a necessary amount of decision-making competence on its currency. The same applied for Finland, the prime minister observed. (*Eurooppakirje* 7/93.) Similarly, EU citizenship was seen as giving additional value to national citizenship rather than replacing it or making it irrelevant. The government explained that '[W]e are also keen to give Finnish nationals additional rights and improve the protection of their interests through the introduction of the citizenship of the Union, which does not in any way take the place of national citizenship.' (*Eurooppa* 1/93.)

It is not that the government would have ignored the elements of supranationality in the Union. Majority decision-making, direct applicability of Community law, citizenship of the Union, common foreign and security policy, eventual common defence and economic, monetary and political union are all taken into consideration. The government report notes as the important constitutional and juridical consequences of membership a significant decrease of the norm-giving powers of parliament and the president, the primacy and direct applicability of EC law and the capacity of the Community to enter into international agreements which partly deprives the state of this capacity, as well as the obligation in the Rome Treaty to resolve conflict situations arising between the commitments of membership and previous international agreements (Appendix 1992: 101, 104, 106).

However, these features are interpreted in a particular way. It is seen that while EU membership entails certain obligations, their amount and nature are controlled by the member states. Similarly, while the Court of Justice obviously has an important role in controlling the compliance of the members, its competencies are limited to these particular obligations. On the

An integration policy turned on its head 291

other hand, the existence of common policies is moderated by stressing the idea that in the framing of these policies, national peculiarities and interests are taken into account, and that they, accordingly, strengthen and complement the national ones.[24]

This is obviously not what the EU maintained. In a sense, the government's evaluation of the consequences of membership seemed to be based on characteristics of the European Community while the EU emphasised that what was actually at stake was membership of the European *Union*. This was particularly emphasised in the *avis*[25] of the Commission on Finland's application and in the declaration on foreign policy made at the end of the negotiations.[26]

The clash of interpretations is well illustrated by the case of Finnish neutrality. In the membership negotiations, questions of foreign and security policy were expected to be eventually problematic because of this policy. The Finnish application had not contained any conditions or reflections on neutrality. However, neutrality was supposed to become an important part of the negotiations (e.g., Rometsch 1993: 44). The Finnish government had stated that the interpretation of neutrality was not a question of negotiation: it would remain in the hands of the government, as would foreign and security policy more generally (Government communication 1992; Rehn 1993: 206-207).

A common understanding on the issue seemed to be reached quite soon, while the main problems turned out to be in the fields of agriculture and regional policy. Relieved, the government concluded that the Finnish position had been accepted: no awkward or impossible commitments were expected (cf. *Eurooppa* 9.3.1993). The Commission, however, questioned the Finnish neutrality policy already in the *avis* on the country's application, asking whether it, even if reduced to its 'core', would not constitute a hindrance to the full acceptance of the foreign policy of the Union, including the defence of the independence and security of the Union and the development towards a common defence. The provisions of the Maastricht Treaty make it clear that new members have to accept common positions in foreign and security policy, including eventually a binding defence policy and imposition of sanctions on third countries. To assume that Finland as a member could still continue its neutrality policy would, thus, be mistaken and possibly also obstruct these policies.[27] Thus, the Commission urged full clarification on the Finnish position to ascertain that it would not hamper the evolution of the common policies. It also recommended specific and binding assurances on the political commitment and legal capacity to fulfil the obligations in this field.

Moreover, as a response to the rather vague Finnish interpretation of the WEU as a means of crisis management to which Finland would take stand later, the Commission recalled that the WEU also had political aims (a*vis,* pp. 22-23).

In reality, however, what was presented as the Finnish position – in foreign policy as well as other issues – was no longer autonomously defined: it could hardly be a position that would conflict with that of the others or be incompatible with the EU stand. In fact, policy redefinitions were demanded; the *avis* emphasises Finland's ability to change the meaning of neutrality and notes that it is also willing to do so: Finnish security and foreign policy are noted to have *developed considerably* since the beginning of the 1990s. Importantly, thus, the country's own policies and interests can be furthered in the context of the Union only with the strong reservation that they have to be compatible with those of the others, or with the common interests; diverging interests can be referred to only exceptionally, as a member country cannot afford to appear obstructive (cf. Tonra 1994).

Although the Finnish government seemed to use the compatibility argument to make the required changes appear less important,[28] effective limitations had to be admitted. Although the furthering of the country's own interests and continued neutrality were not explicitly considered incompatible with membership, the Union posed quite clear restrictions on what these could imply in practice. According to the conditions of membership imposed by the Commission,[29] new members have the duty to accept the *acquis communautaire* in its totality, including the contents, principles and political objectives of the treaties, also the Maastricht Treaty, the legislation adopted in the implementation of the treaties and the jurisprudence of the Court, the declarations and resolutions adopted in the Community framework, as well as the international agreements and the agreements between member states connected with the activities of the Community. Moreover, nothing more than technical adaptations, temporary derogations and transitional arrangements could be agreed in the negotiations, while safeguarding the achievements of the Community.

Unlike the older members of the Community, for instance, Denmark – to which Finland could in many respects be compared – Finland had, in practice, to accept all the baggage of the Union unconditionally. This was made particularly clear before the negotiations were over in a ministerial meeting[30] where a rather pleonastic joint declaration was issued stating that Sweden, Austria, Norway and Finland fully accepted the *acquis communautaire* with its contents, principles and goals, and that there was agreement on the fact that the juridical system of the new members will in the moment of accession be in harmony with the *acquis* (*Eurooppakirje* 1/94).[31] This particular emphasis on the firmly binding commitment makes the position of the new member states different from that of the existing members, which were never bound to accept such an amount of decisions without even the possibility of opting out (see, e.g., the exceptions Denmark was able to make on the Maastricht Treaty).

The consequences of Finland's EU membership are difficult if not impossible to estimate in terms of gains and losses, the complex equations between the costs of commitment and the gains of influence[32] being further complicated in that they are also influenced by external events. It is, for instance, quite hard to calculate whether a country would be more secure allied or not; in the Finnish case, much depends on the development of relations between the EU and Russia (cf. Salovaara 1994). The very nature of the membership as perhaps the most far-reaching change in Finnish constitution since 1919, and, moreover, of a sudden character contributes to making its dimensions impossible to determine (Nousiainen 1992: 262). Similarly, the anticipated effects of EU membership for the Finnish economy are highly contingent on the assumptions about the general effects of integration being true (cf. Eskelinen 1985 on the difficulty in anticipating and evaluating the economic impacts of integration).

Still, some profound changes are quite easily recognisable. Firstly, there are those concerning the power relations between the different state organs; the question of the relationship between the executive and the parliament and the evident transfer of power from the latter to the former observed in other member countries (cf. Jääskinen 1992: 278) also concerns Finland. As a particularly Finnish problem, the relationship between the president and the government, or the prime minister, is brought up through the increasing difficulty in maintaining the distinction between foreign and domestic issues, a distinction which has traditionally constituted the boundary of the powers of the two (cf. Nousiainen 1992: 264). Second, membership becomes increasingly visible in the contents of policies, especially concerning economic and foreign affairs. Since the early 1980s, Finland has indeed voted very much like the EC in the UN General Assembly, even more so than Denmark (Salovaara 1994: 24); the Finnish relations to the WEU were also brought into line very soon after membership as Finland acquired observer status in the organisation in February 1995.

Third, the structure and functioning of the public administration changes through the interplay of the national and the communitarian administrations.

This 'europeanisation', mixing the domestic and the international, as Hyyryläinen (1995: 12, 194-195) argues, requires new coordination of decision-making, regulation and organisational changes. These changes may help improve some features of national administration, but they do not necessarily contribute to, e.g., increasing effectiveness. Moreover, the expanding contacts between administrations challenge the national administrative culture; after all, in areas such as customs administration, the Finnish central administration in fact comes to function as a part of the EU administration (cf. Temmes 1995: 215-216 *et passim*).

What is clear, therefore, is that a commitment has been made to a process of European union and constitution-building which will imply increasing acceleration of change in the Finnish state, most probably towards a growing similarity with other member states in their structures and functions. Strikingly, many features which in Finland would probably be seen as (valuable) particularities of the country were dissipated already in the *avis* on membership application by the fact that in many crucial points, exactly the same wording was used in the two *avis* of Finland and Sweden, especially for the chapter on foreign and security policy.[33] In fact, if reservations and 'exits' conform to national characteristics were formerly possible, the possibility now seems increasingly rhetorical. The nature of the process is demanding: it is not possible to defend the particular if this implies obstructionism; the fact that different issues are interlinked and that the process not only is irreversible but also needs to progress for its own credibility reduce possibilities for unanimity and exceptions.

All in all, the argumentation on continuity in Finnish integration policy has to be seen as purely rhetorical. The appearance of continuity can be seen as based on simplifying reinterpretations or reversed meanings of the central concepts. The arguments have been turned upsidedown: prospering economy, international status and influence are now linked to membership, which even implies 'more sovereignty' in terms of possibilities of participation than non-membership. Neutrality has become suspect and the security of the country is now better guaranteed in some kind of alliance.[34] Even continuity itself is reversed: although the previous policy was based on non-membership, continuity is now seen to lie in membership. In all, the Finnish road to the EU is straightened by explaining the policy choices by very general axioms or principles, such as the 'national interest'. This, however, implies the fallacy that anything can be explained as being 'in the interests' of something; whatever is done reflects the Finnish interests – even supranationalism –

through the simple redefinition of the country's own interests in conformity with a new identity acquired by the membership.[35]

In all, there is no question about the Finnish integration policy having changed dramatically. The remaining question is rather *why* this change took place. An intricate choice remains between seeing the decision either as a necessity or as a deliberate policy option. In the first case, there actually was no choice, and the much-emphasised national decision-making capacity was definitively only apparent, as when the minister for foreign affairs Haavisto underlined that the potential changes in Finnish foreign and security policy in all circumstances will result from national decisions (July 1993; quoted in *Eurooppakirje* 5/93).

In this case, one might point out different factors that made the policy change imperative. Some have referred to general causes such as rapid technological development, structural change in the world economy or the end of the cold war (e.g., Rehn 1993: 168-169). However, these are hardly events which take place at a given time and induce rapid reactions. Thus, they cannot give an adequate explanation of the precise responses, neither do they give any precise indications for policy. Rather, they serve in making the choices understandable afterwards. However, in periods which are seen particularly transformatory, the question of image, that is, how Finland is perceived in other countries, might be accentuated or revived. There might well have been pressure for showing that Finland was able to follow the changes. While a passive 'wait-and-see' policy could have been seen as reactionary or outdated, a rapid decision to join the EC seemed to show that Finland, too, had entered the post-cold war era and enhance the Western identity of the country (Himanen 1993: 29-30; *Eurooppa* 30.10.1992; Väyrynen 1993: 39; cf. Arter 1995).

In the second case, if the decision was a choice reflecting particular interests, perhaps a 'loose elite bargain' between the political and economic elites (Väyrynen 1993: 35, 43-45), it seems that the rapid transformation into an eager and willing supporter of integration (a *Musterknabe;* see Mouritzen 1993b) has taken place without profound consideration of the depth of the ensuing changes or the possible alternatives. Indeed, membership was preceded by much less argumentation concerning the possibility of non-membership, which actually appeared unfeasible. Rather suddenly, the idea of not joining the EU came simply to be associated with fated marginalisation and outstanding economic problems, even decreasing security.

Notes

1. The plan, or the European Recovery Programme (ERP), approved in 1948, consisted of economic aid and loans from the United States. It was aimed at facilitating the reconstruction of Europe after the war, but also at increasing political stability and cooperation in Europe. The ERP was offered to all European countries, including the Soviet Union; a condition was a European plan for trade liberalisation, customs union and a supranational organ for the coordination of the countries' economic policies. Other neutral countries were less cautious towards it; Sweden received Marshall aid, while Switzerland did not. In the end, the resultant efforts towards economic coordination did not involve the supranational features or capacities of interfering in the national economic policies originally proposed; discussions on various customs unions went on, the Benelux being the only one to materialise. (af Malmborg 1994: 70, 79-80, 82-90.)

2. In 1959, the Finnish prime minister Sukselainen had alluded to the possibility of Finland joining the EFTA together with the other Nordic countries: '...if the plan does not include political obligations nor provide for supra-national organs Finland is not less interested in this plan than the other Nordic countries' (cf. Törnudd 1969: 64). The minister for foreign affairs Karjalainen, in turn, noted that Finland could accept an agreement on tariffs and trade, but not political obligations contrasting with the Finnish foreign policy; the basis of Finnish integration policy was that while national interests should be secured in the Western markets, the undertakings should not conflict with the international position of the country or with the bilateral agreements with the Soviet Union. (Antola 1990b: 164, 165; *Ulkopoliittisia lausuntoja ja asiakirjoja* 1959: 52 and 1959: 57.)

3. Finland had abolished war-based restrictions and quotas in its trade with Western Europe only three years earlier, and thus adaptation was longer (Antola 1991a: 148-149).

4. Denmark and the United Kingdom applied in 1961, Norway in 1962; Austria, Portugal, Sweden and Switzerland applied for association. Especially consequential was the policy of the United Kingdom which had been the most important trade partner of Finland from 1946 onwards, followed by the Soviet Union and the Federal Republic of Germany (Antola and Tuusvuori 1983: 176).

5. See Antola and Tuusvuori (1983). In part, the themes greatly resembled those presented in the discussion on membership in the 1990s: the nature (supranationality, common policies, military character) and possible future development of the EEC were among the open questions. Considerations which were important for Finland in the bloc environment and détente of the early 1970s also emerged. For instance, Korpinen alluded to attempts to

change the character of the rivalry between the blocs from military to economic. In his view, there were anti-détente forces in the EEC which feared that a policy of conciliation would weaken the internal unity and the defence willingness of the blocs. These forces aimed to have the Scandinavian countries join the EEC as firmly as possible, and force the socialist countries to separate negotiations with the EEC under the shadow of the Community's common trade policy, cutting the bilateral commercial-political relations between the EEC countries and the socialist ones. Korpinen therefore concluded that 'it goes without saying that Finland will not let herself be used as a weapon of mini-Europe's conjuncture politicians against the socialist countries'. (Korpinen 1973: 26-27.)

6. The Finnish government decided to postpone the signing of the agreement, and this was done only in October 1973; thus, it did not enter into force before January 1, 1974, one year after Sweden's agreement. The postponement evidently had to do with the domestic controversies around the treaty which was seen to jeopardise Finland's neutrality policy; cooperation with the EEC could lead to political dependency, as argued by president Kekkonen in 1970, and the Soviet Union might also see it as a threat (Antola and Tuusvuori 1983: 165-166). President Kekkonen was to guarantee that the agreement did not harm the Finnish-Soviet relations; his mandate was prolonged by a special law in January 1973. Moreover, the FCMA treaty was renewed in 1970, five years before it was due to expire, in order to 'remove any possible doubt about the consistency of our policy' (Kekkonen in Washington, July 23, 1970, quoted in Miljan 1977: 261-262; Muoser 1986: 198-199).

7. The CMEA was established in 1949 as a response to the Marshall Plan. The CMEA charter, which made it a proper international organisation, was signed in December 1959. Finland initiated investigations on possible cooperation with the organisation in the summer of 1971; the official negotiations began in March 1973, leading to the signing of a cooperation agreement on May 16, 1973. The agreement, of rather general character, was essentially a foundation and framework for cooperation in questions of mutual interest in different sectors of economy, including industry, science and engineering. A joint commission was established for the investigation, development and execution of cooperation. (Kekkonen 1973: 29-31.)

8. Bulgaria, Czechoslovakia, Hungary, Poland and the German Democratic Republic (Laine 1973: 22); the treaties, still in vigour, comported the removal of tariffs for industrial products by 1977 and in protected areas by 1985 (Lempiäinen 1994: 138).

9. Finland was ready to develop the free trade system, albeit on the basis of its own agreements and its maintenance of autonomous decision-making capacity: it favoured the enlargement and deepening of EFTA in the limits

of neutrality. (Antola and Tuusvuori 1983: 158; Antola 1991a: 149.) Finland was also slower in developing its relations with the EEC than Norway and Sweden; its agreements with the EEC to supplement the free trade agreement were both fewer and narrower in scope (limited to trade issues) than the Swedish ones (Antola 1989: 60).

10. Integration would increase the efficiency of the domestic economy; it was seen to imply a simplification of administrative measures, increased opportunities for specialisation and thereby comparative advantages, economies of scale, increasing competition through the four freedoms, larger market and thus possibilities for innovation and growth, as well as decreasing price level. International competition was seen to benefit both consumers and the export sector. The report (p. 12) even advanced the idea that the growing supply of foreign labour force would alleviate the expected lack of work force in Finland – a rather fantastic idea to be presented in the wake of a unprecedented unemployment in the country.

11. Although the EEA negotiations were completed already in October 1991, the treaty was not signed before May 1992. The European Court of Justice first rejected the agreement because of the planned common EEA court, which was seen to go against the Rome Treaty and threatened the autonomy of the Community legal order. Instead, a separate EFTA court was established in the framework of EEA. (See the opinions of the Court, 1/91 and 1/92; Cremona 1994: 514-516.) The process of ratification was complicated since Switzerland left the agreement after the referendum in December 1992; the ensuing financial problems were resolved in March 1993. (EFTA Bulletin 1/94: 11; Rehn 1993: 194.)

12. For the EEA institutions and the new EFTA organs, see EFTA Bulletin 1/94: 6-8.

13. The Finnish parliament ratified the treaty in October with the overwhelming majority of 154 votes in favour and 12 against, with one abstention and 32 absent (*Eurooppa* 27.10.1992).

14. The treaty was accompanied by two declarations: a rather weak one about continuing Nordic cooperation and a second one in which the EU member countries and the EFTA countries expressed their will to strengthen the political dialogue in foreign policy, aiming at closer relations in areas of mutual importance, or, in practice, unofficial consultation and discussion. This also implied the introduction of such a dialogue to the relations between the EFTA countries. (*Eurooppa* 27.10.1992, pp. 5-6.)

15. With 108 votes for, 55 against and 32 abstentions.

16. Cf. President Koivisto in the College of Europe in Bruges (October 28, 1992) noting that while the EEA would imply that Finland would need to adapt, EU membership would allow for participation.

17. The collapse of Soviet trade was a major reason for the crisis (see Hjerppe 1993: 72); Rehn (1993: 202) sees as further factors contributing to the crisis the rapidly deteriorating terms of trade with Western Europe, rapid credit expansion after the liberalisation of capital markets and the resulting increase in demand and investment prices together with increase in income and consumption through tax reforms and a permissive credit policy.
18. That the possibility of joining really was quite new is shown by the fact that as late as 1990, two years before the application, Antola (1990b: 172) did not see membership as being among the foreseeable choices but argued that one had to expect rather dramatic changes in Europe before Finland would become an applying country.
19. In the government programmes, the traditional statement on neutrality fell in the 1980s from the beginning of the section concerning foreign policy to the fourth chapter (Lipponen 1990: 9).
20. In a visit to Finland in 1989, the then Soviet president Gorbachev unconditionally recognised that Finland was a neutral Nordic country – thus far, the Finnish-Soviet communiqués had spoken about Finland's striving for neutrality – and that it was Finland's internal matter to decide on its attitude towards EC membership (e.g., Rehn 1993: 205). With a singular burst of activity, Finland unilaterally declared in September 1990 that the stipulations of the Paris peace treaty concerning Germany as well as those concerning certain restrictions on the Finnish armed forces had lost significance and would no longer be applied. Analogously, the allusion to Germany in the FCMA treaty was seen to be obsolete. In the autumn of 1991, Finland negotiated simultaneously with the Soviet Union and Russia a new agreement, signed with Russia in January 1992 (the Soviet Union had ceased to exist in December 1991). At the same time, the FCMA treaty was abrogated. The new treaty differs from the FCMA in that it is based on the principles of the United Nations and the CSCE; it does not involve positive security guarantees or mechanisms of consultation, but instead negative ones, the prohibition of the use of force and assistance in the case of an attack against the other party. (Möttölä 1993: 95-97.)
21. Continuity does have a particular attraction; the logical is often more acceptable than the illogical. It may even be difficult to avoid the perception of continuity in explaining integration policy as somehow logical and rational activity on the part of policy-makers, as when Lempiäinen (1994: 128) claims that the acceptance of the EEA in Finland was made easier by the fact that the EEA has been a 'logical step' in the economic integration in Western Europe. The mere fact that one has traditionally spoken about a 'Finnish integration policy' smooths the adjustment of membership, even though this policy was traditionally constructed on the explicit basis of non-membership.

22. Memorandum by the political department of the ministry for foreign affairs, October 26, 1992, published in *Eurooppa* 30.10.1992, pp. 1-6; this document served as background information for the Commission's *avis* on Finland's application and the ensuing negotiations on foreign policy.
23. Finland's view as stated by Pertti Salolainen, minister for foreign trade, in the ministerial meeting opening the conferences on the accession of Austria, Sweden and Finland to the EU, Brussels, February 1, 1993; quoted in *Eurooppa* 1/93.
24. For example, the Appendix 1992 (pp. 35-37) notes that unanimity or/and essential common interests are important and that the envisaged common defence policy will be based on respect for the basic security and defence solutions of the member states; further, the Maastricht Treaty allows for special bilateral or multilateral treaties between the members. One might question, however, whether the possibility of treaty making *between* the members is as important as the possibility of bilateral relations with countries outside the Union.
25. November 4, 1992; published in the Bulletin of the European Communities, supplement 6/92. Unofficial Finnish translation in *Eurooppa* 4.11.1992.
26. It is interesting to confront the statement by Salolainen (above) with the response by the representative of the EU in which the main message was that the process and structures of the Union should not be weakened and that the whole EU *acquis* had to be accepted. This was repeatedly underlined with expressions such as 'I should make it clear from the outset', 'I would also recall', 'may I remind you also'. (Draft statement by Mr. Niels Helveg Petersen, president-in-office of the Council at the ministerial meeting opening the conferences on the accession of Austria, Sweden and Finland to the European Union, Brussels, February 1, 1993; quoted in *Eurooppa* 1.2.1993.)
27. In fact, the Maastricht Treaty states that '[A] common foreign and security policy *is* hereby *established*' and that '[t]he Union and its Member States shall define and implement a common foreign and security policy, governed by the provisions of this Title and *covering all areas of foreign and security policy*' (articles J and J.1, italics added).
28. The government position (above; esp. pp. 2-4) underlined that the EC countries and Finland share the same values and socio-economic development and have, therefore, also common goals in international relations. For example, the position mentions the similarity of the Finnish and the EPC attitudes regarding the Baltic region. Further, it states that as all European countries are committed to the CSCE values of democracy, human rights and economic liberalism, there is no longer reason for a wide neutrality policy.

29. The report of the Commission on the challenge of enlargement presented to the European Council in Lisbon, June 26-27, 1992; Bulletin of the European Communities, supplement 3/92, pp. 11-12.
30. Brussels, December 21, 1993. The negotiations began on February 1, 1993 and ended on March 1, 1994. The European Parliament accepted the results on May 4, 1994, and the accession agreements were signed on Corfu on June 24-25.
31. The EU also used the new member states as a device for strengthening the credibility of 'the common': the declaration states further that the adhesion *shall strengthen the internal cohesion* of the Union and its capacity to act efficiently in the field of foreign and security policy; the acceding countries shall from the moment of accession be ready and capable of participating fully and actively in the common foreign and security policy as defined in the Maastricht Treaty; the new members accept in its totality and without reservations all the goals of the Union treaty and they are ready and capable of supporting from the moment of accession the policy in vigour of the Union.
32. An illustration of the difficulties in assessing something as elusive as 'influence' is given by the game-theoretical study of Widgrén (1995) about national influence in the EU. The conclusions drawn (e.g., that EU decision-making process strongly favours small countries, p. 18) are based on a host of precise assumptions which are necessary to allow for a quantification of the question, but which, at the same time, oversimplify the situation.
33. Cf. Commission opinion on Sweden's application for membership. SEC(92) 1582 final; Bulletin of the European Communities, Supplement 5/92.
34. Indeed, EU membership quite soon led also to discussions on NATO membership; Finland become NACC observer in 1992 and signed the PFP agreement in 1994 (e.g., Rehn 1993: 212).
35. For instance, the government position according to which Finland considers that it can best secure its national interests and international goals as an EC member and that it will also in the future independently define its own interests (*Eurooppa* 30.10.1992) does not say anything about these goals; moreover, the second part verifies the first: interests can be defined so as to be best furthered in the EU. Integration can be said to be in the interests of the states; what is important, however, is that the interests are not given *ex ante*.

7 EU membership: a new dimension to Finland's integration

The logic of membership

Finnish membership in the EU has been interpreted by many as a fundamental change in the traditional Finnish stance on European integration based on the principles of neutrality and the protection of broad freedom of action. This stance implied that Finland previously avoided all political commitments or institutional obligations, in particular supranationality, in order not to risk these principles and its good relations with the Soviet Union. Membership of the EEC/EC – directly based on confrontation between great powers – was obviously not considered possible. Even Finnish relations to EFTA, OECD and Nordic cooperation had to be defined in fairly cautious terms, even refraining from full membership. Accordingly, membership in the supranational EU would be even less compatible with this policy. Therefore, it has been pointed out, Finland has had to change its policies rather strikingly to make EU membership possible: it has completely renounced the former governing principles of neutrality and avoidance of political commitments.

One should not overlook, however, the extent to which this impression of discontinuity is created by the very accounts of Finnish integration policy which tend to trace clear 'lines' and 'policies' to explain past decisions. In other words, the general principles of the policy might actually be *post hoc* constructions, perhaps supported by some political statements, rather than steadfast guidelines of the concrete actions in practice. Finnish integration policy can be made to appear logical, for example in its consistent avoidance of political commitments. It might also be that, in absence of knowledge of actual intentions, the fact that the country has not been able to join some organisation has been interpreted as confirming that the policy of the country actually excluded joining. Logically, then, EU membership comes to be seen as proof of a change of policy. This logic, however, may divert attention from possible 'counterfactuals' and alternative interpretations. In the case of Finnish integration policy, the problem with the usual description is the insufficient attention paid to the elements of continuity that characterise the policy following membership.

Furthering its interests with the best available means has naturally always been an aim in Finnish integration policy. For a small state, an essential means is participating in the central structures of European cooperation, while protecting, within these structures, sufficient freedom of action and decision-making capacity which enables taking into account the national particularities and specific interests in a given question. These are also the important elements of continuity which form the core of the Finnish attitude towards European integration: avoiding economic and political exclusion and guaranteeing the possibility to further the particular interests. Seen through these elements of continuity, it is no longer curious that Finland has on some occasions actually participated in political cooperation or considered EEC membership possible quite early on. These elements also explain why EU membership – while obviously a novelty – is not a disruptive event. Rather, the Finnish process of accession proved to be too smooth to have represented a real change of policy. As President Koivisto stated in the European Parliament in November 1993, the decision to apply for membership is, on closer inspection, a logical continuation of Finnish integration policy.

At the same time, it is important not to misunderstand this continuity. Although the basic aims remain, it would be strange to suppose that a country would for decades have immutable interests or the same means of furthering them. Its interests are not self-evident and stable through time – even though there clearly are quite permanent interests such as good relations with neighbouring countries. Obviously, they are not defined *a priori,* but according to the situation, as the economic and political environment changes. As with the interests, so the appropriate means for furthering them change as a result of a natural adaptation to the environment. Useful in certain situations or certain periods of time, they may also become irrelevant; their precise meaning may also change in time, as Finnish neutrality and avoidance of supranationality shows. While Törnudd (1995: 101-102) still sees neutrality, even after EU membership, as one of the elements of continuity in Finnish policies, together with an emphasis on the nation state, the Nordic relations and relations to Russia, neutrality has in the meantime been redefined and seems gradually to have lost its usefulness as a tool, perhaps even becoming counterproductive (see below).

Finally, one need not see Finnish policy as a mere submission to external influences, either, as has often been done in the literature. In fact, Finland has often been depicted as driftwood: being just a small country situated near a great power which does not have a real choice of policy, its policies being almost determined by external factors. The accounts of Finnish integration policy have also drawn on this picture. For Antola (1989: 55), adaptation – with some reservations – has been the key to Finnish integration policy and Finland has even been 'pushed into her own decisions' by events in the international environment. Lempiäinen (1994: 139), in turn, sees Finland as being at the mercy of international economy, not being able to have much influence. In general, it has been argued that the limited scope for action has made Finnish policies rather passive in nature. As Väyrynen (1993: 41) notes, the importance of foreign policy considerations has meant that the room for political innovation has been fairly limited for Finland.[1]

These interpretations not only exaggerate continuity but can also become easily tautological: everything is either rational adaptation or decided from outside. They seem to be ways of explaining policy *post hoc* rather than descriptions of policy itself.[2] In reality, policy formulation has been more flexible. In fact, Antola and Tuusvuori (1983: 160-163, 246-247) interpret Finnish integration policy as an active strategy of mutual influence which takes into account changes in the environment. Adaptation is thus not an aim in itself, but a strategy to avoid the threat of exclusion from major markets (Antola 1989: 55). The Finnish attitude has changed in time; as Antola (1991a: 148) notes, economic integration has come to be seen as a factor which contributes to the stability in Europe, and integration policy has become increasingly active and more autonomous from foreign policy. Similarly, even the attitude towards political integration has been flexible: what has been seen as 'political' has not necessarily followed any special logic, but it has depended on the situation. While the Council of Europe has been seen as too political, close political cooperation with the Nordic NATO members has been more than acceptable. Dynamic and characterised by increasing participation and commitments, Finland's integration policy can be seen as following the general development of Finnish foreign policy (cf. Möttölä 1993: 88-89).

In fact, Finland's special interests have been defined according to the possibilities of the situation – any rational action requires this kind of adaptation – and, when looked at more closely, it has been able to further them rather efficiently. Even when full participation has been hampered by political factors, Finland has found several individual arrangements to be able to participate in the process of European integration without compromising its political freedom of action, such as individual loans from the United States instead of joining the Marshall Plan or FINEFTA treaty instead of EFTA membership (see below). Finally, these organisations would not themselves be credible did they not allow for taking into account the specific interests of the participants. This is true also for the EU; therefore, the Finnish decision to join is a further step and logical continuation of its policy in a changed environment. At the same time, it is an important step which gives this policy not only additional dimensions and possibilities, but also presents challenges through the mutual relations of influence between the organisation and its member states.

Neutrality: the cold war means in Finnish integration policy

Following Antola and Tuusvuori 1983 and Antola 1989, the Finnish integration policy of the cold war era can be seen as having developed through four different phases which succeed each other according to a clear logic of increasing participation. These phases are bilateralism, trade liberalisation, the delineation of a Finnish free trade policy and maintenance of a broad integration system. The common denominator of this period from the late 1940s to the late 1980s was neutrality as a means needed for furthering the general aims of avoiding exclusion from cooperation and securing particular interests. As an overriding interest was not to induce a deterioration in relations with the Soviet Union through commitments which might compromise the bilateral treaties, neutrality came to be seen as the only possible foreign policy position. Consequently, neutrality was also the basic means for Finnish integration policy: participation in organisations of a 'Western' character was acceptable as long as it could be seen as conforming to neutrality. What divided the periods, then, were the steps taken towards increasing options and widening the scope of participation and the diminishing centrality of neutrality. The domain of neutrality policy, first defined in very broad terms, was gradually shrinking and towards the end of the cold war, its usefulness as a means came under increasing scrutiny.

Bilateralism (1945-1955)

The period immediately following the second world war was characterised by a reconstruction of both Finnish foreign policy and trade relations, with the subordination of the latter to the former. The centrality of relations to the Soviet Union made Finland's treaties with it, especially the FCMA treaty, the cornerstones of Finnish foreign policy. Trade relations which could compromise the foreign policy were avoided; war reparations to the Soviet Union and the conversion of the wartime economy were dominant. (Antola 1989: 55; Antola and Tuusvuori 1983: 122-124.) In addition to signing bilateral treaties with traditional trade partners, such as Sweden and the United Kingdom, Finland signed in 1947 a bilateral trade treaty based on the principle of most favoured nation with the Soviet Union (Hjerppe 1993: 69). The FCMA treaty with the Soviet Union of 1948, which concerned in essence the defence of Finnish territory in order to prevent its use for attack on the Soviet Union, contained also a mutual commitment not to join alliances directed against the other party. In addition, it mentioned Finland's aspiration to remain out of conflicts between the great powers.

A first instance of how the FCMA treaty was interpreted in practice was the Finnish rejection of the Marshall Plan. Originally, the plan of the United States aimed at facilitating the reconstruction of Europe was offered to all European countries, including the Soviet Union. The Soviet Union, however, rejected it, and the Eastern European countries followed this decision. As the plan therefore concerned only the Western bloc, it came to be seen in Finland as associated with the bloc division in Europe and conflicts between the great powers (see Antola 1991a: 146). Therefore, Finland too rejected the invitation to participate.

However, as a compensation for the lost contribution to Finland's reconstruction, other arrangements were made. As Antola notes, both the reparations and the re-establishment of trade made it important to improve the export capabilities of Finnish industry, for example renewing the machinery of the wood processing industry. This demanded foreign capital. The United States gave a first loan for this purpose in 1948 and Sweden also granted large loans. More credit was obtained when Finland joined the IMF and IBRD – even before Sweden[3] – and despite the fact that the Soviet Union did not join the Bretton Woods organisations. Moreover, Marshall aid helped Finnish industry indirectly by hastening economic growth and thereby increasing the demand for wood and paper.[4] In all, Finland's position did not in the end essentially differ from that of other small countries in Western Europe as far as their relations with Western economic cooperation were concerned. (Antola and Tuusvuori 1983: 122-124; Hjerppe 1993: 67, 69; Hakovirta 1976: 153.)

In addition, Finland joined GATT, also characterised by the absence of socialist countries. Its accession in 1950 was motivated by the chance to secure extensive, multilateral markets and letting the Finnish export industry profit in the best possible way from the increase of economic activities.

However, it was also important for Finland that the GATT agreement allowed the possibility of applying the most favoured nation principle to countries outside the agreement, that is, to the Soviet Union with which Finland already had a MFN agreement. (Antola and Tuusvuori 1983: 124-126.)

Nevertheless, there were limits to Finnish participation in Western European cooperation. Finland could not participate in the organisations which developed more or less directly as a result of the Marshall Plan, that is, the OEEC/OECD and the Council of Europe. Neither could Finland take part in the Nordic negotiations of the late 1940s for a Nordic customs union which also were, at the beginning, a response to pressure from the United States to form regional groupings for qualifying for Marshall aid (e.g., Nielsson 1978: 288). Finland's neutrality excluded projects for supranational integration (the Council of Europe as it was originally planned), coordinating integration (OEEC), and common market integration (Antola and Tuusvuori 1983: 124-126).

Indeed, even Finland's membership of the Nordic Council and the United Nations were first hampered by negative Soviet attitudes. Finland could not join the Nordic Council from the beginning, as the Soviet Union saw it as a tool of forces supporting NATO. In reality, however, Finland had all the time been virtually a member. The original Council statutes stated that on the request of Finland, Finnish representatives may take part in the deliberations and decisions of the Council. In fact, Finland not only participated in the preparatory works but also received the Council documents as if it was a member. (Wendt 1981: 35-37, 343-344.) Together with the more general relaxation of international relations in 1955, however, this view changed and the objections to Finnish membership were removed. In the same year, Finland also became a member of the United Nations as a result of an agreement between the United States and the Soviet Union.[5] In 1956, Finland joined the Nordic economic cooperation committee, and the Finnish national committee for Nordic cooperation was established.

In joining the Nordic Council, the Finnish government made a declaration which aimed at underlining the compatibility of the Council membership with Finnish neutrality. According to this reservation, representatives of Finland should not participate in the discussion if the Council, against accepted practice, were to discuss military questions or questions which would lead to adopting a position on conflicts of interest between great powers (Wendt 1981: 35-37, 343-344). Thus secured, active participation in Nordic cooperation assured, in fact, benefits in both economic and political terms. Antola and Tuusvuori (1983: 126-127) observe that

Nordic cooperation gained an important role in the Finnish economy in the late 1950s, being the only form of Western economic cooperation Finland could participate in. Close cooperation with the other Nordic countries, including in the United Nations, strengthened Finland's international position. As Forsberg and Vaahtoranta (1993: 238) note, Nordic cooperation constituted a counterforce to the Soviet Union, with the effect of raising the threshold of the Soviet Union's ability to exert influence on Finland.

As such, a Nordic orientation was not new for Finland. Already in the 1930s, the country had participated in the regular meetings of the Nordic ministers. Political cooperation with the other Nordic countries was, however, temporarily interrupted: in the period from the second world war to 1956, Finland could not participate in the meetings of the Nordic foreign ministers (Wendt 1959: 24, 39). Before the war, Finland had also participated in the Oslo Agreement on economic cooperation, signed in 1930 by Sweden, Norway, Denmark, Belgium, Luxembourg and the Netherlands (Muoser 1986: 105). Thus, for Finland as well as for other European countries, the years 1945-1955 entailed a gradual return to multilateral cooperation.

The period of trade liberalisation (1955-1959)

The late 1950s saw the establishment of both the EEC and EFTA. While a membership in the former was excluded by Finland's neutrality policy, cooperation with EFTA countries was seen to be possible. Although Finland had not joined the OEEC, Finnish trade with Western European countries was liberalised in 1957 with a special Helsinki Protocol between Finland and the 11 OEEC members. Some 70% of the Finnish imports from Western Europe became free from import regulation, and Finnish exports received an equivalent treatment with those of the other signatories. Finland also participated as an observer in some of the special committees of the OEEC. (Antola and Tuusvuori 1983: 128; see also Rehn 1993: 186-187.)

In addition, Finland participated in the Nordic plans of that period for a Nordic customs union. Despite critical moments in Finnish-Soviet relations linked to the increasing Finnish interest towards Western integration,[6] Finland was in 1959 ready for closer economic cooperation between the Nordic countries. Rather quickly, however, the purely Nordic plans had been transformed into larger European ones, and the other Nordic countries abandoned them in favour of EFTA, which was established the same year.

In economic terms, EFTA membership was without doubt attractive for Finland; it was not politically excluded, either. In a Nordic ministerial meeting in 1959, the Finnish prime minister Sukselainen had alluded to the possibility of Finland joining the EFTA together with the other Nordic countries, stating that '...if the plan does not include political obligations nor provide for supra-national organs Finland is not less interested in this plan than the other Nordic countries' (cf. Törnudd 1969: 64). Actually, the Finnish minister for foreign affairs Karjalainen attended the Stockholm conference where the EFTA agreement was signed, even though Finland did not formally participate in the negotiations. He also repeated the Finnish stand that while national interests should be secured in the Western markets, the Finnish undertakings should not threaten the international position of the country or its bilateral agreements with the Soviet Union. Thus, Finland could accept agreements on tariffs and trade with the EFTA countries, but without political obligations and supranationality. (Antola 1990b: 164, 165.)

Even though EFTA membership could not be seen as too demanding in its political obligations and supranationality, based as it was on the clear will of the members of establishing a non-supranational alternative to EEC integration, Finland could not join the organisation. Finnish EFTA membership was hampered by the attitudes of both the Soviet Union and the United Kingdom. The former expressed doubts about the possible negative effects of such participation in closed economic groupings on the Finnish-Soviet trade. The latter opposed Finnish membership as it would have triggered several new membership requests and further complications in the negotiations. (Hakovirta 1976: 200-202; af Malmborg 1994: 381-383.)

Delineation of a Finnish free trade policy (1960-1972)

In order to benefit from EFTA cooperation, it was important for Finland to organise its relations with the Association in a way which would not hamper trade with the Soviet Union. On the other hand, EFTA members were suspicious about the effects of Finnish-Soviet free trade in combination with a Finnish EFTA membership. Both parties therefore preferred a special solution in the form of an association agreement between Finland and EFTA, the so-called FINEFTA agreement, which was signed in 1960.

The fact that EFTA had other neutral members as well has been mentioned as a factor rendering the FINEFTA agreement possible; the majority of the then members, however, belonged to NATO. In fact, it was considered important not to adopt the text of the Stockholm convention as such to the FINEFTA treaty. While the FINEFTA treaty included all the stipulations concerning trade and economy – with the exception of a slower reduction of duties and the right for import restrictions for certain products (appendices I and II) – an exception of a more political nature was constituted by the omission in FINEFTA of the allusions to economic arrangements between the Western European countries, that is, the aim of developing relations to the EEC. In all, the association responded to the needs of Finnish wood and paper exporters. The Finnish home market industry was given a period of protection because of its weak competitive capacities, and bilateral trade with the East could be continued without disruption, while agriculture was adequately protected. (Antola and Tuusvuori 1983: 131-135, Antola 1991a: 148-149.)

What was essential was that the FINEFTA agreement gave Finland in practice the rights of an EFTA member. Although FINEFTA was conceived as an autonomous organisation with its own joint council, Finland also had an observer in personal capacity in the Council of EFTA (Hakovirta 1976: 219), and from 1968 onwards, the councils of EFTA and FINEFTA met at the same time so that in some cases, Finland could even be outvoted ('*majorisiert*', Muoser 1986: 181).

Finally, the FINEFTA treaty was balanced by a simultaneous Finnish-Soviet agreement about customs reductions (Antola and Tuusvuori 1983: 136) which helped improve relations with the Soviet Union. In fact, the 'Finnish paradox', as stated by President Kekkonen in October 1961, was that the better Finland succeeded in maintaining the confidence of the Soviet Union in Finland as a peaceful neighbour, the better were the Finnish opportunities for close co-operation with the countries of the Western world (Jansson 1973: 23).

Manifestly, these opportunities increased in the 1960s. The Finnish decision to join the OECD in 1968 can be seen as an intentional further strengthening of the Western direction in Finland's integration policy. Once again, the Finnish special arrangements had been comparable to full membership: the decision actually only formalised the existing practice of participation in the work of the organisation. The economic benefits of membership, growing possibilities to influence trade and economic policies and improved access to information – together with the additional motivation of strengthening the country's international status – were secured by a special declaration by the Finnish government in joining the organisation about the intention not to commit itself to anything contrary to its foreign and defence politics and neutrality. In addition, it was stated that membership would not limit Finland's possibilities to develop trade relations with countries outside the organisation. (Antola and Tuusvuori 1983: 142-143; Muoser 1986: 155.)

Antola and Tuusvuori note that Finnish neutrality policy acquired a new interpretation in the late 1960s. In the time of the FINEFTA agreement, neutrality had still been seen as setting limits to Finnish possibilities of action in Western European integration. However, from now on, it was understood that neutrality actually gave the possibility of having an active role in promoting economic integration in Europe. While previously economic and political integration had been closely connected, it was now realized that it was important to keep them separate in order to allow for both participation and neutrality. Thereby, the Finnish interpretation moved closer to that of the other neutral states. (Antola and Tuusvuori 1983: 139.)[7] Finland still stayed outside what it saw as political integration and, thus, outside the Council of Europe. However, it participated increasingly in its activities and obtained in 1964 a special right of observer status in all the organs under the ministerial committee whenever the Finnish government so wished, while the status of observer was normally obtained only by invitation (Serenius 1976: 39).

Political commitments seemed no longer completely excluded from Finnish integration policy. In fact, Finland participated in drafting the treaty for a Nordic customs union, NORDEK, which was intended to have also clear political implications. The NORDEK draft contained provisions including harmonisation of legislation in a broad range of issues from economic policy and regulations on the introduction of common tariffs towards countries outside EFTA to agriculture, labour market and competition rules. It also contained the establishment of a Nordic Council of Ministers which had the right of making binding decisions and of the NORDEK secretariat, which was to receive no instructions from national authorities, being actually comparable to the EEC commission. (Wendt 1981: 125-129; Solem 1977: 83.)

NORDEK was seen to strengthen Finland's position *vis-à-vis* the developments in the EEC. Soon after the establishment of EFTA, in fact, the United Kingdom – the most important trade partner – applied for EEC membership, followed by Denmark and Norway. Thus, the question of the relations between EFTA and the EEC as well as the proper position for Finland was far from being settled. As Antola and Tuusvuori put it, the blurring of the boundary between common market integration and free trade integration was a particularly intricate problem for Finland. In the late 1960s, the Finnish policy was to support the development of economic cooperation in Europe between all the three organisations, EFTA, EEC and CMEA (Antola and Tuusvuori 1983: 137, 139-140, 247-250). While for Denmark in particular, the NORDEK draft was a bridge to the EEC, Finland stressed the value of Nordic cooperation in itself; it was important for Finland that NORDEK be kept separate from the EEC.

Törnudd (1969: 70-71) notes that the question of Finnish relations with the EEC appeared quite complex. The possibility of membership was not totally rejected; the national scene was characterised by lack of agreement on the meaning of the 'political' nature of the EEC and the political implications of membership or association.[8] Moreover, there was at first hardly any public debate; Törnudd argues that the government deliberately avoided stimulating debate by not divulging studies made by the authorities on Finnish relations with the EEC.

As a way of assuring that this renewed interest in Western integration would not harm the relations with the Soviet Union − or, 'in order to remove any possible doubt about the consistency of our policy'[9] − the FCMA treaty was renewed in 1970, five years before it was due to expire. This notwithstanding, Finnish integration policy suffered some setbacks. First, as the possibilities of Danish and Norwegian EEC membership had considerably improved, it no longer seemed evident that the NORDEK treaty could be kept sufficiently apart from the EEC to allow for Finnish membership. In fact, Finland declared that if one of the Nordic countries were to begin membership talks with the EEC, Finland would leave the negotiations on NORDEK; similarly, if some of them were to join the EEC after the treaty was signed, Finland required the possibility not to apply the whole agreement. Finally, in March 1970 when the NORDEK treaty was ready for approval, the Finnish government announced that Finland could not sign the treaty.[10] (Antola and Tuusvuori 1983: 144-146.)

This, however, did not mean a halt to Finnish integration policy. On the one hand, Nordic cooperation was given a firmer and politically more important character: even though NORDEK did not materialise as such, much of its contents did, including the Council of Ministers. On the other hand, negotiations on a free trade agreement between Finland and the EEC were started on a Finnish initiative as early as the spring 1970. Once again, the Finnish aim was to avoid possible discrimination and isolation while maintaining neutrality, Soviet trade, EFTA free trade, Nordic cooperation and its international agreements, especially GATT. Thus, in comparison to Sweden which was ready to discuss all possible areas of cooperation, Finland intended to stay outside the EEC economic policy, agreeing only on the removal of duties for industrial products. In all, the treaty should not limit economic or political sovereignty or decision-making capacity, being compatible with neutrality and not infringing upon the doctrine of foreign policy. (Hakovirta 1976: 290.) The free trade agreement was initialled on July 22, 1972, but a second setback occurred in that the Finnish government decided temporarily to postpone signing the agreement. The treaty was finally signed on October 5, 1973, and entered into force at the beginning of 1974. Finland also signed an agreement with the European Coal and Steel Community which entered in force a year later.

Maintaining a broad integration system (1973-late 1980s)

The essential contents of the Finnish free trade treaty with the EEC were the gradual removal of duties for industrial products and agreement on not creating new import duties. The exceptions included the question of quantitative restrictions on fuel and fertilisers and the protection of weak industries for both parties. Finland could also retain the restrictions concerning payments and credits which it had in the OECD. Moreover, the Finnish free trade agreement did not include the so-called evolution or development clause (art. 32) which meant that Finland was committed only to the free trade treaty, not to the possible future extension or intensification of relations with the EC. (Antola and Tuusvuori 1983: 147-156; Antola 1991a: 149.)[11]

In order to make it acceptable both internally and in terms of foreign policy, the free trade agreement was accompanied by protective legislative measures against the possible harmful effects of free trade and by parallel measures taken in trade with the socialist countries. These measures consisted of a special system of bilateral treaties on the reciprocal removal of barriers to trade with the socialist countries other than the Soviet Union – the so-called KEVSOS treaties which had scarce practical significance (Antola 1991a: 149; Hjerppe 1993: 71) – and a cooperation agreement with the Council for Mutual Economic Assistance (CMEA). In addition, a bilateral trade agreement was signed guaranteeing the Soviet Union an equal treatment with the EEC countries on the Finnish market. (Hakovirta 1976: 290; Antola and Tuusvuori 1983: 156-157; Antola 1989: 56-57.)

EFTA soon came to be seen as a suitable instrument in Finnish integration policy. It had proved to be less temporary than had perhaps been thought, and it became a useful forum for consultations in international economic relations such as common preparations for the Kennedy Round of GATT. Since 1965, Finland had been participating in internal EFTA discussions on European integration (Törnudd 1969: 67). In the 1970s, EFTA was strengthened and it developed relations to countries outside the free trade area, becoming increasingly an actor of its own (Antola and Tuusvuori 1983: 97-103).[12] Finland was in favour of both enlargement and deepening, being ready also for the development of free trade and relations with the EEC in the limits of neutrality; the EEC relations were to be based on own agreements and decision-making. (Antola and Tuusvuori 1983: 157-158; Antola 1991a: 149.)

In fact, Finnish integration policy was shifting from special arrangements to an EFTA-based approach. In this development, the Luxembourg meeting between EFTA and the EC in 1984 constituted an important new step. In 1985, Finland became a full EFTA member – something that in practice did not entail departure from its previous status as associate member (Muoser 1986: 182-183). Finnish reservations regarding the political nature of the organisation and its relations to the EC were no longer particularly relevant. According to the new Finnish 'EFTA-card policy', EFTA should be the main tool in the integration policy of its members; a strengthened EFTA was seen to be in the interests of all of them as a way of sharing costs and reducing the threat of marginalisation. (Antola 1991a: 149-150; see also Government report 1988.) Finland was assuming an active role in the promotion of economic cooperation (cf. Antola 1989: 61-62).

The end of the cold war and the EEA

Towards the 1990s, full participation was visibly replacing neutrality as a means of Finnish integration policy. Throughout the latter part of the 1980s, there had been signs of change in the way neutrality was interpreted. Although no political aspects of integration had officially been taken up, practical informal integration and cooperation with the EC had increased, and this informal participation even involved elements of political cooperation.

The formal avoidance of political commitments notwithstanding, Finland had in reality been participating in European cooperation on a broad front. Nordic cooperation kept Finland in pace with the larger developments, facilitating, subsequently, also EEA and EU membership (cf. Temmes 1995). The individual ministries participated through direct contacts increasingly in the coordinative integration both in the OECD and in the Council of Europe. In fact, without even being observer, Finland had participated in and hosted from 1963 onwards meetings and projects of the Council of Europe on the initiative of the member states (Antola and Tuusvuori 1983: 229-240); Finland joined the Council in 1989.

As regards the EEC, Finland had been rather slow in developing its relations in comparison to, for instance, Sweden, limiting the agreements with the EC to trade issues (Antola 1989: 60). Yet, the EEC's importance for Finland was recognised, and Finland accredited an ambassador to the EEC as early as in 1964 (Antola and Tuusvuori 1983: 138). Finland joined the EC's cooperation programme for high technology (EUREKA) in 1985, the year it was established, despite the potential political implications of such cooperation, and pursued additional bilateral agreements with the EC to supplement the free trade agreement (Antola 1991a: 150 and 1991b: 17-18). Both economically and politically, the importance of participation was recognised. National business leaders were increasingly aware of the necessity of establishing their companies in the European market. In the mid-1980s, the economic elite was tacitly using the 'exit option', investing in Europe, and was becoming largely independent of the political leadership (Väyrynen 1993: 35, 43-44). At the same time, the 'political dialogue' between Finland and the EC also began. From 1988 onwards, meetings of a joint committee with the Commission were held at the level of heads of political departments of the ministers for foreign affairs, then at ministerial level. In 1988, Finland invited the Community to open a mission in Helsinki. (Antola 1989: 60; *Eurooppa* 27.10.1992, pp. 5-6).

The margins of interpreting the requirements of a policy of neutrality had grown visibly larger. On the one hand, the Soviet attitude towards Western European integration was changing in the 1980s.[13] Hakovirta observes how the Soviet posture developed from intense hostility to occasional mild criticism, selective positive commentary and indications of its own interest in cooperation, even participation.[14] Consequently, he argues, the control of the 'acceptable limits of neutrality' remained increasingly in the hands of the neutrals themselves. On the other hand, the EC was also changing its view on neutrality. Previously, the reticence of the EEC to let the neutral countries select some economic benefits of membership without sharing the economic responsibilities and political goals of the ordinary members had limited the relations of the neutral countries to the EEC. The United States was also negative towards such special conditions.[15] Hakovirta argues that the EC came to expect a flexible, 'Irish-type' interpretation of neutrality: no-one claimed that neutrality would be an obstacle to membership, provided a suitable interpretation was given. (Hakovirta 1976: 117 and 1987: 268, 270-271.)

In fact, the Finnish prime minister and the minister for foreign affairs asserted in the autumn of 1987 that participation in West European

EU: new dimension to Finland's integration 317

integration was no longer part of Finnish policy of neutrality. In other words, neutrality was redefined as no longer affecting integration policy; consequently, it did not hamper the deepening of Finnish participation. In practice, increasing integration with the West was no longer seen to require parallel measures with the East. However, it was still emphasised that integration should not undermine the possibilities of autonomous decision-making – domestic autonomy was considered necessary to maintain good relations with the Soviet Union (Väyrynen 1993: 36). From the maintenance of a broad integration system, thus, Finland openly concentrated its participation on the Western European scene. This new stand received a confirmation from the Soviet Union in 1989, when it stated that it was Finland's own matter to decide on its attitude towards EC membership (cf. Rehn 1993: 205). In all, neutrality came to be reduced to a narrow field of security and military policy, but also in a geographical sense through the notion of 'neutrality in the neighbouring regions'. (Möttölä 1993: 90-95, 101; cf. Törnudd 1995: 91, 93.)[16]

In this changed environment, the plan to establish the European Economic Area (EEA) between the members of EFTA and the EC, presented in 1989, suited Finnish policy particularly well. First, it was designed so as to allow for neutral states' full participation in the common market without having to accept the political aims of the Community. In fact, the Finnish support for the EEA was seen as a logical outcome of the Finnish EFTA-policy. It was also a fitting compromise in that it excluded the sensitive areas of agriculture and foreign policy while meeting the needs of business to gain access on an equal basis to the EC's internal market. In fact, the EEA agreement met practically no political resistance in Finland, in contrast to Norway and Switzerland. (Antola 1991a: 150-151; Väyrynen 1993: 39.) Secondly, it brought the eventual EC membership much closer as the agreement implied the acceptance of a large part of the *acquis communautaire*. In fact, it seemed to be clear almost from the outset that there were practically no hindrances to full Finnish EC membership, either. From an eager supporter of the EEA agreement, Finland thus very soon passed, together with the other EFTA members, to the preparation of its membership application.

The EEA negotiations began in the autumn of 1989 and the treaty was signed in May 1992, coming into force on January 1, 1994. The EEA agreement involves the equal participation of the EFTA countries in the 'four freedoms' and cooperation in other areas, such as environment, education, research and development. It contains the EU legislation adopted before

August 1, 1991. Subsequent legislation having impact on the operation of the EEA, that is, concerning the internal market, is successively added to the EEA norms in order to maintain a homogeneous and dynamic economic area.

Considering that the EEA agreement entails a considerable part of the *acquis communautaire,* its unproblematic acceptance in Finland clearly shows both the compatibility of the *acquis* with the Finnish legislation, and, above all, the efficiency of the preceding informal adjustment of Finnish norms to those of the EC, which took place in part in the fora of Nordic cooperation. Together with the economic contents, the political part of the agreement was also quite acceptable. Indeed, a declaration was given in which the members of EU and EFTA expressed their will to strengthen political dialogue in foreign policy aiming at closer relations in areas of mutual importance. However, security and defence were kept outside the treaty. At the same time, the EEA implied that political dialogue between EFTA countries began (*Eurooppa* 27.10.1992, pp. 5-6). An EFTA court was established, and the EEA also imposed a much stricter regime in competition policy than in the earlier free trade agreements with the EC, enforced by the European Commission and the new EFTA surveillance authority (Cremona 1994: 512-513).

However, the EEA came to be viewed as a temporary solution already in the course of the negotiations. In Finland, intensive discussions about EC membership started in the beginning of 1990. Austria had applied for EC membership in 1989, before the initiation of the formal negotiations, Sweden applied in 1991 and Finland and Norway in 1992.

In essence, the problem of the envisaged EEA arrangement was that the members of EFTA and the EC were not based on an equal footing. In comparison to EC membership, the membership of the EEA gave fewer possibilities to influence the EC norms. In the creation and modification of community norms, EFTA members had only the right of being informed and participating in the preparatory work, while the EU Commission had the monopoly of initiative. Thus, Finland could in the EEA influence the contents of EC law only indirectly and with the support of other EFTA countries. In addition, although Finland had the possibility to hinder unacceptable decisions and impede the adoption of new norms, doing this in practice could lead to pressure from the other EC/EFTA states, perhaps also to the partial annulation of the treaty. (Appendix 1992: 103-104; cf. *Eurooppa* 27.10.1992, p. 18; EFTA Bulletin 1/94, esp. pp. 6-7; EFTA News 1/1994.) In fact, the EEA was drafted in order not to require amendments to the EC treaty or to threaten the institutions of the Community. Therefore, consultation with the

EFTA states had not been made a formal part in the process of adaptation of Community legislation (Cremona 1994: 512).

The government, having first favoured the strengthening of EFTA (Government report 1988), emphasised increasingly participation in the EC integration process. In its report of 1990, the government stressed the economic benefits of the possible EEA agreement while noting the negative consequences which remaining outside of it would have. (Cf. Antola 1991a: 151-153.) In March 1992, however, the EEA phase had come to an end: in declaring to parliament its intention to apply for EC membership, the government stated that there was a risk of the EEA being only temporary. Therefore, the Finnish interests seemed best secured by EC membership. Politically, participation in the EC decision-making was considered essential. As for the Finnish economy, equal opportunities with the competitors were vital. Integration was also seen to contribute to sound economy. (Government report 1992; *Eurooppa-tietoa* 153/1994; Himanen 1993: 27.) The immediate reason for the application was the preceding Swedish application which caused fears for worsened position for Finnish export industry (cf. Salovaara 1993: 36-37). Not only economic arguments were used in favour of membership: also the effect of strengthening the image or international identity of Finland as a Western country and strengthening the security of the state through increased capability of influence and commitment to mutual solidarity were mentioned (Himanen 1993: 29-30; *Eurooppa* 30.10.1992; Möttölä 1993: 98-100).

Finally, the increasing informal integration of the Finnish economic and political system to the Community had been paving the way to membership, realised in 1995. In practice, Finland had been adjusting its policies to membership in several ways. Among the many examples, the full liberalisation of capital movements, a first step towards economic and monetary union, had been undertaken in Finland simultaneously with the Community, in July 1990 (*Eurooppa-tietoa* 153/1994: 13). In 1991-1992, the convergence criteria of Maastricht became the guidelines for the economic policy of the Finnish government (Väyrynen 1993: 44-45); in June 1991, the Finnish *markka* was bound to the *ecu*. The legislative harmonisation needed for EC membership had also been under way both as a result of the EEA negotiations and as a part of adaptation by the single countries and the Nordic countries together in matters such as foreign ownership (see Hjerppe 1993: 73). In foreign policy, Finland had voted since the early 1980s very much in line with the EC members in the UN general assembly (Salovaara 1994: 24).

The implications of membership

During the cold war, neutrality had been a means that allowed Finland to further its central aims in relation to integration: being able to participate in, and thus not risking the exclusion from decision-making, while, at the same time, being able to defend its own primary interests. Towards the 1990s, neutrality was no longer needed to make Finnish participation possible. Indeed, neutrality was even becoming a burden in that it could be interpreted in a way that questioned Finland's willingness fully to share the duties and rights of participation. During the membership negotiations, this view was put forward quite clearly. It was noted that neutrality was not a value in itself, but a means in realising national interests. After the cold war, neutrality no longer widened the possibilities for action, but narrowed them, thereby losing its original function (cf. Lempiäinen 1994: 160). Similarly, the undersecretary of state Jaakko Blomberg asserted that the old principle according to which one should not rely on receiving help from the others is suspicious in today's world: it gives the idea that Finland acts alone without taking into consideration the interests of the Community, thereby jeopardising the support and the stabilising effect the Community membership can provide for Finland as a neighbour to Russia.[17]

Once EU membership became politically possible for Finland, it was also understood that it was an outstandingly efficient way to further Finnish interests, and that an efficient EU would serve these interests particularly well. As an EU member, Finland can directly influence decision-making and so can contribute to questions concerning the development of the Union, even the policies of the other member states. This attitude has since become increasingly apparent,[18] but it was clear already in the negotiations where Finland did not make any exceptions or restrictions in adhering, but accepted the *acquis communautaire*, the Treaty on European Union and the *finalité politique* as such.

The Finnish government admitted that membership would reduce the freedom of action and the capacities of the state due to, in particular, the primacy and direct applicability of EC law and the EC's capacity to enter into international agreements that partly deprives the state of this capacity, and that leaving the EC could in practice prove impossible. Nevertheless, it was seen that Finland as a member could pursue its own policies more efficiently than before: membership would be a stronger means of enforcement and it would also increase the importance of Finland to other EC countries. In trade, Finland as member would carry out the national trade policy in the framework of EC membership, benefiting from the EC which, as a great power in trade policy, can effectively defend the interests of its members. (Government report 1992, esp. 10, 12; Appendix 1992: 101, 104, 108.)

Further, as the government pointed out, membership would not change the essential aims of Finnish foreign and security policy, either. Neutrality policy, now restricted to military and security matters only, and defined as military non-alliance and credible independent defence, was to be continued. Instead of being a hindrance to political cooperation, neutrality aims at – as the government expressed it – furthering international cooperation, avoiding involvement in a European conflict and furthering stability in Northern Europe. The government also emphasised continuity in the relations with the Eastern countries and the importance of Nordic cooperation. Developing neighbourly relations with Russia, strengthening the Nordic community and the creation of Baltic Sea cooperation would contribute to the aim of stability and security in Northern Europe. 'Nordicity' was seen as one of the cornerstones of Finnish national *Eigenart* and international position. Therefore, it was important for Finland to continue to develop Nordic foreign and security policy cooperation between the governments and in the Nordic Council, anchored to European security structures and aiming at safeguarding Nordic values in Europe. (Government report 1992: 5, 10, 25; Appendix 1992: 34, 36.)[19]

It could be argued that this view on the consequences of membership is somewhat over-optimistic in that the effectiveness of the Union, majority decisions and strong common institutions actually contradict the possibilities claimed for furthering the country's own particular interests and continuing traditional policies. Several instances could be found in the process of enlargement that depict the EU in rather demanding terms on this point. For example, the principles laid down before the enlargement on relations with third countries aim at securing the integrity of the Community by stating that no area of cooperation should be excluded *a priori*, that integration within the Community had absolute priority over any agreements with third countries, that the decision-making autonomy of the Community must be safeguarded and that cooperation with the EFTA countries should be based on 'real reciprocity' in all areas (COM (85)206, COM (86)298, quoted in Pedersen 1991: 118). Similarly, in the EEA agreement, the position of the Court of Justice and the autonomy of the legal system of the Community was defended against the influence of EFTA states. The EC further required in the course of the EEA negotiations the acceptance of the *acquis communautaire* with at most temporary exceptions and emergency clauses (see Pedersen 1991: 137-138).

In fact, the EC position seemed hardly less demanding in the membership negotiations. Particularly in the case of foreign and security policy, the Commission[20] questioned the compatibility of Finland's neutrality policy with the full acceptance of the foreign policy of the Union, including defence of the independence and security of the Union and development towards common defence. It questioned the credibility of Finland's assurances recommending specific and binding guarantees on the political commitment and legal capacity of the country to fulfil its obligations in this field. In fact, the provisions concerning common foreign and security policy in the Maastricht Treaty seem to imply that the new member states have to accept the common positions in foreign and security policy, eventually also in defence, having to renounce the possibility of formulating separate foreign policies. A joint declaration to this effect was actually given at the end of the membership negotiations by the EU member states and the applicant countries stating that the new members have to be ready and capable of participating fully and actively in the CFSP from the very beginning, of accepting its contents without reservations, and of supporting the prevailing policies at the time of entering the Union.[21]

Nevertheless, the understanding of the compatibility between Finland's own interests, even neutrality, and the CFSP prevailed. The discussions and the opinions expressed by the EU member countries and by the Commission indeed enhanced the view that membership would not imply any particular difficulties of adaptation.[22] As stressed by the Finnish government, the common foreign policy is formulated on the basis of unanimity or essential common interests, and the (thus far only envisaged) common defence policy will be based on the respect for the national security and defence policies of the member countries. Moreover, the Maastricht Treaty allows for special bilateral or multilateral treaties between the members and commitments such as those stemming from NATO membership. It is also remarked that Austria and Sweden see military non-alignment as compatible with the treaty. (Government report 1992; Appendix 1992: 35-37.)[23]

In fact, according to the Maastricht Treaty, the aim of the CFSP is to strengthen the security of the Union and of the member states and to safeguard the common values, fundamental interests, independence and security of the Union (art. J.1). These are rather abstract notions and reducible to the safeguarding of the interests of the members. As it is the European Council that defines the principles and general guidelines of the CFSP, deciding what issues shall be included under joint action and defining a common position whenever the Council deems it necessary (art. J.2), the member governments can be seen as the major agents of systems transformation in this field (Petersen 1993: 20-23). Accession to the CFSP thus implies above all the possibility of participating in decisions about its contents. In fact, the Finnish government frequently alluded to the benefits of becoming a member before the intergovernmental conference of 1996 in allowing for participation in shaping the policies. In addition to active participation in the development of the common foreign and security policy, Finland also assured its readiness to contribute constructively to the development of the defence dimension of the Union.[24]

In addition, adaptation to the CFSP causes few problems not only because of its present limited range – it comprises a few questions of general common interest such as democracy in South Africa, on which the Finnish position is already similar (cf. Törnudd 1995: 103) – but also because its particular interests in the field have in practice been acknowledged. Nordic cooperation serves here as a useful example. In the EEA, a declaration was made about the continuation of Nordic cooperation after the entering into force of the treaty. While this declaration might have seemed rather weak in that it imposed on Nordic cooperation the condition of not impairing the good functioning of the agreement (article 121, part IX), the actual strength of the Nordic *acquis* is shown by the fact that the EU accepted the condition of the Nordic member states of acceding to the Schengen treaty only if the Nordic non-members could also associate themselves to the treaty.

In all, Finnish foreign policy might not have been the actual target of the Commission's urge to compliance; rather, what was aimed at was neutrality in general, the most difficult case among the neutral applicants being Austria. Actually, the fact the *avis* on the Swedish and Finnish applications are almost identical concerning foreign and security policy makes the Commission's view appear more one of principle than one pointing to a concrete problem. One could see the part of the negotiations concerning foreign policy as a tossing of the coin of the critical definitions which both sides actually want to avoid. While the Commission asks for the specification of Finnish foreign and security policy in order to ascertain its compatibility with the CFSP, Finland, in declaring in turn its willingness to accept all the contents of the EU is, in a way, asking for a specification of what this 'all' actually is – a question which hardly could be answered without intense and disruptive debates.

In this light, the negotiations between Finland and the EU can be seen as part of a special rhetoric; the specific assurances about common foreign policy can be used to add credibility to the Union by giving some authority and weight to the Maastricht provisions. This was particularly visible in the declaration of December 1993 (see above) which was seemingly strict but which, in the end, was made less demanding than the original EU position according to which the applicant countries were to declare that they would accept not only all existing but also all *potential* rights and duties deriving from the Union's foreign and defence policy. This idea was subsequently abandoned since it would have meant that the new member states would have had to accept more obligations than the original members.

Thus, the contradiction which Antola (1991a: 155) points out between Finnish aims of simultaneously guaranteeing access to real influence, the possibility of some opting-out and the retention of a meaningful role by the national institutions, notably the parliament and the president, does not seem to be a real contradiction. The process of integration actually builds on a combination of these elements: it cannot thrive without taking the participant's goals and interests into account. In essence, the EU accommodates different views about the process and the institutions and reflects the needs of the participants.[25] All of them – including the common institutions – bring their views to the process, with sometimes even a competition for influence. What the 'meaningful role of national institutions' is, then, changes little by little; it can be seen as a part of the natural adaptation or adjustments which form the actual implications of membership.

This adaptation as such is nothing new or particular for Finland. In the above, several examples were given on how Finland has adapted to different forms of international cooperation and how it has, at the same time, influenced them through its policies, as when it sought to limit the possible harmful effects of participation by special reservations and conditions, such as the declarations in Nordic Council and OECD. Nordic cooperation, in particular, has for a long time been an additional dimension in Finnish policy-making, legislation and international activities. Now that also the EU constitutes such a dimension, the similarities between the contents of the two may facilitate Finland's adaptation to EU integration. For instance, the contents of the CFSP do not greatly differ from those of traditional Nordic cooperation in foreign policy (cf. Helsinki Agreement).[26]

In broader terms, the influence of EU structures and agendas on Finland can be seen as an instance of the process of state formation through participation in various forms of cooperation. This concerns not only the interests of the country, but also the tasks, methods and procedures in the administration, and, finally, also the state structures – such as the structure of central administration or the relative power of the parliament, prime minister and president. In this sense, statehood is in constant evolution, and with it, also the meaning of sovereignty or neutrality. What is regarded as the proper domain of an individual state or as its interests is not static or purely endogenous. Ultimately, it is participation – and not autonomous isolation – that constitutes the state as a sovereign or a particular entity in international relations.

This process can be seen very specifically by analysing, for example, the role of the national administration. The Finnish public administration needs to adjust to the tasks which its new role in integration implies, both as part of the EU administration in fields such as customs, border control or statistics, and as a support for the national decision-makers in the preparation of national goals and in the control and management of the implementation of common norms. The increasing links between national and EU administration are likely to influence not only the practical methods and tasks of administration, but also the national administrative culture and values. (Temmes 1995: 197-198, 215-216; cf. more generally Hill 1991: 90-92.) Adjustment implies strengthening features which help to cope with these tasks while modifying others. In the Finnish case, Temmes points out in particular the need for more 'management' and high-profile technocratic experts, and the need for more flexibility over the boundaries between different administrative fields and between the 'domestic' and the 'foreign'. Further, the centrality of policy-coordination in the state apparatus and the need to plan for national long-term strategies are new elements for the Finnish political and administrative culture. (Temmes 1995: 210-216, 218-219.)

While EU membership is a logical continuation in Finland's policies of furthering its interests through participation in international cooperation, the special characteristics of the EU, its effectiveness and political weight, give Finland additional possibilities of concrete influence and, thus, also more importance for the other participants. As a member country, Finland contributes to the process of integration with its own features and by bringing its special concerns to the common agenda. At the same time, these very interests and features are influenced by the process. Without doubt, Finland will exert influence on EU policies and the EU administration addressing the features which from a Finnish perspective are seen as problematic, for instance, excessive bureaucracy, vague implementation and weak follow-up, or the undue importance of informal contacts, favours and counterfavours.

The Finnish contribution in this sense could, then, consist of advancing the features of Finnish administrative system and administrative culture which are considered particularly valuable. Among these, Temmes sees the general Nordic features of legality, neutrality and openness of the administration, open recruitment and wide municipal autonomy, and the typically Finnish presidential powers, minority protection and broad coalition governments. (Temmes 1995: 175-176, 192, 213.) The extent to which Finland actually succeeds in promoting these features, then, depends on the final sum of the mutual influence between the EU and its new member state.

Notes

1. Finland, particularly Finnish foreign policy, often appears as an example in theories of political adaptation. For instance, Rosenau sees Finland as an example of acquiescent adaptation in that it has been adapting to one factor in the environment, acknowledging the dependency on the interests of the Soviet Union. (See Rosenau 1981: 63, 119-120 and Mouritzen 1988; cf. Möttölä 1993: 83-88.) While the constraints by the Soviet Union on the Finnish participation in international organisations during the cold war imposed on Finland the need to ascertain that its arrangements could not be interpreted as implying political commitments, capable of jeopardising the Finnish-Soviet relations, the logic of adaptation has subsequently been extended to seeing Finland – still a small state with limited resources – as having now to adapt to the policies of the EU (e.g., Mouritzen 1993b).
2. The characterisation of Finnish integration policy as a 'wait-and-see' strategy, a strategy consisting essentially in waiting for a clarification or a favourable change in the situation before taking important decisions (cf. Hakovirta), seems also an example of the wisdom of hindsight. On the other hand, there need be nothing especially Finnish about this attitude. In fact, in another context, Jervell (1991a: 40) notes that it can be appealing for a small country to wait until more is known about the 'new Europe' before deciding on its own attitude, but that this increases the risk that the others decide about the role of these countries in Europe.
3. Finland became a member of the IMF in 1948 and of the IBRD in 1949, whereas Sweden joined them only in 1951 (see af Malmborg 1994: 64).
4. Muoser (1986: 152) argues that Finland was also given a boost, *Zuschuß*, from the Marshall funds ($500 000) for the export of wood products to the Federal Republic of Germany.
5. Having been a member of the League of Nations, Finland had applied for UN membership in 1947; the application had, however, met with the veto of the Soviet Union in the Security Council. The Soviet Union linked the

approval of Finnish membership with the acceptance of those of Bulgaria, Rumania and Hungary, which the United States did not wish (e.g., Wendt 1981: 368).
6. The so-called 'night frost crisis' was perhaps a result not only of economic reorientation and increasing links to the Nordic countries and the 'group of seven', but also of Soviet suspicions concerning Finnish domestic politics (Antola and Tuusvuori 1983: 129-130), the increasing NATO activities since 1957, the remilitarisation of Germany and the establishment of the EEC (Maude 1976: 18).
7. President Kekkonen stated in 1967 that integration and neutrality were not to be regarded as mutually exclusive alternatives, while prime minister Koivisto stated in a Nordic prime ministers' meeting in Oslo in 1968 that neutral countries had a constructive role to play in economic integration. Thus, a verbal policy similar to that of other neutral countries was used. (Hakovirta 1976: 230-231; Törnudd 1969: 68.) Hakovirta even claims that neutrality actually required participation in West European cooperation to be credible (Hakovirta 1976: 302).
8. Interestingly, Törnudd refers to some potentially self-fulfilling estimations, observing that the government can make predictions which are both plausible and favourable from the Finnish point of view – e.g., when it predicts that 'continued integration will be compatible with a policy of neutrality', 'neutral countries will have a constructive role in future European integration', 'it is inconceivable that tariff barriers could be re-established between the Nordic countries' and that 'an enlargement of EEC is improbably at the present time and will have to wait'. If these statements can help shape actual developments accordingly, Törnudd adds, they are obviously useful elements in Finnish integration policy.
9. President Kekkonen in Washington on July 23, 1970, quoted by Miljan (1977: 261-262).
10. The reason was Soviet opposition; according to the formulation used by the government, the treaty corresponded to Finnish aspirations, but it did not fulfil the demands of stability and permanence.
11. The authors note that Finland thereby succeeded in organising its relations with the Community on the basis of mere free trade, and not of common market integration; they attribute this success partly to the favourable conditions created by the climate of détente and the fact that the other neutrals too opted for a free trade agreement instead of membership.
12. By the 1990s, the results of this development were clearly visible. By 1993, EFTA had signed eight free trade agreements with third countries (e.g., Hungary) and a cooperation declaration with the 11 countries of Central and Eastern Europe, while the Baltic countries had asked for negotiations on association. (Press release from EFTA ministerial meeting in Geneva, June

15-16, 1993, quoted in *Eurooppakirje* 4/93.)
13. Soviet criticism had not been directed solely towards Finnish participation in European integration, but towards the process in general; Muoser (1986: 177) alludes to the opinions the Soviet Union communicated to other Scandinavian countries and the notes it sent to the (future) EEC member states in 1957 criticising the EEC for being an economic basis for NATO and EURATOM for being an instrument for German rearmament; in the Soviet view, the EEC was dominated by capitalist monopoly, it had neocolonialist intentions through the association treaties, and polarised trade for the disadvantage of third parties (*idem:* 194).
14. Although the Soviet Union had recognised the diplomatic capacity of the EC already in the CSCE conference of 1975 where Italy signed in the name of the organisation (Iloniemi 1990: 98), a real turning point in the EC-Soviet relations was a basic treaty signed in 1988 on the relations between the EC and the CMEA; on this occasion, the Soviet Union officially recognised the EC (Antola 1990a: 116). An economic frame treaty between the EC and the Soviet Union was signed in 1989 (Appendix 1992: 33).
15. Hakovirta quotes the EFTA Bulletin (XII, No. 9, p. 3) according to which the United States sent in November 1971 a note warning the EEC not to conclude trade relations discriminating against the US with countries unwilling to join the EEC as full members.
16. Cf. the Finnish term *lähialuepuolueettomuus*. 'Neighbouring regions' can be seen as denoting above all relations to Russia. These relations acquired a new basis when the FCMA treaty was replaced by a treaty with Russia in January 1992, based on the principles of the United Nations and CSCE (Möttölä 1993: 95-97).
17. In Joensuu on February 11, 1993; quoted in *Eurooppa* 1/93. - Cf. Antola (1991a: 157).
18. Judging from the Finnish position in the IGC, Finland is ready for a reduction of unanimity in favour of majority decisions to increase effectiveness, as it is for an improved position of the Commission and the Court in matters of justice and home affairs, or internal security. However, Finland clearly does not aim at a federation; it underlines the possibility of opting out when vital national interests so require. (Antola in *Helsingin Sanomat,* March 8, 1996.) Even though Finland does not associate itself with some of the small member states, notably the Benelux, that emphasise the need to pursue federative, supranational arrangements as a way of having real influence on the more powerful partners, it is also in Finland's interests to be a part of an effective and strong union, which is, however, intergovernmental in nature with respect to foreign and security policy (cf. Törnudd 1995: 98). Thus, Finland did not confirm the expectations that other Nordic countries would, as EU members, follow Denmark's minimalism (cf.

19. Cf. Törnudd (1995: 101-102) who sees as the elements of continuity in Finnish integration policy – and as elements which give an own profile for its security policy – neutrality, an emphasis on the nation state, the Nordic relations and relations to Russia.
20. Opinion on the Finnish membership application, November 4, 1992; Bulletin of the European Communities, supplement 6/92.
21. Ministerial meeting on December 21, 1993; see *Eurooppa* 1/1994, *Helsingin Sanomat*, December 17 and 22, 1993.
22. The minister for foreign affairs Väyrynen in parliament in response to a question on negotiation goals, March 9, 1993, quoted in *Eurooppa* 9.3.1993. – The problems encountered in the negotiations did not reflect the apparent difference between the principles of Finnish integration policy and the character of the EU, but, instead, more concrete and practical matters, in particular agriculture and regional policy. This could be seen as a portrait of the Union itself: agriculture and regional policy are, indeed, for the time being, an essential part both of national decision-making or sovereignty and of the European Union.
23. The Maastricht provisions for the CFSP establish systematic cooperation between member states and joint action (art. J.1). Joint action, the goal or target of the CFSP, is more ambitious and binding and includes the possibility of majority voting, but it is confined to areas in which the member states have important interests in common (art. J.1,3). Moreover, the Council's decision on majority voting must be unanimous. Issues with defence implications shall not be subject to the procedure of joint action (art.2 J.4), and the policy of the Union shall not prejudice the specific character of the security and defence policy of certain member states and shall respect the obligations of certain member states under the North Atlantic Treaty and be compatible with it (art. J.4).
24. Minister for foreign trade, Pertti Salolainen, in the ministerial meeting opening the conferences of the accession of Austria, Sweden and Finland in Brussels, February 1, 1993; quoted in *Eurooppa* 1/93. – As to defence policy, the official stand has been that no alternatives are in principle excluded in its development (cf. Möttölä 1993: 101).
25. The need to accommodate particularity in the Union may also lead to increasing 'variable geometry'. As Cremona notes, while the internal market legislation probably requires an equal submission by all to the rules of the game, the extension of the scope of Community activity 'make it harder to argue that the entire Community system is really a seamless web of policies'. In her view, it is difficult to see why, e.g., the CFSP should be a precondition for joining the internal market. (Cremona 1994: 525, *passim*.)

26. A example of practically identical provisions is the article J.6 of the Maastricht Treaty, which states that the member states shall inform and consult each other on any matter of foreign and security policy of general interest and coordinate their action in international organisations and at international conferences, and that diplomatic and consular missions of the member states and the Commission delegations in third countries and international conferences and organisations shall cooperate in ensuring that the common positions are complied with.

8 Conclusion: the plurality of interpretation

Constructing knowledge

This study started with the observation that increasingly numerous and central research problems in political science require an understanding of the nature of the relationship between the state and integration. The role and functions of the state in today's Europe, the future of the state in general, or the development of the EU are but a few examples of problems which either explicitly involve the need to define this relationship or implicitly contain an understanding of the matter. To find answers to these questions, one must take into consideration how the state is influenced by integration and vice versa.

In chapters four and five, two particular research problems of this kind were presented. It was asked, first, whether Nordic cooperation is likely to continue in the wake of Finnish and Swedish EU membership, or whether Nordic cooperation is still profitable or possible when conducted in parallel with EU integration. Second, it was asked whether EU membership has constituted a major departure from Finnish integration policy. What these questions have in common is that they concern the consequences of EU integration. These, it was seen, could be assessed only with knowledge about both the nature of the process of integration, of Nordic cooperation, and of the state in question. In other words, to understand the consequences, we need to know, for example, to what extent the process of integration is under the control of the participating states, or whether integration can proceed even against the will and aims of its participants. Our knowledge on these questions, then, depends on our understanding of the relationship between the state and integration, and thus, on how we understand and define these loaded terms.

Seeking answers to these questions, however, easily leads to definitional twists over the proper way of understanding these terms. In such debates, some tend to argue that the questions cannot be reasonably answered at all because defining the terms is a hopeless task, or else that they are not meaningful since the term 'state' is outdated and should not be focused on. Others stress the need to arrive at a shared understanding, something that was repeatedly found to be impossible. Both stands are equally problematic. The issue of the state should not simply be overlooked, as might happen if it is put aside for definitional reasons. On the other hand, to search for one definition and one answer is not only difficult but also counterproductive, as we will see. The same applies to debates on theories. Integration studies are characterised by theoretical debates that centre on conceptions of the state-integration relationship. Here, too, theories are often seen as obsolete, and the aim of arriving at a shared understanding appears unattainable. In fact, the contentions of the two extreme positions in this debate, that integration either strengthens or weakens the state, is a typical example of potentially delusive theoretical debates. They might go on endlessly without getting anywhere if the problem of the assumptions, the meanings of the two basic terms, remains hidden in the background as if it was in some way a secondary issue.

Both debates actually divert attention from the abundance of available answers and the fact that several correct views have been presented. The manifold meanings of the two terms allow for several different answers to the questions. The problem, then, is what attitude to take to this plurality. For conventional research practice, plurality has to be eliminated: several different views cannot all be true at the same time. Therefore, the thinking goes, it is the scholar's task to point out the right view. This calls for clear criteria for evaluating the different views, and above all requires knowledge about how and why they emerged. Thus, in chapter one, the presence of contradictory views led one to underline the need for examining more closely the research on the subject, the ways in which it approaches the question and its results. In practice, this means examining the origins of particular views and the conditions for them to be correct, or how our knowledge on the question is conditioned by assumptions. This examination of how and why certain research results are achieved helps reach a better understanding of the variety of different results, not only concerning the relationship between the state and integration, but of many questions in social sciences that involve the same problems of different interpretations and outcomes. Therefore, this examination can be seen as relevant in illustrating some general problems in research in the field.

Chapter one delineated an approach to the study of research which essentially consists of examining *choice*. In cases such as the 'state' and 'integration', the scholar has a wide array of definitions of the terms to choose from. This choosing is not necessarily intended; yet, it cannot be avoided.

Thus, the reasons for opting for a particular meaning and the array of alternatives become particularly interesting. A proper evaluation of the results involves, then, considering not only the actual outcomes, but also the possible ones, that is, what *can* be achieved. These features – in short, the potential and limits of research practice – will be examined below.

In chapter two, literature on the state and integration was analysed emphasising the importance of chronological analysis. Four different conceptions were identified; the succession of theories revealed, moreover, important features of research practice, the way results are attained and the nature of the links between the theories. When the different views are analysed chronologically, and not just by individuating the different views as separate theories, their connections are revealed. On the one hand, this succession was functional: understandably, the views emerged through a consideration of the preceding literature, its criticism and the comparison of its conclusions with the reality observed by the researcher. Typical of the research was a search for the common, generally accepted and shared in particular in relation to definitions; the ideal of the accumulation of knowledge together with the need to eliminate debunked alternatives were seen as fundamental. In appearance, the different views were all presented as new and improved in that they reflected reality better than the preceding ones and better met the requirements of good scientific explanation. On the other hand, this succession also had negative effects: knowledge often seemed sedimented rather than properly evaluated, with the result that leaning on previous research has induced circularity and predictability rather than new interpretations. At the same time, the concepts used and the questions posed have tended to converge and thereby become fewer due to the aim of shared research premises.

In all, then, research on the state and integration appeared rather inadequate in terms of its self-understanding or faculty of self-reflection. The search for one answer through the elimination of rival views seems to mislead research to suggest that results should be evaluated by comparison with reality and by some explanatory standards. These two criteria, however, can hardly explain the emergence of the varying views. As argued in chapter three, they might be the least applicable of evaluative criteria in that they simply cannot be claimed to be sufficiently unambiguous. Reality suits most theories – not least as shown in chapters four to seven – while scientific standards were seen to differ from author to author and from one time to another. Instead, four other reasons or factors were identified which better explained the four different views: methodological considerations, the view of science and theory, disciplinary features, and values. These factors directed the basic choices of assumptions which, then, led to the emergence of particular interpretations of the state-integration relationship.

The nature or type of these influencing factors leads to an important conclusion: it is not possible to sort the views into some order of correctness. How can one compare values or disciplines? Yet, this does not mean that the views are all false or that they are somehow less important in that if they are all true, then none is really true. All are applicable, and they were seen to make a profound difference when applied to empirical research questions. This was done in chapters four and five where the two cases of Nordic cooperation and Finnish integration policy were examined, both from two different points of view. Even though they were based on the same facts and same material, the accounts yielded dissimilar, even opposite accounts.

The contribution of the four accounts

The case studies brought the question of plurality from an abstract theoretical level to the level of how we actually describe and write about real events. They can be summarised as follows:

According to version 4, Nordic cooperation is seriously challenged by the increasing involvement of the Nordic countries in the EU. A review of the development of Nordic cooperation shows that all the most important attempts at closer coordination between the Nordic countries in central policy areas and the great schemes such as for a defence union have failed. This can be attributed to the different interests of the countries and to the fact that a purely Nordic solution in economic or security issues has never been viable. The achievements have been of a rather low profile, and facilitated by the great similarity of the Nordic countries. Nordic institutions are weak and do not have an independent potential for developing cooperation much further. In the new situation following Finnish and Swedish EU membership, the usefulness of and political will to continue Nordic cooperation are likely definitively to evaporate. 'Nordic cooperation' seems increasingly a mere rhetorical device in the politics of the Nordic countries. The measures and declarations apparently aimed at guaranteeing a role for Nordic cooperation in the future lack credibility. Indeed, they may even be counterproductive in practice.

The second version, then, claims that Nordic cooperation is not challenged. Its structures are actually strong, although different from the respective European ones; the achievements are of a high profile, and, indeed, also the similarity of the Nordic countries is to a great extent a result of the past 100 years of experience in close cooperation in different fields. An analysis limited to the formal part and institutions of Nordic cooperation does not give an adequate picture of the Nordic integration process. Having started earlier, proceeding in a different way and being both deeper and more extensive than integration in the EC/EU, the nature of Nordic cooperation seems to evade the normal analyses of integration. However, there exists an '*acquis nordique*', even Nordic citizenship; Nordic cooperation is a widely recognised factor in foreign policy formulation and it has been successfully used as a tool by the Nordic countries both collectively and individually. In the context of the EU, Nordic cooperation will play an increasingly important role both for the countries themselves and for the development of the EU integration.

In version 6, Finnish EU membership constitutes an unexpected rupture in the traditional Finnish policy towards European integration. It reverses the principles of that policy, independent decision-making and autonomy, secured through avoidance of political commitments. The rapidity and unconditionality of the decision seem to imply a change in the national political 'style'. The causes and direction of this change are difficult to explain; above all, however, the claimed continuity of Finnish policies has to be seen as mere rhetoric. The claim that Finland is actually able to continue furthering its interests misinterpret the nature of the integration process which largely changes the view on what these interests are, as it also changes the practical functioning and tasks of many state organs. In 7, finally, Finnish integration policy is seen as a series of logical steps stemming from the aim to find the best possible ways to safeguard the national interests and to participate in international cooperation to the widest extent possible. The decision to apply for EU membership is therefore not a rupture, but a continuation of this policy in an environment which has changed making membership politically possible. The difference between EU integration and the forms of cooperation in which Finland thus far has participated is a matter of degree. The EU is uniquely effective and powerful and this gives Finland as a member country an enhanced international status and greater leverage to influence the environment in which it acts.

Presented one after the other, these accounts seem confusing. Again, like in chapter two which presented discordant views on the state-integration relationship, a plurality of contrary answers appears. We may discern a clear difference in the purchase of any one of these alone in comparison to presenting all of them together: even though the facts are correct, the very presence of opposite interpretations makes all of them appear incomplete, even faulty. The conclusions seem unsatisfactory, as the two versions seem to falsify each other. The effect of presenting two alternative accounts might, in fact, be that although the first might have been accepted as such as a fair account of the case, the presence of a second version shows that also the first is also nothing more than a version, one possible account (cf. Allison in chapter 1). The details on Nordic cooperation and Finnish integration policy that have been duplicated presenting them in different contexts and with different emphases in the accounts serve as a reminder that they indeed have been interpreted in the first place, that they do not automatically appear in a certain role in the account.

Furthermore, the procedure highlights the scarcely self-reflective character of the accounts and the ensuing benefits to be drawn from such a reflection or explanation of the premises of the interpretations. Clearly, even these empirical accounts rely on assumptions which can be spelled out. At all the points where the accounts differ, one can find an allusion to the reasons for which they differ, and thus a key to their proper evaluation. In this evaluation, the central theoretical background questions individuated in chapter three are immediately useful. Thus, we can find certain basic choices as to the stands taken on the theoretical questions and crucial assumptions which become visible when two contrasting interpretations are given. Among them, there are well-known debates in international relations literature, notably on whether (certain kinds of) institutions matter and how to differentiate between the domestic and international, or between low and high politics. They are broadly the same for both cases, and can all be seen as instances of the debate on how to define 'the state' and 'integration', with consequent differences as to the understanding of a host of subconcepts such as 'supranational', 'cooperation', 'neutrality' or 'national interest'. In essence, the cases illustrate the basic oscillations outlined in chapter three about the nature of the state, its efficiency, the actor capacity of states and other institutions, state similarity, the nature of international relations, the states' role in them and whether integration belongs to international relations, and the nature of integration as a general *versus* unique phenomenon, its consequences, controllability and reversibility.

In fact, when looked upon more analytically, the reasons for the differences between the accounts appear. Versions 4 and 5 deem differently the need for and ways to safeguard Nordic cooperation due to the different interpretations of the value and role attributed to it. Version 4 is essentially institution-centred; it points out general patterns in previous Nordic efforts and their tendency to fail, noting that the current situation is not new, but that European integration has always been more attractive to the Nordic countries than pure Nordic arrangements. In comparison to the picture given on the EU – characterised through its long-term goals and ambitions, supranationality and effectiveness – the Nordic institutions have a low profile. Were they strengthened, the situation would be different, and while importance is given to the measures taken in this direction, they are reckoned to be inadequate. It is seen that the more efficient the institutions are, the more useful they are for the states; the basis of the strength of the institutions lies in their independence and the possibility of making binding decisions. It is also seen impossible to reverse the Nordic tradition of concentrating on consensual matters such as culture or passport union, which are interpreted as belonging to low politics. The alert reader will have noticed the interpretation of details such as the assessment of the Council's right to discuss foreign policy as a mere formality, or the scarce importance given in this version to Nordic coordination in the Kennedy round.

Version 5 starts in a dialogue-like manner, criticising the framework of the preceding version, which is a usual way of presenting one's contribution in integration literature. It sees cooperation within the EU as a new possibility for the Nordic countries. Different levels of cooperation are presented in parallel, and the institutions are not highlighted, as they are only one part of the whole. Bureaucratic interpenetration is thought more important than independent institutions: the strength of the common institutions is seen in that they do not constitute a separate level or actor: they are rather a part of the domestic policy-making structures and processes.[1] The time perspective changes from that implicitly given by the institutions to that given by all the different forms of cooperation. Evidence for the vitality and importance of Nordic cooperation is gathered through pointing out its hundred years' traditions; frequently, early dates and details from the 19th century are mentioned. This presentation inverts causes and consequences in relation to the previous version: the starting point of the first version here appears as an outcome. Thus, Nordic cooperation seems to involve far more successes than failures; at the same time, the Nordic institutions and the commitment expressed by the Nordic countries appear much more credible and are taken seriously. Where the first version identifies a weakness in that Nordic cooperation concentrates on unimportant matters, this version sees that the limitless field of Nordic cooperation is a proof of its unquestioned and domesticised role. It also avails itself of a different classification of matters as 'high' or 'low' politics. Similarly, the variability of the participants in

Nordic cooperation is here a strength in that it removes an important encumbrance to reaching agreement, that is, the requirement of the participation of all. Finally, distance from the EU is diminished through applying without hesitation concepts which are normally used about EU integration, for instance, 'spill-over' and *acquis nordique*.

Account 6 claims that to view membership as a continuation of Finnish integration policy is only rhetoric; unavoidably, EU membership makes the traditional policy impossible in that the common policies and majority voting of the supranational and progressive EU replace autonomous policies and make it impossible for Finland to continue safeguarding its decision-making power. The traditional Finnish policies are seen as having an inherent value. Therefore, the profound changes in Finnish policy seem difficult to explain. It is argued that the reason for this change was perhaps a misinterpreted necessity to join the EU in order to avoid marginalisation. The consequences of membership are seen to be profound and to a considerable extent unintended. In brief, Finland is seen to lose its particular features and become increasingly similar to the other member states not only as to its policies but also its understanding of the state's functions. This stems from a need to have coinciding bureaucracy, authorities with the same competencies and functions in the different countries, and by policies such as common standardisation and mutual recognition which in time have structural consequences.

Version 7, then, sees EU membership as a logical continuation of Finnish integration policy, since Finland has always strived for that kind of participation as a means of furthering its interests. Finland is seen as a normal small state, and not as exceptionally keen on preserving its autonomy. Until the end of the cold war, however, its policies were constrained by the need to follow a policy of neutrality, an impediment to joining political and supranational integrative arrangements. The EU is a particularly effective framework for furthering Finnish interests. While it has an influence on the other members, as a member itself Finland is also capable of influencing the EU and contributing to changing it according to its specific aims. In this account, continuity in Finnish integration policy is built on an emphasis of the tradition of pragmatic, informal participation in cooperation even when or before formal membership or agreement was politically possible. Finland's chances of influencing decision-making and policies at the EU level, then, are grounded on interpretations of the EU that differ from those of the precedent version as to both the nature of the EU institutions and of the impact of supranationality. Here, EU institutions are not an autonomous factor which competes with the authority of the member states; similarly, supranationality does not curtail the states' powers but is seen as a feature that strengthens the positive effects of the EU. For example, the stipulations of the Maastricht Treaty concerning the common foreign and security policy are here interpreted as an instance of community rhetoric, whereas they are taken literally in the first account.

In all, the cases show the concrete implications of a series of theoretical problems. They make the role of choice more tangible, helping to evaluate how it affects the results. What is seen as the logic behind a policy, what time-span and what perspective are chosen are questions where at some point a choice is made – with sometimes unexpected repercussions. Decisive and broad divergencies emerge in the assessment of similarity and comparability and the distinctions between change and continuity, failure and success, and between rhetoric and fact.

A first crucial choice for the unfolding of the accounts concerns the assumptions about similarity, in particular, whether states are examined as essentially similar to or as essentially different from each other. The versions concerning Nordic cooperation differ in that in the first, similarity was seen as a factor which explains the success of cooperation, while it was seen as an achievement of long-lasting cooperation in the second version. This contributed to undermining the achievements of Nordic cooperation in the first version, while in the second, Nordic integration (note the choice of term) was seen as still a rather distant model for the EU which does not have an equally long history behind it. The versions on Finnish integration policy, then, differed in that the first tended to underline the specific characteristics of the state in question, confronting it with the influence of the EU which makes the states increasingly similar, whereas the second sees Finland as a normal small state.

Essentially, the cases show how 'similarity' depends on what is looked at. Therefore, the understanding of questions such as whether small states differ from the large ones as to, e.g., their 'vulnerability' to integration or possibilities to influence it, and whether integration has similar consequences for all states are also questions which essentially depend on or are relative to the theoretical assumptions made. In addition, the study also shows the relative nature of comparability: the definitions used form the basis for comparison, determining the degree of similarity. In the cases presented, this is illustrated by questions such as whether Nordic cooperation and European integration can be compared and whether different member countries can be compared regarding their position in the process of integration and its consequences for them.

The distinctions between change and continuity, failure and success, and rhetoric and fact, then, depend to a great extent on the time-span and logic employed in the study. The case of Finnish integration policy shows clearly the way in which the policy comes to be constructed in the account. What kind of policy emerges depends on the time-span used; this, in turn, is contingent on the definition used. Obviously, the main thread of the account changes in function to what is known and what has been chosen as the beginning and the end. New facts tend to change the interpretation of older ones: the decision to join the EU easily makes the previous developments seem logically to lead to this decision, whereas before knowing about the decision this kind of interpretation would have been improbable.[2] Where the first version perceives change, the second sees continuation. When analysing the membership negotiations from a 'realist' viewpoint as a national policy choice, the change in policy disappears; the same terms (state, sovereignty) can be used both before and after membership, even though with different (latent) contents. The time perspective in describing Nordic cooperation, in turn, changes according to the definition: when the formal institutions are concentrated on (as a consequence, e.g., of comparison with the EU institutions), Nordic cooperation will tend to be limited in time to the existence of those institutions, and thus coincide with the cold war. This can further lead to equating the favourable conditions for Nordic cooperation with the conditions of that period, seeing, therefore, a consequential negative change threatening after the end of the cold war. In the second version, however, Nordic cooperation is a rather different phenomenon for which the institutions are not so central. In this case, the cooperation of the 19th century becomes very relevant, and the cold war period can be seen more as an exception, a temporary limitation of the extension and depth of Nordic cooperation.

The evaluation of consequences, for instance, those of EU membership, is also a good example of observing and interpreting change. On the one hand, the cases point to the difficulty in assessing what actually changes as a result of integration, or deciding whether some important changes take place. Understandably, the manifest changes which integration causes appear in rather concrete and limited questions – such as changes in working practices or in particular norms – and as such, they can be seen as relatively unimportant. The large-scale changes that can be and often are expected of integration – a redefinition of the areas of exclusive competence between member states and the Union, the amount of resources, decisions on policies, power relations between different state organs – are less visible. The larger changes obviously consist of a number of smaller ones, but the chain of causes and effects, such as the reverberation of general economic decisions to education or culture, are not necessarily clear, and they can be constructed in different ways.

On the other hand, the perception of change – as that of any movement – seems to require a stable point of comparison in order to become visible. In the cases shown here, it is seen how a rather stable 'Finnish integration policy' has to be constructed if a radical change in it is to be shown; conversely, continuity is facilitated by letting in some incoherence instead of drawing too clear a line when depicting past policies. Interestingly, the first, 'rupture' view presents a more solid view on Finnish integration policy than the second one. It may accentuate the continuity to a point where it appears exaggerated and therefore prompts criticism. In fact, a parallel can here be drawn with the discussion on the withering away of the state (chapter 3) where the critics of the state, or those arguing that it withers away, construct a particularly powerful state, a more robust image of it than those accused of over-stressing the state and refusing to see its 'withering' taking place.

Finally, the choices lead the versions to diverging assessments of what is success and what is failure, as well as of what is a fact and what is mere rhetoric. Nordic cooperation in the fields of security and economy is seen as a failure in 4, but rather successful in 5, because the latter emphasises more the actual contents than the form: it is not so relevant in which fora cooperation takes place, provided that it does, and therefore it is a minor setback if plans for specific Nordic arrangements have failed. Finnish integration policy may appear successful in both accounts, but on different grounds. In 6, Finland had until very recently pursued a successful policy of neutrality; the successfulness of that policy makes the sudden change of policy all the more surprising. In 7, EU membership is an achievement of the traditional Finnish policy that has not so much aimed at maintaining neutrality than at participation, but which has often met obstacles.

In 4, statements on the importance of continued Nordic cooperation are seen as rhetorical. They are put in an unfavourable light by the weight given to the repeated failures of grand common plans, the diverging policies of the countries and the modesty of the proposed improvements that are made follow a logic which has been seen to fail many times earlier. In 5, on the contrary, the statements are really seen to reflect the policies of the countries: what appears rhetorical, on the contrary, is the EU's insistence on common policies. In 6, then, claiming that Finnish integration policy has continued undisturbed is seen to be pure rhetoric: evidence is accumulated against seeing any similarities between the Finnish policies before and after EU membership by presenting the Finnish pre-EU policies as coherent and having as their undisputed aims neutrality and the avoidance of political commitments. In 7, finally, rupture is a product of erroneous interpretations, while the facts show that Finnish policies have throughout been geared towards maximum possible participation, including political participation, and that neutrality has been a mere aim towards this, not an aim in itself.

Conclusively, the cases highlight the plurality of truth in the form of plurality of reality; they ease the proper understanding of plurality and its implications through linking the abstract, theoretical plurality to concrete events, showing that the versions lead to quite different conclusions, political prescriptions, and further research questions. In other words, the cases show the actual importance of implicitly chosen assumptions in directing further research, but also their political relevance.

First, it is important to notice how different conclusions can be drawn on the basis of the versions when used as a ground for generalisations or prognostications. The chapter on Nordic cooperation leads to two opposite conclusions as to what might be the right or most effective method of integration, a functional and pragmatic or a teleological and intangible one. The first version on Finnish integration policy leads us to conclude that states are gradually becoming more similar to each other and also more clearly limited and defined as to their functions and role. Instead of belonging to one and the same system, integration is a separate process which defines the state and curtails its independence. The second version, on the contrary, leads one to expect that integration and the state are approaching the same extension since integration is defined by the states and used as an agency in their policy. Integration will thus not surpass the state, but will hardly remain more restricted in extension than the states are as to their functions and fields of activities – in a way, the two are part of the same political system.

Further, the choices concerning conceptualisations obviously shape what are seen as important questions for further research. While a certain question is central in one version, it may be a non-issue in the other, or answered latently by omission. For instance, if an account of a state's policy is written using the state's own perspective and definitions, the question of the good or effective nature of the state might well not appear at all. Further, while version 7 proposes that one could study the mutual influence between the state and the EU institutions as a contest of who has greatest influence, version 6 starts looking for possible explanations for why the change took place – a change which was not even observed in 7. Similarly, the arguments on similarity may lead to the question of whether similarity is functional, and what kind of similarity is functional, necessary or important. From the perspectives of 5 and 7, the capacity for accommodating differences rather than eliminating them seems central to the very success of the EU enterprise.

Finally, the cases portrayed one by one show the same inadequacy that the four theories did when they were presented independently of the others. They suggest that an adequate account of any related case has to take into consideration diverging interpretations. Moreover, they suggest that the familiar debate on whether integration strengthens or weakens the state might, as a debate, be somewhat misleading, even rather futile. It could be seen as a pseudo-discussion which undoubtedly keeps the research going on in that it cannot be concluded in the favour of any of the contenders; at the same time, it diverts attention from more basic questions.

Indeed, when the views are analysed according to the assumptions, as above, one can also see how the various background choices are linked to the insuperable problem of whether to give priority in conceptualisation to the state or to integration, that is, which of them comes first as a constant to define the other. One can see the states as having always been defined by their environment and the international organisation having grown simultaneously with the assertion of the state (in which case integration obviously also plays a part in this definition); one can also see the states as having defined their environment, in which case the state is defined *a priori*. In any case, one of the two has to be made constant to explain the other. Although the state has usually been in this role in the analysis of integration, it is interesting to note that integration also appears, perhaps even increasingly, as a constant which explains the state. Despite the difficulties in explaining integration, or perhaps because of these difficulties, 'integration' seems to be acquiring some of the features of 'the state' as to its functions in theory construction. It comes to define the state or explain the different changes that take place in the states. While the theories first aimed at explaining integration, they now use integration in explaining different phenomena, such as regionalism, the strengthening of the executive *versus* the legislative, or the states' policies and structures. Moreover, integration becomes something isolable or independent, while, at the same time, EU integration is increasingly analysed as unique or incomparable.

Possibilities and limits of scientific analysis

The plurality of truth which the theories and cases examined in this book reflect helps to understand the process by which knowledge is constructed, leading to important observations concerning the possibilities and limits of research. These, evidently, do not regard solely the research on the state and integration. Quite tangibly, the case studies exemplify this construction of knowledge by showing the internal dynamism implied in different theoretical stands and, thus, the crucial importance of the basic choices: they do lead the interpretation in a particular way. We also see how, in practice, the accounts 'hide' some points, or minimise their importance even though they do take them into consideration and do not really 'misrepresent' them.

In practice, the cases show how the analysis of Finnish integration policy actually constructs that policy, and how a particular stand taken makes even the history of that policy appear in different forms in the search for evidence, or credibility, for the interpretation given. Thus, the history of Finnish integration policy is unavoidably drawn into the picture. The first account depicts the period until membership as following the same, immutable principles; this makes membership appear as a rupture. The second, in turn, constructs the policy as a logical sequel: the general aim is to participate, and the policy gradually changes in this direction. Similarly, Nordic cooperation is constructed twice through its very definition as an institution-bound or as a more ubiquitous type of cooperation. This definition changes the time perspective, while it also determines in precise terms what aspects of Nordic cooperation are concentrated on in the account.

At this point, we can summarise the particular sense in which this study is entitled as a critique. The object of criticism has obviously not been any of the views on the state and integration as such. Instead, the study points out three main features of conventional research practice – the understanding of accumulation, objectivity and empirical research – which together contribute to the main and most consequential shortcoming of integration studies in answering the question about the relationship between the state and integration: the attitude towards the plurality of different views that result. First, plurality is seen as something negative and inconclusive; second, relations between different views are seen as contradictory; and third, progress is understood as accumulation of evidence in favour of one view, making it the right answer, implying that one of the views is the best and that it is possible to find out which one it is.

In all, integration studies seem not to possess a particularly well-developed self-understanding. First, it is usually said that the problem with integration studies and the reason for their scarce results is the dearth of an accumulation of knowledge. This study would rather claim that the problem is excessive accumulation: the same choices are repeated and different factors (indicators, variables) accrue into long, rather useless lists, becoming a heavy package of persistent features which research has to take into account. The cases encourage alertness from the scholar about the often compelling forces of quantity and logic or continuity in deciding which of the available theories is the best. Indeed, accumulation involves the problem that the original relation between assumptions and results is not necessarily taken into account when results, conclusions or judgements are taken over to subsequent research. Accumulation tends to turn assumptions into facts and theories into evidence, for instance when a view on institutions leads one to judge the Nordic innovations aiming at more efficiency as useless.

Second, being objective is seen as a self-evident aim of research (as opposed to other forms of knowledge), and objectivity is most often seen to require that only one truth is possible. It is also stressed that the results have to be objectively attained to be scientific. Yet, it was seen that very unobjective, and thus unscientific, factors in reality shaped the views, namely values, preferences and trends inside disciplines. It seems, in fact, reasonable to claim that what is scientific is precisely taking a stand on these features, which in the final analysis are so characteristic of scientific enterprise, and being aware of their influence, not putting them aside. The unscientific, thus, is scientific. Similarly, one might also think that objectivism needs 'permissivism'. A view is not objective if it eliminates equally good ones; a scientific view therefore should treat different views objectively, that is, equally.

Finally, the cases do not solve the problem of the relationship between the state and integration; they are not helpful in the traditional view of deciding which view is better. Indeed, no case would be, as empirical evidence cannot do that: it is impossible to say that some view is *not* valid as long as the differences are in the realm of assumptions and the interpretation of facts. In other words, recourse to empirical cases does not solve the kinds of problems it is thought to do. Most studies are characterised by strong empirical tendencies or beliefs in the possibility of empirically solving problems of a profoundly theoretical character, such as whether integration has a similar influence on all states (which implies a decision on whether all states are to be considered as essentially similar) or whether some change in the state means that there no longer is a state (which implies a stand on whether the state previously has been something different). Empirical studies, however, scarcely bring anything new to the question; they only strengthen an idea – as deductive method could be said to do: deducing something from certain assumptions does not increase knowledge. In other words, as the domain of the empirical is given beforehand, it cannot uncover but what has been prespecified (cf. Weber 1995: 17-28). Instead, one could argue with Feyerabend (1975: 37) that the possibility for progress lies in finding facts which contradict the theories, and that in order to find these facts, research methods may also have to be modified, as one method is conducive to one type of results. In sum, the cherished ideals of research do not necessarily yield the results expected.

Thus depicted, research has its possibilities and limitations which have to be taken into account in its evaluation, be it for the aim of applying the knowledge acquired or of increasing it. On the one hand, that knowledge is constructed implies that it can be constructed in different ways. It is, in other words, possible for conventional research practice to attain a number of different, but still correct, interpretations of the same facts; these interpretations may have consequential practical implications. This is true for all the views; thus, the theories of integration cannot be seen as mere 'bad old theories' which do not work, or as 'mere theories': they are examples of the actual possibilities of constructing knowledge.

On the other hand, research also has its limitations. In particular, it is limited in its ability to reflect the plurality of truth. The rules of conventional research practice is conducive to one view at a time, producing chains of views – such as exemplified in chapters two, four and five – in which all pieces are as such rather imperfect. At the same time, the different views or versions seem credible only when presented alone; they try to falsify other views, accumulating evidence in their support. This 'scientific' proof of their being 'evident' rests on the fact that they do not reveal any conditionality; thus, they may also create 'necessary' links between phenomena. Plurality therefore threatens the credibility of these views: they are questioned by the presence of other interpretations which show how knowledge actually is conditioned and relative to the assumptions. In the end, however, the understanding of what creates credibility implied in the conventional research practice can be questioned. It can be argued that research which is able to reflect the plurality of truth and which is aware of its limits and possibilities is preferable to research which is not in that it actually is more credible.

The plurality of truth and credibility of research

Usual research practice leads, thus, quite understandably to one answer at a time, irrespective of whether or not it is assumed that the questions ultimately have *one* (right) answer. This is because of the rules concerning unequivocal definitions and logic; research requires a stand taken on the definitions and indicators used, as well as on questions of priority. These elements are normally identified as parts of the theoretical part of research. Theory enters the research process by providing alternative frameworks: different theories lead to different views, or answers, through different conceptualisations and assumptions. The truth of each view is ascertained, in the final analysis, through these assumptions. However, they seldom, if ever, support just one view: often, the basis consists of choices between two equal alternatives, and therefore gives rise to at least two different, equally motivated views.

This kind of 'internal relativism' of a piece of research is generally well understood: the terms can be defined in but one way at a time, and the rest of the study should conserve and follow the choices made, thus making the results relative to the initial choices. The idea of theoretical plurality is similarly customary: while the empirical world is one, there are different competing theoretical pictures of it. Actually, however, the logical consequence of the 'internal relativism' and the plurality of theoretical views is that the results produced, the outcomes of research, are clearly incomplete, partial, as pieces of one whole. Therefore, it is important to stress the plurality of truth as a way to increase the usefulness of research as effectively making reality more understandable through first making itself more understandable.

The term 'plurality', however, needs to be given a more precise meaning. It is important to note that what is meant here by plurality is not complete relativism. The decision to present alternative accounts might seem useless, anti-problem-solving: juxtaposing different versions, which alone could be convincing pieces of research, has the effect of rendering both somehow 'optional' or speculative, as if what would have been 'facts' no longer were such. However, it is not meant as support for the view that anything goes, all results being equally good or bad, or that nothing (conclusive) can be achieved – which in the end amount to the same. As Carr (1961: 30-31) has noted, that a mountain appears to take different shapes when looked at from different angles does not mean that it has objectively either no shape at all or an infinity of shapes.

There is, however, relativism in the sense that it is not difficult to see that the validity of statements is relative to or depends on the definitions used, or on the angle of vision one has chosen to look at the mountain. It is also quite clear that one cannot find any single objective or absolute meaning for terms such as 'state' and 'integration'. That the concepts are 'relative' in this sense, however, does not reduce their importance or the importance of the results obtained. While one theory cannot encompass the variety of meanings because of the rules of research practice which reduce the meanings of the central concepts, it is understandable that there might be several 'correct' theories on the same subject. In fact, the problem actually is the tendency of theory to substitute a single meaning for the original variety of meanings. Theories simplify, but this does not necessarily mean that they are incomplete; it could rather be that they are too complete in that they succeed in 'universalising' some conceptualisations, excluding all competing ones. Therefore, several theories together render the reality better than a single theory despite the fact that accepting different theories and meanings apparently relativises the very value and authority of the scientific explanation.

Again, the empirical cases help to understand why a variety of views is needed to explain reality. In the practice of international relations, the actors represent different views which themselves are not stable, and their action certainly requires taking into consideration more than one perception of a given fact at the time. The cases in this study raise the question of whether the views and definitions expressed by the object of research itself should be taken into account or not, and whether it is possible not to take them into account. It is also seen how political actors not only use definitions to suit their purposes, but also often avoid definition altogether. In politics, definitions of concepts, rules or goals may, indeed, be rather counterproductive, as exemplified in the study of Finnish membership negotiations.[3]

It is essential to realise that this plurality is not a sign of weakness. In the end, the importance of plurality is not based on the idea of one empirical reality and a plural theoretical reality, but on the thought that this plurality resides in the empirical, the description. This study, in fact, questions the conventional way of distinguishing between theory and facts, or drawing a boundary between the theoretical and the empirical. Even a description which in no way aims at theory construction and which does not even contain references to theories involves what could be called *theoretical elements*. A 'mere' description is also a way of rendering something understandable; it requires decisions, or choices, concerning conceptualisation and the relative importance of different facts. As here, different choices lead to different versions, the number of which is certainly not limited to two. 'Theory' itself may have to be given a wider meaning than is usually the case. It is difficult to say whether the 'cases' of this study are more empirical than theoretical in character. The 'pure facts' do not constitute a narrative or description: they do not 'mean' anything or have any 'importance' as such. The meaning and importance stem from their placement into a context and their configuration to each other. This, one could argue, is already 'theoretical' or optional in the sense that it involves choosing between different possibilities. It is, in fact, difficult to locate the boundary between the general and particular: the distinction between theoretical and empirical studies does not seem meaningful in that both actually imply the need of choosing and ordering facts. In all, the domain of the objective or the absolute seems rather limited in comparison to that of the 'relative'.

In this book, the contradictory interpretations are shown to increase knowledge rather than to diminish or question it. On the one hand, they increase knowledge tangibly in that they tend to stress different facts and therefore tell more than any single account alone. As Peirce has noted, it is better to trust the multitude and variety rather than any one view: a cable made of all views together is stronger than a chain which is as weak as its weakest part (cf. Bernstein 1983: 224). On the other hand, the different accounts increase knowledge in that they point out the choices made; thus, they increase the transparency of the views, helping to understand their origins. They also help to individuate the limits and possibilities of research, the 'options', such as the basic oscillations identified in chapter three concerning the nature of state or the role of institutions, and, thus, may also draw attention to the need to explain why some views appear in the literature less often than others, for instance, the reasons for the prevalence of views which give a negative view on the state over the positive ones. When increasing their own credibility, however, they also increase the credibility of the other views. Thus, the versions make each other understandable and acceptable and have to depend on each other for their credibility.

This might seem to be a rather 'shaky' ground for research to be credible. Yet, conventional research practice can in this respect hardly be seen as less shaky. In fact, it leads to results that can easily be contested by the simple juxtaposition of different views; it is therefore not surprising that the results of social sciences are often interpreted as artificial or irrelevant for practical politics. The self-portrait of conventional research, maintaining that results are relevant in that they reflect reality and conform to scientific standards, cannot be very convincing since these can easily be shown to be contradictory. Thus, the opaqueness or impenetrability of conventional research reduces its credibility.

In the end, acknowledging that the grounds of research practice – concepts, methods, assumptions, values – are mere choices and, thus, relative and shaky, does not make the results or the enterprise as such dubious or less worthwhile. In reality, the results become criticisable and are bound to be found shaky if and when these grounds are hidden in some assumed objectivism. An increased 'transparency' regarding the way research actually proceeds and the choices it involves will only increase its credibility. It also increases the possibilities of seeing the biases of research and allows for progress in research, not in the sense of accumulating evidence for one view and against some other, but as a development of the understanding of the foundations for the single views and their interrelations.

Objectivity, and thus credibility, can be seen to lay in understanding the 'unobjectivity' of what one does, in mastering, as it were, one's own perspective. In Carr's (1961: 163, 175) view, a historian is objective if he has capacity to rise above the limited vision of his own situation, being capable to recognise the extent of his involvement, the impossibility of total objectivity and the interaction between facts and values. This is certainly true also in social science, where, as shown in this study, the scholar faces the challenge of mastering a wealth of implicit choices which lead and constrain the studies.

One could think of research as a kaleidoscope which through a certain mechanism produces several different pictures from the same elements. Understanding the working principles of this 'scientific kaleidoscope' contributes to evaluating the results; thereby, it also helps to avoid blind accumulation, the uncritical adaptation of methods, definitions and theories that constrain the results of analyses. The conventional scholar, however, tends to mistake the kaleidoscope for a telescope. Trying not to shake it in order to keep the picture it shows immutable, this rather serious character aims at an increasingly sharper image and discovering further details of the picture with additional binoculars. Obviously, however, the very purpose of a kaleidoscope is its ability to produce a seemingly infinite number of different figures out of the same material according to its specific way of functioning. The point is to shake it. Similarly, one should see the meaning of the scientific enterprise in the totality of the different constellations the scientific kaleidoscope can produce when it is moved: this variety is the true result of science. A more transparent and self-reflective research practice, that is, a distance from the scientific work which permits us to see how and why particular results are reached would, thus, constitute a ground for increasing the objectivity and credibility of research, in single cases as well as in the field of social sciences in general.

Notes

1. In the absence of strong central institutions, Nordic cooperation has often been characterised as 'cobweb integration'. This metaphor is particularly interesting in that it 'explains' the different impressions the scholars have had when looking at it. Indeed, if one happens to gaze *through* the cobweb, one might not see it at all.
2. The nature of knowledge about past facts is different from that about the present: the more ancient the facts are, the less numerous and the more firmly chosen (generally agreed) become the important facts. Conversely, the newer the facts are, the more numerous and disparate they are (which also gives the impression of the speeding up of history).
3. On a more general level, Weber (1995: 60) points to the preferability of leaving the aims and rules of common undertakings unstated; similarly, Der Derian argues that definitions are sometimes counterproductive even in research (see his example of a UNESCO conference on cultural policy which decided not to define 'culture' or 'cultural politics'; Der Derian, James, *On Diplomacy. A Genealogy of Western Estrangement.* Basil Blackwell, 1987, p. 31).

Bibliography

General references

Abi-Saab, Georges (ed.) (1981): *The concept of international organization*. Unesco, Paris.
Alger, Chadwick F. (1981): 'Functionalism and integration as approaches to international organization', in Abi-Saab, Georges (ed.): *The concept of international organization*. Unesco, Paris.
Allison, Graham T. (1971): *Essence of Decision. Explaining the Cuban Missile Crisis*. Little, Brown and Company, Boston.
Andersen, Svein S. – Eliassen, Kjell A. (1993): 'The EC as a new political system', 'Policy-making and institutions in the EC', and 'Policy-making in the new Europe', in Andersen, Svein S. – Eliassen, Kjell A. (eds.): *Making Policy in Europe. The Europeification of National Policy-making*. Sage Publications, London, Thousand Oaks, New Delhi.
Anderson, Jeffrey J. (1995): 'The State of the (European) Union. From the Single Market to Maastricht, from Singular Events to General Theories'. *World Politics*, vol. 47 (3), pp. 441-465.
Aron, Raymond (1962): *Paix et guerre entre les nations*. Calmann-Lévy, Paris [1975].
Aron, Raymond (1963): 'Old Nations, New Europe', in Graubard, Stephen R. (ed.): *A New Europe?* Oldbourne Press, London.
Baker, John – Kolinsky, Martin (1991): 'The State and Integration', in Navari, Cornelia (ed.): *The Condition of States. A Study in International Political Theory*. Open University Press, Milton Keynes, Philadelphia.
Banks, Michael – Shaw, Martin (eds.) (1991): *State and Society in International Relations*. Harvester Wheatsheaf.
Bartelson, Jens (1993): *A Genealogy of Sovereignty*. Stockholm Studies in Politics 48. University of Stockholm, Department of Political Science.
Bayles, Michael D. (1991): 'Definitions in Law', in Fetzer James H. – Shatz, David – Schlesinger, George N. (eds.): *Definition and definability: philosophical perspectives*. Synthese library, vol. 216, Kluwer Academic Publishers.
Beloff, Max (1963): 'International integration and the modern state'. *Journal of Common Market Studies*, vol. II (1), pp. 52-62.
Bernstein, Richard J. (1983): *Beyond Objectivism and Relativism: Science, Hermeneutics, and Praxis*. Basil Blackwell, Oxford.

Booth, Ken – Smith, Steve (eds.) (1995): *International Relations Theory Today*. Polity Press, Cambridge.
Brown, Seyom (1988): *New Forces, Old Forces, and the Future of World Politics*. Scott, Foresman and Company.
Bull, Hedley (1966): 'International Theory. The Case for a Classical Approach'. *World Politics*, vol. XVIII (3), pp. 361-377.
Bull, Hedley (1979): 'The State's Positive Role in World Affairs'. *Dædalus (Journal of the American Academy of Arts and Sciences)*, vol. 108, (4) (Fall), pp. 111-123.
Bulmer, Simon (1983): 'Domestic Politics and European Community Policy-Making'. *Journal of Common Market Studies*, vol. XXI (4), pp. 349-363.
Bulmer, Simon J. (1993): 'The Governance of the European Union: A New Institutionalist approach'. *Journal of Public Policy*, vol. 13 (4), pp. 351-380.
Burley, Anne-Marie – Mattli, Walter (1993): 'Europe Before the Court: A Political Theory of Legal Integration'. *International Organization*, vol. 47 (1), pp. 41-76.
Caporaso, James A. (1971): 'Theory and Method in the Study of International Integration'. *International Organization*, vol. 25 (2), pp. 228-253.
Caporaso, James A. (ed.) (1989): *The Elusive State. International and Comparative Perspectives*. Sage Publications.
Carr, Edward Hallett (1961): *What is History?* Vintage Books, Random House, New York.
Cassese, Sabino (1986): 'The Rise and Decline of the Notion of State'. *International Political Science Review*, vol. 7 (2), pp. 120-130.
Cerny, Philip G. (1990): *The Changing Architecture of Politics. Structure, Agency, and the Future of the State*. Sage Publications, London, Newbury Park, New Delhi.
Colliard, Claude-Albert (1985): *Institutions des relations internationales*. 8ème éd. Dalloz, Paris.
Connolly, William E. (1974): *The Terms of Political Discourse*. Second edition. Martin Robertson, Oxford.
Cox, R. W. (1965): 'The Study of European Institutions: Some Problems of Economic and Political Organization'. *Journal of Common Market Studies*, vol. III (2), pp. 102-117.
Cox, Robert W. – Jacobson, Harold K. (1974): 'The Anatomy of Influence', in Cox, Robert W. – Jacobson, Harold K. (eds.): *The Anatomy of Influence. Decision Making in International Organization*. Second edition. Yale University Press, New Haven and London.
Czempiel, Ernst-Otto (1989): 'Internationalizing Politics: Some Answers to the Question of Who Does What to Whom', in Czempiel, Ernst-Otto – Rosenau, James N. (eds.): *Global Changes and Theoretical Challenges. Approaches to World Politics for the 1990s*. Lexington Books.

Czempiel, Ernst-Otto - Rosenau, James N. (eds.) (1989): *Global Changes and Theoretical Challenges. Approaches to World Politics for the 1990s.* Lexington Books.
Dessler, David (1989): 'What's at stake in the agent-structure debate?' *International Organization,* vol. 43 (3), pp. 441-473.
Deutsch, Karl et al. (1957): *Political Community and the North Atlantic Area. International Organization in the Light of Historical Experience.* Greenwood Press, New York. (Reprint 1969).
Deutsch, Karl W. (1968): *The Analysis of International Relations.* Prentice-Hall, Inc., Englewood Cliffs, New Jersey.
Deutsch, Karl (1974): 'Between Sovereignty and Integration: Conclusion', in Ionescu, Ghita (ed.): *Between Sovereignty and Integration.* Groom Helm, London.
Deutsch, Karl W. (1986): 'State Functions and the Future of the State'. *International Political Science Review,* vol. 7 (2), pp. 209-222.
De Vree, Johan K. (1972): *Political integration: the formation of theory and its problems.* Mouton, The Hague and Paris.
Dougherty, James E. - Pfaltzgraff, Robert L., Jr. (1981): *Contending Theories of International Relations. A Comprehensive Survey.* Second edition. Harper & Row, Publishers, New York.
Dunn, John (1994): 'Introduction: Crisis of the Nation State?'. *Political Studies,* vol. XLII, pp. 3-15. (Special issue.)
Easton, David (1971): *The Political System. An Inquiry into the State of Political Science.* Second edition. Alfred A. Knopf, New York.
Eco, Umberto (1995): *Come si fa una tesi di laurea.* 23th edition. Bompiani, Milano.
Etzioni, Amitai (1965): *Political Unification. A Comparative Study of Leaders and Forces.* Robert E. Krieger Publishing Company, Huntington, New York. (Reprint 1974.)
Evans, Peter B. - Rueschemayer, Dietrich - Skocpol, Theda (eds.) (1985): *Bringing the State Back In.* Cambridge University Press.
Evans, Peter B. - Rueschemayer, Dietrich - Skocpol, Theda (1985): 'On the Road toward a More Adequate Understanding of the State', in Evans, Peter B. - Rueschemayer, Dietrich - Skocpol, Theda (eds.): *Bringing the State Back In.* Cambridge University Press.
Evans, Peter B. - Jacobson, Harold K. - Putnam, Robert D. (eds.) (1993): *Double-Edged Diplomacy. International Bargaining and Domestic Politics.* University of California Press.
Ferguson, Yale H. - Mansbach, Richard W. (1989): *The State, Conceptual Chaos, and the Future of International Relations Theory.* Lynne Rienner Publishers, Boulder and London.
Feyerabend, Paul K. (1975): *Against Method. Outline of an anarchistic theory of knowledge.* Lowe & Brydone (Printers) Ltd, Thetford, Norfolk.
Feyerabend, Paul (1987): *Farewell to Reason.* Verso, London and New York.

Galtung, Johan (1967): 'A Structural Theory of Integration'. *Journal of Peace Research*, vol. 4 (4). Reprinted in Galtung, Johan: *Peace and World Structure. Essays in Peace Research*. Vol. IV. Christian Ejlers, Copenhagen 1980.

Grant, R.A.D. (1988): 'Defenders of the State', in Parkinson, G.H.R. (ed.): *An Encyclopedia of Philosophy*. Routledge.

Graubard, Stephen R. (ed.) (1963): *A New Europe?* Oldbourne Press, London. (Cf. *Dædalus*, Winter 1964.)

Grieco, Joseph M. (1988): 'Anarchy and the limits of cooperation: a realist critique of the newest liberal institutionalism'. *International Organization*, vol. 42 (3), pp. 485-507.

Grieco, Joseph M. (1990): *Cooperation among Nations. Europe, America, and Non-tariff Barriers to Trade*. Cornell University Press, Ithaca and London.

Grieco, Joseph M. (1991): *The Renaissance of the European Community and the Crisis of Realist International Theory*. Duke University Program in Political Economy, Working Paper 151.

Grieco, Joseph M. (1995): 'The Maastricht Treaty, Economic and Monetary Union and the neo-realist research programme'. *Review of International Studies*, vol. 21, pp. 21-40.

Guzzini, Stefano (1992): *The Continuing Story of a Death Foretold. Realism in International Relations/International Political Economy*. EUI Working Paper in Political and Social Sciences 92/20. European University Institute, Florence.

Haas, Ernst B. (1948): 'The United States of Europe. Four Approaches to the Purpose and Form of a European Federation'. *Political Science Quarterly*, vol. LXIII (4), pp. 528-550.

Haas, Ernst B. (1958): *The Uniting of Europe. Political, Social, and Economic Forces 1950-1957*. Stanford University Press, Stanford, California 1968. (Originally published by Stevens & Sons Limited, London.)

Haas, Ernst B. (1961): 'International Integration. The European and the Universal Process'. *International Organization*, vol. 15, pp. 366-392.

Haas, Ernst B. (1963): 'Technocracy, Pluralism and the New Europe', in Graubard, Stephen R. (ed.): *A New Europe?* Oldbourne Press, London.

Haas, Ernst B. (1964): *Beyond the Nation-State. Functionalism and International Organization*. Stanford University Press, Stanford, California.

Haas, Ernst B. (1970): 'The Study of Regional Integration: Reflections on the Joy and Anguish of Pretheorizing'. *International Organization*, vol. 24 (4), pp. 607-646.

Haas, Ernst B. (1975): *The Obsolescence of Regional Integration Theory*. Institute of International Studies, University of California, Berkeley.

Haas, Ernst B. – Schmitter, Philippe C. (1964): 'Economics and Differential Patterns of Political Integration: Projections about Unity in Latin America'.

International Organization, vol. XVIII (4), pp. 705-737. (Revised in *International Political Communities: An Anthology.* New York 1966.)
Haass, Richard (1979): 'The Primacy of the State... or Revising the Revisionists'. *Dædalus*, Fall, pp. 125-138.
Halliday, Fred (1991): 'State and society in international relations', in Banks, Michael – Shaw, Martin (eds.): *State and Society in International Relations.* Harvester Wheatsheaf.
Halliday, Fred (1994): *Rethinking International Relations.* Macmillan.
Hansen, Roger D. (1969): 'Regional Integration. Reflections on a Decade of Theoretical Efforts'. *World Politics*, vol. 21 (2), pp. 242-271.
Hanson, Norwood Russell (1965): *Patterns of Discovery. An Inquiry Into the Conceptual Foundations of Science.* Cambridge University Press. (First printed in 1958.)
Harrison, Reginald J. (1974): *Europe in Question. Theories of Regional International Integration.* George Allen & Unwin Ltd, London.
Held, David (1989): *Political Theory and the Modern State. Essays on State, Power and Democracy.* Polity Press.
Héritier, Adrienne – Mingers, Susanne – Knill, Christoph – Becka, Martina (1994): *Die Veränderung von Staatlichkeit in Europa. Ein regulativer Wettbewerb: Deutschland, Großbritannien und Frankreich in der Europäischen Union.* Leske + Budrich, Opladen.
Herz, John H. (1957): 'Rise and Demise of the Territorial State'. *World Politics*, vol. 9, pp. 473-493.
Hill, Christopher (1991): 'Diplomacy and the Modern State', in Navari, Cornelia (ed.): *The Condition of States. A Study in International Political Theory.* Open University Press, Milton Keynes, Philadelphia.
Hix, Simon (1994): 'The Study of the European Community: The Challenge to Comparative Politics'. *West European Politics*, vol. 17 (1), pp. 1-30.
Hoffmann, Stanley (1966): 'Obstinate or Obsolete? The Fate of the Nation-State and the Case of Western Europe'. *Dædalus*, vol. 95 (2), pp. 862-915.
Hoffmann, Stanley (1982): 'Reflections on the Nation-State in Western Europe Today'. *Journal of Common Market Studies*, vol. 21 (1-2), pp. 21-37.
Hoffmann, Stanley (1995): 'Introduction', in Hoffmann, Stanley: *The European Sisyphus. Essays on Europe, 1964-1994.* Westview Press, Boulder, San Francisco, Oxford.
Hollis, Martin – Lukes, Steven (eds.) (1982): *Rationality and Relativism.* Basil Blackwell, Oxford.
Hollis, Martin – Smith, Steve (1990): *Explaining and Understanding International Relations.* Clarendon Press, Oxford.
Ionescu, Ghita (ed.) (1974): *Between Sovereignty and Integration.* Groom Helm, London.

Jackson, Robert H. - James, Alan (eds.) (1993): *States in a Changing World. A Contemporary Analysis.* Clarendon Press, Oxford.

Jackson, Robert H. - James, Alan (1993): 'The Character of Independent Statehood', in Jackson, Robert H. - James, Alan (eds.): *States in a Changing World. A Contemporary Analysis.* Clarendon Press, Oxford.

James, Alan (1986): *Sovereign Statehood. The Basis of International Society.* London.

James, Alan (1989): 'The realism of Realism: the state and the study of International Relations'. *Review of International Studies,* vol. 15 (3), pp. 215-229.

Kahler, Miles (1987): 'The survival of the state in European international relations', in Maier, Charles S. (ed.): *Changing boundaries of the political. Essays on the evolving balance between the state and society, public and private in Europe.* Cambridge University Press.

Kaiser, Ronn D. (1972): 'Toward the Copernican Phase of Regional Integration Theory'. *Journal of Common Market Studies,* vol. 10 (3), pp. 207-232.

Kaplan, Morton A. (1966): 'The New Great Debate. Traditionalism vs. Science in International Relations'. *World Politics,* vol. XIX (1), pp. 1-20.

Kelstrup, Morten (1992): 'European integration and political theory', in Kelstrup, Morten (ed.): *European Integration and Denmark's Participation.* Institute of Political Science, University of Copenhagen. Copenhagen Political Studies Press.

Keohane, Robert O. - Nye, Joseph S. Jr. (eds.) (1973): *Transnational Relations and World Politics.* Harvard University Press, Cambridge, Massachusetts. (Third printing; originally appeared in *International Organization,* vol. XXV (3) 1971.)

Keohane, Robert O. - Nye, Joseph S. (1977): *Power and Interdependence. World Politics in Transition.* Little, Brown and Company, Boston and Toronto.

Keohane, Robert O. (1984): *After Hegemony. Cooperation and Discord in the World Political Economy.* Princeton University Press, Princeton, New Jersey.

Keohane, Robert O. (1988): 'International Institutions: Two Approaches'. *International Studies Quarterly,* vol. 32 (4), pp. 379-396. (Also published in Keohane, Robert O.: *International Institutions and State Power. Essays in International Relations Theory.* Westview Press, Boulder, San Francisco & London 1989.)

Keohane, Robert O. - Hoffmann, Stanley (eds.) (1991): *The New European Community. Decisionmaking and Institutional Change.* Westview Press.

Keohane, Robert O. - Hoffmann, Stanley (1991): 'Institutional Change in Europe in the 1980s', in Keohane, Robert O. - Hoffmann, Stanley (eds.): *The New European Community. Decisionmaking and Institutional Change.* Westview Press, pp. 1-39. (An earlier version of this chapter in Wallace, William (ed.) (1990): *The Dynamics of European Integration.*)

Koskenniemi, Martti (1989): *From Apology to Utopia. The Structure of International Legal Argument.* Lakimiesliiton Kustannus/Finnish Lawyers' Publishing Company, Helsinki.
Koskenniemi, Martti (1991): 'The Future of Statehood'. *Harvard International Law Journal,* vol. 32 (2), pp. 397-410.
Koskenniemi, Martti (1994): 'The Wonderful Artificiality of States'. *American Society of International Law, Proceedings,* pp. 22-29.
Krasner, Stephen D. (1984): 'Approaches to the State. Alternative Conceptions and Historical Dynamics'. *Comparative Politics,* vol. 16, pp. 223-246.
Krasner, Stephen D. (1989): 'Sovereignty: An Institutional Perspective', in Caporaso, James A. (ed.): *The Elusive State. International and Comparative Perspectives.* Sage Publications.
Kratochwil, Friedrich – Ruggie, John Gerard (1986): 'International organization: a state of the art on an art of the state'. *International Organization,* vol. 40 (4), pp. 753-775.
Kuhn, Thomas S. (1962): *The Structure of Scientific Revolutions.* The University of Chicago Press.
Lasok, Dominik – Soldatos, Panayotis (eds.) (1981): *Les Communautés Européennes en fonctionnement/The European Communities in Action.* Bruylant, Bruxelles.
Laudan, Larry (1977): *Progress and its Problems. Towards a Theory of Scientific Growth.* Routledge & Kegan Paul, London and Henley.
Lessnoff, Michael (1988): 'The Philosophy of Social Sciences', in Parkinson, G.H.R. (ed.), *An Encyclopedia of Philosophy.* Routledge.
Lijphart, Arend (1974): 'The Structure of the Theoretical Revolution in International Relations'. *International Studies Quarterly,* vol. 18 (1), pp. 41-74.
Lijphart, Arend (1981): 'Karl W. Deutsch and the New Paradigm in International Relations', in Merritt, Richard L. – Russett, Bruce M. (eds.): *From National Development to Global Community. Essays in Honor of Karl W. Deutsch.* George Allen & Unwin, London.
Lindberg, Leon N. (1963): *The Political Dynamics of European Economic Integration.* Stanford University Press, Stanford.
Lindberg, Leon N. – Scheingold, Stuart A. (1970): *Europe's Would-Be Polity. Patterns of change in the European Community.* Prentice-Hall, Inc., Englewood Cliffs, New Jersey.
Lowi, Theodore J. (1992): 'The State in Political Science. How We Become What We Study'. *American Political Science Review,* vol. 86 (1), pp. 1-7.
MacCormick, Neil (1993): 'Beyond the Sovereign State'. *The Modern Law Review,* vol. 56 (1), pp. 1-18.
Marks, Gary (1995): *European Integration and the State.* EUI Working Paper RSC No. 95/7. Robert Schuman Centre, European University Institute, Florence.

Matlary, Janne Haaland (1993a): 'Now you see it; Now you don't'. Expose and critique of approaches to the study of European Integration', in Tiilikainen, Teija - Damgaard Petersen, Ib (eds.): *The Nordic Countries and the EC*. Copenhagen Political Studies Press, Copenhagen.

Matlary, Janne Haaland (1993b): 'Beyond Intergovernmentalism: The Quest for a Comprehensive Framework for the Study of Integration'. *Cooperation and Conflict*, vol. 28 (2), pp. 181-208.

Matlary, Janne Haaland (1994): *The Limits and Limitations of Intergovernmentalism: From De-Constructive to Constructive Criticism*. Paper prepared for the ECPR Joint Sessions, Madrid.

Matlary, Janne Haaland (1995): 'New Forms of Governance in Europe? The Decline of the State as the Source of Political Legitimation'. *Cooperation and Conflict*, vol. 30 (2), pp. 99-123.

Merritt, Richard L. - Russett, Bruce M. (eds.) (1981): *From National Development to Global Community. Essays in Honor of Karl W. Deutsch*. George Allen & Unwin, London.

Milward, Alan S. (1990): 'États-Nations et Communauté: le paradoxe de l'Europe?'. *Revue de synthèse*, IVe S., (3), pp. 253-270.

Milward, Alan S. (1992): *The European Rescue of the Nation-State*. Routledge, London.

Milward, Alan S. - Sørensen, Vibeke (1993): 'Interdependence or integration? A national choice', in Milward, Alan S. et al.: *The Frontier of National Sovereignty: History and Theory 1945-1992*. Routledge, London and New York.

Mitrany, David (1943): *A Working Peace System. An Argument for the Functional Development of International Organization*. The Royal Institute of International Affairs, London.

Mitrany, David (1963): 'Delusion of Regional Unity', in *Limits and Problems of European Integration*. Stichting Grotius Seminarium, May 30 - June 2, 1961; with an introduction by B. Landheer. Martinus Nijhoff, The Hague.

Mitrany, David (1975): *The Functional Theory of Politics*. London School of Economics & Political Science, Martin Robertson.

Moravcsik, Andrew (1991): 'Negotiating the Single European Act: national interests and conventional statecraft in the European Community'. *International Organization*, vol. 45 (1), pp. 19-56.

Moravcsik, Andrew (1993a): *Liberalism and International Relations Theory*. The Center for International Affairs, Working Paper Series No. 92-6, revised. Harvard University.

Moravcsik, Andrew (1993b): 'Preferences and Power in the European Community: A Liberal Intergovernmentalist Approach'. *Journal of Common Market Studies*, vol. 31 (4), pp. 473-524.

Moravcsik, Andrew (1994): *Why the European Community Strengthens the State: Domestic Politics and International Cooperation*. Center for European Studies, Working Paper Series #52. Department of Government, Harvard University.
Morgan, Roger (1972): *West European Politics since 1945. The Shaping of the European Community*. B.T. Batsford Ltd., London.
Morgan, Roger (1994): 'European Integration and National Interests'. *Government and Opposition*, vol. 29 (1), pp. 128-134.
Morgenthau, Hans J. (1985) [1948]: *Politics among Nations. The Struggle for Power and Peace*. Sixth edition, revised by Kenneth W. Thompson. Alfred A. Knopf, New York.
Morin, Edgar (1982): *Science avec conscience*. Fayard, Paris.
Mutimer, David (1989): '1992 and the political integration of Europe: neofunctionalism reconsidered'. *Journal of European Integration*, vol. 13 (1), pp. 75-101.
Navari, Cornelia (ed.) (1991): *The Condition of States. A Study in International Political Theory*. Open University Press, Milton Keynes, Philadelphia.
Navari, Cornelia (1991a): 'Introduction: The State as a Contested Concept in International Relations', in Navari, Cornelia (ed.): *The Condition of States. A Study in International Political Thepry*. Open University Press, Milton Keynes, Philadelphia.
Navari, Cornelia (1991b): 'On the Withering Away of the State', in Navari, Cornelia (ed.): *The Condition of States. A Study in International Political Theory*. Open University Press, Milton Keynes, Philadelphia.
Nettl, J.P. (1968): 'The State as a Conceptual Variable'. *World Politics*, vol. 20 (4), pp. 559-592.
Nordlinger, Eric A. (1981): *On the Autonomy of the Democratic State*. Harvard University Press, Cambridge (Massachusetts) and London.
Nye, Joseph S. (1968): 'Comparative Regional Integration: Concept and Measurement'. *International Organization*, vol. XXII, pp. 855-880.
Nørgaard, Ole - Pedersen, Thomas - Petersen, Nikolaj (1993): *The European Community in World Politics*. Pinter Publishers, London and New York.
Olsen, Johan P. (1994): *Europeisering av nasjonalstaten*. ARENA Working Paper No. 1. Oslo.
Oppenheim, Felix E. (1981): *Political Concepts. A Reconstruction*. Basil Blackwell, Oxford.
Palan, Ronen (1990): *Non-Governmental Interactions Among Social Formations as the Bridge between the Structuralist Theory of the State and the Study of International Relations*. Ph.D. Thesis, London School of Economics, University of London.

Pedersen, Thomas (1991): 'Community Attitudes and Interests', in Wallace, Helen (ed.): *The Wider Western Europe. Reshaping the EC/EFTA Relationship.* Pinter Publishers, London.
Pentland, Charles (1973): *International Theory and European Integration.* Faber and Faber, London.
Pentland, Charles (1981): 'Political Theories of European Integration: Between Science and Ideology?', in Lasok, Dominik - Soldatos, Panayotis (eds.): *Les Communautés européennes en fonctionnement/The European Communities in Action.* Bruylant, Bruxelles.
Pinder, John (1986): 'European Community and nation-state: a case for a neo-federalism?' *International Affairs,* vol. 62 (1), pp. 41-54.
Poggi, Gianfranco (1990): *The State. Its Nature, Development and Prospects.* Polity Press.
Puchala, Donald J. (1972): 'Of Blind Men, Elephants and International Integration'. *Journal of Common Market Studies,* vol. 10 (3), pp. 267-284.
Puchala, Donald J. (1981): 'Integration Theory and the Study of International Relations', in Merritt, Richard L. - Russett, Bruce M. (eds.): *From National Development to Global Community. Essays in Honor of Karl W. Deutsch.* George Allen & Unwin, London.
Puchala, Donald J. (1993): 'Western Europe', in Jackson, Robert H. - James, Alan (eds.): *States in a Changing World. A Contemporary Analysis.* Clarendon Press, Oxford.
Putnam, Robert D. (1988): 'Diplomacy and domestic politics: the logic of two-level games'. *International Organization,* vol. 42 (3), pp. 427-460.
Robertson, A.H. (1973): *European Institutions. Co-operation : Integration : Unification.* Third edition. The London Institute of World Affairs. Stevens/Matthew Bender, London and New York.
Rosamond, Ben (1995): 'Mapping the European Condition: The Theory of Integration and the Integration of Theories'. *European Journal of International Relations,* vol. 1 (3), pp. 391-408.
Rosecrance, Richard (1996): 'The Rise of the Virtual State. *Foreign Affairs,* vol. 75 (4), pp. 45-61.
Rosenau, James N. (1989): 'The State in an Era of Cascading Politics: Wavering Concept, Widening Competence, Withering Colossus, or Weathering Change?', in Caporaso, James A. (ed.): *The Elusive State. International and Comparative Perspectives.* Sage Publications.
Ruggie, John Gerard (1983): 'Continuity and Transformation in the World Polity: Toward a Neorealist Synthesis'. *World Politics,* vol. XXXV, pp. 261-285.
Ruggie, John Gerard (1993): 'Territoriality and beyond: problematizing modernity in international relations'. *International Organization,* vol. 47 (1), pp. 139-174.
Scheingold, Stuart A. (1970): 'Domestic and International Consequences of Regional Integration'. *International Organization,* vol. 24 (4), pp. 978-1002.

Schmitter, Philippe C. (1991): *The European Community as an emergent and novel form of political domination.* Estudio/Working Paper 1991/26, Centro de Estudios Avanzados en Ciencias Sociales, Instituto Juan March de Estudios e Investigaciones, Madrid.
Schmitter, Philippe C. (1996): 'Imagining the Future of the Euro-Polity with the Help of New Concepts', in Marks, Gary - Scharpf, Fritz W. - Schmitter, Philippe C. - Streeck, Wolfgang: *Governance in the European Union.* Sage Publications, London, Thousand Oaks, New Delhi.
Sjöstedt, Gunnar (1981): *The external role of the European Community.* Gower.
Skinner, Quentin (1989): 'The state', in Ball, Terence - Farr, James - Hanson, Russell L. (eds.): *Political innovation and conceptual change.* Cambridge University Press.
Skocpol, Theda (1985): 'Bringing the State Back In: Strategies of Analysis in Current Research', in Evans, Peter B. - Rueschemayer, Dietrich - Skocpol, Theda (eds.): *Bringing the State Back In.* Cambridge University Press.
Smith, Steve (1987): 'Paradigm Dominance in International Relations: The Development of International Relations as a Social Science'. *Millennium*, vol. 16 (2), pp. 189-206.
Smith, Steve (1995): 'The Self-Images of a Discipline: A Genealogy of International Relations Theory', in Booth, Ken - Smith, Steve (eds.): *International Relations Theory Today.* Polity Press, Cambridge.
Stopford, John - Strange, Susan (with John S. Henley) (1991): *Rival states, rival firms. Competition for world market shares.* Cambridge Studies in International Relations: 18, Cambridge University Press.
Strange, Susan (1988): *States and Markets.* Pinter Publishers, London.
Strange, Susan (1989): 'Toward a Theory of Transnational Empire', in Czempiel, Ernst-Otto - Rosenau, James N. (eds.): *Global Changes and Theoretical Challenges. Approaches to World Politics for the 1990s.* Lexington Books.
Strange, Susan (1995): 'The Defective State'. *Dædalus*, vol. 124 (2), pp. 55-74.
Sørensen, Georg (1991): 'A Revised Paradigm for International Relations: the "Old" Images and the Postmodernist Challenge'. *Cooperation and Conflict*, vol. XXVI, pp. 85-116.
Taylor, Paul (1975): 'Introduction', in Mitrany, David: *The Functional Theory of Politics.* London School of Economics & Political Science, Martin Robertson.
Taylor, Paul (1978): 'Elements of supranationalism: the power and authority of international institutions', in Taylor, Paul - Groom, A.J.R. (eds.): *International Organisation. A Conceptual Approach.* Frances Pinter Ltd, London.
Taylor, Paul (1983): *The Limits of European Integration.* Columbia University Press, New York.

Taylor, Paul (1991a): 'British Sovereignty and the European Community: What is at Risk?'. *Millennium: Journal of International Studies,* vol. 20 (1), pp. 73-80.

Taylor, Paul (1991b): 'The European Community and the state: assumptions, theories and propositions'. *Review of International Studies,* vol. 17, pp. 109-125.

Taylor, Paul - Groom, A.J.R. (eds.) (1978): *International Organisation. A Conceptual Approach.* Frances Pinter Ltd, London.

Thomson, Janice E. - Krasner, Stephen D. (1989): 'Global Transactions and the Consolidation of Sovereignty', in Czempiel, Ernst-Otto - Rosenau, James N. (eds.): *Global Changes and Theoretical Challenges. Approaches to World Politics for the 1990s.* Lexington Books.

Tilly, Charles (1985): 'War Making and State Making as Organized Crime', in Evans, Peter B. - Rueschemayer, Dietrich - Skocpol, Theda (eds.): *Bringing the State Back In.* Cambridge University Press.

Tonra, Ben (1994): *Ireland, Denmark and the Netherlands in European Political Cooperation.* Paper presented to the European Consortium for Political Research (ECPR), Madrid Joint Sessions, April 17-22, 1994.

Toulmin, Stephen (1972): *Human Understanding. Volume I: The Collective Use and Evolution of Concepts.* Oxford University Press, Oxford.

Toulmin, Stephen (1990): *Cosmopolis. The Hidden Agenda of Modernity.* The Free Press, New York.

Twitchett, Carol - Twitchett, Kenneth J. (1981): 'The EEC as a framework for diplomacy', in Twitchett, Carol - Twitchett, Kenneth J. (eds.): *Building Europe: Britain's Partners in the EEC.* Europa Publications Limited, London.

Virally, Michel (1981): 'Definition and classification of international organizations: a legal approach', in Abi-Saab, Georges (ed.): *The concept of international organization.* Unesco, Paris.

Walker, R.B.J. (1993): *Inside/outside: international relations as political theory.* Cambridge Studies in International Relations 24, Cambridge University Press.

Wallace, Helen (1973): *National Governments and the European Communities.* Chatham House, European Series No. 21, April. London.

Wallace, Helen (1990): 'Making multilateral negotiations work', in Wallace, William (ed.): *The Dynamics of European Integration.* Pinter Publishers, London and New York, for the Royal Institute of International Affairs.

Wallace, Helen (ed.) (1991): *The Wider Western Europe. Reshaping the EC/EFTA Relationship.* Pinter Publishers, London.

Wallace, William (1977): 'Walking Backwards Towards Unity', in Wallace, William - Wallace, Helen - Webb, Carole (eds.): *Policy-Making in the European Communities.* John Wiley & Sons: London, New York, Sydney, Toronto.

Wallace, William (1982): 'Europe as a Confederation: the Community and the Nation-State'. *Journal of Common Market Studies,* vol. 21 (1-2), pp. 57-68.

Wallace, William (ed.) (1990): *The Dynamics of European Integration.* Pinter Publishers, London and New York, for the Royal Institute of International Affairs.

Wallace, William (1990): 'Introduction: the dynamics of European integration', in Wallace, William (ed.): *The Dynamics of European Integration.* Pinter Publishers, London and New York, for the Royal Institute of International Affairs.

Wallace, William (1994): 'Rescue or Retreat? The Nation State in Western Europe, 1945-93'. *Political Studies,* vol. XLII, pp. 52-76.

Wallace, William (1996): 'Government without statehood: the unstable equilibrium', in Wallace, Helen – Wallace, William (eds.): *Policy-Making in the European Union.* Third edition. Oxford University Press, Oxford 1996.

Waltz, Kenneth N. (1979): *Theory of International Politics.* Random House, New York.

Waltz, Kenneth N. (1990): 'Realist Thought and Neorealist Theory'. *Journal of International Affairs,* vol. 44 (1), pp. 21-37.

Webb, Carole (1983): 'Theoretical Perspectives and Problems', in Wallace, Helen – Wallace, William – Webb, Carole (eds.): *Policy-Making in the European Community.* John Wiley & Sons Ltd. 2nd edition.

Weber, Cynthia (1995): *Simulating Sovereignty: Intervention, the State, and Symbolic Exchange.* Cambridge University Press (Cambridge Studies in International Relations 37).

Weiler, J.H.H. (1991): 'The Transformation of Europe'. *The Yale Law Journal,* vol. 100 (8), pp. 2403-2483.

Wendt, Alexander E. (1987): 'The agent-structure problem in international relations theory'. *International Organization,* vol. 41 (3), pp. 335-370.

Wendt, Alexander (1994): 'Collective Identity Formation and the International State'. *American Political Science Review,* vol. 88 (2), pp. 384-396.

Wessels, Wolfgang (1990): 'Administrative interaction', in Wallace, William (ed.): *The Dynamics of European Integration.* Pinter Publishers, London and New York, for the Royal Institute of International Affairs.

Wessels, Wolfgang (1992): 'Staat und (westeuropäische) Integration. Die Fusionsthese', in Kreile, Michael (ed.): *Die Integration Europas.* Politische Vierteljahresschrift, Sonderheft 23, 33.Jg.

Winch, Peter [1958]: *The Idea of a Social Science and its Relation to Philosophy.* Second edition, 1990. Humanities Press International, Inc.

Wind, Marlene (1996): *The Structuration Theory of European Legal & Political Integration. Integrating agency and structure: a Sociological alternative to Neofunctionalism and Intergovernmentalism.* Paper presented at a research course for Ph.D. students arranged by the Copenhagen Research Project on European Integration (CORE) in Humlebæk, May 28 – June 1, 1996.

Wæver, Ole (1992): *Introduktion til Studiet af International Politik.* Forlaget Politiske Studier, København.
Wæver, Ole (1994): *The Rise and Fall of the Inter-Paradigm Debate.* Working Papers 13/1994, Centre for Peace and Conflict Research, Copenhagen.
Wæver, Ole (1995): 'Identity, Integration and Security. Solving the Sovereignty Puzzle in E.U. Studies'. *Journal of International Affairs,* vol. 48 (2), pp. 1-42.
Zimmern, Alfred (1939): *The League of Nations and the Rule of Law 1918-1935.* Russell & Russell, New York. (Reproduced from the second revised edition of 1939, reissued 1969.)

Nordic cooperation

Literature

Almdal, Preben (1986): *Aspects of European Integration. A View of the European Community and the Nordic Countries.* Odense University Press, Odense.
Anderson, Stanley V. (1963): 'Negotiations for the Nordic Council'. *Nordisk tidsskrift for international ret og jus gentium,* vol. 33, pp. 23-33.
Anderson, Stanley V. (1967): *The Nordic Council. A Study of Scandinavian Regionalism.* University of Washington Press, Seattle and London. (Based on an unpublished doctoral dissertation *The Nordic Council: an institutional analysis,* University of California, Berkeley 1961.)
Andrén, Nils (1967): 'Nordic Integration - Aspects and Problems'. *Cooperation and Conflict,* vol. II, pp. 1-25.
Andrén, Nils (1984): 'Nordic Integration and Cooperation - Illusion and Reality'. *Cooperation and Conflict,* vol. XIX, pp. 251-262.
Andrén, Nils (1991): '*Norden* and a New European Security Order', in Huldt, Bo - Herolf, Gunilla (eds.): *Towards a New European Security Order.* The Swedish Institute of International Affairs, Yearbook 1990-91, Stockholm, pp. 279-292.
Drzewicki, Krzysztof (1980): 'The Conception of Administrative Organs in the Nordic Council of Ministers'. *International Review of Administrative Sciences,* vol. 46 (4), pp. 341-353.
Engman, Max (1994): 'Är Finland ett nordiskt land?'. *Den Jyske Historiker,* vol. 69-70, pp. 62-78.
Franzén, Gösta (1944): 'Will There Be a United States of Scandinavia?'. *World Affairs Interpreter* (Los Angeles, California), n. 2, pp. 147-158.
Goldschmidt, Ernst (1990): 'The European Community and the Nordic countries: a view from the Nordic Council of Ministers', in Laursen, Finn (ed.): *EFTA and the EC: Implications of 1992.* European Institute of Public Administration, Maastricht.

Gustafsson, Sven (1968): 'Norden i GATT', in Landqvist, Åke (ed.): *Norden på världsarenan.* LTs förlag, Stockholm.
Haskel, Barbara G. (1976): *The Scandinavian Option. Opportunities and Opportunity Costs in Postwar Scandinavian Foreign Policies.* Universitetsforlaget, Oslo, Bergen and Tromsø.
Hettne, Björn - Käkönen, Jyrki - Lodgaard, Sverre - Wallensteen, Peter - Wiberg, Håkan (1991): *Norden, Europe and the Near Future.* Report from the Directors of Nordic Peace Research Institutes. PRIO Report No. 3, Oslo.
Hveem, Helge (1992): *The European Economic Area and the Nordic Countries - End Station or Transition to EC Membership?* Jean Monnet Chair Papers, The European Policy Unit at the European University Institute, Florence.
Jervell, Sverre (1991a): 'Norden og samarbeid mellom nordiske land', in *Norden i det nye Europa. En rapport fra det danske, finske, norske og svenske utenrikspolitiske institutt og universitetet i Reykjavík.* Helsingfors, København, Oslo, Reykjavík, Stockholm, juli 1991.
Jervell, Sverre (1991b): 'Elementer i en ny nordisk arkitektur', in *Norden i det nye Europa. En rapport fra det danske, finske, norske og svenske utenrikspolitiske institutt og universitetet i Reykjavík.* Helsingfors, København, Oslo, Reykjavík, Stockholm, juli 1991.
Joenniemi, Pertti (1990): 'Europe Changes; The Nordic System Remains?' *Bulletin of Peace Proposals,* vol. 21 (2), pp. 205-217.
Joenniemi, Pertti (1992b): 'Norden as a Mystery. The Search for New Roads into the Future', in Øberg, Jan (ed.) (1992): *Nordic Security in the 1990s. Options in the Changing Europe.* Pinter Publishers, London.
Joenniemi, Pertti (1994a): *Det nya Norden: svanen bland de europeiska regionerna.* Occasional Papers, No. 60, Tampere Peace Research Institute, Tampere.
Joenniemi, Pertti (1994b): 'Norden - en europeisk megaregion?', in *Norden är död. Länge leve Norden!* Nordisk debatt, Nordiska Rådet, Stockholm.
Karvonen, Lauri (1981): 'Semi-Domestic Politics: Policy Diffusion from Sweden to Finland'. *Cooperation and Conflict,* vol. XVI, pp. 91-107.
Kivimäki, Erkki (1992): *Pohjoismainen yhteistyö uuteen vaiheeseen.* UM Taustat 4/1992, Ulkoasiainministeriö/Ministry for Foreign Affairs, Helsinki.
Landqvist, Åke (ed.) (1968): *Norden på världsarenan.* LTs förlag, Stockholm.
Landqvist, Åke (1968): 'Norden i Nationernas Förbund', in Landqvist, Åke (ed.): *Norden på världsarenan.* LTs förlag, Stockholm.
Lange, Christian (1965): 'Nordisk offentlig samarbeid - en regional integrasjonsprosess?'. *Internasjonal Politikk,* (2), pp. 151-164.
Lange, Halvard (1954): 'Scandinavian Co-operation in International Affairs.' *International Affairs,* vol. XXX (3), pp. 285-293.
Laursen, Finn (ed.) (1990): *EFTA and the EC: Implications of 1992.* European Institute of Public Administration, Maastricht.

Laursen, Finn (1993): 'The Maastricht Treaty: Implications for the Nordic Countries'. *Cooperation and Conflict*, vol. 28 (2), pp. 115-141.
Lidström, Jan-Erik – Wiklund, Claes (1968): 'Norden i Förenta Nationernas generalförsamling', in Landqvist, Åke (ed.): *Norden på världsarenan*. LTs förlag, Stockholm.
Milas, René (1978): *Les institutions de la coopération nordique: les pouvoirs du Conseil Nordique et du Conseil des Ministres*. Conseil Nordique, Stockholm 1978.
Miles, Lee (ed). (1996): *The European Union and the Nordic Countries*. Routledge, London and New York.
Miljan, Toivo (1977): *The Reluctant Europeans. The Attitudes of the Nordic Countries towards European Integration*. C. Hurst & Company, London.
Mouritzen, Hans (1993a): *The 'Nordic' Model: Its Usefulness and Its Downfall as a Tool of Statecraft. Reflections on a Silent Revolution*. Working Papers 7, Centre for Peace and Conflict Research, Copenhagen.
Neumann, Iver B. (1992): *Regions in International Relations Theory. The Case for a Region-Building Approach*. NUPI, Norsk Utenrikspolitisk Institutt (Norwegian Institute of International Affairs), Research Report No. 162.
Neumann, Iver B. (ed.) (1995): *Ny giv for nordisk samarbeid? Norsk, svensk og finsk sikkerhetspolitikk før og etter EUs nordlige utvidelse*. Norsk Utenrikspolitisk Institutt, TANO, Oslo.
Neumann, Iver B. (1995): 'Konklusjon: Sikkerhetspolitisk samarbeid som nordisk samarbeid efter den nordlige EU-utvidelse', in Neumann, Iver B. (ed.): *Ny giv for nordisk samarbeid? Norsk, svensk og finsk sikkerhetspolitikk før og etter EUs nordlige utvidelse*. Norsk Utenrikspolitisk Institutt, TANO, Oslo.
Nielsson, Gunnar (1978): 'The Parallel National Action Process: Scandinavian Experiences', in Taylor, Paul – Groom, A.J.R. (eds.): *International Organisation. A Conceptual Approach*. Frances Pinter Ltd, London.
Pedersen, Thomas (1990): 'Denmark as a bridge-builder', in Laursen, Finn (ed.): *EFTA and the EC: Implications of 1992*. European Institute of Public Administration, Maastricht.
Petrén, Gustaf (1959): 'Nordiska rådet, ett egenartat folkrättssubjekt'. *Nordisk Tidsskrift for International Ret og Jus Gentium*, vol. 29, pp. 112-126.
Rosas, Allan (1988): 'PGOs and Nordic Co-operation', in Hood, Christopher – Schuppert, Gunnar Folke (eds.): *Delivering Public Services in Western Europe. Sharing Western European Experience of Para-government Organization*. SAGE Publications.
Solem, Erik (1977): *The Nordic Council and Scandinavian Integration*. Praeger Publishers, New York.
Stålvant, Carl-Einar (1988): 'Nordic Political Co-operation'. *Nordic Journal of International Law*, vol. 57 (4), pp. 442-456.

Stålvant, Carl-Einar (1990): 'Nordic cooperation', in Wallace, William (ed.): *The Dynamics of European Integration*. Pinter Publishers, London and New York.
Stålvant, Einar (1991): 'Vägar till inflytande', in *Norden i det nye Europa*. En rapport fra det danske, finske, norske og svenske utenrikspolitiske institutt og universitetet i Reykjavík. Helsingfors, København, Oslo, Stockholm, juli 1991.
Stråth, Bo (1980): 'The Illusory Nordic Alternative to Europe'. *Cooperation and Conflict*, vol. XV, pp. 103-114.
Sundelius, Bengt A. (1977): 'Trans-governmental Interactions in the Nordic Region'. *Cooperation and Conflict*, vol. XII, pp. 63-85.
Sundelius, Bengt (1978): *Managing Transnationalism in Northern Europe*. Westview Press, Boulder, Colorado.
Sundelius, Bengt (1982): 'The Nordic Model of Neighborly Cooperation' and 'North European Foreign Policies in a Comparative Perspective', in Sundelius, Bengt (ed.): *Foreign Policies of Northern Europe*. Westview Press, Boulder, Colorado.
Sundelius, Bengt - Wiklund, Claes (1979): 'The Nordic Community: the Ugly Duckling of Regional Cooperation'. *Journal of Common Market Studies*, vol. XVIII (1), pp. 59-75.
Sverdrup, Bjørn Otto (1996): *Nordic cooperation and Europeanisation: The politics of integration and disintegration*. Paper presented at the CORE seminar 'The Study of European Integration: Domestic and International Issues', May 28 - June 1, Humlebæk.
Sæter, Martin (1993): 'The Nordic Countries and European Integration. The Nordic, the West European and the All-European Stages', in Tiilikainen, Teija - Damgaard Petersen, Ib (eds.): *The Nordic Countries and the EC*. Copenhagen Political Studies Press, Copenhagen.
Tiilikainen, Teija - Damgaard Petersen, Ib (eds.) (1993): *The Nordic Countries and the EC*. Copenhagen Political Studies Press, Copenhagen.
Tunander, Ola (1991): 'The Two Nordens: The North and the South, or the East and the West?' *Bulletin of Peace Proposals*, vol. 22 (1), pp. 55-63.
Turner, Barry (with Gunilla Nordquist) (1982): *The Other European Community. Integration and Co-operation in Nordic Europe*. Weidenfeld and Nicolson, London.
Værnø, Grethe (1993): *Lille Norden - hva nå? Splittelse og samling i EFs kraftfelt*. J.W. Cappelens forlag a.s/Europa-programmet, Oslo.
Wallensteen, Peter - Vesa, Unto - Väyrynen, Raimo (1973): *The Nordic System: Structure and Change, 1920-1970*. Tampere Peace Research Institute Research Reports, n. 6; Department of Peace and Conflict Research, Uppsala University, Report n. 4.

Wallmén, Olof (1966): *Nordiska rådet och nordiskt samarbete.* P.A.Norstedt & Söners förlag, Stockholm.
Wendt, Frantz (1959): *The Nordic Council and Co-operation in Scandinavia.* Munksgaard, Copenhagen.
Wendt, Frantz (1973): *The Nordic Council and the Nordic Council of Ministers. Structure and Functions.* Nordic Council, Danish secretariat, Copenhagen.
Wendt, Frantz (1981): *Cooperation in the Nordic Countries. Achievements and Obstacles.* The Nordic Council; Almqvist & Wiksell, Uppsala.
Wiberg, Håkan (1986): 'The Nordic Countries: A Special Kind of System?' *Current Research on Peace and Violence,* vol. IX (1-2), pp. 2-12. Tampere Peace Research Institute (TAPRI).
Wiberg, Håkan (1992): 'An Alternative Scenario: Dissolution of Norden', in Øberg, Jan (ed.): *Nordic Security in the 1990s. Options in the Changing Europe.* Pinter Publishers, London.
Wiberg, Håkan – Wæver, Ole (1992): 'Norden in the Cold War Reality', in Øberg, Jan (ed.): *Nordic Security in the 1990s. Options in the Changing Europe.* Pinter Publishers, London.
Wiklund, Claes (1968): 'Norden i ILO', in Landqvist, Åke (ed.): *Norden på världsarenan.* LTs förlag, Stockholm.
Wiklund, Claes (1970): 'The zig-zag course of the Nordek negotiations'. *Scandinavian Political Studies* (Yearbook), vol. 5, pp. 307-336.
Wiklund, Claes (1984): 'Nordiskt samarbete', in Lindblad, Ingemar – Stålvant, Carl-Einar – Wahlbäck, Krister – Wiklund, Claes (eds.): *Politik i Norden. En jämförande översikt.* Liber Förlag, Stockholm. (Edition 3:1.)
Wæver, Ole (1992a): 'Nordic nostalgia: Northern Europe after the Cold War'. *International Affairs,* vol. 68 (1), pp. 77-102.
Wæver, Ole (1992b): 'Norden Rearticulated', in Øberg, Jan (ed.) (1992): *Nordic Security in the 1990s. Options in the Changing Europe.* Pinter Publishers, London.
Wæver, Ole (1994): *Balts, Books and Brussels: Nordic Identity and Cooperation after the Cold War.* Centre for Peace and Conflict Research, Copenhagen; Working Papers 11/1994.
Øberg, Jan (ed.) (1992): *Nordic Security in the 1990s. Options in the Changing Europe.* Pinter Publishers, London.
Ørvik, Nils (1974): 'Nordic Cooperation and High Politics'. *International Organization,* vol. 28 (1), pp. 61-88.

Documents and reports

Erklæring fra de nordiske lands statsministre. (Århus 10.11.1992.)
NORD 1988/78. Nordiska Rådets verksamhet 1971-1986. Översikt över rådets rekommendationer och yttranden. Nordiska Rådet, Stockholm.

NORD 1988/100E. *Nordic Council. Rules and Procedures. An introduction to co-operation within the Nordic Council.* Stockholm 1988. (Quoted: *Rules and Procedures.*)
Norden i det nye Europa. En rapport fra det danske, finske, norske og svenske utenrikspolitiske institutt og universitetet i Reykjavík. Helsingfors, København, Oslo, Reykjavík, Stockholm, juli 1991.
Norden og nordisk samarbeid i et Europa i forandring. Rapport fra en arbeidsgruppe nedsatt av statssekretærutvalget for europautredningen. Utenriksdepartementet, Oslo 1992.
Nordens folk om nordiskt samarbete – en attitydundersökning i Sverige, Norge, Danmark, Finland och Island våren 1993 för Nordiska Rådet och Nordiska Ministerrådet. Testhuset marknad opinion TEMO ab, Stockholm 1993.
Nordic Cooperation. An introduction. The Nordic Council, Stockholm 1972.
Nordiska samarbetsavtal 1993. Stockholm 1993.
Nordiskt samarbete 1993. Nordiska ministerrådets verksamhetsberättelse. Nordiska rådet, 44:e sessionen 1994. (C1) København 1993. (Quoted: *Verksamhetsberättelse.*)
NU 1969/21. *Nordic Economic and Cultural Cooperation.* Third Conference organized by the Nordic Council for international organizations in Europe, September 29 - October 2, 1969. Nordic Council, Stockholm 1970.
NU 1983/8. Organisation och arbetsformer för Nordiska rådets presidiesekretariat. Stockholm 1983.
NU 1988/4. *Internationella samarbetsfrågor i Nordiska rådet.* Betänkande avgivet av Nordiska rådets internationella samarbetskommitté. Nordiska rådet, Stockholm 1989. [The English version NU 1988:4E, The Nordic Council and International Co-operation. In Finnish, NU 1988:4F.]
NU 1989/7E. *The Nordic Council and European Co-operation.* Report of the Nordic Council's Committee on International Co-operation. Nordic Council, Stockholm 1989.
NU 1990/7. *Det nordiska samarbetet. Internationalisering och effektivisering. Förslag till reformer.* Betänkandet avgivet av Nordiska rådets organisationskommitté. Nordiska rådet, Stockholm 1990. [Partly in English with the title 'Nordic co-operation. Internationalisation and improved efficiency. Proposed reforms. Report of the Organisation Committee of the Nordic Council'.]
Oppfølginsgruppen för nyvurdering av det nordiske samarbeidet. Rapport til de nordiske lands statsministre. Århus, 11. november 1990. (Quoted: *Oppfølginsgruppen.*)
Planer for det nordiska samarbetet. Redogörelse överlämnad av Ministerrådet. Nordiska rådet 44:e session 1994 (C2), Köpenhamn 1993. (Quoted: *Planer 1993.*)

Rapport till statsministrarna av statsministrarnas personliga representanter för nyvärdering av det nordiska samarbetet 14.8.1992 ('Iloniemi-rapport'). [Report to the prime ministers by their personal representatives on re-evaluation of Nordic cooperation.] Published in NKextra 'Det nordiska samarbetes framtid'. (Quoted: *Rapport.*)

UD informerar 1979: 2: Nordiskt samarbete. The Ministry for Foreign Affairs of Sweden, Stockholm 1979.

UD informerar 1986: 3: Nordiskt samarbete. The Ministry for Foreign Affairs of Sweden, Stockholm 1986.

Working Programme Norden in Europe until 1992. Nordic Council of Ministers, Copenhagen 1990.

Finnish integration policy

Literature

Antola, Esko (1989): 'The Finnish Integration Strategy: Adaptation with Restrictions', in Möttölä, Kari - Patomäki, Heikki (eds.): *Facing the Change in Europe. EFTA Countries' Integration Strategies.* The Finnish Institute of International Affairs, Helsinki.

Antola, Esko (1990a): 'Euroopan muutoksen ulottuvuudet', in Väyrynen, Raimo (ed.): *Suomen puolueettomuuden tulevaisuus.* WSOY, Juva, pp. 112-133.

Antola, Esko (1990b): 'Finnish perspectives on EC-EFTA relations', in Laursen, Finn (ed.): *EFTA and the EC: Implications of 1992.* European Institute of Public Administration, Maastricht.

Antola, Esko (1991a): 'Finland', in Wallace, Helen (ed.): *The Wider Western Europe. Reshaping the EC/EFTA Relationship.* Pinter Publishers, London.

Antola, Esko (1991b): 'The End of Pragmatism: Political Foundations of the Finnish Integration Policy under Stress'. *Yearbook of Finnish Foreign Policy* 1991. Finnish Institute of International Affairs, Helsinki.

Antola, Esko - Tuusvuori, Ossi (1983): *Länsi-Euroopan integraatio ja Suomi.* Ulkopoliittinen instituutti, Turku.

Arter, David (1995): 'The EU Referendum in Finland on 16 October 1994: A Vote for the West, not for Maastricht'. *Journal of Common Market Studies,* vol. 33 (3), pp. 361-387.

Cremona, Marise (1994): 'The "Dynamic and Homogeneous" EEA: Byzantine Structures and Variable Geometry'. *European Law Review,* vol. 19, pp. 508-526.

Eskelinen, Heikki (1985): 'International Integration and Regional Economic Development: The Finnish Experience'. *Journal of Common Market Studies,* vol. XXIII (3), pp. 229-255.

Forsberg, Tuomas - Vaahtoranta, Tapani (eds.) (1993): *Johdatus Suomen ulkopolitiikkaan. Kylmästä sodasta uuteen maailmanjärjestykseen.* Gaudeamus, Tampere.

Forsberg, Tuomas - Vaahtoranta, Tapani (1993): 'Lähialuepolitiikan tuleminen', in Forsberg, Tuomas - Vaahtoranta, Tapani (eds.): *Johdatus Suomen ulkopolitiikkaan. Kylmästä sodasta uuteen maailmanjärjestykseen.* Gaudeamus, Tampere, pp. 232-260.

Hakovirta, Harto (1976): *Puolueettomuus ja integraatiopolitiikka. Tutkimus puolueettoman valtion adaptaatiosta alueelliseen integraatioon teorian, vertailujen ja Suomen poikkeavan tapauksen valossa.* Acta Universitatis Tamperensis, ser. A, vol. 78. University of Tampere.

Hakovirta, Harto (1987): 'The Nordic Neutrals in Western European Integration: Current Pressures, Restraints and Options'. *Cooperation and Conflict,* vol. XXII, pp. 265-273.

Himanen, Hannu (1993): 'Poliittisesta yhteistyöstä yhteiseen politiikkaan. Suomen EY-jäsenyyden ulkopoliittisesta merkityksestä'. *Ulkopolitiikka,* vol. 30 (1), pp. 26-34.

Hjerppe, Riitta (1993): 'Finland's Foreign Trade and Trade Policy in the 20th Century'. *Scandinavian Journal of History,* vol. 18 (1), pp. 57-76.

Hurni, Bettina (1989): 'EFTA-EC Relations after the Luxembourg Declaration', in Möttölä, Kari - Patomäki, Heikki (eds.): *Facing the Change in Europe. EFTA Countries' Integration Strategies.* The Finnish Institute of International Affairs, Helsinki.

Hyyryläinen, Esa (1995): *Integraatiopolitiikka hallintopolitiikkana. Tutkimus organisaatiomuutoksen, päätöksenteon koordinoinnin ja sääntelyn eurooppalaistumisesta Euroopan unionissa ja Suomessa.* Hallintotieteen lisensiaatintutkimus, Vaasan yliopisto, Vaasa. (Unpublished licentiate thesis, University of Vaasa.)

Iloniemi, Jaakko (1990): 'Suomen integraatiopolitiikka ja puolueettomuus', in Väyrynen, Raimo (ed.): *Suomen puolueettomuuden tulevaisuus.* WSOY, Juva.

Jansson, Jan-Magnus (1973): 'Finland and Various Degrees of Integration'. *Yearbook of Finnish Foreign Policy 1973.* The Finnish Institute of International Affairs, Helsinki.

Joenniemi, Pentti (1992a): 'Suomen uusi ulkopolitiikka'. *Rauhantutkimus* (1), pp. 56-63.

Joenniemi, Pentti (1995): 'Finland i det nya Europa: Granne till en stormakt eller småstat bland småstater? in Neumann, Iver B. (ed.): *Ny giv for nordisk samarbeid? Norsk, svensk og finsk sikkerhetspolitikk før og etter EUs nordlige utvidelse.* Norsk Utenrikspolitisk Institutt, TANO, Oslo.

Jääskinen, Niilo (1992): 'EY-jäsenyyden vaikutus eduskunnan valtaan'. *Politiikka,* vol. 34 (3), pp. 271-279.

Kekkonen, Taneli (1973): 'Finland's CMEA Policy'. *Yearbook of Finnish Foreign Policy* 1973. The Finnish Institute of International Affairs, Helsinki, pp. 29-31.
Korpinen, Pekka (1973): 'Finland and the Enlarging EEC'. *Yearbook of Finnish Foreign Policy* 1973. The Finnish Institute of International Affairs, Helsinki, pp. 25-29.
Laine, Jermu (1973): 'The Finnish Model for Foreign Trade Policy'. *Yearbook of Finnish Foreign Policy* 1973. The Finnish Institute of International Affairs, Helsinki, pp. 20-23.
Lempiäinen, Petri (ed.) (1994): *Suomen ulkosuhteet 1990-luvun Euroopassa*. Painatuskeskus, Helsinki.
Lempiäinen, Petri (1994): 'Vapaakauppastrategiasta sitoutumiseen. Kansainvälisen talousintegraation syveneminen ja Suomi', in Lempiäinen, Petri (ed.): *Suomen ulkosuhteet 1990-luvun Euroopassa*. Painatuskeskus, Helsinki.
Lipponen, Paavo (1990): 'Esipuhe', in Väyrynen, Raimo (ed.): *Suomen puolueettomuuden tulevaisuus*. WSOY, Juva, pp. 7-12.
Majander, Mikko (1991): 'The Finnish-Soviet Treaty of Friendship, Cooperation and Mutual Assistance in Finland under President Koivisto. Two Rounds of Discussion', in *Yearbook of Finnish Foreign Policy*, Finnish Institute of International Affairs, Helsinki.
af Malmborg, Mikael (1994): *Den ståndaktiga nationalstaten. Sverige och den västeuropeiska integrationen 1945-59*. Lund University Press.
Maude, George (1976): *The Finnish Dilemma. Neutrality in the Shadow of Power.* Oxford University Press for the Royal Institute of International Affairs.
Mouritzen, Hans (1988): *Finlandization: Towards a General Theory of Adaptive Politics*. Avebury, Gower Publishing Company, Aldershot.
Mouritzen, Hans (1993b): *The Two Musterknaben and the Naughty Boy: Sweden, Finland and Denmark in the Process of European Integration*. Working Papers 8, Centre for Peace and Conflict Research, Copenhagen.
Muoser, Toni (1986): *Finnlands Neutralität und die Europäische Wirtschaftsintegration*. Nomos Verlagsgesellschaft, Baden-Baden.
Möttölä, Kari – Patomäki, Heikki (eds.) (1989): *Facing the Change in Europe. EFTA Countries' Integration Strategies*. The Finnish Institute of International Affairs, Helsinki.
Möttölä, Kari (1993): 'Puolueettomuudesta sitoutumiseen. Turvallisuuspoliittisen perusratkaisun muutos kylmästä sodasta Euroopan murrokseen', in Forsberg, Tuomas – Vaahtoranta, Tapani (eds.): *Johdatus Suomen ulkopolitiikkaan. Kylmästä sodasta uuteen maailmanjärjestykseen*. Gaudeamus, Tampere.
Nousiainen, Jaakko (1992): 'EY-jäsenyyden vaikutus Suomen valtiollisten laitosten keskinäisiin toimivaltasuhteisiin'. *Politiikka*, vol. 34 (3), pp. 262-270.
Patomäki, Heikki (1991): 'Suomen ulkopolitiikan genealogia'. *Rauhantutkimus*, vol. 7 (1), pp. 60-111.

Pedersen, Thomas (1991): 'EF-Unionen og det bredere Europa: associering eller udvidelse?', in *Norden i det nye Europa*. En rapport fra det danske, finske, norske og svenske utenrikspolitiske institutt og universitetet i Reykjavík. Helsingfors, København, Oslo, Reykjavík, Stockholm, juli 1991.

Penttilä, Risto E.J. (1994): Suomen ulko- ja turvallisuuspolitiikan muutos 1985-1992. In: Lempiäinen, Petri (ed.): *Suomen ulkosuhteet 1990-luvun Euroopassa*. Painatuskeskus, Helsinki.

Petersen, Nikolaj (1993): 'The European Union and Foreign and Security Policy', in Nørgaard, Ole - Pedersen, Thomas - Petersen, Nikolaj: *The European Community in World Politics*. Pinter Publishers, London and New York.

Rehn, Olli (1993): 'Odottavasta ennakoivaan integraatiopolitiikkaan? Suomen integraatiopolitiikka kylmän sodan aikana ja sen päätösvaiheessa 1989-92', in Forsberg, Tuomas - Vaahtoranta, Tapani (eds.): *Johdatus Suomen ulkopolitiikkaan. Kylmästä sodasta uuteen maailmanjärjestykseen*. Gaudeamus, Tampere, pp. 166-231.

Rometsch, Dietrich (1993): 'Finnlands Außen- und Sicherheitspolitik - reif für die Europäische Union?' *Integration*, vol. 15 (1). Beilage zur Europäischen Zeitung 1/1993, pp. 44-46.

Rosenau, James N. (1981): *The Study of Political Adaptation*. Pinter, London.

Salovaara, Jukka (1993): 'Suomen integraatiopolitiikka Euroopan murroksessa'. *Ulkopolitiikka*, vol. 30 (1), pp. 35-42.

Salovaara, Jukka - Rumpunen, Juha - Salmimies, Okko-Pekka (1994): *Suomi ja Euroopan Unioni: vaikutukset ulko- ja turvallisuuspolitiikkaan, ympäristöpolitiikkaan ja pakolaispolitiikkaan*. Ulkopoliittinen instituutti, Helsinki.

Salovaara, Jukka (1994): 'Suomi ja Euroopan Unioni. Jäsenyyspäätöksen vaikutus ulko- ja turvallisuuspolitiikkaan', in Salovaara *et al.*: *Suomi ja Euroopan Unioni: vaikutukset ulko- ja turvallisuuspolitiikkaan, ympäristöpolitiikkaan ja pakolaispolitiikkaan*. Ulkopoliittinen instituutti, Helsinki.

Serenius, Maria (1976): 'Euroopan Neuvosto ja Suomi'. *Ulkopolitiikka* (4), pp. 37-40.

Temmes, Markku (1995): 'EU:n vaikutukset Suomen hallintoon', in Paul, Jan-Peter *et al.*: *EU ja kansallisvaltio. Suomen hallinto 2000-luvun haasteiden edessä*. Hallinnon kehittämiskeskus; Painatuskeskus, Helsinki.

Tiilikainen, Teija (1992): 'Suomen doktriini murtuu. Suomalaisen politiikan kulku Paasikiven-Kekkosen realismista kohti yhteisöllisyyden Eurooppaa'. *Ulkopolitiikka* (4), pp. 15-22.

Tiilikainen, Teija (1996): 'Finland and the European Union', in Miles, Lee (ed.): *The European Union and the Nordic Countries*. Routledge, London and New York.

Törnudd, Klaus (1969): 'Finland and Economic Integration in Europe'. *Cooperation and Conflict*, vol. IV (1), pp. 63-72.

Törnudd, Klaus (1995): 'Bindningar. Historiska erfarenheter och nuvarande fronter i Finländsk säkerhetspolitisk debatt om EU-medlemskap och nordiskt samarbete - En dryftning av argumentation och polarisering', in Neumann, Iver B. (ed.): *Ny giv for nordisk samarbeid? Norsk, svensk og finsk sikkerhetspolitikk før og etter EUs nordlige utvidelse.* Norsk Utenrikspolitisk Institutt, TANO, Oslo.

Väyrynen, Raimo (ed.) (1990): *Suomen puolueettomuuden tulevaisuus.* WSOY, Juva.

Väyrynen, Raimo (1993): 'Finland and the European Community: Changing Elite Bargains'. *Cooperation and Conflict*, vol. 28 (1), pp. 31-46.

Widgrén, Mika (1995): *National Interests, EU Enlargement and Coalition Formation. Four essays on National Influence in the EU.* ETLA Series A 20; Taloustieto Oy, Helsinki.

Documents and reports

Eurooppa. (Later *Eurooppakirje*; also *Eurooppa-tietoa*). 4.8.1992 - 14.1.1994. Documentary newsletter on European integration and the Finnish membership negotiations published by the Finnish ministry for foreign affairs.

Europe and the challenge of enlargement. *Bulletin of the European Communities*, Supplement 3/92.

The challenge of enlargement. Commission opinion on Sweden's application for membership. Document drawn up on the basis of SEC(92) 1582 final. *Bulletin of the European Communities*, Supplement 5/92.

The challenge of enlargement. Commission opinion on Finland's application for membership. Document drawn up on the basis of SEC(92) 2048 final. *Bulletin of the European Communities*, Supplement 6/92.

Suomi ja Euroopan talousalue. Valtioneuvoston selonteko eduskunnalle Suomen suhtautumisesta Länsi-Euroopan yhdentymiskehitykseen 1990. (Quoted: Government report 1990.)

Suomi ja Euroopan yhteisön jäsenyys. Valtioneuvoston selonteko eduskunnalle EY-jäsenyyden vaikutuksista Suomelle 9.1.1992. (Quoted: Government report 1992.)

Suomi ja Euroopan yhteisön jäsenyys. Taustaselvitys. Liite valtioneuvoston selontekoon eduskunnalle EY-jäsenyyden vaikutuksista Suomelle 9.1.1992. (Quoted: Appendix to the report 1992.)

Suomi ja Länsi-Euroopan yhdentymiskehitys. Valtioneuvoston selonteko eduskunnalle Suomen suhtautumisesta Länsi-Euroopan taloudelliseen yhdentymiskehitykseen 1.11.1988. (Quoted: Government report 1988.)

The Stockholm Convention on the Establishment of the European Free Trade Association. January 4, 1960, in *Den Europeiska frihandelssammanslutningen.* EFTA Secrerariat, Geneva 1988. WSOY, Juva.

Valtioneuvoston tiedonanto eduskunnalle Suomen suhtautumisesta Länsi-Euroopan yhdentymiskehitykseen. Helsinki 1989. (Quoted: Government communication 1989.)

Valtioneuvoston tiedonanto Eduskunnalle Euroopan yhteisön jäsenyydestä. Valtion painatuskeskus, Helsinki 1992 (March 16). (Quoted: Government communication 1992.)